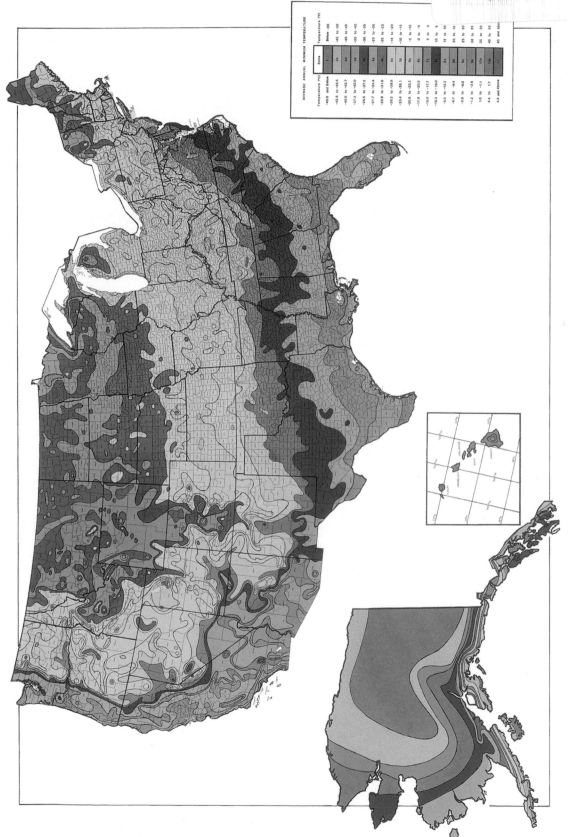

GREAT GROWING
AT HOME

Other Books by Allan A. Swenson

101 Old Time Roses
Everything Gardening
Everything Landscaping
Cultivating Carnivorous Plants
Flowers of the Bible
Foods Jesus Ate and How To Grow and Use Them
Fruit Trees for the Home Garden
Fun To Grow series
Gardener's Book of Berries
Herbs of the Bible
Inflation Fighter's Victory Garden
Landscape You Can Eat
My Own Herb Garden
Only Gardening Book
Plants of the Bible and How To Grow Them
Practical Book of Organic Gardening
Terrariums, Your Complete Guide
Your Biblical Garden

GREAT GROWING AT HOME

THE ESSENTIAL GUIDE TO GARDENING BASICS

Allan A. Swenson

taylor trade publishing
Lanham • New York • Boulder • Toronto • Plymouth, UK

Published by Taylor Trade Publishing
An imprint of The Rowman & Littlefield Publishing Group, Inc.
4501 Forbes Boulevard, Suite 200, Lanham, Maryland 20706
www.rlpgtrade.com

Distributed by NATIONAL BOOK NETWORK

Library of Congress Cataloging-in-Publication Data

Swenson, Allan A.
 Great growing at home : the essential guide to gardening basics / Allan A. Swenson.
 p. cm.
 ISBN-13: 978-1-58979-265-4 (pbk. : alk. paper)
 ISBN-10: 1-58979-265-3 (pbk. : alk. paper)
 1. Gardening. I. Title.

SB453.S8955 2008
635—dc22   2007032824

∞™ The paper used in this publication meets the minimum requirements of
American National Standard for Information Sciences—Permanence of
Paper for Printed Library Materials, ANSI/NISO Z39.48–1992.
Manufactured in the United States of America.

This book is dedicated to America's dedicated gardeners everywhere
who aspire to have more blooming beauty, productive
vegetable gardens, flavorful herbs, and glorious landscapes.

May your dreams grow into the tasteful delights you deserve.

CONTENTS

PREFACE

This is the only gardening book you'll need, for several reasons. Not only does it offer the best gardening facts, tips, and ideas from my experiences as a longtime gardener, but it also includes great growing ideas and advice I've harvested from hundreds of garden experts all around our country. Top arborists, horticulturists, plant breeders, and other authorities as well as neighborly good gardeners have shared their knowledge and advice, which you'll find in this fact-packed book.

You'll discover how to grow the tastiest vegetables, most glorious flowers, and most flavorful herbs. You'll find out how to improve your landscape to boost property values and have gardens that are the envy of the neighborhood. In addition, you'll discover the best varieties of vegetables from asparagus to zucchini and flowers from azaleas to zinnias. Tips to attract birds for tuneful gardens, solve garden problems, enjoy international flavors, garden in containers, and grow wildflowers are included. This book is an easy-to-follow compilation of gardening know-how in one convenient volume to help you grow more tastefully, productively, and beautifully wherever you live.

ACKNOWLEDGMENTS

My heartfelt thanks to all the wonderful gardeners, young and old, all across America who have shared their wit and wisdom about gardening with me, so that I may share it with readers of my newspaper columns, magazine articles, and books over the years.

Special thanks to hundreds of county agricultural agents and state college horticulturists who have given of their time and talent to answer my myriad questions. And to the well-focused folks at the National Garden Bureau, National Gardening Association, many different garden clubs and organizations, friends and associates of the Garden Writers Association, and thousands of down-to-earth, dedicated gardeners. You all have been of much help during the forty-plus years that I've been writing about gardening. The worthwhile, productive ideas and advice you willingly offered, which I was able to share with readers, are proof of your dedication to the hobby we all love so much: tilling, planting, cultivating, and tending the good earth. Thanks again.

I

PLAN TO GROW BETTER

Congratulations! You came to the right garden spot. In this book you'll find and enjoy a wealth of great growing information that has been harvested from all around America and from international sources. For more than 40 years, I have been an avid gardener and garden writer, and I have had the pleasure of meeting and interviewing top horticulturists, plant breeders, veteran gardeners, and a variety of other leading authorities on all phases of gardening. They have graciously shared their knowledge and provided copious, worthwhile ideas, tips, and advice from their areas of expertise. And in the more than 25 years that my nationally syndicated garden columns appeared in over 150 newspapers all around the country, many talented home gardeners—who are a sharing group of like-minded people—sent me more useful information.

From that abundance of great growing information, I've compiled the best how-to know-how in this special book. You'll discover how to grow the tastiest vegetables and most glorious flowers, as well as how to improve your landscape for beauty and to boost your property values. In addition, you'll discover the best new All America Selection hybrids, both vegetables and flowers, plus practical ideas to create the most stunning gardens in the neighborhood.

There's much more. You'll find tips to attract birds for tuneful gardens, discover how to identify and solve garden problems, and be introduced to international food flavors from world-favorite veggies and fruits you can grow in your own backyard. Plus, you'll find an abundant harvest of growing advice about herbs and wildflowers, berries and tree fruits, annual and perennial flowers, roses, and bulb plants for yearly pleasure. This book is an easy-to-follow compilation of gardening know-how in one convenient volume. It has taken me nearly 40 years to assemble it in one place, and now it is yours to enjoy as your growing guide for more beautiful home grounds, tastier eating, glorious living, and all the other pleasures that gardening provides.

Some of the tips you will find are historic and time-proven over generations. Others are based on new discoveries and ways to help make gardening easier and more fun. You're not alone in your enthusiasm for gardening. You are one of the more than 80 million Americans who love digging in the ground, planting, cultivating, and enjoying growing experiences of all types.

As a veteran garden writer, I receive dozens of garden catalogs a year. Many of them do more than mention new varieties. There are worthwhile gardening tips tucked into the pages of specialty catalogs. Some feature rare heirloom varieties that are making a comeback as Grandma and Grandpa gardens gain new popularity. In the "good old days," wonderful plants graced America's gardens and fed us well. Fortunately some mail order firms have saved these rare, heirloom species and varieties and are making them available again.

However, America's tastes are changing. For instance, more salsa is sold these days than ketchup. As a home gardener, you can grow your own salsa ingredients for delicious dips and snacks. More Americans are thinking globally. Seed firms are aware of that fact. You can now grow a wider range of international vegetables than ever before. One catalog lists 58 international varieties. With the tips available in this book, your own backyard can produce the vegetables and herbs for tasty stir-fry meals, Tex-Mex dinners, French gourmet treats, and Asian delights for family and friends.

Many folks today are focusing more on natural foods and natural gardening too. Fine. Life can be well worth living if you'll tune in to what kindly old Mother Nature has to teach us. But she works best with your help.

Natural, organic gardening is a practical and wholesome approach to producing an abundant, nourishing, and flavorful food supply. Having known both J. I. Rodale, the founder of Rodale, Inc., and of *Organic Farming and Gardening* magazine, and his son, Robert, I studied some of their methods at their farm in Emmaus, Pennsylvania. Then I put that knowledge to work in tandem with other talented gardeners' tips. You'll find many valuable lessons in these pages, happily harvested from help-ful gardeners all around our country, and some from overseas for international good measure.

To some, organic gardening means growing plants without using any commercial pesticides or fertilizers. The purists rely on manure, bone meals, fish and seaweed fertilizers, and other basics. Other organic gardeners use pyrethrum insecticide, made from South African flowers, and sulfur or copper to beat bugs. Others accept commercial fertilizers of nitrogen made from the nitrogen in the air into a solid form for garden use with phosphates and potash. Today there is a wide range of opinions of what is really organic gardening, so I'll provide a better understanding of those techniques too.

Another fact merits attention. More people want to restrict fats, salt, and chemical additives in their foods. That accounts for the appeal of natural gardening. Yet people still ask if it is possible to control destructive garden insects without using pesticides. Nature has some answers, including beneficial insects that naturally eat and control the nasties that attack your flower, vegetable, and fruit plants.

There's lots more to know about gardening today. The good news is that plant breeders have been introducing new hybrids with built-in genetic ability to resist diseases and repel insects. You'll read in this book about these improved vegetables, tree fruits, and berries for home gardens. Happily, these scientists also have focused on retaining flavors in these improved varieties. Another advantage is that some of the new hybrid fruits are ever-bearing varieties. You get crops from summer right up to fall, and in tasty abundance.

Some people wonder if their soil is right for a garden. Not to worry! If it isn't what your plants need, you'll discover in this book how to improve it, use cover crops, make compost, thwart weeds with mulches, and use many other handy ideas for more productive and rewarding gardening. Soil improvement is an important key to better gardening. Compost is one way to make your garden ground better. Soil requires humus and ample organic matter to provide the right environment for best plant growth. Compost becomes humus as organic matter decays naturally. You'll learn how to use many types of organic matter to make valuable compost.

Plants must eat well to feed you well. Animal manure provides valuable nutrients for plants. If you have access to animal manure, that's great. However, major chain stores now offer a variety of composted, dried manure for gardeners. Fertilizer manufacturers also have been at work developing improved materials. You can now have designer fertilizer for a variety of different type plants. Water-soluble, plant-feeding systems have been perfected to make plant nutrition easier and faster.

Birds can be insect-eating allies for gardeners. It pays to encourage insect-eating types of birds. They'll reward you with their singing as they help win your battle against nasty bugs, naturally. The more insect-eating birds you can attract, the more bugs will be eaten. Think about the advantages. Tree and cliff swallows, swifts, wrens, and flycatchers are good friends. In a given day, one swallow can gulp a thousand assorted flying and jumping pests on the wing. House wrens devour hundreds of spiders and caterpillars each day. Juncos, kinglets, and song sparrows dine on scale and other minute insects. Warblers, scarlet tanagers, vireos, flycatchers, and phoebes all eat insects and sing merrily as they do.

You'll find ideas for attracting these feathered friends, including planting some of the shrubs and trees that they prefer and that will add to the look of your landscape. You'll also learn more about multipurpose landscaping. Picking decorative shrubs and trees that offer dramatic bloom in spring and colorful fall foliage is another way to build a more attractive plantscape.

Speaking of landscape ideas, plantings offer more advantages than beauty and display. Shrubs, flowers, trees, and vines can be used as windbreaks. They also clean the air, and they provide shade in summer. Evergreens act as wind barriers in winter. Certain trees are better than others for city homes, and you'll find specifics in this book to help all who live in small towns and big cities.

Annuals offer beauty for every garden, but they must be replanted each year. Still, they have advantages that shouldn't be missed. Perennial flowers are becoming more popular, mainly because of the simple fact that once planted, they return every year. That includes most of the spring-flowering bulbous plants, from crocus and hyacinths to daffodils, iris, and tulips. Other bulb plants work well for mass displays, including day lilies and oriental lilies.

Wildflowers deserve consideration. Some may require special attention at first, but once established, they become blooming beauties to grace your yard for years. As natives, they grow well naturally in their own habitats.

A rose is a rose is a rose, Gertrude Stein once said. Roses offer more than that. Hundreds of different types, from hybrid tea and floribunda to climbers and miniature beauties, are available to grace your gardens. Ground-hugging roses offer ways to carpet slopes with color. Plant breeders once focused on perfecting bigger blooms and sometimes sacrificed fragrance. Not anymore. Gardeners spoke out, loudly and clearly. Now more roses are available with wonderful perfumes that fill the air. One of my earlier books, *101 Old Time Roses*, told their story. I've included the best information from that book for you here.

Other fragrant plants also are available. From ground covering lily of the valley to tall, dramatic lilac bushes, you can add both beauty and refreshing fragrance to your outdoor dining and recreation areas. Other fine shrubs help you plant a meditation garden where you can escape the woes of the world and regain peace and sanity for a time.

Biblical gardens have gained ground and popularity. Hundreds of them grow at churches and other places of worship as well as at individual homes. You'll discover that many of the most beautiful flowers actually have their roots in the Holy Land. From bits of floral and herbal lore, you'll learn how to grow these plants that have scriptural reference.

Children learn from gardening. You'll pick up some wonderful child-pleasing ideas in this book and also links to many sources for ideas to grow better with your kids and grandkids. Brag patch gardens, super sunflowers, prize pumpkins, mouthwatering melons are all part of the fun of growing together with children. We've done it with ours and provide here some of the best ideas for you to enjoy. Plus, I've included fun growing ideas gathered from parents all around America. Our writing theme has long been "Let's Grow Together."

Often gardeners like to have statistics about their favorite hobby. So be it. According to research by the National Gardening Association (NGA), during 2005 an estimated 91 million households participated in one or more types of do-it-yourself indoor and outdoor lawn and garden activities. That 83 percent of all U.S. households set a new record in terms of the percentage and number of households participating in lawn and garden activities. That surge was the biggest increase in lawn and garden activities seen in a single year since 2001. From 2000 to 2004, household participation in lawn and garden activities ranged from a low of 76 million in 2000 to a high of 85 million in 2001 and 2002, and averaged 82 million households.

Some other trends are interesting. Lawn and garden participation in 2005 was highest among married households, people 55 years of age and older, college graduates, those with annual incomes over $50,000, those with children at home, and among households that are employed full-time or are retirees, according to NGA research.

From 2000 to 2005, average spending on lawns and gardens ranged from a low of $387 in 2005 to a high of $466 in 2002 and averaged $440. Total lawn and garden retail sales ranged from a low of about $33 billion in 2000 to a high of more than $39 billion in 2002 and averaged $36.885 billion. According to NGA Research Director Bruce Butterfield, households that spent the most on their lawns and gardens in 2005 included those with no children at home, married households, college graduates, two-person households, those with annual incomes over $75,000, and people 45 years of age and older.

There are other gardening trends of note. The Garden Writers Association recently released some very interesting insights on consumer gardening attitudes and expectations. Here are those key facts from nationwide polls.

- Better mental health, nutrition, or fitness is the primary reason 36 percent of households have gardens.
- More perennials and more vegetables are the two leading additions that households plan to make to their garden in the next gardening year.
- The number of consumers planning to increase their lawn areas rose by 5 percent over 2005, while the number planning to decrease their lawn areas dropped from 11 percent to 9 percent.

- Fewer households plan to use weed and insect control.
- Manure is the most frequently planned means of fertilizing gardens and container plants in the 2006 poll (31 percent), followed by slow-release fertilizer (27 percent), potting soil with fertilizer (19 percent), and liquid fertilizer (16 percent).
- One in four households planned to prepare their garden area with store-bought soil mixes (26 percent).

There's lots more to know and learn about gardening. Consider this just a preview of some of the great growing topics you'll find in this book. Equally important, you'll find a list of nearly a hundred different colorful, free garden catalogs you can order. Just a few of them, especially those with rare and specialty plants, will provide marvelous winter nights as you plan for spring growing time. In addition, you'll find my personal favorite garden websites. For years, the phone was my best communication system, beyond visiting in person with garden experts and authorities. Now I frequently let my fingers do the walking and the Internet do the talking. Seems fair to share these sites with you so you can let your own fingers walk the garden knowledge paths that I've discovered. You'll find ways to get answers to your garden questions and even some toll-free telephone numbers to call so you can talk to a human garden expert.

Even better in today's high-tech world, websites have links around the country and the globe. You can spend an afternoon walking through glorious gardens, selecting the flowers you wish to grow from the dramatic colorful illustrations and descriptions.

We all have our own reasons for gardening, but it may be useful to consider the many other reasons people garden and the values it provides.

Gardening is good exercise. The digging, lifting, pulling, and twisting in our backyards use major muscle groups and help us stay in shape. Studies at Stanford University reveal that 30 minutes in the garden can burn the equivalent amount of calories as 30 minutes of light jogging. Another fact is that gardening has proved especially helpful for people with physical injuries or disabilities to regain their mobility and dexterity. The American Horticultural Therapy Association is a nonprofit organization developed to support professionals in horticultural therapy with educational programs and latest research. Details are available at their website: www.ahta.org.

The nonprofit Cancer Lifeline Center in Seattle provides support groups, classes, and activities aimed at optimizing quality of life for cancer victims and their families. They have developed a Celebration Garden of herbs, a Reflection Garden featuring a quiet nook, and an Earth and Sky Garden with a healing circle where people go to paint or draw or take workshops.

Sue Casey of Portland, Oregon, came up with a Remember Me rose garden in memory of victims of September 11, 2001. Each garden at New York, Washington, and Pennsylvania crash sites will have 3,000 roses. Rose breeders are creating new roses to salute the heroes of 9/11. One such rose is Firefighter, a fragrant scarlet rose from Edmunds Roses.

Gardeners are naturally inquisitive, seeking new ideas, sharing them with others, and encouraging youngsters to join their growing ranks. Gardens teach vital life lessons about cooperation, patience, persistence, and responsibility. National Garden Month celebrates those who created school gardens as tools for learning, as Roberta Paolo of Loveland, Ohio, did with her Granny's Garden. A lifelong gardener, she wanted her grandchildren to enjoy that hobby. They brought friends to see what they were growing. As the news spread, gardens sprouted at the school and around town, bringing many people together. Granny's Garden is just one of thousands of school programs that have begun growing across America. The National Gardening Association has awarded hundreds of Youth Garden Grants to kid's gardening programs over the last 15 years. Details about other worthwhile community and individual cultivating projects are readily available at the National Garden Month website, worth a looksee at www.nationalgardenmonth.org. It celebrates people who see beauty in gardens and love to create them for public places.

Because gardening can become a bit confusing with strange names and terms, you'll find a glossary in this book. Look it over, study the terms, and you'll be able to talk "gardenese" as well as anyone. Seriously, some garden terms do need explanation, so the glossary can be a useful aid to understanding the basic scientific jargon in the field.

As you'll learn in this book, gardening today is easier and more productive than ever, if you take advantage of all the opportunities available. That's one purpose of this book, to put together a collection of the best ideas, tips, and advice that I've been able to find over the years. So read on, dig in, and get yourself growing—better than you ever have before.

2

DIG DEEP TO GROW BETTER

The most important Green Thumb tip is to pick the right location for your garden. You have options even if you are limited in space available, have poor exposure to the sun, and face problems from nearby trees, buildings, wet areas, or other situations. Use this chapter to plan for successful gardens, whether flowers, veggies, herbs, fruits, or just lovelier landscapes. And then dig in to prepare your growing ground for the best gardens possible.

First key point: select an area with at least 6 hours of sun each day, access to the water that plants need to thrive, and space to enjoy your gardens. We've seen the most unlikely areas bloom gloriously when a person sets his or her mind to good gardening.

The ideal location is a sunny, well-drained site with at least 6—8 hours of direct sun each day. Southern exposures are best, followed by eastern, western, and finally northern exposure plots. Plan vegetable beds running north to south, so plants receive equal amounts of sunlight.

Avoid shaded areas or areas near large trees that compete for water and nutrients. Be sure your garden spots will get ample sun at least 6 hours daily. However, also consider trees to provide shade so you can enjoy watching your garden grow.

Next, examine existing soil where you plan new gardens. Don't despair if it isn't rich and fertile: you can improve what you have. One key point is improving organic matter. Compost is a key to doing that. Natural gardeners know that soil improvement is an ongoing project. You'll discover how to make your gardens productive by improving soil condition and fertility too. Another key fact is that insects dislike healthy plants growing in healthy, fertile soil.

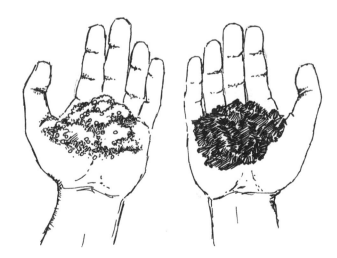

Soil should feel crumbly, as shown on the right. Don't dig or till when soil is overly wet. You can improve what you have by following tips in this book.

To be a productive gardener, you must start where it all begins, in the good earth. Frankly, what you have may not be very good. Your soil may be too sandy or even rocky. It may be muddy from excess clay content. Don't worry. Whatever soil you have can be improved. It has been well said: "and they made the deserts to bloom, and it was good." You can apply the techniques of accomplished gardeners to improve your own growing ground. As you improve and nourish your soil, your plants will reward you with more productive growth. Apply ideas from this chapter to build a fertile foundation for years of glorious gardening.

First the down-to-earth basics. Every soil has a profile. Layers in it are called horizons. These horizons differ in color, texture, structure, and porosity. In shallow soils, horizons may be only an inch thick. In deeper soils, they may be several feet but are usually about a foot or so. Scientist identify three major horizons as A, B, and C. True soil is the combined A and B horizons, which form the major portion of the soil profile. They are the direct result of the soil formation process and are the growing area for your plants. Soil is truly alive. Millions of bacteria and fungi as well as plant roots, small animals, and insects are at work in the soil.

Take a spade and cut into your garden soil to see its profile. When you examine the soil profile, you can better understand ways to improve it. Next step as a dedicated gardener is to get down on your knees and examine your soil. We all do lots of crawling around as we garden, so take this tip: buy a pair of sturdy knee pads. They're especially helpful when you crawl through rocky soil.

Look carefully at the soil texture. Texture refers to the size of the majority of particles that make up soil. These range from microscopic clay particles to small gravel. Clay soils can be stony clay, gravelly clay, sandy clay, or clay, depending what other ma-

terials are mixed with the clay. Clay soils tend to hold excess water, so they must have organic material added to open them up.

Loamy soils can be sandy loams and medium loams to clay loams. Sandy soils can be gravelly sands, coarse sands, or even loamy sands. This may sound confusing at first. Remember, this chapter is designed to help you focus on what it takes to improve your garden ground. Happy fact is, all soils can be improved more easily than you may think.

What is the ideal garden soil? Gardening experts advise that a loamy garden soil is best for practically all plants. Therefore, your goal should be to focus on producing that ideal. A loamy soil combines all three of the major classifications of soil particles: sand, silt, and clay, in about equal parts.

Whether your garden soil is too sandy or contains too much clay, the remedy lies in the addition of organic matter, including peat moss, compost, and animal manure. Today, garden centers provide dried animal manure of various kinds.

Another good way to improve your soil is by growing and turning under cover crops, such as winter rye, hairy vetch, or buckwheat. Organic matter increases the water- and nutrient-holding capacity of sand, as well as improving drainage and aeration of clay soil.

Be patient. Soil improvement is not a one-shot deal. It truly is part of a sound, ongoing gardening program. Your goal should be a balance in structure, texture, and porosity. When you pick up a handful of rich soil in the spring and it crumbles freely in your palm, you are approaching the ideal.

SOME SOIL TEST FACTS

Plants benefit from balanced diets. To grow plants well, you must feed them properly. First step is to find out what nutrients are in the soil you have. Soil tests provide the answers. You can get help from your local County Extension agent or local garden center advisors. Testing is the easy part. Interpreting results can be confusing. It pays to learn more about this process.

If your present gardens are growing well, you may question why soil testing is needed. There are two good reasons. First, know what you have so you can learn what adjustments may be needed in fertilizer to provide a balanced diet to your different plants. Some plants require different ratios of nutrients to perform best. Fruiting crops like tomatoes have different needs than leafy crops like lettuce or root crops like carrots. Naturally, if your plants aren't growing as well as you'd like, or you're concerned about using the right amount of fertilizer, a soil test is the place to start.

Tests don't solve your problems. They do show you what your soil has so you can improve it to give plants in various garden areas what they need to prosper. Most authorities recommend soil testing 3–4 years, in the fall when fertility is lowest. Use the same kit or source to have consistent comparisons.

The most accurate tests are conducted by university and private soil laboratories. These labs have had years of experience testing the soils in your state and giving specific fertilizer recommendations based on the soil types and crops grown. Basic tests usually cost less than $20 but can vary. However, you may also wish to have your soil evaluated for any toxic materials from construction backfill or other problems that may exist. Test results will indicate relative levels of each nutrient, including the basic elements nitrogen, phosphorus, and potassium or potash. It is important to test different garden area because there can be wide variations in soils around your home grounds.

UNDERSTAND THE SOIL'S PH

Soil pH is important to know because some plants prefer neutral soil while others require more acidic conditions. Soil pH is measured on a scale of 1 (acid) to 14 (alkaline). Most garden crops grow well at a pH of 6–7, but specific plants such as blueberries and azaleas may need a lower (more acidic) pH. In general, lime is used to raise pH, while sulfur is recommended to lower it.

pH CHART

1 2 3 4 5 6 ⑦ 8 9 10 11 12 13 14

ACID   NEUTRAL   ALKALINE
SLIGHTLY   SLIGHTLY
ACID   ALKALINE

Plants have their preferences for soil condition. Make regular soil tests to see what fertilizer nutrients you should add and the proper acid/alkaline balance for best plant growth. Most plants prefer conditions near the middle of this chart, but check each plant's special needs and improve your soil accordingly.

Most plants grow best in slightly acid soils of pH 6.1–6.9 because nutrients needed for plant growth are most available in soil water at pH 6.5. Above that level some nutrients become bound to soil particles and therefore are unavailable to plants. Lime sweetens soils that are too acid. However, soil nutrients are most readily dissolved and therefore available to your turf and plants when the soil is slightly acidic. Since plants grow best in slightly acid soil, you should never add lime unless a soil test recommends it.

BASIC ABC'S OF NPK

It is important to know the ABC's of NPK. These are the Big Three nutrients. By law they must be listed in the same order on all fertilizer containers you buy.

N is for **nitrogen**, a key nutrient needed for plant growth. It tends to leach out of the soil easily, which means levels can fluctuate during the growing season. Nitrogen deficiency symptoms usually are pale yellow leaves and stunted growth.

P stands for **phosphorus**. Soil may have adequate levels of phosphorus, but it may be tied up by soil pH conditions. Often, just raising or lowering the pH to the ideal 6.5 will free up phosphorus for plant use. Excess phosphorus can create problems, running off during rain or garden irrigation and causing pollution. Phosphorus deficiency is indicated by purple leaves, brittle roots, skinny stems, and late fruit set and plant maturity.

K is for **potassium**, which is vital for stem strength, root growth, and disease resistance. Many soils are naturally high in potassium, making it readily available to plants. Sandy soils often can be deficient. Signs of potassium shortage are irregular yellowing of lower leaves and poor root growth.

Other nutrients also are needed for proper plant growth. Each has its own function. **Calcium** is important for cell-wall integrity and for root and leaf growth. Symptoms of calcium shortage are deformed leaves and branches and weak stems and roots. Lime adds calcium.

Another minor element is **magnesium**, which is needed for chlorophyll and green leaf development. Pale leaves with green veins are a sign of magnesium deficiency. Most modern fertilizers have trace amounts of calcium and magnesium. Ask your plant test person or fertilizer supplier about best combinations for your area and gardens.

Another key factor in building soil fertility is the percentage of organic matter. Organic matter usually has little nutritional value but is essential for nitrogen absorption and release and as a food for microorganisms that help make other nutrients available. A level of 3–5 percent organic matter is considered ideal. Organic gardeners believe that soil can't have enough organic matter. It opens clay soils and also helps sandy soils retain moisture for plants. Be aware that soils high in some undecomposed organic matter, such as wood chips or sawdust, actually tie up nitrogen because it gets used as cellulose materials break down. That means you may need to add extra nitrogen. Generally, compost is the best soil-improving additive.

As you review soil test results, you'll find most labs provide recommendations for adding specific nutrients to bring garden soils up to their optimum levels. These nutrient levels are usually given in pounds of that element per 1,000 square feet of garden.

For modern gardeners, new types of plant foods are readily available. There isn't room to provide details of all of them, but some key considerations should be noted. Liquid fertilizers have won popularity. You just mix according to package directions and spray on. One problem is being sure to get the right amount applied to meet plant needs, without repeat applications. Pellet or pill fertilizers are handy. They are easier to spread and come in slow-release formulations. That means the plant food is released over a period of time to nourish your plants over many weeks. I favor these types of fertilizer. They save work and are reliable.

Read and heed instructions for whatever type of fertilizer you use. Some fertilizers are designed for flowers, others for fruiting plants, still others for shrubs and trees. Buy smaller quantities of the types you need for the variety of plants you have for best results for all of them. Avoid using high-nitrogen lawn fertilizers for other purposes, because nitrogen promotes foliage growth. You'll get leaf growth at the expense of flower or fruit or veggie production.

At this point, make a mental note: too much fertilizer is often as bad as too little. You waste money if you add unneeded fertilizer, and it may overstimulate plants. Excess nitrogen forces excess leaf growth at the expense of fruit and flower production.

WATER FACTS TO KNOW

Understanding basic points about water can be helpful as you plan your soil improvement projects. There are several types of water. That may seem odd but is a fact worth noting as you garden.

Gravitational water is water that drains out of soil after it rains or when you water your garden. In sandy and sandy loam soils, water may leave too quickly from the pore spaces, causing plants to wilt. On the other hand, in heavy soils with lots of silt and clay, water may remain too long, which can rot roots. Both conditions can be corrected with soil amendments as you improve your garden soil. In very soggy spots, it may be necessary to install drainage tiles.

Peat moss is one of the best materials to quickly improve sandy and clay sail. It comes in small to huge bales, most about 6 cubic feet. Peat opens heavy soils and helps retain moisture in sandy soils. Talk to neighbors. Perhaps you can buy in truckload lots as you all begin soil improvement projects.

Hygroscopic soil water is chemically bound with soil materials and is unavailable to plants. It may be bound more or less closely, depending on the chemical composition of your soil. As you work on soil improvement and fertilizer balance for your gardens, you can adjust this situation.

Capillary water is moisture that is available to your plants. It is chemically free to leave the soil to enter plant roots. There it carries the dissolved nutrients to roots, stems, stalks, leaves, blooms, and fruit. This is the water you want. The more you improve your soil's texture and structure, the greater will be its capacity to hold and transfer capillary water. That is the vital water that transports the needed nutrients to your plants.

To learn more about soils, check out U.S. Department of Agriculture resources. They have some excellent documents. Other good local literature is available from the information office at your own state agricultural college. County agricultural agents can also provide gardening information that relates to your particular state and area. Much of this information is free. Better yet, state agricultural colleges have garden literature that focuses on specific soil and climatic conditions in your own state.

FIGURING FERTILIZER FACTS

Plants need food to grow well, just as people do. Fertilizer recommendations often refer to pounds of nutrients rather than pounds of material in a bag. This allows for consistent recommendations that can be used with a variety of fertilizer formulations. Note that fertilizers are identified by their analysis, such as 5-10-5 or 10-10-10. The numbers refer to the percentage of nitrogen, phosphorus, and potassium, respectively, in the fertilizer.

Read the directions for the fertilizer that you buy, and apply the amounts specified around plants or along rows.

In a 100-pound bag of 5-10-5, there are 5 pounds of total nitrogen, 10 pounds of available phosphorus, and 5 pounds soluble potassium. The volume of filler in the bag acts to ensure proper and even distribution.

A fertilizer of high analysis such as 10-10-10 is generally more expensive than a fertilizer of low analysis such as 6-8-8. Plant nutrition experts note that, in general, mineral fertilizers such as 5-10-5 act more quickly than organic types. Since they are salts, the nutrients are available to your plants as soon as they dissolve in the soil water. Organic fertilizers such as dried blood, bone meal, and manure materials must be broken down by soil bacteria to release the nutrients.

There is an ongoing debate between organic or natural gardeners and others over what are organic gardening techniques. That includes fertilizer. Mineral fertilizers are widely available in chain stores nationwide and are relatively inexpensive. Organic gardeners favor natural materials, and now many garden centers carry bags of dried blood, bone meal, and cottonseed and composted manure for natural gardening, but prices are usually higher. Because of increased interest in organic gardening, today you can find many organic fertilizers in chain stores as well as local garden centers.

To help you pick the best fertilizer, here are some guidelines from plant nutrition experts.

Readily soluble types of fertilizers are good for houseplants, for applying at transplanting, or as a

Apply proper amounts of fertilizer for the type you use according to label directions, whether you side dress along rows or around individual plants.

side dressing after the first fruits are set on plants. The most common types of fertilizers, such as 5-10-5, 10-6-4, and 12-12-12, are useful for applying plant nutrients to large areas.

Be aware that fertilizer alone doesn't guarantee adequate plant growth. For example, it will not compensate for poorly drained soil, poor plant material, improperly placed plants, poor cultural practices, excess weed competition, or the wrong acid level, or pH, of the soil.

Side-dressing is a time-honored term. It simply means applying fertilizer to garden plants, mainly referring to vegetables, during the growing season after the plants have become established. Normally it is applied in a band about 6-12 inches from the plants, or placed on the soil surface and carefully worked in with a light raking. After applying fertilizer, water the soil so the fertilizer gets into the root zone where plants can pick it up. One side dressing per season is recommended. The usual rate for a side dressing is about one-half pound of a 10-10-10 or equivalent fertilizer per 100 feet of row. Veteran gardens usually apply side dressing to leafy crops once they are well established and to tomatoes, eggplants, peppers, squash, and similar fruiting plants once the first fruit have set. For broccoli, cauliflower, cabbage, and similar vegetables, it can be done once buds or heads have begun to form. And side dressing can be done once vine crops begin to set runners.

Details about fertilizing roses, ornamental shrubs, fruit crops, and trees are included in chapters about those specific plants. However, here's a summary of quick tips.

Be aware that many modern fertilizer promotes "ease of application," so carefully read and follow directions for the types you buy.

Avoid fertilizing trees and shrubs as growing season ends. That could result in late, tender growth that won't be tough enough to survive cold winter and you'll have winter kill on plants. However, a fertilizer application later in the fall can benefit trees and shrubs if you wait until these plants have lost their leaves and entered a state of rest but before the ground freezes. It will be available to promote good spring growth. Roots continue to take up nutrients and moisture and store carbohydrates that plants will need during the next growing season. Landscape specialists explain that fertilizer applied at that time helps develop a healthy, vigorous root system which will benefit the trees the following year.

Here's another good growing basic to keep in mind. Soil is actually alive. There are thousands of bacteria, microorganisms, and other minute creatures in every square foot. They help form new and better soil and humus. When you help them, providing more organic matter, you can improve all types of soil. Sandy and gravely soils don't hold the moisture that your plants need. Clay soils give plants wet feet. Richer soils are usually filled with valuable organic matter that makes soil nicely friable. Plant roots need air to breathe, just as leaves do. Try growing plants in wet clay soil and you'll realize that plant roots do need air. Fortunately, organic matter is nature's way of creating better soil. Dig in and help Mother Nature help you and your plants.

TAP ORGANIC MATERIAL VALUES

Organic matter, all growing parts of plants, decays in time. As it decomposes, it naturally breaks down into minute particles, which improves soil tilth and adds some nutrients too. Good sources of organic matter are leaf humus, composted manure, humus from your compost pile, peat moss, and green manure crops. Manure should be well composted and have no ammonia smell. Peat moss is suitable for all garden soil. It holds a lot of water within the soil.

Green manure is a term for crops grown to be turned under to feed the soil microbes. When growing, green manure crops reduce weed growth and help loosen soil. Favored green manure crops commonly grown during fall months to protect the garden soil during the winter include annual rye, oats, and winter rye. These also can be sown in the spring and turned under two weeks prior to planting the garden. Whatever you do, or whatever combinations you apply, improving soil begins with adding organic matter anytime of the year. Mulching your garden with grass clippings or composted leaves is another good way to incorporate organic matter. Probably the best soil improvement material is compost. It's easy to make and you should put it on the top of your Green Thumb to-do list. I use all types of organic matter and add to my compost piles every week as a standard practice. Get into that habit and you'll have compost for uses all around your garden.

FOCUS ON COMPOST MAKING

Composting offers multiple advantages. It helps protect the environment, saves you money, and improves your soil at the same time. It truly is a practical and convenient way to handle yard trimmings such as leaves, grass, thatch, chipped brush, weeds, and plant cuttings. Veteran gardeners agree, compost is a gardener's best friend. Compost returns organic matter to the soil in a usable form. Organic matter in the soil improves plant growth by stimulating the growth of beneficial microorganisms, loosening heavy clay soils to allow better root penetration, and improving soil capacity to hold water and nutrients, particularly in sandy soils.

Besides grass clippings, fall leaves, and weeds, you can include well-ground brush, wood ash, fruit and vegetable peelings, egg shells, and coffee grounds. Do not compost meat, bones, fatty foods, or cooking oil. With those ingredients in mind, here's how the process works. Bacteria, the most numerous and effective microbes, are the first to break down plant tissue. Fungi and protozoans join them. Often, a white layer forms just beneath the surface of the compost. This is usually due to fungi and actinomycetes, a class of filamentous bacteria. As organic material decays, it heats up, killing most weed seeds. Small insects as well as earthworms aid decomposition once the compost has cooled.

The Indore compost method is ages old. It was perfected by Sir Albert Howard, a founder of the organic gardening movement. This simple, easy system can work well for everyone. It does require periodic turning of compost layers, but that speeds up the decay process so you get finished, usable

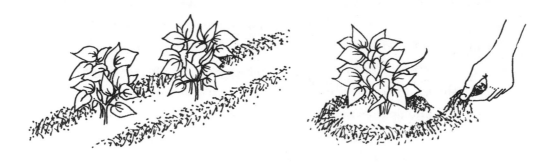

Compost is a great way to improve growing ground.

compost faster. Begin with 4–6 inches of green matter. Next add a 2-inch layer of manure. Then add another 2–3 inches of soil, sod, or garden trash. Build the pile in layers several feet high and about 4 feet across. I've liked that size and system for decades. You should turn the pile with a spading fork every 5–7 days to encourage aerobic soil bacteria to work their wonders along with the anaerobic types. Keep the pile moist. Leave a depression on top to collect rain. That helps organic material decompose better.

If you don't have sufficient material, look around. Many towns ban burning, so you can often collect bags of fall leaves, grass clippings, and other

SNOW FENCE COMPOST PILE

Two simple compost piles turn weeds, grass clippings, and other organic material into soil-enriching humus. You can use a simple cinder-block structure, a snow fence, or a wire frame.

useful organic material. Several garden friends have a pickup route among nongardeners to collect and use bags of organic material others throw away during summer and fall. Good for gardeners and nongardeners alike.

Composting activists explain that the more surface area microorganisms have to work on, the faster materials decompose. Chopping garden wastes with a shovel or running them through a shredding machine or chopping with a lawn mower speeds composting. As decay begins, a compost pile builds up heat from microbial activity. Piles smaller than 3 feet across and 3–4 feet tall have trouble holding heat in the winter. Larger piles, 5–6 feet, don't let enough air reach the microbes at the center. We've found that several piles about 3–4 feet across and 3–4 feet high work best. As one is ready, we use the compost and begin making alternate composting sites.

Water is vital to making compost, as is air, so both types of microbes, aerobic and anaerobic, can function properly to form humus from the organic materials. Microbes work best when the compost heap has many air passages and is about as moist as a wrung-out sponge. Generally, moisture content of the compost should be 50–60 percent on a total weight basis. Overly wet piles are deficient in oxygen and may cause odor problems.

Compost piles aren't attractive garden sights, so find a hidden spot or plan to conceal piles with decorative fencing or landscape plants. Remove sod from the spot for your piles, or till the ground so soil microorganisms can penetrate the pile. You can "inoculate" a new pile with a few spadefuls of completed compost, or use compost-making kits from mail order firms.

An avid Midwest gardener friend offered this composting recipe for constructing your compost pile. For the first layer, put in about 4 inches of chopped brush or other coarse material on top of the soil surface. This allows air circulation around the base of the heap. For the next layer, add 6–8 inches of mixed scraps, leaves, grass clippings, kitchen parings, or weeds. These materials should be moistened. Then, add a third layer of an inch of soil as an inoculant that puts microorganisms into the compost pile. To speed things up, add a fourth layer of 2–3 inches of rotted manure. That provides nitrogen needed by microorganisms. Then, sprinkle a few handfuls of lime, wood ash from a wood stove or brush pile burning, or rock phosphate over the manure to reduce acidity. If you can't obtain manure, add 1 pound of urea fertilizer per square yard of leaves or ground brush unless organic sources of nitrogen are available.

Once you have this sandwich of organic materials in place, repeat these steps until your compost pile is full. Remember to add water to keep the pile as moist as a damp sponge. Leave a depression at the top to catch rainwater.

Naturally, your own system will depend on the types and quantities of materials you have available. Don't be surprised that a properly made compost pile will reach internal temperatures of about 140°F in 4–5 days. As it heats up, the pile will settle, which is a sign that the decay process is working properly. That temperature also kills any bad bugs and often weed seeds too.

In this slower, "pile on" process, turn the material after 3–4 weeks, mixing inner and outer materials, and add water so all is moist. Then, step back and let it rot. It will decay slowly and steadily over several months. To speed things up, it is best to turn your compost a second or third time. When you do, compost should be ready to use within 3–4 months. Therefore, a pile you start in late spring can be ready for fall use. Consider beginning another pile in autumn, when natural materials such as raked leaves, weeds, and prunings are available, for spring application.

By following the Indore method and turning the piles more often, you can speed up the decomposition process. Nice idea if you have time. Many gardeners prefer the slower system. A final thought about turning compost piles. Winter weather can cause a soggy pile that doesn't decompose properly. When you have had several days of temperatures above 32°F, turn over the pile or loosen with a gardening fork to help dry it out and improve air circulation. This helps it thaw out more quickly in the spring and begin composting sooner than a pile that's left wet and too compressed.

CONSIDER FIELD LAYERING

There is another compost method called field layering. Just spread a few inches of organic material over an unused area or under shrubs and trees, and add more as clippings, weeds, and organic refuse become available. Remove any weeds that may sprout, and let the layers decay in time, in place. Lazy gardeners like this system for mulching around shrubs and trees to improve soil, as the material suppresses weeds from sprouting and retains moisture in the soil too. Another term for this is mulch gardening. It is much easier to control weeds in gardens mulched with compost between rows of plants. Have your compost-mulched plant beds soil tested for pH and major nutrients N, P, and K every 2–4 years. Then, adjust the amount of lime and fertilizers to nourish your plants adequately. Many types of fertilizers are now available to boost soil nutrition and feed plants the diets each type needs for optimum growth during the growing season.

Some gardeners still like to use manure. Composted manure of various kinds is readily available in chain stores and garden centers. Here are some considerations when using manure in your garden. Manure is the oldest fertilizer known, and many gardeners, especially those following organic growing methods, believe manure is superior to mineral fertilizers. Always use manure that has composted for at least one year or has been incorporated into a compost pile so it is thoroughly broken down. When adding composted manure to your garden soil, spread the material 1–2 inches deep in the spring or fall. Work it into the soil so that it is mixed thoroughly and uniformly with soil. Composted manure has and will continue to be an excellent garden fertilizer.

TAP VALUES OF GREEN MANURE

Green manure can be a confusing term for beginner gardeners. Actually, it isn't a new kind of manure. Green manure is the term for cover crops planted in the spring or fall and then turned under to improve the growing ground. By planting a crop and tilling it under, you add organic matter. This added organic matter loosens up clay soil and makes nutrients more available to the roots. It also improves sandy soil by holding things together and prevents minerals and nutrients from leaching away. Veteran veggie gardeners are enthusiastic about planting green manure in an area they will use for crops the next year.

Others plant cover crops every fall and till them under in the spring. It doesn't matter what type of plant you choose, although legumes such as clover and vetch can improve nitrogen levels by pulling nitrogen from the air and fixing it on nodules on their roots. Other useful green manure cover crops are cowpeas, soybeans, buckwheat, and winter rye. Except for winter rye, turn under green manure crops when they begin flowering. You can speed decay by mowing the crop before tilling. You'll want to mow winter rye and turn it under as soon as possible in the springtime. It is wise to let the soil rest for 2 weeks after turning the green manure crop under before planting your vegetables. This gives soil bacteria ample time to break down the crop into organic matter for your plants.

MUCH WORTHWHILE ABOUT MULCH

Mulch is another invaluable garden aid. Many types of mulching material can be used along beds and borders to prevent weeds from sprouting, hold vital moisture in the soil, and make your gardens look nicer. Some mulches are attractive, while others are purely functional. You can spread peat moss or a decorative mulch over unattractive black plastic sheets to disguise them. Look around and see how neighbors put mulch to good use. Then get into the mulching act yourself.

Water shortages or droughts show up periodically, but your plants need moisture to grow properly, bloom, and bear abundantly. A mulch conserves soil moisture and reduces water usage around landscape plantings and in fruit and vegetable gardens. Several organic materials may be used as mulches. An added benefit is that these organic materials will eventually decay to improve your soil. Lawn clippings are useful for mulching, but allow them to dry before applying to garden areas. Fresh, green material will settle and form a dense mat but may produce an unpleasant odor. Note this caution: if your lawn has been treated with herbicides for weed control, don't use grass clippings until the lawn has been mowed two or three times after treatment. Grass clippings are not long-lasting and are best used in the vegetable garden or annual flower bed.

Straw that is free from crop and weed seed is an excellent mulch, especially for vegetable gardens and berry beds. Ground and rotted tree bark depresses weed seeds and also looks nice. Be aware, however, that bark or wood chips tend to take nitrogen out of the soil as they decompose. You must compensate for that in your plant fertilizing plans. Peat moss is an attractive mulch, and 2–3 inches around plants and along borders will set off flowers well.

You also can use leaves and newspapers as mulch around landscape plantings and in fruit and vegetable gardens. Leaves are readily available in the fall and should be shredded or composted before being applied as a mulch. Shredded leaves don't mat down as readily as whole leaves but do decompose more quickly. Shredded or composted leaves are an excellent mulch for vegetable gardens, berry plantings, perennial flower beds, and around trees and shrubs.

Unattractive as it may seem, shredded newspaper or whole sheets may be used in the vegetable garden. Most newspaper publishers use organic inks today, so gardeners need not worry about lead contamination. When placing sheets between plant rows in the garden, weigh them down to prevent them from blowing away in the wind. A top layer of natural-looking peat moss or wood chips disguises the newspapers and serves a useful second purpose as mulch.

Other cellulose materials are often readily available. Sawdust is easy to apply, is weed free, and decomposes slowly. Generally, sawdust should be allowed to age or weather for a year before being applied. Never use sawdust from chemically treated lumber. Wood chips are another excellent mulching material and sometimes may be available free from communities that have recycling programs. Chips are produced by passing tree and shrub trimmings through a mechanical chipper. Warning: if communities chip all types of wood, including painted wood, don't use these materials.

In addition to locally available wood chips from brush and prunings and those sold in chain stores, commercially packaged bark mulches are available shredded or as chips, nuggets, or chunks. Bark mulches are attractive, weed free, and decompose slowly. Bark mulches are best used around trees and shrubs and in perennial beds.

A key point deserves repeating. Sawdust, wood chips, bark, and ground corncobs may deplete nitrogen in the soil during their natural process of decomposition in the garden. Bacteria in the soil that gradually break down organic materials require large quantities of nitrogen. Since the woody materials contain only small amounts of nitrogen, the bacteria may use some of the available nitrogen in the soil and produce a nitrogen deficiency. You can adjust for this by sprinkling a small amount of complete fertilizer, such as 10-10-5 or 10-6-4, on the soil surface prior to applying the mulch. In this way, you provide sufficient amounts of nitrogen to meet the needs of both the bacteria and plants. The type of mulch you use determines the depth at which to use it. Apply most organic mulches 2–4 inches in depth.

Weeds grow faster than we realize. Count on that fact of life. It pays to remove them when they first sprout. Otherwise, July becomes a horror show as weeds compete for nutrients and water that your valued plants need. Mulching can be your first line of defense against weeds.

Mulching involves covering soil around vegetables so light cannot reach the soil surface. When done correctly, this eliminates all but the most persistent weeds. Your mulch choices are wide. Black plastic is most effective around large and widely spaced plants such as cucumbers, melons, squashes,

tomatoes. These crops really benefit from the weed control and extra warmth the black plastic provides.

There is a drawback. Black plastic provides an ideal environment for slugs, and in wet growing seasons these pests can be troublesome. However, on the plus side, it completely stops weeds and keeps soil beneath it nicely moist. Black plastic mulch also absorbs heat in spring to give plants a warmer starting environment.

Organic alternatives including grass clippings, old leaves, compost, and weed-free straw. These help moderate soil temperature, reduce evaporation from the soil, and can be incorporated into the soil. Actually, I use both organic and inorganic types, and you should consider which will work best for your own garden sites.

Before applying mulch, remove all weeds. Then water the garden to get moisture into the soil. If you prefer black plastic, cut slits in the sheets to permit air and water movement. Anchor the plastic with soil or wood strips. Then, cut slits in the plastic where you will plant your seedlings. To conceal the plastic, toss on a light layer of grass clippings or peat moss, at least 2 inches thick. Organic mulch materials may need a second application during the season as the first layer decays.

CONSIDER CROP ROTATION

Farmers know that crop rotation can break insect and disease cycles in many crops. Gardeners can use that technique too. To reduce the likelihood of plant diseases becoming an ongoing problem in your vegetable garden, do not grow the same crop in the same area of your garden each year. Rotate the crops by family, not by individual vegetable. And plant related crops in the same family in the same place only once every 3 or 4 years. For example, follow tomatoes with peas or pole beans, followed by trellised cucumbers or squashes the second year, sunflowers the third year, and then back to tomatoes, peppers, eggplant, or tomatillo. For a quick guide, here are some related crop families.

Composite Family: lettuce, endive, salsify, Jerusalem artichoke, chicory, sunflower, celtuce.

Gourd Family: pumpkin, squash, zucchini, cucumber, melon, gourd.

Mustard Family: cabbage, cauliflower, broccoli, Brussels sprouts, kale, collards, kohlrabi, bok choy, Chinese cabbage, turnip, broccoli raab, mustard greens, rutabaga, radish, horseradishes.

Nightshade Family: eggplant, potato, tomato, pepper, tomatillo.

Pea Family: peas, beans, peanuts.

Also rotate shallow-rooted crops with deep-rooted ones, to aid in soil aeration and improve water movement in the garden. Some of the popular shallow-rooted crops are broccoli, Brussels sprouts, cabbage, cauliflower, celery, Chinese cabbage, corn, endive, garlic, leek, lettuce, onion, parsley, potato, radish, spinach. Moderately deep rooted are bush bean, pole bean, beet, carrot, Swiss chard, cucumber, eggplant, muskmelon, mustard, pea, pepper, rutabaga, summer squash, turnip. These have deep roots: lima bean, parsnip, pumpkin, winter squash, sweet potato, tomato, watermelon.

THINK ABOUT RAISED BEDS

If you have a bad back, or really poor garden soil, raised beds may be worth trying. Many seniors garden in raised beds and containers. These let you tend crops more easily, grow more intensively by fertilizing plants being grown closer together, control weeds, and harvest more conveniently. You can fill raised beds with good loam that you buy.

Raised beds have historic roots. Remember the Hanging Gardens of Babylon? This centuries-old technique increases the soil depth to improve the health and productivity of a garden. If they're properly constructed, raised beds have better soil structure and drainage than ordinary garden beds. Soil in raised beds also dries out earlier in spring to give you an earlier start.

Permanent raised beds have supported sides. You can use a variety of materials, including wood, concrete blocks, bricks, or stones. Most raised beds are 3–4 feet wide for ease of cultivation. They can be any length. In raised beds, gardeners can plant, tend, and harvest their crops without walking on and compressing the soil. That means air and water can move easily into the soil to let you grow healthier, more vigorous plants.

Once you build or have a contractor frame the beds, the most important consideration is the soil mix. Don't economize on this vital growing ground. Raised-bed fans recommend a mix of approximately two-thirds topsoil and one-third leaf humus. First calculate how much you will need to fill your beds, leaving 3 inches from the top boards so soil doesn't wash out. Calculate the volume of the bed in cubic feet by multiplying the length times the width times the depth in feet. A typical depth for raised beds is 8 inches, which equals 0.67 feet. A raised bed 3 feet wide, 16 feet long, and 8 inches deep is 32 cubic feet. Now, divide 32 cubic feet by 27 because there are 27 cubic feet in 1 cubic yard and you'll have the volume in cubic yards, which is how most topsoil is sold.

To fill that bed, you'll need one yard of topsoil and one-half yard of leaf humus or compost.

Happily today, garden centers and landscape contractors are offering premixed raised-bed soil mixtures. Check around for them.

With soil mixture in place, you're ready to plant. Try growing some flowers for beauty and cutting amid your veggies. Some gardeners like to set up a drip watering or soaker hose system to provide moisture for plants. With a timer at the tap, you can tend your raised-bed crops more easily.

Even veteran gardeners who have spent years growing in the ground are pleased with raised beds, which have been popular in Europe for decades. Transplanting such a good idea to your home grounds might be worth a try.

3

BERRY TREASURED GARDENS

You'll love berry treasures that you can pick sun-kissed ripe from plants in your own yard: blushing blackberries, rosy raspberries, bright blueberries, and the sweetest strawberries you ever tasted. Most of the tastiest berry varieties aren't suitable for commercial production, but you can grow the most flavorful in your garden. In this chapter, berry experts around the country share their secrets with you.

All you need to enjoy berry tasty gardens is a few berry bushes or rows of strawberries that can yield many quarts of fruit. Follow the easy steps here. Choose the berries you prefer. Then, select the prime varieties to give you early, mid, and late season harvests and you'll be berried in tasteful delights for many weeks each year.

Because you are planting perennials that you want to thrive for years, take the time to plant properly. Prepare soil deeply. Dig or till 10–12 inches deep. Spread compost you've made or composted manure from garden supply stores. If you have heavy clay or sandy soil, add peat moss, which works wonders to open heavy soils and help hold moisture in sandy soils.

Buy your plants locally or from reputable mail order firms that specialize in berries. Most mail

order firms ship bare-root berry plants wrapped in sphagnum moss or similar material to protect plant roots.

Dig holes twice as large as the bare root ball or size of the container-grown plants you buy. Next, pour a half-gallon of water into each hole. Carefully position your plants in the holes to avoid disturbing their roots, especially when working with bare-root plants. Mail order firms usually provide helpful, illustrated instructions to follow.

After positioning the plant and carefully arranging the roots, fill the hole half full of soil. Tamp down the soil to eliminate air pockets, and water again. After the water soaks in, add soil to fill the hole, firm it well, then water. Always leave a saucer-shaped depression around each berry plant to catch rain and direct it to the new plant.

Finally, mulch with compost, grass clippings, rotted leaves, or peat moss. Mulch helps hold soil moisture, which newly planted bushes need. It also helps stop weeds that would compete for moisture and nutrients.

Water at least once every week, so plants establish a good foundation. Be aware that most berry bushes won't develop much fruit the first year. That's nature's way. But as they set fruit in future years, plan for weekly watering to produce the lush, sweetest fruit crops. Adequate water is especially vital when fruit forms and ripens.

To achieve the most bountiful harvests, you must nourish your berry plants. There are many excellent balanced fertilizers especially formulated for berry bushes. Check garden centers and chain-store garden departments and ask for suggestions. Follow directions on the package for amounts to use. Don't be heavy handed. Too much plant food can be as bad as too little.

Berry plants and bushes need a good growing year to set their roots and prepare to give you years of bountiful harvests. Most will bear only a few berries the first year, and many more the next. By the third and future years, you'll be amazed how prolific berries can be.

BLUSHING BLACKBERRIES

Gardeners often overlook blackberries as a backyard berry crop. One reason is that the canes are thorny, making picking a sticky business. Today, however, thanks to plant breeders, you have a wide choice of tasty, thorn-free blackberries. Try one of these marvelous new varieties as a test plot in your garden. Consider early and late ripening varieties to extend your picking season.

Blackberries are a native plant that plant breeders have perfected to provide easier culture, large harvests of delicious, plump berries, and few or no thorns. Blackberry bushes are the heaviest bearing of bramble fruits. They ripen from June to mid-summer. Most varieties tend to spread by underground suckers, so you may need to trim back the plants to control their spread.

Blackberry is the common name for several of the plants of a genus of the rose family. Darrow was one of the most favored and productive for years,

but it is very thorny. Thornless new varieties include early Arapaho, featuring very small seeds, which ripens in June. Kiowa bears the largest black-berries, up to 3 inches long, and bears in early June.

Apache is a thornless variety introduced by the University of Arkansas. Chester, another thornless, is considered the hardiest and most productive for the upper Midwest. It offers firm berries ripening in July. Illini, developed in Illinois, was bred for northern areas and has vigorous growth and abundant crops of shiny berries ripening in late July. Triple Crown thornless has large, glossy black fruit and can yield up to 30 pounds per plant in early August.

Two Green Thumb award winners deserve your attention: Prime Jim and Prime Jan blackberries. These are revolutionary new blackberry plants that bear on both old and newer canes. These plants therefore produce quality berries in a wider range of climates, since winter damage to canes no longer means a poor crop the following summer. Second-year canes bear the heaviest crops in mid-June; first-year canes bear berries that start to ripen in mid-July and continue to frost. These new varieties cost a bit more but certainly offer major advantages. Keep an eye open for newer types being introduced by plant breeders.

Blackberries are perennials that live for years. But the canes of most popular varieties are biennial, growing one year and producing fruit the following year. Then these fruit canes die and should be removed. Take heart, though: new canes are produced each year from roots. First-year canes are called **primocanes**; the second-year canes are called **floricanes**.

There are two types of blackberries, erect and trailing. Erect blackberry types have stiff, arching canes that are somewhat self-supporting. Trailing

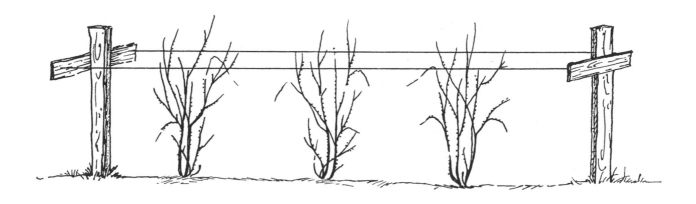

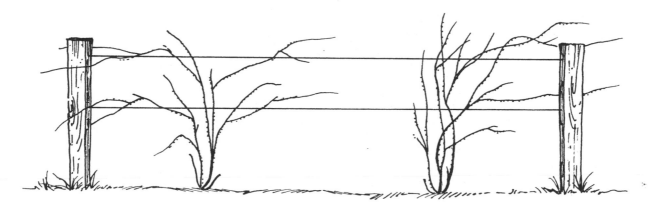

Here are two good ways to train and control blackberries. Use two parallel wires to contain the plants (top), or position one wire above the other, with canes tied by twist-ties to cord (bottom).

blackberries, called dewberries by some gardeners, have canes that are not self-supporting. For most gardens and best harvests, focus on erect blackberries, which are more cold hardy and produce more abundantly, according to berry experts.

Blackberries prefer full sun but can tolerate partial shade. They are sensitive to wet soils. They do best in a well-drained, fertile, loamy soil with moderate water-holding capacity. However, even in heavy, poorly drained soil, blackberries perform fairly well. When you improve the soil with compost and keep the plant area weeded and mulched, black-

berry bushes will amaze you with their productivity. Once planted, they'll produce for 15–20 years.

Do a soil test before planting. Blackberries prefer soil with a pH between 5.5 and 7, so if your soil is below 5.5, add lime as recommended by the soil analysis. Best planting time is early spring. If your soil has low fertility, add one pound of 5-10-5 per 100 square feet as you till the area. When starting new berry beds, I like to deeply till the entire area to incorporate any sod plus fertilizer and soil-improving compost into what will be the permanent berry bed.

New thornless blackberries are easy to grow, very productive, and tasty.

Dig shallow holes large enough to accommodate each plant's roots. Space plants 4–5 feet apart and rows 8–10 feet apart. Berry plants send out underground suckers that will fill in the row, so you need room to weed and harvest from each side. Remove any damaged root parts and spread the root mass evenly around in the hole. Set plants the same depth they were in the nursery, then cover the roots with soil. Press firmly to eliminate any air pockets.

Next, water the plants to settle the soil. Then, cut the canes to 6 inches. Water every week so your blackberries get a good roothold. Be patient. Berries usually don't yield the first year but after that crops should be abundant.

You may wish to use a trellis of parallel wires from cross posts to keep berry bushes under better control, but most erect types don't really need such extra effort. Proper pruning keeps them in shape and gives you room to reach in to harvest even hidden berries.

Blackberries respond well to fertilizer, producing more abundant crops of larger, sweeter berries. Apply fertilizer in early spring when new growth be-

gins. I spread granular fertilizer along each side of the row in the amount recommended for the type used. Typically, 5–6 pounds of 10-20-20 fertilizer per 100 feet of row or the equivalent rate of a similar fertilizer is sufficient. Organic gardeners prefer manure. It is best to apply rotted manure in late fall or early winter so it penetrates the soil. We applied horse manure one year and the berry patch production exploded in tasty profusion. Unfortunately, horse manure tends to carry many weed seeds that can create problems by adding weeds to beds.

Mulch is a good, labor-saving way to thwart weeds. Use rotted bark, straw, or composted leaves 2–3 inches deep along rows to control weeds and retain soil moisture. Cultivate no deeper than 1–2 inches to prevent root damage.

As ripening time arrives, be sure to provide water, especially during dry periods. Blackberries plump up to sweetest taste with ample water. Give them about 1 inch of water per week from mid-June onward, and especially through harvest. Be watchful for harvest time. Pick berries every few days, using a breaking motion rather than pulling.

Blackberry bushes need periodic pruning to boost productivity. Each summer, remove the top 1–2 inches of new primocanes when they're 3 feet tall. This forces them to branch, and these branches will produce fruit the next year on floricanes. After harvest, remove dried old floricanes that have died.

As friends admire your blackberries and their exceptional taste, they may want some plants. You can easily create new plants by digging up suckers that are formed from underground root systems, so your friend can have blackberry treasures too.

TRULY TASTY BLUEBERRIES

Blueberry pancakes start a day right. Delicious blueberry pie caps a day perfectly. To enjoy those

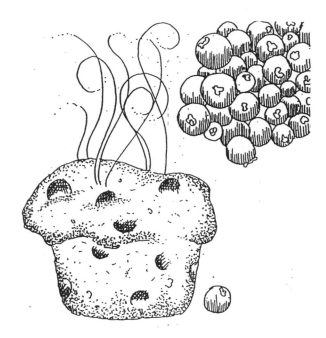

Blueberry muffins for breakfast are one reason to grow blueberries. Once well-rooted, the plants yield abundant crops every year.

treats and blueberry muffins in between, add blueberries to your landscape plans.

Many prolific blueberry varieties are available that give you more fruit for less effort than other bush berries. Happily, they also make delightful ornamental shrubs, bearing distinctive bell-shaped flowers every spring followed by clusters of berries each summer. In the fall, attractive reddish leaves grace the plant.

Blueberry is the common name for several related North American shrubs and their fruit. Lowbush blueberries (*Vaccinium angustifolium*) average less than 3 feet tall. Highbush blueberries (*Vaccinium corymbosum*) range 6–15 feet tall. Bushes bear sweet blue or blackish berries, usually in clusters. Blueberries belong to the family Ericaceae.

Plan to extend your blueberry pleasure time by selecting early, mid, and late ripening varieties. Early types bear in June, and late varieties bear right up to October. Some varieties are better for fresh use, others for pies and preserves, while oth-

ers are nicely multipurpose. Check nursery catalogs and you'll be able to enjoy blueberries for many weeks.

Earliblue offers the first blueberries of summer. These are vigorous, upright plants that produce clusters of large, firm berries. Pollinate with Bluecrop for larger berries. Blue Ray is another early variety that is vigorous, somewhat spreading, with smaller, tight clusters of firm, light-blue berries. For large berries, try Patriot or Darrow. Bluecrop is known for its extreme hardiness, vigor, and consistent production. Jersey has big yields on hardy bushes, and is crack-resistant too, but the plants need pollination with Earliblue or Bluecrop for larger fruit in June. Climax and Tifblue are Rabbiteye blueberries (*Vaccinium ashei*), favored south of the Mason-Dixon line to produce tasty, abundant berries. Check plant catalogs for other varieties newly introduced. As blueberries have won popularity, plant breeders continue to develop even more productive varieties.

Because their roots are fibrous and grow close to the surface, blueberry bushes have special requirements. Their growing area should have loose, well-aerated, somewhat acid soil, between 4.8 and 5.0 pH. Blueberries have such a hairlike, fine, root filament system, it pays to prepare the planting area a year in advance. Dig or till under compost, manure, peat moss, and rotted oak and maple leaves to produce a light, fluffy, acid soil condition.

You can continue to meet blueberries' special needs by adding acid fertilizer and mulching with acid-producing oak and maple leaves, pine needles, and rotted manure. Important note: it pays to buy two-year-old stock because this has better root development to give the plants a faster, more successful adjustment.

Blueberries do best in full sun and sandy loam soil. Avoid low land pockets where frost may nip

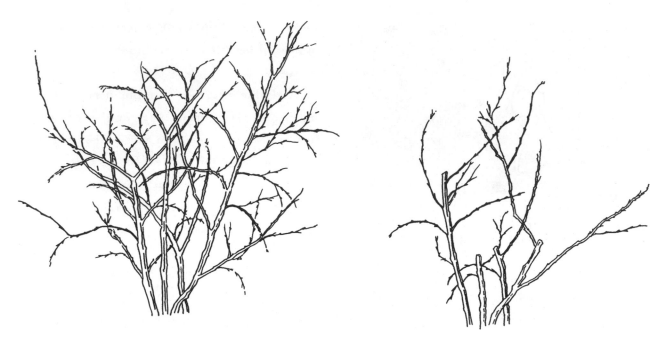

The blueberry bush on the left is wasting energy. When properly pruned as on the right, it produces more berries

tender spring blooms. They also prefer slightly acid soil, between 4 and 4.5 pH, and lots of moisture, especially at fruit-bearing time. Highbush blueberry plants can be very prolific. Be patient the first two years as plants develop their spreading, fibrous root system. By the second and third year, you'll be amazed at the bountiful harvests. Some mature bushes when 4–6 feet tall can produce up to 20 pints over 2–3 weeks. By selecting early, mid, and late ripening varieties, you can really stretch the season from early June into the fall. Cross pollination isn't needed, but it has a curious advantage. It seems to encourage plants to produce bigger berries.

Plant your blueberry bushes in early spring. Dig a hole 18 by 18 inches. Fill it with a mixture of 50 percent compost and peat moss with 50 percent topsoil, and leave 4 inches to spare. Spread plant roots in the hole and cover with remaining soil mix. Set plants about 5 feet apart, water well, and mulch with a 4-inch layer of bark mulch, oak leaves, pine straw, or other acidic material.

Continue watering each week until the roots take hold and the bushes seem thriving. Soaker hoses or drip irrigation are especially helpful to provide the larger amounts of moisture these plants need. If you cultivate, do it lightly and very carefully to avoid damaging the fibrous surface-area root system.

Blueberries respond to pruning during the winter dormant system. By the fourth year, remove weak and dead branches, and thin out small pencil-sized ones and unproductive older branches.

Picking is easy. Gently roll berries between your thumb and forefinger and the ripest will come off, leaving others to ripen fully for later picking. When in prime production, blueberries may be so prolific that you can roll them off into a pot, just like a bunch of grapes.

Blueberry bushes reward you with often brilliant foliage in the fall and bright stems in winter. They make an appealing addition as ornamentals within landscape plantings as well as in berry patches. Some varieties are low and shrubby, only

24 inches tall. Others grow 6–8 feet high. Since they prefer acidic soil, keep them away from masonry walls where soil may be somewhat alkaline.

RELISH RADIANT RASPBERRIES

Black raspberries, or "blackcaps," are an overlooked treat. Black raspberries have arched canes and tend to grow in a cluster-type bush. These plants are natives, growing wild from Quebec to the Dakotas and south to Georgia. They lost their appeal for years but finally are making a deserved comeback. Typically, black raspberry bushes yield 3–4 pints per plant over 10–15 days of ripening time, usually at the end of the normal strawberry season and a bit earlier than most red raspberries begin bearing.

Raspberry is the common name for certain plants of the rose family and their cap-shaped fruits. Raspberries are native to the North Temperate Zone. The European red raspberry (*Rubus idaeus*) was one of the first European plants to be introduced into America. Our American red raspberry (*Rubus idaeus* var. *strigosus*), native to the eastern United States, produces fruit that is slightly inferior in quality to the European species. America's native black raspberry (*Rubus occidentalis*) is hardy and productive.

Over the years, many raspberry varieties have been developed from these three species. Fruits range from black through purple and red to yellow. Among the best-rated black raspberries is the virus-free Allen, which ripens in a concentrated period so all fruit can be picked at once. Blackhawk was introduced in Iowa and is one of the hardiest varieties. Bristol is widely planted. Jewel, a virus-free type with upright growth, is very productive. Munger is an extremely disease-resistant variety with small seeds and is noted for large, sweet fruit.

It also is tops for preserving and freezing. It ripens in mid to late season.

Purple raspberries are hybrids of red raspberries and blackcaps. They have the same growth characteristics as blackcaps. Some raspberries have yellow fruit and are variations of red raspberries. Except for fruit color, they have all the characteristics of red raspberries, and they are grown chiefly by homeowners in northern states.

Purple Royalty, a virus-free gourmet-type purple raspberry, has large fruit with a high sugar content. It bears late, avoiding spring frost damage. There is also Kiwigold, bearing large gold berries that ripen in August. It is disease resistant and reportedly more flavorful than earlier gold rasps. Another treat is Fall Gold, an ever-bearing type that yields from July to late October. It is especially hardy for cold climates.

Red raspberries are perhaps the best known and most widely grown of the raspberries. Heritage is the most widely planted worldwide. It is virus free and a truly outstanding ever-bearing raspberry. It has vigorous upright canes that don't require staking or a trellis. That's a big plus. Fruit is superior; the berries are large, bright red, and firm. Some of the berries mature in early July, and a fall crop begins in early September and continues to frost. That late crop often is better than the first.

Killarney is a virus-free, subtly sweet berry from Canada, so it handles cold winters well. Burgundy-red berries burst with flavor and aroma for eating fresh or freezing. Latham, Taylor, Laure, and Tulameen are other top varieties. Ever-bearing Fall Red is a New Hampshire development, ripening first early in July then with a fall crop by August to frost. In the past few years, plant breeders have been introducing ever-bearing varieties, so check mail order catalogs for the latest developments.

Try a few different types so you can compare them and learn which you like best. Again this perennial advice: extend your berry dining season with early, mid, and late ripening varieties, or with ever-bearers.

As you dream of raspberry turnovers, tarts, and jam, look though catalogs and plan your raspberry beds. Raspberries are easily grown and thrive in almost any type of soil, but all rasps prefer full sun for peak performance. You can grow them in beds, along property lines, or in clusters among other landscaping.

When you buy plants, order tissue-cultured plants, because they are certified virus free and should be free of Verticillium wilt and crown gall. Be cautious about accepting plants from a neighbor's garden. They may have hidden disease problems. It pays to buy virus-free varieties directly from leading producers. And get the tastiest, most productive varieties.

All raspberries are self-fertile, so they may be planted alone; they don't need a companion for cross-pollination. Canes of raspberries, like blackberries, are biennial. They grow for one year and then produce flowers and fruits during the second year. Remove the old dead canes after harvest.

All raspberries produce new canes to replace those that die. Some are from crown buds and from buds along roots, called root suckers. These suckers arise randomly and may result in a thick bramble patch if not controlled. Black and purple raspberries, however, produce primocanes only from crown buds on the original plant and remain as bushes where you first planted them.

Although most red raspberries bear in July, some such as Heritage are ever-bearing. Heritage may be annually pruned by simply mowing or cutting off all canes at or slightly below ground level each fall. Next spring, new shoots begin to grow,

which will produce fruit on the tops in late summer through early fall. New varieties also have improved growing and bearing habits, so check fruit mail order catalogs for them.

When planning your beds, don't select a site where tomatoes, potatoes, or eggplants have been grown, since those plants may have left some disease organisms in the ground that can harm raspberries. Raspberries grow best in deep, sandy loam soils that have ample amounts of organic matter. Actually, rasps will grow in any sunny, good garden soil if it is well drained and has high moisture-holding ability. A pH range between 5.8 and 6.5 is considered optimum. It helps to mix about 3 pounds of 10-10-10 or equivalent fertilizer per 100 square feet into the soil to give the plants a better, faster start.

Place red raspberries 3 feet apart in rows, and leave 8–10 feet between rows. Set black raspberries 2.5 feet apart with 8–10 feet between rows. Red rasps will tend to form hedgerows that you can cultivate and pick from both sides. Suckers from the roots will fill in the rows. Blacks and purples will remain as bushy specimens. However, you can propagate new plants by bending canes to insert the tips into the ground. Cover with soil and let them set roots. When they have, cut the new plants away from the parent, and dig up to transplant.

To plant rasperry bushes, dig holes 12 inches deep. Mix in compost and peat moss, since you are preparing permanent beds that your plants will occupy for many years. For potted or root-balled plants, set them to a depth of about 3 inches. Plant bare-root plants 5–6 inches deep, which should be about 1 inch deeper than the plants were grown in the nursery. Water well every week to give the plants a strong start and encourage them to set roots deeply. Mulch around black and purple bushes to preserve soil moisture and smother weeds.

Pruning improves red raspberry performance. Cut back the bearing floricanes during winter to 4–5 feet, which is a good height for picking. That also avoids having tall canes bend over with the crop weight.

New canes as well as fruiting canes occur together in the row from spring to the end of harvest, competing for light, water, and nutrients. Thin out weak new shoots, and remove old, dead canes in late winter or early spring before growth begins. However, many gardeners prefer removing fruiting canes after harvest. Cut close to the ground, leaving about three or four of the sturdiest canes per foot of row.

Black and purple raspberries do not need trellises or support if they are pruned periodically. Cut off the tips of new shoots when individual canes reach 24–30 inches. By the end of the first season, canes send out laterals. Next year, small branches

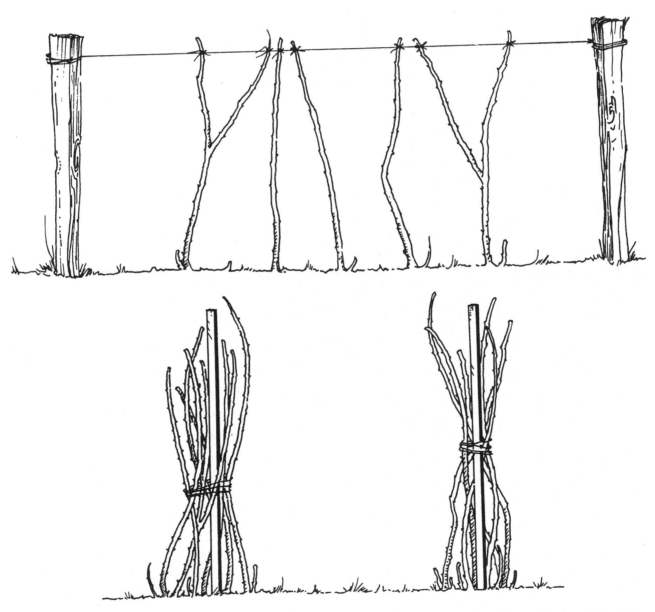

These drawings show training and pruning needed for a hedge system for growing red raspberries (top) and the hill system (bottom).

A black raspberry plant that looks like the one on the left becomes more productive when pruned as shown on the right.

grow from buds on laterals, and fruit is produced on these. With black rasps as with red, canes die after fruiting, so remove them when convenient.

Imagine months of delicious raspberry harvests. Look over catalogs and plan your feasts. Extend your raspberry treat time by selecting early, mid, and late season. Consider varieties that offer two crops a year:—one in spring, another usually bigger crop in fall. Even better are ever-bearing varieties that begin ripening in early summer and yield ongoing crops up to frost. Heritage is popular because it is vigorous and ever-bearing, with moderate summer crops followed by a prolific fall crop of medium-size berries. New varieties keep coming along.

Remember that raspberries are shallow rooted. Mulching is a worthwhile practice along beds or around bushes to stop weeds and conserve soil moisture. If you cultivate, be certain to do it lightly and carefully to avoid damaging roots.

Finally, focus on that tasty harvest. Unless they are ever-bearing, varieties usually ripen over 2–3 weeks. Check regularly for readiness when they look ripe. When berries slide easily off the small white core, they are ready for harvest. Do a taste test. Pick into small containers so you don't crush those on the bottom with the weight of others. Then, enjoy as you wish on cereal or for pies, jams, and any other recipes you prefer.

SUPER SWEET STRAWBERRIES

Prepare to be berry, berry happy. Think about strawberry shortcake or strawberry-rhubarb pie. Strawberries really are the most productive of any berries. They can be grown in any fertile, well-drained soil with ample sun. One warning: they can be killed by late spring frost. Never plant them at the bottom of a hill where frost gathers. Slopes are good. You can edge a walk, interplant with flowers, or prepare regular strawberry beds. If you live in a city, grow strawberries in barrels or tubs on your porch or patio. Today, special

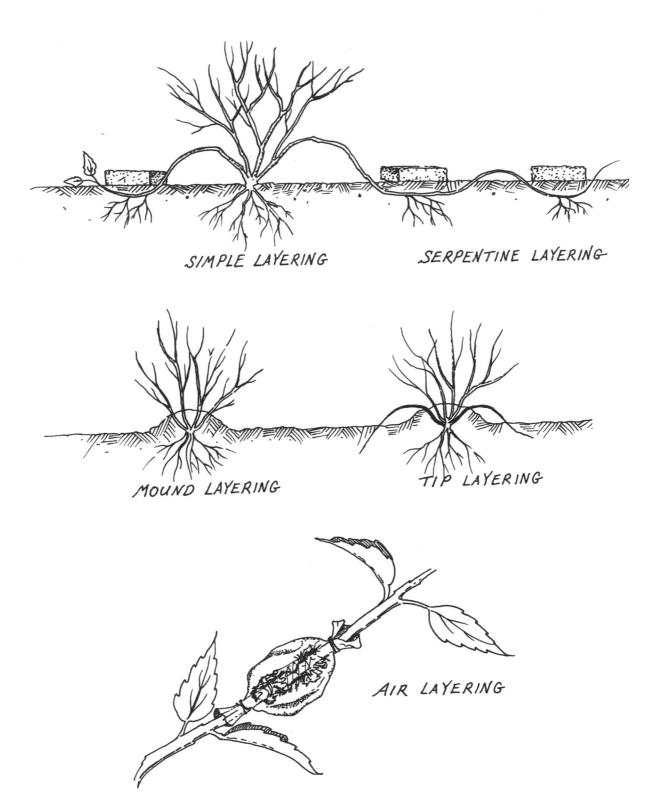

SIMPLE LAYERING   SERPENTINE LAYERING

MOUND LAYERING   TIP LAYERING

AIR LAYERING

Propagating pays by producing new plants. Here are several ways to propagate new plants: simple layering, serpentine layers, mound layering, tip layering, and air layering.

strawberry planters are available to grow up where space is scarce.

Strawberry is the common name for low, perennial herbs of a genus of the rose family and for the fruit of these herbs. Strawberries are native to temperate regions throughout the world and were first cultivated in the United States about 1835. There are so many strawberry varieties that selecting the best ones to grow may seem impossible. Check in mail order catalogs to find the ones that best fit your location and needs. Ever-bearing varieties now make strawberry pleasure a summer-long treat.

Annapolis is a delicious early strawberry variety with plump, firm fruit that bears well in northern climes. Earliglow is another top flavor berry for desserts, freezing, or preserves, ripening in June. Other early bearers include Jewel, Allstar, Stark Crimson King, Surecrop, and Eversweet. Surecrop has been a favorite for years and lives up to its name for production reliability. Cavendish and Sparkle are delights too.

Ever-bearing ability is on everyone's mind these days. Tribute blooms and sets fruit without regard to length of days and nights. You pick the first crop in early spring and additional crops at about 6-week intervals. It also resists cold weather and diseases. Ozark Beauty is a virus-free ever-bearer for abundant crops from spring until snow flies; the berries are tasty, deep red, firm, and sweet. Tristar is yet another reliable strawberry, bearing spring to fall.

Space strawberries 12 inches apart in rows or beds. Be sure that the crown, the point where roots grow down and leaves sprout up, is right at the soil surface. Spread roots well, and keep them moist while planting. Lay a wet cloth over unplanted plants or keep them moist in a bucket.

The number of plants to set depends on how many strawberries you want. One plant yields about 1–2 quarts of berries, providing you satisfy their needs. If you start ten plants and they each produce five daughter plants, you'll have 50–100 quarts of berries the next year. Best to have a bit more in case of weather or growing problems. Besides, then you'll have extra to share with friends or make more delicious strawberry jam for toasty winter morns.

After plants have rooted well, they'll usually send out runners the first year. Most first-year parent plants may yield a few berries, but let them develop their new plants to fill in thick rows. Strawberries will bear larger crops the second and third year but then tend to decline. Cut back or remove older plants. That allows new plants to develop fully from runners. They will be the bearing plants for the next few years.

One easy way to renovate is to mow the beds. Young plants will emerge to become the new producing plants. They too will send out more runners that you can transplant if you wish. Unlike berry bushes, strawberry plantings need periodic renovation. Look for young runners and position them in new areas, or cut and plant them for new beds. By keeping beds well mulched, you'll prevent most weeds, retain soil moisture, and provide a cushion for a cleaner berry crop.

When berries begin to form and ripen, they need ample moisture to set largest, sweetest fruit. Provide an inch of water each week, and a bit more during dry periods to insure plumpest, sweetest fruit.

Many strawberry lovers keep two beds in rotation so that every year they can count on 50–100 quarts of super-delicious berries. That's enough for about 30 shortcakes and 50 pints of preserves. Keep in mind that strawberries are in full production their second year. Within 5–6 weeks after planting, they send out runners. When these reach 8–10 inches, they begin to form a new daughter

Strawberries must be planted at the correct depth to produce well. The plant on the left is too deep, the next is too shallow, and the third is correct with plant crown at the surface.

You can grow strawberries in the hill system as shown above or the row system below. Either way you must renovate strawberry beds, removing older plants every few years to let new ones perform at their peak.

plant. They in turn produce more plants, which produce the crop the following year. June bearers normally yield more than ever-bearers but over a shorter period. That's why many gardeners grow early bearing berries and also have ever-bearer varieties to extend their strawberry feasting time.

As with other berries, try strawberry varieties that will give you early, mid, and late harvests. And evaluate one of the new ever-bearing varieties that begin with small crops in spring and continue producing luscious strawberries up to frost. Dig in and begin growing your homemade strawberry short-cake this year.

BE GRATEFUL FOR GRAPES

Grapes are one of the world's favorite fruits. You can find historic records of them and the wine they provide as far back as written records exist. Grapes and wine are widely mentioned in the Bible, and that dates back 5,000 or so years. The European grape has been used as food since prehistoric times. Grape seeds have been found in remains of lake dwellings of the Bronze Age in Switzerland and Italy and in tombs of ancient Egypt. Today, grapes are commercially cultivated in warmer regions all over the world.

As you think about colorful grapes and the joys they provide for eating fresh and making great grape jam, jelly, and juice, it is good to know how valuable grapes are to health. Grapes are fat free as well as sodium and cholesterol free. Red grapes especially are recognized as being very beneficial for preventing heart problems. Scientific studies reveal that fresh grapes, grape jams and juices, and wines have important health benefits. We all can be grateful for grapes.

Grapes belong to the family Vitaceae. American and French hybrid types are best for northern growing conditions because they tend to be more winter hardy. Recommended American cultivars include Niagara, Delaware, and Canadice.

Among seedless grapes, consider these white ones: Neptune, Lakemont, and Marquis. Among seedless blue grapes, consider Glenora, a very hardy, Concord-type grape. Jupiter is a reddish blue seedless, and Flame is a reddish one.

The prized Concord grape, a classic since 1843, is the flavor standard for prize-winning jams and jellies. It ripens in late September. Several French-American hybrids, such as Seyval Blanc and Vidal Blanc, are recommended for their wine-making qualities and good winter hardiness. Several other cultivars to try are Golden Muscat, Marechal Foch, Chardonel, and Frontnac.

For colorful grapes with different flavors, read through mail order catalogs. Depending on the cultivar, grapes may be red, blue, white or greenish-yellow, purple, or black. You can chose among seeded and seedless types.

Keep in mind that harvested grapes don't store well. To enjoy them over a longer period, select early, mid, and late ripening varieties, as you would with other fruits. Earliest cultivars ripen beginning about mid-August, while the latest cultivars ripen from late September to early October. Ontario, Seneca, Fredonia, and Hardy Worden are early ripeners. Mid-seasons include Delaware, Niagara, and Steuben. Late ones include Sheridan and Golden Muscat. Concord is the most widely planted grape east of the Rockies. It is hardy in most northern areas except truly cold winter states. For cold areas, consider Bluebell, Fredonia, Van Buren, and Worden.

Grape growing requires long-term dedication. Vines take several years from planting to first harvest. Some don't reach full production until the fifth or sixth year. Good news is that grape plants can survive for 50–100 years. Several generations of your family can enjoy them. It is important to carefully select both the vine site and devote time to proper soil preparation.

Avoid frosty areas. Commercial grape areas are located on sloping land that faces south, so any cold air drains away to the bottom of the slope. The first step toward producing high-quality fruit is a sunny location. Sheltered home surroundings usually are warmer. A sloping area, especially a south or south-west slope, usually has higher temperatures and is less likely to get frost. Plant rows north to south so that fruit and leaves will be better exposed to sunlight than in east–west rows.

You can grow grapes in a wide variety of soil types but drainage is important. Your grapes won't prosper if you have heavy, soggy clay soil. It pays to select areas with deep, well-drained, loamy soils for your arbor. Also, grapes need full sunlight and high temperatures to ripen. Shielding vines from

prevailing winds is worthwhile. Avoid sites where there will be standing water, especially in spring.

Spring planting is best, according to experts, as soon as the soil can be worked. Before planting the vines, remove all except the most vigorous cane. Trim off any broken or overly long roots. Next, dig a hole large enough so you can spread the root system out without bending the roots. Space plants 6–8 feet apart. Plant vines at the same depth as in the nursery. Spread roots evenly and cover them completely with soil. After planting, shorten the remaining cane to two strong buds. Each bud will develop into a cane.

Firm the soil well around the roots to remove air pockets. Then water thoroughly. Leave a slight depression around the base of the plant to catch rain. Young grapevines can't compete with weeds or lawn grass for water and nutrients, so keep the planting free of all weeds. Mulching for a foot or more around newly planted vines is useful. If you

A grape plant should be placed in a hole that accommodates its roots. Then fill with improved soil mix and water well until the vine is established.

cultivate the ground, do it no deeper than 1–3 inches, to avoid root injury. Grapes require patience, several years' worth. It takes about 3–5 years to establish a grape planting. Some varieties take more time.

Space vines for training on a trellis 8 feet apart. Space those for training on an arbor 4 feet apart. Grapes require some type of support. You should have support in place before planting, or at least before vine growth begins the second year.

Feed grape vines well and they will feed you with abundant, delicious harvests. Grapes do best where soil pH is between 5.0 and 6.0. Apply lime only if soil analysis indicates a need. To properly feed new

vines, apply 8 ounces of 10-10-10 fertilizer per plant about 7 days after planting. Then increase the amount to 1 pound of 10-10-10 in the second year and 1.5 pounds per vine in the third and later years. Apply fertilizer about 30 days before new spring growth begins. Spread the fertilizer evenly 6–12 inches from the trunk of the vine.

Water plants after planting and during dry periods. An inch per week the first year is advisable. Mature vines seem to thrive with rain water, except during droughts or in dry climates, when you should irrigate vines, especially as they set fruit and as the fruit matures.

Grape vines need special attention to pruning. Actually, they need more than most gardeners believe or are willing to do. You must achieve a balance between vegetative growth and fruiting. The best time to prune vines is when they are dormant during winter, using either cane or spur pruning. The most common problem with grape growing is that gardeners don't prune hard enough. For grapes, remove the majority of wood produced the previous season, which will be about 90 percent. That's right! Read that again. In proper pruning, very little wood is left to produce the following year's crop.

Now for the good part—picking and enjoying your grape crops. Learn to pick at proper maturity. Fruit color isn't the best indication of maturity. With table grapes, taste is the best test. All grapes become sweeter and usually less acidic as they mature. The average temperature must be greater than 50°F for grapes to continue to mature on the vine. Fruit does not ripen further once picked. So sample some grapes as they appear to be mature. When you like what you taste, it is harvest time. Write down the date. Watch the calendar the next year and you'll be able to focus on the best grape-picking period for your crops. Bon appetite!

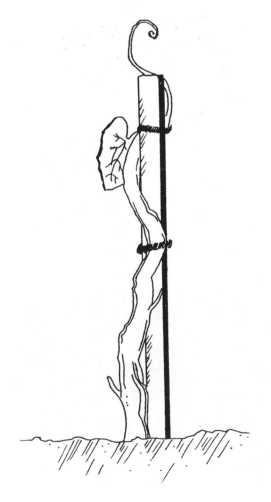

A new grape vine needs support as it begins to set permanent roots.

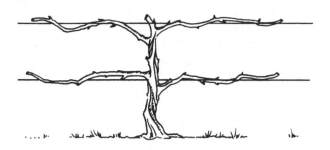

FOUR ARM, SINGLE TRUNK KNIFFIN SYSTEM.

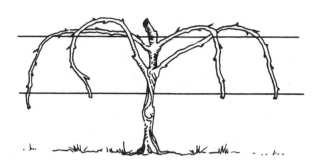

FOUR ARM, SINGLE TRUNK UMBRELLA SYSTEM.

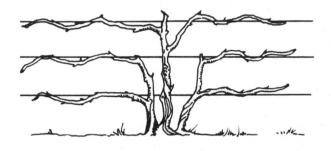

SIX ARM, THREE TRUNK, THREE WIRE,
MODIFIED KNIFFIN SYSTEM.

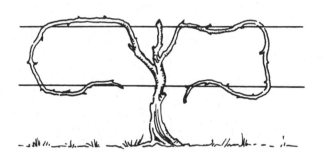

TWO ARM, SINGLE TRUNK UMBRELLA SYSTEM.

Here are basic forms for training and pruning grape vines. Use the one that appeals to you, but remember to prune well every year to encourage the most productive crops.

COLORFUL CURRANTS AND GREAT GOOSEBERRIES

Currants and gooseberries are highly tolerant of less-than-perfect sites. Full sun gives the healthiest, most productive results, but the shrubs can perform quite well on as little as a half-day of sun. A soil pH between 5.5 and 7, which is moderately acidic to neutral, is optimal.

Currant and gooseberry plants both have fibrous and shallow root systems, so they must have extra water during their growing time. Another disadvantage is that currants and gooseberries bloom very early in spring. Therefore, their flowers are susceptible to late-season frosts that can seriously reduce crops.

Prepare your planting site the fall before you actually plant. Because currants and gooseberries do not perform well in dry or waterlogged conditions, you may have to improve your soil with the addition of organic material such as shredded peat or compost before planting. Rid the proposed planting site of all perennial weeds, as they are much more difficult to control after planting. Test the site soil for pH and nutrient needs. Professional soil testing may be done through local garden centers or with help from your County Extension office.

Currants and gooseberries are self-fertile, but research suggests that planting more than one cultivar results in better yields. Plants from mail order sources are usually sent as bare roots. Those purchased from a local nursery may be bare roots or potted. Set out plants in spring as soon as the soil can be worked. When handling bare-root plants, be certain to keep the plants cool and moist until they go into the ground. Delicate root systems must not be allowed to dry or become waterlogged. Just before planting, soak the roots of bare-root plants in a bucket of clean water for 3–4 hours.

Plant currants and gooseberries at least an inch deeper than they were in the nursery, in holes deeper and wider than their root systems. If lower canes are covered with soil to a depth of two to three buds, this will encourage a larger root system and the development of numerous renewal canes to maximize the useful lifespan of the plant. Plants may be spaced as close as 3 feet apart for a hedge-type system in rows at least 6 feet apart. Black currants are more vigorous and should be spaced 4–5 feet apart in rows at least 8 feet apart.

After planting, prune all canes back to 4–6 inches above-ground buds; the resulting low bud count encourages development of vigorous new canes. You should also spread 2–4 inches of an organic mulch such as wood chips, pine needles, or compost around new plants. Mulching cools the soil, conserves water, and suppresses weeds, actions that are preferable in a partially shaded site and essential in a sunny spot. Renew mulch annually. If you use a low-nitrogen mulch such as wood chips or sawdust, you may need to apply extra nitrogen at

fertilization. Signs of nitrogen deficiency include yellowing leaves and poor growth. Note that older leaves yellow first.

Fertilize currants and gooseberries in early spring, before growth begins. Apply between one-quarter to one-half pound of a balanced fertilizer. The ratio of nitrogen, phosphorus, and potassium is indicated by the numbers on the bag, so look for three numbers that are the same or close to it, such as 10–10–10. Apply fertilizer in a band around each bush, working it lightly into the soil from near the canes to a foot or so beyond the branch tips. A composted material rich in nitrogen, such as manure, also makes an excellent fertilizer and may be substituted for a balanced synthetic fertilizer. Because composted materials release their nutrients more slowly than synthetic fertilizers, apply such materials in late fall.

Prune established currant and gooseberry shrubs to encourage vigor and fruit production, improve sun penetration into the bush, and maintain good air circulation to minimize disease. During the first three years of growth, allow four or five canes to develop per year, removing only weak or damaged wood. Beginning in the fourth year, prune out the oldest wood annually in early spring before growth begins. In addition, remove any weak new growth. A mature bush should have nine to twelve canes once pruning is completed. Fruit is produced on one-, two-, and three-year-old wood.

There is no simpler way to tell when currants and gooseberries are ripe than to monitor the color and flavor of the fruits as they develop. When using the fruit for jam, you should harvest it before it is fully ripe so that natural fruit pectin levels will be higher.

Cool picked fruit quickly, placing it in covered containers or closed bags to maintain humidity levels and prevent drying when storing fruit in a refrigerator. Promptly cooled berries will keep in the refrigerator for up to several weeks.

A few states don't allow import and cultivation of currants and gooseberries because they may be hosts for diseases that could attack valuable commercial berry crops. Check your state rules with your County Extension agent. If you can grow currants and gooseberries, you are among the lucky gardeners. Both are delicious and worth trying.

4

FRUITFUL PLANTSCAPES

Fruitful gardening is a delicious goal. In this chapter, you'll learn how to grow sun-ripened, juicy fruit you can reach out and pick at its flavorful peak from trees or shrubs in your backyard. Just a few trees of your favorite fruits will give you many years of pleasure.

A talented American nurseryman, Clay Stark Logan, gave us fruitful food for thought when he noted, "Few of us realize how importance an abundance of trees is to man and his environment. They are nature's principal factories for converting carbon dioxide into oxygen. Trees add beauty to our homes. Their many distinctive shapes and forms provide variety for more attractive landscape designs. But trees do even more. They release moisture that cools the air and washes it. They keep water and wind from carrying away the topsoil that support all life. They help to keep pollution from washing into our streams."

Add to that the fact that fruit trees give you blooming beauty in spring and delicious taste treats from summer through fall. You have a marvelous choice of many varieties of apples, cherries, peaches, pears, and plums plus nuts that you can grow in your own backyard. You can grow

tastier varieties than supermarkets sell because the tastiest fruits often don't ship well but are available to grow where you live. Plan an edible landscape this year. It doesn't take as much space as you think.

Today you have a choice of miniature, dwarf, semi-dwarf, or standard fruit trees. These smaller trees fit nicely into limited space and bear full-size fruit. Miniature fruit trees are ideal for patios and decks because they grow only 6–8 feet tall. Dwarf trees grow to 8–10 feet high.

Semi-dwarf fruit trees are the most productive, reaching 12–15 feet tall and yielding abundant fruit per limb and per tree. Standard fruit trees bear most of the crop on outside branches and grow 18–25 feet tall. Pick whichever size best fits your available space. All types yield full-size fruits. You can find out more about specific varieties of each type of fruit in mail order catalogs.

Trees also have a proved monetary value, as you will realize when you read about landscaping in chapter 7. Real-estate agents know that lovely shrubs and trees add to the dollar resale value of a home. Trees should be one of your first investments as you begin landscaping. When you add up

You can enjoy a fruitful landscape with a variety of fruit trees as well as berry bushes that produce an abundance of fruits and berries right in your own backyard.

the advantages, fruitful plantscaping makes sense and tastes good too.

Select a sunny spot so your fruit trees receive eight hours of sun each day to thrive and produce the sweetest natural sugars in the fruit. Treat yourself to tastier living all summer and into fall by choosing varieties that ripen early, mid, and late season. Local nurseries can advise you which are best for your locality. Mail order nurseries like Stark Bro's, Miller Nurseries, and others provide a wide choice of truly tasty fruit varieties. Each year new, improved varieties are introduced.

Take a walk around your home grounds. Make a plot plan. Record which areas get the most sun. Examine your soil. If it needs help, determine to improve it with the helpful hints in chapter 2. Consider where a peach or apple or plum tree might prosper. You can set a miniature orchard along a drive, bordering your vegetables, or as specimen trees to enjoy in bloom as you look out your windows.

Home mini-orchards are easier than ever. Plant breeders have developed new varieties that resist diseases and reduce the need for chemical sprays. Look through favorite mail order catalogs for the different fruits and varieties that you want to savor for years. Shop locally if you wish.

According to experts at Stark Bro's, the sooner you plant after trees arrive, the better. You can plant trees even when the outdoor temperatures are quite cool. So long as your soil is workable, it is fine to plant. If you must delay planting until the weather breaks in spring, you can safely store the plants for a short period. Open the package, cover the roots with newspaper, moisten the roots and newspaper to keep them damp, then rewrap the plants in their shipping plastic and store in a cool, dark place. A temperature of 40°F is ideal, but anything under 60°F will work for a short period of time.

If planting must be delayed for more than 10 days, "heel in" the plant in your garden ground. Simply dig a sloping trench long and wide enough to hold the roots. Lay the plants in the trench with roots against the steep side, and cover the roots with soil. Then, soak with water. That can hold plants for a week or so until you have time to get them into their spot in your home grounds.

Here's another important tree planting tip from the Stark experts. Before planting, soak the roots in a tub or large trash can full of water for 1–2 hours. But do not soak more than 6 hours.

Be patient with your new trees. All bare-root stock will begin root development soon after plant-

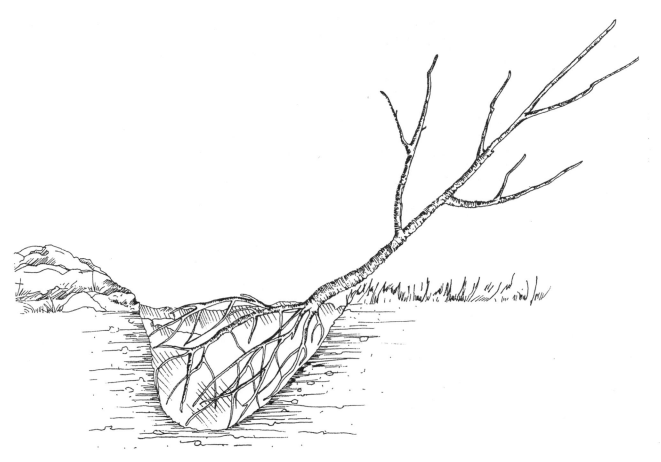

If you can't plant trees or shrubs when they arrive, heel them in for a week or so with their roots beneath moist soil in a shady area.

ing. However, plants need time to develop before top growth is sizable. Most spring-planted items need 3–6 weeks before new sprouts appear. Fall-planted trees may not show any new top growth until spring.

Note these key points. Digging may not be your favorite project, but when planting trees that will be permanent and beautiful parts of your landscape, take time to dig deep and plant well so trees get a good, early roothold and will prosper.

It's a fact that roots grow faster when they are spread out than when they are cramped. So dig the tree hole sufficiently deep and wide enough to give the root system plenty of room. Roots grow better in soil that has been loosened. Mix dehydrated cow manure, garden compost, or peat moss into your pile of topsoil. Make sure the peat moss you get is baled sphagnum or granular peat. Stark Bro's has a Gro-Brick tree starter nutrient that is worthwhile.

Next, put the top few inches of topsoil in a separate pile and use it in the bottom of the hole, where it will do the most good. After positioning the tree roots, work the fine soil carefully around the roots. Then tamp well to firm the soil and eliminate air pockets. For optimum growth and performance, add time-released fertilizer pills to the hole when you backfill. Because these are time released, they will continuously nourish your tree for two years. Then, fill in the hole with soil, tamp down, and water well.

Once planting is done, make a rim of soil around the tree. This allows water to soak in rather than running off. Come fall, fill in that depression around the plant with soil to prevent damage from water freezing around your plant.

For good growth, fruit trees require fertile soil with a pH of 6.0–7.0. Look over your established trees. If they look healthy and are growing well, follow the recommended fertilization program for fruit trees. Many garden centers and chains have reliable fertilizer and fertilizer spikes for use with fruit trees.

Fruit trees from reliable firms usually have been grafted or budded, which are the only methods for growing true-to-name planting stock. Check your new trees and you'll see where the fruiting variety on top is joined to the root variety on the bottom by a bump in the bark, a change in the bark color, or a slight offset angle. For certain dwarf fruit trees, it is very important to keep this graft above the ground. Otherwise roots could develop from above the graft, and then the tree could grow to full size by bypassing its dwarfing parts. Be sure to plant dwarf apple trees about 1 inch deeper than the soil line from the nursery row. Their grafted dwarfing interstem is high enough to keep the top from rooting.

APPLES ARE ALWAYS APPEALING

There is no doubt that apples are as American as apple pie. The true original home of apples is not

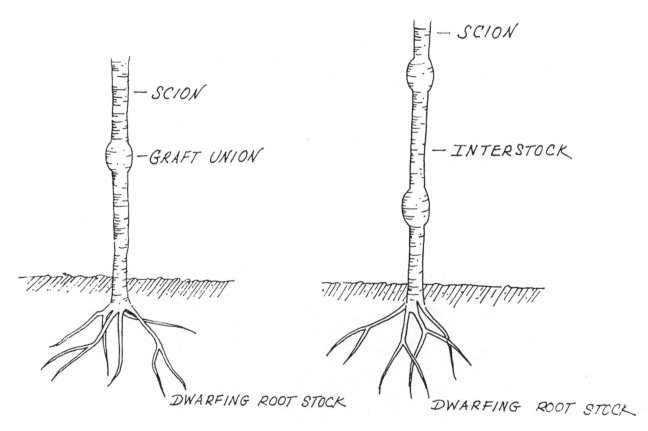

Be sure graft unions, which can be noted by a slight swelling and change in bark color, are above ground. Be sure not to cut off or bury graft unions, because they are what give you the special variety or dwarfing capacity of the rootstock for your tree.

definitely known, but they probably originated somewhere between the Caspian and the Black seas.

Charred apple remains have been found in prehistoric lake dwellings in Switzerland. From ancient writings, we know that apples were a favorite fruit of the ancient Greeks and Romans. Early European immigrants brought apple seeds to the New World, according to Massachusetts Bay Company records that show apples were grown in New England as early as 1630. John Chapman, dubbed Johnny Appleseed, was responsible for extensive plantings of apples throughout the Midwest.

Apples are a member of the rose family They are high in fiber, vitamin C, and potassium, but low in sodium and almost fat-free. Fresh apples are a healthy snack that quenches thirst, and their acid content makes them a natural mouth freshener. And 25 percent of an apple's volume is air, which helps explain why they float. It is best to store whole apples in the refrigerator. However, sliced apples keep their fresh color longer if dropped in a bowl of water containing 2 tablespoons of lemon juice. As you plan your apple plantings, note that it takes 2 pounds of apples to make one 9-inch pie.

Supermarkets offer only a limited selection of apple types. The choice of varieties to plant is far wider and much tastier. Just consult mail order firms that specialize in fruits and choose the delights you want to enjoy. Focus on varieties that will bear in early summer, late summer, early fall, and

Apples are appealing, and you can grow many varieties that are tastier than those you might find in a supermarket.

later to have apples for many months. Fortunately, plant breeders have developed productive varieties resistant to common diseases. These let you save time and reduce need for sprays.

Among the literally hundreds of apple varieties, some are worth special note. For early eating, Lodi is marvelous fresh and for pies. Summer Rambo, dating to sixteenth-century France, is attacked less by insects and disease than varieties that ripen later. Prima ripens midseason with a dark red color on a yellow background. Macoun is a midseason, red-striped apple with crisp, white flesh. Starkspur Golden yields especially flavorful fruit and bears more heavily than others. Zestar is a flavorful large apple that stores well and ripens around August.

Two newer apples developed in Minnesota are the Honeycrisp and Honeygold. Honeycrisp, an excellent, large dessert apple with crisp flesh, ripens in September. It survives cold northern areas and produces reliably. Honeygold has sumptuous flavor as a dessert apple, similar to a Golden Delicious with added honeysweet taste. It also is hardy in northern areas, bearing golden to yellowish green fruit that keeps well. Both these varieties cross-pollinate with Jonared and Jonafree, two reliable disease-resistant apples.

Red Fuji was developed in Japan and is reputedly tastier than Red Delicious. It is available as a semi-dwarf tree and usually ripens in mid-October. September Wonder Fuji ripens earlier. Redfree is bright red, resistant to apple scab and other problems, and ripens in early August. Sweet for fresh use, it stores well in refrigerators. Jonafree is an improved, bright red apple that also resists diseases. Especially hardy, it ripens in mid-September. Grimes Gold is a rugged, hardy, disease-resistant variety that is tasty fresh and wonderful for applesauce. It ripens in mid to late September.

Empire also resists disease. It has the sweetness of Delicious apples combined with McIntosh flavor and ripens in mid-September. Liberty is another extra disease-resistant McIntosh type that produces big crops in late September. Granny Smith is a tart, green-colored apple that resists cedar rust and diseases and ripens in early November.

The best disease-resistant apples are Dayton, Enterprise, Freedom, GoldRush, Jonafree, Liberty, Macfree, McShay, Nova Easygro, Novamac, Prima, Priscilla, Pristine, Redfree, Sir Prize, and Williams' Pride. Look them up in a catalog or plant encyclopedia to find details of color, flesh, flavor, and ripening time.

Want some really different apples? Hawaii is a large, yellow apple with the tang and scent of pineapple. Chenango Strawberry, which dates to 1850, has a scent of strawberries and ripens in early September. Winter Banana is a beautiful pale yellow fruit with an aroma of bananas. You can try other exotic types, from Thomas Jefferson's favorite, the Spitzenburg, to Sops of Wine, one of the oldest apples known. Thumb through fruit catalogs this year and decide which unique apples you can plant to wow your gardener friends.

By the way, if you like apples but live in warmer climates, take heart. Tropical Beauty was discovered in South Africa and has proved successful in warm areas, including Florida and Hawaii. It produces medium-size, carmine-red fruit with a mild flavor.

TREE PLANTING TIPS

Fruit trees do best when they receive full sun, have a well-drained, loamy soil, and are sheltered from prevailing winds. Your fruit trees, as all trees, are permanent parts of your home landscape. It pays to prepare soil well for proper planting. If you have

Leave a saucer-shaped depression around a newly planted tree to hold rainwater. Be sure to water new trees weekly so they gain a strong roothold.

poor soil that is too sandy or has excess clay content, add well-rotted manure, peat moss, compost, or humus to improve growing conditions. The soil improving tips in chapter 2 will help you turn even poor soils into productive growing environments.

Table 4.1, based on information from the leading mail order firms, shows the planting distances for fruit trees, their height at maturity, and the estimated bearing age after planting. Fruit varieties may differ, so keep a record of the types you order and their expected performance.

For apples, choose the special flavors you prefer, and look for disease-resistant varieties to reduce care problems. Remember, apple trees are not self-pollinating, so plant at least one other variety that blooms at the same time. Buy dormant, bare-root, 1-year-old trees. With apples, there really is no advantage to paying a high price for older stock. Younger trees establish themselves quickly and let you control their growth pattern by early pruning.

Table 4.1. Fruit Tree Spacing Guide, Height, and Bearing Age

	Planting Space	Mature Height	Bearing Age
Apple (s/d)	12 x 12 feet	12–15 feet	2 years
Apple (s)	35 x 35 feet	20–25 feet	3–10 years
Apricot (d)	10 x 10 feet	8–10 feet	2 years
Apricot (s)	20 x 20 feet	15 feet	3 years
Cherry, Sour (d)	10 x 10 feet	8 feet	2 years
Cherry, Sour (s)	20 x 20 feet	20 feet	3 years
Cherry, Sweet (s)	25 x 25 feet	30 feet	3–4 years
Peach/Nectarine (d)	10 x 10 feet	8–10 feet	2 years
Peach/Nectarine (s)	20 x 20 feet	20 feet	3 years
Pear (s/d)	12 x 12 feet	12–15 feet	2 years
Pear (s)	20 x 20 feet	25–30 feet	3–4 years
Plum (d)	10 x 10 feet	8–10 feet	2 years
Plum (s)	20 x 20 feet	20 feet	3 years

s = standard size   s/d = semi-dwarf   d = dwarf

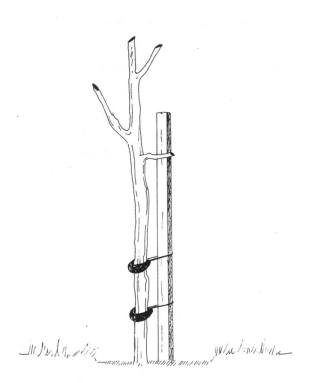

Newly planted trees benefit from staking support. Loop wires through pieces of old garden hose to avoid damaging tender bark on saplings.

Always dig a hole large enough to accommodate the roots or root ball of a container-grown plant. Add soil, water, fill the hole, and add more water.

Key reminder: be sure to keep the graft union on dwarf and semi-dwarf trees at least 1 inch above ground level. Spring is the preferred apple planting time in most parts of the country. By selecting different varieties, you can have delicious apples ripening from July through late fall.

Several apple pests must be controlled. These include codling moths and plum curculio. Combination fruit tree pesticides with Sevin and Imidan have proved effective for home gardeners. Follow mixing and application directions whenever using chemical sprays of any kind. County agents have the latest recommendations.

ENJOY COLORFUL CHERRIES

Cherries have been popular for centuries. Happily, we now have a wide range of deliciously different cherries that will grow well in almost any area.

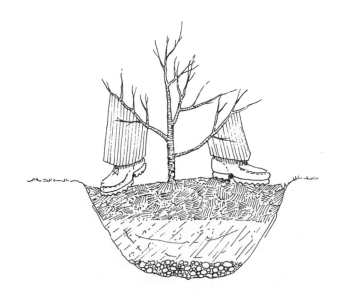

After planting a tree, water again and tamp down the soil to eliminate air pockets. Leave a saucer-shaped area to collect water or rain as the new tree begins to grow.

Whether you want sweet for eating or sour for cooking, cherries have a charm we all can enjoy.

Botanical scholars say the Romans discovered sweet cherries in Asia Minor about 70 BCE and introduced them to Britain in the first century CE. The German word for cherry, *Kirsche*, may come from *karshu*, the name for the first cultivated cherries in Mesopotamia circa 8 BCE. Nutritionally, cherries are free of fat, sodium, and cholesterol and are a good source of fiber.

You can grow two types of home orchard cherries: either the sweet dessert cherry or the sour pie cherry. Sour cherries are lower in calories and higher in vitamin C and beta carotene than sweet cherries.

Cherries may be grown in many parts of the United States. Once well planted, trees bear fruit for about 25 years. Originally, the sweet cherry was planted for its flowering beauty and fruit, plus its value as a timber tree. It grows rapidly, with close-grained wood favored by cabinetmakers and musical instrument makers. The most famous sweet cherry variety is the Bing, which got its name from one of the Chinese workers at the Henderson Lewelling farm in western Oregon, a farm known for its sweet cherries in the 1870s. Bing cherries are a dark burgundy color. Rainier and Queen Anne are light-color, sweet cherry varieties.

Tart or sour cherries are better for pies. Montmorency is the primary sour cherry variety. There are about 7,000 cherries on an average sour cherry tree, depending on the tree's age, the weather, and growing conditions.

Cherry trees begin to produce fruit about five years after planting, but full fruit-bearing capacity is not reached until 10 or 15 years. Be very patient. Once bearing, a fully mature cherry tree is capable of producing more than 100 pounds of fruit in a season.

Check out old favorites and newer varieties to decide which you want. Among sweets, Black Tartarian is a beautiful tree that bears dark purplish-black to cherry-red fancy fruits. Star Stella trees bear younger than other sweet cherries and is self-pollinating.

The wine-red, firm, juicy BlackGold and the red blush over yellow WhiteGold are two cherries developed by Cornell University that merit attention. Royalton Sweet and Starkrimson Sweet are two others worth considering. The Stark Gold sweet cherry is a golden treat that can take cold weather and confuse birds that prefer red cherries.

Among tart pie cherries, evaluate North Star, Balaton, and Starkspur Montmorency. Dwarf North Star is hardy, producing large, bright-red fruits that are great for pies. And it is self-fruitful, ripening mid to late July. Montmorency is perhaps the finest sour pie cherry, a heavy bearer, and self-fruitful.

Cherry trees grow to medium height, between the size of standard peach and apple trees, and they bloom earlier than most fruits. They have a graceful shape, an abundance of spring blossoms, and of course their fruitful harvests. Sweet cherry trees grow larger than the sour cherries, with upright growth for appeal in the landscape, and they are tastier for eating fresh, but they have one disadvantage. Sweet cherries are not self-fruitful, so you must grow two compatible varieties that will cross-pollinate each other to produce crops.

In contrast, the sour pie cherry varieties pollinate themselves. It is true they make great pies, but unfortunately birds love them. Birds prefer sour cherries rather than sweet ones, so you'll need netting to solve that problem. Birds also seem to prefer red-colored cherries, so consider growing yellow cherries like Stark Gold to thwart feathered friends.

Cherries prefer full-sun locations with well-drained and sandy loam. Protection from winds is helpful, such as the sunny backyard of a house. Follow basic planting directions for fruit trees. You now can select semi-dwarf ones to save space. The new Damil rootstock from Belgium has made smaller trees possible, maturing around 10 feet in 15 or so years, which makes picking easier. Gisela rootstock from Germany also produces smaller cherry trees. Check out details if you want tasty cherries but have limited space. Reports indicate that some cherry rootstock varieties not only dwarf a tree but also provide some disease resistance and improved growth in poor soils.

Standard-size cherry trees begin bearing in about their fourth year. Dwarf trees may bear by the third year. A standard tart or sweet cherry tree yields 30–50 quarts per year. A space-saving dwarf tree yields 10–15 quarts.

Spring is the best planting time. Refer to table 4.1 for plant spacing and height at maturity. Keep graft unions at least an inch above ground level to avoid sucker growth. Prune trees each year, dwarfs to a central leader and semi-dwarf or standard to a modified leader. Pruning each year in winter encourages growth of new fruiting wood. Cherry trees respond to fertilizing, but do it after harvest each year. Follow directions for the type of fruit tree fertilizer you purchase. Avoid over or under feeding.

Sugar content in cherries rises dramatically in the last few days of ripening. For the tastiest treats from sweet cherries, wait until the cherries turn the final full color for the variety. Test pick a few as they do. Then, harvest as cherries on specific trees ripen over about a week's time. Pick with stems attached, and be careful not to tear off the fruit spur that produces fruit each year.

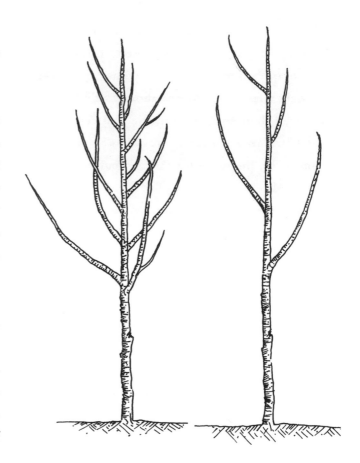

On the left is a young cherry tree with too many branches. The one on the right has been properly pruned.

PERFECTLY PEACHY PEACHES AND NICE-TO-KNOW NECTARINES

Many gardeners believe peaches are a southern fruit and won't thrive in northern areas. Not so. Michigan, New Jersey, and Canada have major peach-growing areas. You can enjoy delicious peaches when you choose the correct, cold-hardy varieties bred for northern states.

Peaches appear in Chinese illustrations from the tenth century BCE. Supposedly, the peach was named around 300 BCE by the Greek philosopher Theophrastus, who thought the fruit came from Persia, now Iran. Other historic archives mention that peach trees were growing alongside nectarines

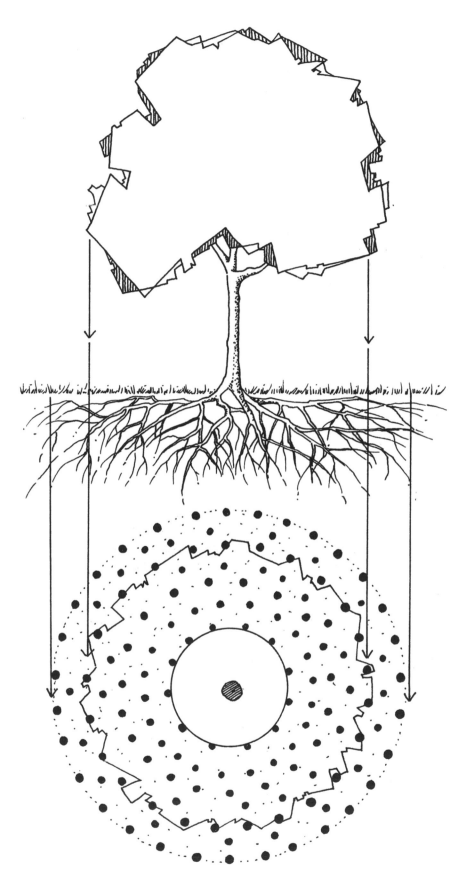

Roots extend much farther than most gardeners realize, so be sure to apply fertilizer in circles out to the drip line of established trees.

in Virginia in 1720. Nutritionally, peaches are free of fat, sodium, and cholesterol, and they are high in Vitamin A and are a good source of vitamin C. Peaches ripen well in a brown bag at room temperature and then can be stored in a refrigerator crisper for up to 6 days.

A peach and a nectarine are very similar genetically. Botanical scholars say that nectarines may have originated as a sport of peaches. The main difference is that a peach has fuzz on its skin while a nectarine does not. Some people object to the fuzzy feeling of peaches. If you do, simply peel them before eating. Or grow nectarines. But be aware that nectarines are a bit more likely to be affected by diseases such as brown rot and bacterial spot.

Today, you have many tasty options to grow, including delicious peach varieties from improved, disease-resistant trees. Hardy peach varieties have been perfected that thrive in Michigan and Canada. However, although some peach varieties can survive cold, their fruit buds are more tender than other fruit trees. For that reason, careful site selection is essential. Peaches love sun, so pick a spot with well-drained soil that gets full sun 8 hours a day. Avoid low frost pockets. Best site is a well-protected, sheltered, sunny area warmed by day and shielded from extremes of winds or frosty night air. A southern side of a garage or neighboring house works well.

Catalogs offer wonderful adventures. Consider extending your peach-eating pleasure with early, mid, and late ripening varieties. Burbank July Elberta is a peach of a peach perfected by Luther Burbank. It has rose-red blossoms in spring, and the bright-red peaches have golden-yellow flesh that is a taste treat. The Stark Early White peach is a winner, and the Gala peach is another firm-fleshed July ripener. Candor,

Collins, Harbinger, and Garnet Beauty are early maturing.

Prairie Dawn, Reliance, Redhaven, and Raritan Rose bear later. Many veteran peach growers say mid-season peaches are best flavored. They salute Red Globe, Loring, Madison, Jefferson, and the white peaches Nectar and Late Crawford. For other mid-season peaches consider Trigem, Eden, Glohaven, or Vanity. Varieties like Reliance, China Pearl, and Intrepid tolerate low temperatures. There are others in catalogs, so for cold areas, plant varieties known for their hardiness to survive harsh winters.

Nectarines grow in the same type soil and conditions as peaches. There are cold-hardy varieties too. Be certain to select those that are recommended for their winter survival in northern states.

Buy vigorous 1-year-old saplings. Standard-size trees begin fruiting at 3 years of age and dwarfs at 1–2 years. Most varieties are self-fertile, but check when you buy if you may need pollinator trees. See table 4.1 for spacing, mature height, and bearing age of peach and nectarine trees.

Peaches respond to fertilizing with 10-10-10 or equivalent about 6–8 weeks after planting. In following years, three-quarters of a pound of fertilizer in spring and again in summer helps. Follow package directions for proper amounts. Peaches benefit from pruning that opens the center of the tree for better air flow and ample sun. Remove any dead limbs. It also pays to remove excess tiny peaches that form, so space them 6–8 inches apart about 5 weeks after trees have bloomed and set fruit.

Peaches and nectarines are much more tender than apples or pears. There should be no green on the fruits when ready for harvest. If you use the tips of your finger to hold the peach, you will put little dents in the peach. Instead, pick a peach using the sides of your fingers. Simply grab the peach firmly and pull it straight off the branch.

PEAR PLEASURES

Growing pears, especially some of the newer varieties, provides pleasures no supermarket can offer. There are more than 5,000 varieties of pears, and not all of them are pear shaped. You can chose varieties from nearly a hundred different types and treat your family to truly exotic pear flavors from around the world.

Pears are one of the world's oldest cultivated fruits, recorded as far back as 5000 BCE. In *The Odyssey*, Homer lauds pears as a "gift of the gods." The common pear is native to Europe, the Chinese sand pear to the Orient. Both species are extensively cultivated for their fruit in cool, humid, temperate regions throughout the world. The Seckel pear, that tasty winter favorite, was discovered growing near the Delaware River in Pennsylvania in the early eighteenth century by a farmer named Seckel. Amazingly, pear trees can produce fruit for up to 100 years.

Pears are pomes and vary from apple shape to teardrop shape. Their thin skin varies in color from light yellow and green through red and brown, depending on the variety. Today, thick-fleshed Asian pears have become popular for home gardens. The flavor varies among varieties. Unlike sweet, conventional pears, in Asian pears the flesh contains numerous gritty cells called stone cells.

Unlike other tree fruits, pears should be picked before they are completely ripe, then allowed to ripen in storage. That improves the flavor and is the natural way to handle pears for best taste.

Classic European-type pears grown by early American settlers are still available for home gardens. New varieties have been perfected and introduced that are worth trying. Asian pears are a large group of pear varieties having crisp, juicy fruit. When mature, the fruit is good to eat at harvest or can be kept for several months after picking if held in cold storage. The crisp texture of an Asian pear remains unchanged after picking or storage. That contrasts with the flesh of European pears such as Bartlett or Comice. There are three basic types of Asian pear: round or flat fruit with green to yellow skin; round or flat fruit with bronze-colored skin and a light bronze-russet; and pear-shaped fruit with green or russet skin.

Pears have fewer problems from diseases or insects than other fruits. Once they are well established, pear trees require less pruning and care to produce abundant harvests. Also, pears offer markedly different flavors and ranges of texture, size, and shape compared to other fruits. Some are self-pollinating while others are not. Usually you need two varieties so they cross-pollinate to insure adequate fruit set.

Among the best, most productive varieties is Moonglow, which bears early. The trees are vigorous and upright and are strong pollinators for other pears. The fruit of this Bartlett-type pear is large, soft, juicy, and blight-resistant. Starkrims and Shinseiki also ripen early. Midseason varieties include Jumbo, Stark Honeysweet, and French Grande. For later picking, consider Dutchess, Beurre Bosc, and Magness, which bears late on spreading trees. Magness pears are oval shaped, medium size, and have a soft, very juicy, sweet taste.

Colette is an ever-bearing pear with ripe fruit from August until fall frosts. Another delight is Red Anjou, a dwarf hybrid that matures in September and keeps for several months after picking. Seckel pears mature late on vigorous trees. They are productive but yield small, smooth fruit with white to slightly yellow, aromatic flesh. These are often called winter keepers since they store fairly well and are somewhat spicy. Bosc pears also ripen late. These large pears with dark yellow undercolor and a russet veil have white, aromatic, sweet, tender flesh.

Most home gardeners usually focus on varieties not available in stores. However, even home-grown Bartlett and Clapps are especially tasty when sun ripened and picked from home garden trees. Bartlett is a superior pear tree bearing large, golden-yellow pears early and abundantly. Clapps Favorite looks similar but has pale lemon-yellow fruit with a bright pink cheek. Tyson is an early sugar pear that is blight resistant for northern and central areas. Comice is a delight. It is the kind you see in fruit gift baskets, a long, golden pear blushed with red. Kieffer is a good winter pear.

Among Asian pears, Shinseiki is a dwarf variety that ripens in mid-August. Chojuro is an extra juicy, dwarf variety for backyard gardens. These pears look like apples but taste like pears. Both need another Asian pear or Bartlett for proper pollination. Ya Li and Hosui are other Asian pear options.

As you plan your pear production, look for fire blight-resistant varieties and rootstocks, especially in areas outside dry western regions. Note that most pear varieties will start to bear significant harvests after 5–6 years. Be sure to check pollination facts, because you often need at least two different varieties for cross-pollination.

Once you select your favorite varieties to plant, find a site with full sun, moderate fertility, ade-quate air circulation, and good water drainage. Pears will do well in a wide range of soil types. You'll find that pears do best with a small amount of fertilizer early in the year. Frosts during bud and blossom time can damage blooms and reduce yields. If possible, plant pears on a slope for better drainage. Check table 4.1 for spacing, height, and bearing age.

Keep young trees weed free until they get well rooted. Mulching helps. Also, water well during dry times. That helps roots get established quickly. Then, fertilize lightly in early spring the second and succeeding years about 2 weeks before bloom. Follow package directions for the fertilizer. However, if new shoot growth on the tree is more than 12 inches in a season, use less fertilizer next spring. If leaves appear pale green or yellowish, add slightly more fertilizer next year.

Dwarf pears should be trained to a central leader. Semi-dwarf and standard trees seem to do best when trained to a central leader too, but many gardeners report that they usually use a modified leader, because that type of pruning is easier to maintain with a large tree. Pear branches tend to grow nearly straight up. Therefore, it is best to prune regularly but lightly to encourage your tree's scaffold branches to grow in a more outward, hori-

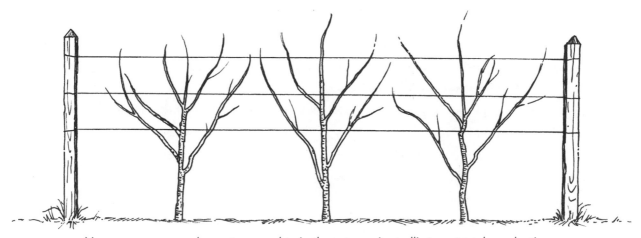

You can grow several pear trees and train them to a wire trellis to get peak production.

CHAPTER 4

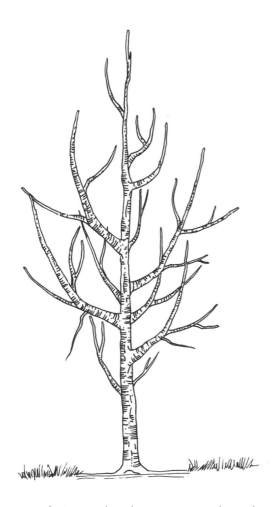

This young fruit tree has become scraggly and over-branched. It should be pruned to encourage best growth and productivity.

zontal direction and encourage development of fruiting spurs.

Remember that unlike most other fruits, pears should be picked "hard ripe" on the tree and allowed to reach their peak flavor off the tree. Check trees when pears seem to be ripening. Pick a few and store them in the house. Taste test in a few days. That way you'll learn when it is best to pick your pear pleasure.

PLUM DANDY DELIGHTS

Plums are an overlooked backyard fruit crop that may surprise and reward you deliciously. They can be grown in more parts of America than practically any other fruit tree. Give some a try. You have a great choice of species and varieties.

One type of plum originated in Syria and Persia and was originally brought to England by a member of the Gage family, hence that name for a type of plum. Wild plums native to North America were gathered and eaten by native peoples and early colonists alike. European and Japanese plums are more recent introductions to home gardens. Japanese types were brought to America in the late 1800s.

History records plums in antiquity, and Crusaders in the twelfth century brought Damson trees back to Europe from the Mideast. The monks in the Abbey of Clairac, crossing a Damson tree

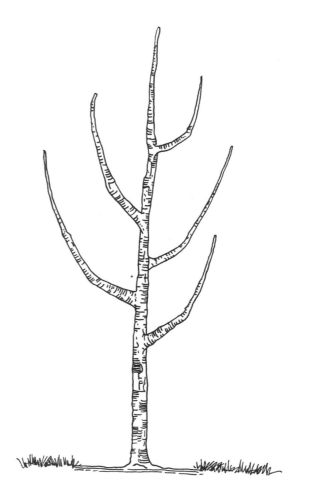

This illustration shows a pear tree after proper pruning.

Here are the proper pruning steps for an apple or pear tree from left to right, its second, third, fourth, and fifth or sixth year.

with a local plum, created a new variety which they called the Ente plum, from a French word meaning "to graft."

The common European plum, the most important species and most widely known, probably originated near the Caspian Sea. It was introduced into North America probably by the Pilgrims and is the most widely grown type. Fruits of this species range in color: varieties may be yellow, red, or green, but purplish-blue is most common.

The Japanese plum, which probably originated in China, was introduced to the United States circa 1870. This fruit is more pointed at the apex than the European plum, and varieties are yellow or light red, but never purplish-blue. The Damson plum, which is a small, oval, sweet fruit used mostly in jams, was first cultivated in ancient times in Syria.

Plums fit nicely in most home landscapes because their small tree size lets you enjoy plums both as decorative accents and for their abundant fruits. There are five basic plum groups descended from European plum families. The Prune group provides plums that can be picked and dried with the pit intact. Green Gage plums are identified by round fruit with yellow, green, or reddish flesh, which is sweet and juicy. Yellow Egg plums are mainly commercial canning types, so forget about them.

Imperatrice plums include most of the blue-colored ones that bear heavily. They yield medium-size, oval-shaped fruit with firm flesh. Lombard plums are smallish, reddish, and somewhat lower in quality, so you may forego them too.

Japanese plums have appeal because the trees are more attractive during bloom. Generally speaking, European plums have the best flavor and offer a wider range of varieties. Montfort is an old French blue plum with dark purple, juicy fruit.

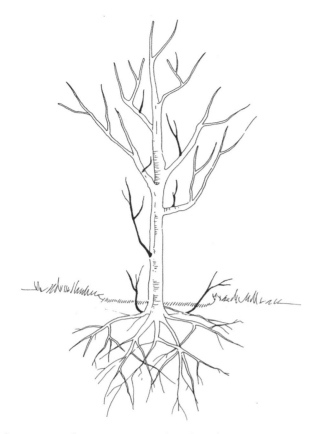

Sprouts can form on trees and suckers from root areas. Remove as shown so your tree attains the best growth for peak performance.

French Damson is vigorous, productive, and yields large plums. Green Gage is a favorite with medium, yellow-green fruit mottled with red. In colder areas, Mount Royal is good for dessert and survives even Canadian winters. You can find many other varieties, such as Bluebyrd, Earliblue, Empress, Fellemberg, Redheart, Santa Rosa, Shiro, Starking Delicious, Stanley, and even the cold-hardy Japanese Superior, which is fire-red with yellow flesh. For fun, you could try the Yellow Egg plum too.

For warmer areas, Abundance yields heavily, with large, cherry-red fruits. Burbank produces bright reddish-purple fruit and bears late. Pick your plum pleasures, and plant this year for future tasty harvests. Plums are delicious fresh, baked in pies and cakes, or made into jams and jellies.

As you plan, look for a site with loamy, well-drained soil in full sun, and avoid frost pockets. Be aware that some plums are self-fertile but all yield better if planted with a second variety to insure good cross-pollination. Once well established, plum trees yield up to 2 bushels of plums each year.

Plant the tree in the prepared hole with any graft union an inch above the ground level. See table 4.1 for spacing requirements. Fertilize as you would for peaches, lightly and according to the directions on the package.

Watch the water. Plums like deep watering the first two years, 6–8 gallons per tree about once each week if no rain falls. As trees begin bearing in a few years, add about 1 gallon of water per square foot of root area between bloom and harvest. That's about 2 inches per week. Plums are rather pest free and need only moderate pruning to produce abundantly. Aim to keep the trees open for sun and air to reach all fruiting branches well. Actually, plums are one of the easier fruit trees to grow.

Come harvest time, pick European and American type plums when they are tree ripe. Test pull. If they come off with a slight twist, they are ready. Japanese-type plums need picking a bit earlier than tree ripe and then should be allowed to fully ripen in a cool place indoors.

FIG, PAWPAW, AND QUINCE

This fruitful gardening chapter wouldn't be complete without some brief notes about several overlooked fruits for home landscapes. You can find more details in garden catalogs. Thanks to my friends at Stark Bro's nurseries, here are some highlights about fig, pawpaw, and quince trees.

Figs can be grown in a variety of soils from light, sandy types to heavy clay in warmer areas. They do not like alkali soils, so a pH between 6.0

and 6.5 is suggested. Plant them 2–4 inches deeper than in the nursery row and space at least 20 inches from other trees, since they are heavy feeders. Mulch the ground around the tree to keep it free of weeds. However, don't cultivate so deeply that surface roots will be damaged. Figs need fertilizer, but too much nitrogen will result in vegetative growth at the expense of fruit production. Also, the ground should be kept moist.

Figs are ever-bearers. They produce fruit on shoots that grow this year. Next year, they will produce the first crop of the season on wood that grew last year, with a second crop growing on the new season's growth.

North of USDA hardiness zone 7, it is best to provide figs with winter protection. After leaves have fallen, prune out any unwanted branches and wrap the remaining ones with several layers of paper or burlap. It is wise to tie the branches together as tightly as possible without breaking them. Finally, use a layer of tar paper or plastic film. Secure the top so water cannot seep in. Come spring, remove the wrapping just before new growth starts in spring. Figs also may be grown in pots for summer pleasure, then stored in an unheated basement or garage for the winter. If grown in pots, figs should be repotted every second year with fresh soil.

Pawpaws are a rather exotic fruit for many people. They can be grown up to hardiness zone 5. Sometimes called the Hoosier banana, the fruit's flavor is like a banana but its texture is like custard. Pawpaws grow in almost any kind of soil with a pH balance near neutral. Pests don't bother it. Dark purple flowers open in late spring. Oval fruits weigh half a pound or more. A mature tree yields 25–50 pounds of fruit per year. Plant two for proper pollination. They ripen in late September in zone 5.

You can grow pawpaws in full sun to light shade at the depth grown in the nursery pot. The hole should be extra large across and deep to encourage fast root development. The first year is critical. Fertilize sparingly with Stark Tre-Pep Fertilizer at planting time. Water thoroughly every 7–10 days unless you get at least 1 inch of rain per week. Avoid letting the soil dry completely but do not overwater. Give plants protection from direct sunlight the first few growing seasons. Use a wooden shingle, evergreen bough, screen, or similar method to offer shade. Pruning is similar to that for an apple tree with a central leader with wide-angle crotches for sturdy limbs. Have patience. Pawpaws start bearing fruit in year 6 or 7.

Quince trees need full sun and well-drained, humus-rich soil. Gently remove the quince from the nursery pot and plant it at the same depth it was growing in the pot. Pruning is only necessary for shaping. Fruit ripens in October and needs to be stored by a window until it softens.

A chapter on fruits wouldn't be complete without a salute to two of the major fruit tree nurseries in America. Both took root decades ago and have served home gardeners well for more than 100 years each.

In 1816, James Hart Stark and a small band of pioneers moved west from Kentucky and settled on the west bank of the Mississippi in what would later become the town of Louisiana, Missouri. He brought with him a bundle of apple scions. From this bundle grew a thriving nursery business that became the world famous Stark Bro's. By carefully selecting and propagating only the best varieties, James Stark started a tradition. The most famous of these was the Stark Red Delicious apple in 1893. In 1914, the Stark Golden Delicious was developed.

This early work led to an association with famed plant wizard Luther Burbank. He selected Stark Bro's to carry on his work and willed over 750 varieties to the company. Paul Stark Sr. was instrumental in writing U.S. legislation creating plant patents in the 1930s. Today, new fruit varieties may be patented just like other products. The Stark Bro's website is www.starkbros.com.

Miller Nurseries began on the shores of Canandaigua Lake in New York State more than a century ago. Through the years, the Miller family has continued a tradition of offering a wide selection of hardy plants, including Olde-Tyme apple varieties, berries, pears, cherries, nut trees, grape vines, and much more. Miller Nurseries remains a family-owned business. Their website is www.millernurseries.com.

I've bought fruit bushes and trees from both companies over the years for our gardens in New Jersey and Maine. Both introduce exciting, tasty new varieties regularly, and their catalogs are a welcome treat every year.

5

SPICE YOUR LIFE WITH HERBS

Do you want a spicier life? Try herbs in your garden and savor great new flavors whenever you cook a meal. Herbs require little space to produce big flavor treats. They perk up salads and soups, stews and veggies. In these days when we're told to cut back on salt, fat, and carbs, herbs have come to the rescue. Actually, herbs have been rediscovered and welcomed by millions of gardeners.

Some herbs are annuals. Others are perennials. A few add appealing blooms and offer the option of scenting your home with dried herb displays. Try your hand at herb growing and wake up your appetite. Pick a small plot near the kitchen so you can step out, snip some herb sprigs, and use them immediately for culinary delights. Or select an area near your vegetable garden. Herbs can be planted in the flower border too, adding distinct decorator touches. Tall herbs make fine background plants. Low ones work as garden edges. But the closer they are to your kitchen, the more tempted you'll be to step outside, snip a sprig of thyme, a stalk of mint, or some summer savory to upscale meals.

Six herbs, well named "les fine herbs" by the French, are excellent starters. These include basil, chervil, marjoram, rosemary, tarragon, and thyme. Depending on your tastes, you can add others, such as chives, parsley, summery savory, and ever popular mints. As you perfect your herb growing skills and your taste buds coax you on, you may add anise, fennel, lemon balm, borage, and other herbs. Just a few dollars invested in herbs may reward you with million-dollar flavors. In this chapter, you'll find herb growing basics to get you started, along with some tempting ideas to try.

A loamy soil with organic content for good drainage will produce best results. Sun-loving herbs need 5–8 hours per day. Those that prefer partial sun or shade need only about 3–4 hours of sun. Some prefer dry areas but mints like moist growing conditions. Many herb fanciers grow herbs in window boxes, tubs, or individual pots by a kitchen window. Growing herbs indoors can add fragrance to your home.

Outdoors, pick a spot that has well-drained soil and provides a sunny area and some shade too. A 6-foot-square plot will yield herbs all season. With care to keep weeds out and improve fertility, you'll have surplus to dry too. To dry herbs, cut several sprigs, tie them together with string, and hang them upside down in a dry corner of the garage or basement. Or hang them in your kitchen for fragrance. Be sure there is good air circulation wherever you dry herbs.

TIPS FOR SEEDS, SEEDLINGS, AND CUTTINGS

Be patient with herbs—sometimes, very patient—because many herb seeds are slow to germinate. Some seeds are very tiny, so mixing with fine sand helps spread them. You only need a few seeds to plant outdoors, or in peat pots with seed starting mix to begin seedlings indoors. Be sure to keep soil moist outdoors or in pots while the seeds take their time to sprout, set true leaves, and set roots.

When potted seedlings are ready and frost danger has passed, dig a hole in the garden big enough to accept the entire peat pot. Cover lightly with soil and keep moist. Roots will grow right through the peat sides, and this method avoids the transplanting setback that can occur if seedlings are transferred from starter trays. It pays to have several seeds in a pot. When the plants have rooted, simply snip off the extra, smaller seedlings in each pot.

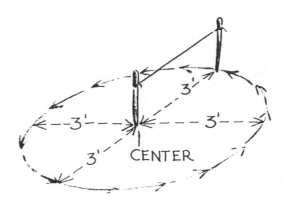

Make a circle and divide it as a wagon-wheel herb bed.

A third way to grow herbs is to obtain cuttings of plants. Friends often love to share good taste, so when you have enjoyed an herb-flavored meal, don't be surprised that you may be offered a cutting of that herb to grow in your own garden. To take a cutting, snip off about 4–5 inches of stem from the growing top of a parent plant. Remove lower leaves and put stems into a glass of water. Check daily until tiny roots begin forming. Then transfer the cutting into potting soil in a peat pot. When it matures enough, plant it into its home in your garden. You can plant a cutting directly into potting mix in a peat pot, water regularly, and when it begins growing, move it outdoors.

Some herbs send out underground runners and new plants arise. You can dig these volunteer herbs to share with friends. Pot them up also for church fairs and fund-raising events for organizations.

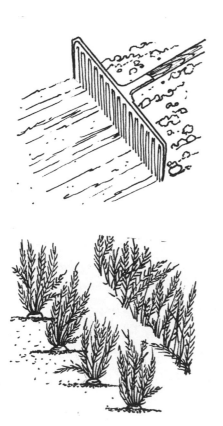

Level soil evenly for your herb bed.

HERB PLANT COLLECTIONS

The Herb Society of America (HSA) has many worthwhile programs and projects for all who want to put more spice in their lives. The organization's National Herb Garden, part of the National Arboretum in Washington, D.C., stands as one of the finest examples of how a diverse group of people working together can achieve a dream. For more than twenty years, the National Herb Garden has fulfilled the HSA's mission to promote the knowledge, use, and delight of herbs. The garden includes hundreds of species and cultivars of herbs used for everything from perfume and cooking to flower arranging. Every plant is labeled, and interpretive signage helps visitors understand the herbs in the context of their history and use. Visit the National Arboretum website, www.usna.usda.gov/Information/index.html, for a detailed description of the garden and additional information.

In 1996, the HSA established a series of plant collections held by units or groups of members. The purpose was to recognize the role that living herb plants have for our existence and to encourage cultivation and preservation of the living germ plasm of herbs. These collections expose members and the general public to a wide variety of herbs. The collections are available for study, and a limited number of cuttings, seeds, or plants are available through HSA Seed Exchange and commercial sources. The HSA plant collections also encourage cultivation, reintroduction, and preservation of uncommon herbs for posterity and as a repository of authentically labeled taxa.

Collections may be generic, a division with a genus, cultivars within a species, native herbs, or international herbs. The HSA also explains that parallel, complementary, or duplicate collections are desirable to cater to our range of climates and to encourage sharing between and among collection holders. In addition, growing three plants of each taxon in any one collection, hopefully in different gardens, will ensure that enough plant material is available.

Plant material from the collections may be sold, exchanged, or donated at the discretion of the collection holder, bearing in mind that wide distribution of plant material is desirable. Further information is available from the Herb Society of America Plant Collections, 9019 Kirtland Chardon Rd., Kirtland, OH 44094, Telephone (440) 256-0514.

TIPS TO GROW TEN POPULAR HERBS

Surveys around the country reveal that America's ten most popular herbs are basil, chives, dill, mint, oregano, parsley, rosemary, sage, marjoram, and thyme. Each is described below. You can find more details about these and other herbs on seed packets, in plant catalogs and gardening books, and from the HSA.

Here are good growing tips for the most popular herbs. Some are annuals; others are perennials. Some like sun, while others prefer shadier areas. Give them the conditions they need and they'll reward you tastefully. Later in this chapter, you'll find notes on a range of other flavoring herbs. Try some easy, popular ones. Then expand your tastes to others. Some gardeners just like the look and fragrance as garden plants. That's fine, but for most folks, herbs give their best rewards when you dine.

BRAVO FOR BASIL

Basil, or sweet basil, has a romantic heritage. It has been called a sign of love. In France it is called *herb royale*. It is an annual that has a bushy look and especially fragrant leaves. Basil prefers rich, moist soil and full sun. The leaves give a rich, spicy flavor to sauces. For salads, use fresh whole leaves. For cooking, crush or chop leaves.

When spring ground has warmed, sow tiny basil seeds an inch apart and one-quarter inch deep and cover lightly with soil. When seedlings are 2–3 inches high, thin to 6–8 inches apart. Basil matures 1–2 feet tall in gardens, but less in containers. Water every week, to keep soil moist and ensure succulent, tastiest leaves. Regular pinching back forces a bushier plant.

Shiny, pointed green basil leaves are spicy, somewhat like cloves. Try freshly chopped or dried leaves with fish, soups, stews, and favorite tomato recipes. Gourmets recommend basil with lamb and poultry, or to perk up zucchini, summer squash, and other veggies. Try taste tests yourself.

Hang a spray of basil in a cool room until dry, then remove and crumble leaves and seal in an airtight glass jar. Freezing works well too.

CHEER FOR COLORFUL CHIVES

Beyond their mild oniony flavor, chives offer colorful purple flower displays each summer and serve as a tasty flower display. Plants mature 12–20 inches tall with stemlike, hollow leaves.

Start seeds directly outdoors in moist soil in spring. Plant 8–10 inches apart or several seeds to form a cluster. For containers, use about 4–6 seeds in 8–10 inch pots. Water outdoor seedlings well, and pots too. Chives love sun, so place pots in southern or eastern windows. Outdoor chives tend to spread, so dig up extra clumps and trade with friends for their favorite herbs, or sell at fundraising plant bazaars. Chives need ample moisture, so water weekly and mist them periodically for most succulent growth. Cutting forces the plants to produce more.

Clip stems 3–4 inches from the soil. Try chopped chives in salads and soups and with other veggies too. As gourmets know, chives and sour cream are a favorite topping for baked potatoes. Check recipe books for other tasty uses.

DILL IS DELIGHTFUL

Although an annual that must be planted each year, dill deserves a garden spot. You'll use both leaves and seeds, especially for making dill pickles. Dill grows 3–4 feet tall and has attractive, lacy foliage. Flower clusters are 3–6 inches across. This herb prefers moderately rich, well drained, moist soil in full sun.

Plant outdoors when frost danger is over. Space several seeds per inch. Water well and be patient, since dill seems slow to grow. When the seedlings are a few inches tall, thin to 6 inches apart. Dill can be self-seeding like some flowers, so think of it as a potential perennial. Plant early to ensure a good summer seed crop.

To pick so-called dillweed, clip leaves close to the stem in early morning. To collect seeds, keep a close watch on the plants. Seeds ripen in mature, brown, umbrella-shaped clusters within 2–3 weeks after flowering and are very tiny. Place an old cotton sheet under the plants. Then rub dry seed heads to release seeds and remove chaff later. Another way to harvest seeds is by cutting stems after flowers have died, then hanging them in a dark, dry area over a sheet. Some seeds will drop, but you can then rub others off by hand. Pick dill leaves and dry them on a nonmetallic screen in a dark area for several days. Store dried seeds and leaves in separate airtight containers.

ENJOY MARVELOUS MINT

Famed ancient scholar Pliny called mint the loveliest of herbs, and Romans crowned themselves with peppermint wreaths. Today mint is a favorite flavor for chewing gum. Happily, mint it is one of the easiest perennial herbs to grow. It grows almost anywhere, but it thrives in rich, moist soil in full to partial shade. You can enjoy peppermint to spearmint in soggy places where few other plants will grow. Mint can spread far beyond where you plant it, however, so be prepared. Because mints are intrusive, some herbalists recommend growing mint in pots in the ground outdoors to prevent its spreading. Most mints mature 2–3 feet tall and bear lavender to purplish blooms on distinctively square stems.

Start mint from seeds, or use cuttings or transplants. Mints require ample moisture, so water at least once a week, more in dry periods. They need little care or fertilizing, but ample water is their special requirement.

Pick after young plants reach 12 inches tall. On mature plants, just snip away for iced tea, mint sauces, or just a mouth-freshening chew. Chop and crush mint leaves to make a traditional sauce for lamb. Mint is best used fresh.

ABOUT OREGANO

Oregano is praised primarily for use in tomato recipes, to which it adds a peppery flavor. Herbalists say that oregano also improves beef, pork, poultry, and game recipes. Oregano prefers full sun and well-drained, average loamy soil. This perennial matures 1–2 feet tall and has erect, hairy, squarish stems bearing dark-green leaves. In summer it has pinkish to purplish blooms. Older plants get woody, but if you cut such parts away, new tender growth appears. You may also want to try growing oregano in 8-inch pots as a kitchen houseplant.

Sow seeds several inches apart outdoors in spring, about one-quarter inch deep. Cover lightly with soil, and water well. Oregano seeds typically require several weeks to sprout, so cuttings from underground roots are often a better bet for new plantings.

Harvest oregano leaves and flower tops for use fresh or to dry as flavoring. Oregano is a treat in salads, soups, and stews. To dry, hang a bunch in a cool area. Remove leaves when they are dry, then crumble them and store in airtight jars. You also can freeze oregano.

PICK PLEASING PARSLEY

Parsley is praised not just for its use in cooking but also for its value to freshen the mouth and hide bad breath. There are several common types of this popular, bright-green biennial, such as the flat-leaf Italian type and the curly-leafed varieties. The plants have dark-green, feathery leaves. Most mature about 18 inches tall. Parsley prefers fertile, well-drained soil with a pH of 7 and partly sunny to somewhat shady conditions. This popular, useful herb grows well as a house plant.

Sow seeds outdoors 2 inches apart in rows and cover with one-quarter inch of soil. Thin to 8–10 inches apart. Snip what you want and the plant grows more. For a kitchen herb house plant, either transplant from your outdoor garden or start a few seeds in pots. For juiciest parsley, water well. For peak performance, if you snip plants regularly, use a basic foliage house plant liquid fertilizer according to directions. Flowers are tiny.

RAVE ABOUT ROSEMARY

Herbalists praise rosemary as one of the more beautiful perennial herbs. Even better, it is hardy and tolerates poor, dry soil yet continues to produce its delightful pine-scented foliage. Rosemary bears lovely lavender-blue tall flower clusters in spring. Leaves are needlelike and shiny on upright stalks that grow 2–5 feet tall. Older outdoor plants become gnarled. In containers, rosemary stays compact.

Sow rosemary seeds one-quarter inch deep in sunny, well-drained soil. Thin to 6–8 inches apart, and select the best permanent plants later. Outdoors, dig or till deeply, because this perennial sets deep roots. As a house plant, set seeds in a 10–12 inch pot and keep in a sunny window. Prune away top shoots to encourage bushy plants. Water moderately, because excess water causes leaf fall. Give rosemary a side dressing of balanced fertilizer once a year. Indoors, fertilize like other house plans.

Collect, dry, and crush the leaves for use in soups and gravies. Just use a pinch or two, because rosemary is very flavorful. Try a fresh sprig to brush barbecued chicken, steaks, and burgers. Herbalists favor rosemary on roasted poultry, fish, lamb, beef, pork, and game. Rosemary combines well with chives, thyme, and parsley in recipes. Drying is simple. Cut and tie stems and hang them upside down in a dry, cool area. Remove dried leaves and store in glass jars.

SING PRAISE OF SAGE

Sage is a hardy, distinctive perennial herb with pungent aroma and taste. It has slightly bitter, fragrant leaves that have been a classic for sage and onion dressings with poultry. Sage plants mature into a 2-foot-tall shrub. Coarse, oval leaves are 3–4 inches long and usually a grayish green color. You can enjoy several types of sage, from typical green to golden, purple, and tricolor. All prefer full sun and dry soil.

Sow seeds one-quarter inch deep and 3 inches apart. Be very patient, since it may take 4 weeks for seeds to sprout. Water sparingly. Thin seedlings to 10–12 inches apart. Cut back woody stems after plants bloom to encourage new branches that bear more tender leaves. As an indoor plant, sow a few seeds in an 8-inch pot, thin to the strongest when 3–4 inches tall, and place in a sunny window. Remember, sage doesn't like much water.

You can enjoy sage leaves fresh or dried. Cut sage and hang it in sprays to dry. Then, strip leaves from stems, spread on a clean surface, and crush the leaves. Store in a glass jar. Try growing different sage varieties for distinctive dining.

SAVOR SWEET MARJORAM

Marjoram, or sweet marjoram, was praised by ancient Greeks as being favored by Aphrodite, the goddess of love. This herb is a sweet-smelling perennial in southern areas but needs annual replanting in northern states. It has a dense but shallow root system that produces unusually bushy growth. Plants mature 12–24 inches tall in outdoor gardens but stay smaller in containers. Frequently branching stems are square and covered with tiny hairs. This herb prefers dry, well-drained soil in full sun.

Sow about 6 seeds per inch and lightly cover with soil after the last spring frost. It usually takes several weeks for seeds to start and the seedlings are ready to thin to 6–8 inches apart. Water to moisten soil for seedlings. In containers, plant a few seeds in a pot, keep the soil moist, and wait. When seedlings are a few inches tall, thin to the strongest two and place in east or south windows for proper sunlight.

Harvest your marjoram for salads, soups, meats, stews, and veggies. It is versatile, so give it lots of culinary tries. To dry, hang branches in a dry, warm room. Strip the dry leaves off, and pack them either whole or chopped in glass jars.

TIME FOR THYME

There is worthy wisdom from good cooks: "When in doubt, use thyme." Fact is, thyme does blend with many herbs, which is why it has remained so popular with home gardeners. Thyme is a low-growing, sturdy, shrubby perennial ideal for beds and borders. It has a neat spreading growth habit as a ground cover. The numerous tiny leaves appear along the upright stalks. Lovely lilac to pink flowers form on terminal clusters. The foliage is attractive too, from green to silver leaves, and some varieties have a lemony fragrance. Plant it in light, dry, well-drained soil in full or partial sun. If you like common thyme, expand your growing horizons to the nutmeg, lemon, or other thyme varieties.

Start thyme in peat pots indoors because it favors about 70°F for good germination. Once established outdoors, it can survive well below zero. For potted thyme, plant a few seeds in an 8-inch pot, cover with soil, and wait about 15–20 days for sprouting. Outdoors, thin to 2 inches apart when seedlings are 3 inches tall. Thyme tends to spread, so thin as needed to control growth. Unlike mint, which also can be invasive but prefers moist growing conditions, thyme prefers dry areas.

Try thyme fresh or dried to flavor vegetables, soups, stews, fish, poultry, and other meats. Be aware that thyme can be strong, so use it lightly at first, then more as you wish.

Pick stems of thyme on a dry day, then spread them on a clean sheet or hang in sprays. When dry, strip off leaves and store in airtight containers.

A special note: Herbs look surprisingly alike when dried and stored in glass jars. It pays to clearly label your herbs so they are easy to identify when you want some for cooking.

MORE HERBS TO TRY

Here are some hints for plants to grow that can lead you down a longer and even tastier herbal path.

Anise is an annual that somewhat resembles Queen Anne's lace with its delicate foliage. It does well in full sun and even in poorer but well-drained soil. The plant matures in about 75 days and grows 18–24 inches tall. Seeds are used whole or ground to flavor applesauce, soups, and stews. Anise leaves are nice in salads.

Borage is an annual herb maturing in 80 days. Its leaves when young can be used in salads or as flavoring for lemonade and other summer drinks. It is faintly aromatic and grows 18 inches all.

Caraway is a biennial, maturing in 70 days, and bears the second year. Its seeds are widely used to flavor bread, pastry, cakes, and cheese. Caraway is fine in sauces and soups and often added to salads as a seasoning. It grows 1–2 feet tall.

Catnip is a perennial that matures in 80 days and grows up to 2 feet tall. Useful fresh or dried for making tea or as a seasoning, it is better known as an animal tonic. Cats love it.

Fennel, or finocchio, is an annual that matures in 90 days and reaches 2–3 feet. It produces an enlarged oval base with a pleasing aniselike flavor. It is best used in salads, eaten raw, or boiled.

Horehound is a perennial that matures in 75 days and grows 12-to 18 inches tall. You may know the name from horehound candy. The leaves are used for flavoring.

Lavender is a perennial that matures in 60 days. Sweet scented, this lovely herb with beautiful flowers grows 18–34 inches tall. Lavender flowers are dried and used to perfume linens as well as to repel moths. New varieties are especially beautiful as additions to flower gardens and perennial borders.

Summer savory is an annual maturing in 60 days. It reaches 12–18 inches. The leaves are used fresh or dried for flavoring in salads, dressings, gravies, and stews.

There are many more herbs, as you will note when scanning mail order catalogs. Dozens of focused herbal books and cookbooks about herbs are available to help you follow this tasteful gardening path to new growing and eating adventures.

HERBS FOR ZESTY VEGETABLES

If you grow vegetables, you soon realize that some produce surplus crops. Zucchini and tomatoes are two that tend to overbear. Veggies can taste the same when you grow too many. Herbs are an answer to whet the appetite and provide new dining delights. Here's a list of veggies matched with herbs that will give them new life and flavor.

Lima beans	Marjoram, oregano, sage, savory, tarragon, thyme
Snap beans	Basil, dill, marjoram, mint, oregano, savory, tarragon, thyme
Beets	Caraway, dill, savory, thyme
Broccoli	Caraway, dill, tarragon
Cabbage	Caraway, dill, mint, savory, tarragon
Carrots	Caraway, dill, fennel, marjoram, mint, thyme
Cauliflower	Dill, tarragon
Cucumbers	Basil, dill, mint, tarragon
Onions	Caraway, oregano, sage, thyme
Peas	Basil, dill, marjoram, oregano, rosemary, sage, savory
Potatoes	Basil, dill, marjoram, mint, oregano, rosemary, sage, savory
Squash	Basil, fennel, rosemary
Tomatoes	Basil, oregano, sage, thyme
Green salads	Basil, chives, dill, tarragon

Perk up those appetites. Innovate a little. There are dozens of ways to improve on the old boil, fry, or bake methods you have used. Look over a few recipes for sauces and seasonings in your favorite cookbooks. Often all it takes is a dash of this, a pinch of that or a spoonful of something else to make a vegetable sparkle in a new way. Let your imagination take you in tasty new directions, in your garden and around your dinner table. You can win applause from family and friend when you grow and cook herbally.

HERBS TO LURE BUTTERFLIES AND HUMMINGBIRDS

Whether you are a parent hoping to share your love of herbs and gardening with your children, an educator planning to add herbs to your classroom, or a child ready to discover the magic and wonder of herbal plants, the HSA's Family Herb Corner will provide you with ideas and inspiration. Butterfly and hummingbird gardens are popular. Here are some herbs included in the HSA's list of suggested nectar plants, followed by a list of herbs that are food plants for butterfly larvae.

Nectar Plants

Botanical Name	Common Name
Achillea spp.	yarrow
Agastache foeniculum	anise hyssop
Allium schoenoprasum	chives
Lavandula spp.	lavender
Mentha spp.	mint
Monarda didyma	bee balm
Nepeta spp.	catmint, catnip

Larval Food Plants

Anethum graveolens	dill
Foeniculum vulgare	fennel
Petroselinum crispum	parsley
Tagetes hyb.	marigold

HERBS FOR INTERNATIONAL APPEAL

Perhaps you wish to try some of the best international herbs for gardening and cooking. Here are HSA recommendations.

Allium christophii	star of Persia
Allium fistulosum	Welsh onion
Allium sativum var. *ophioscorodon*	French garlic
Artemisia dracunculus	French tarragon
Lavandula angustifolia	English lavender
Lavandula stoechas	French lavender
Matricaria recutita	German chamomile
Nepeta sibirica	Siberian catmint
Origanum vulgare subsp. *hirtum*	Greek oregano
Petroselinum crispum var. *neopolitanum*	Italian parsley
Tagetes erecta	African marigold

PLANTS FOR A BACKYARD PIZZA GARDEN

We Americans love our pizza, so here are some herbs and vegetables to plant for your own backyard pizza garden.

Allium sativum	garlic
Allium cepa	onion
Brassica oleracea var. *botrytis*	broccoli
Capsicum annuum	pepper
Coriandrum sativum	cilantro
Cynara scolymus	artichoke
Lycopersicon esculentum	plum, or Roma, tomato
Ocimum basilicum	basil
Origanum vulgare subsp. *hirtum*	oregano
Petroselinum crispum var. *neopolitanum*	Italian parsley
Spinacia oleracea	spinach

As you think about tastier living, focus on herbs. *Bon appetit!*

6

GROW MORE
MARVELOUS MEALS

Gardening has a multitude of values. You can enjoy booming beauty from flowers and more delicious meals from homegrown veggies as two major benefits. From a health standpoint, doctors recommend gardening for exercise and relaxation. In fact, doctors are one of the largest single groups of avid gardeners. Even mental hospitals have discovered that gardening has therapeutic benefits, relaxing patients and rekindling their sense of accomplishment.

Equally important, home gardening, even in small plots and containers, provides you with richer supplies of healthier, tastier food. There are more vitamins in freshly picked vegetables and fruit you can pick and cook right away. Supermarket foods must be shipped long distances to the store and lose quality along the way. The longer food sits around, the greater the loss of food value, mainly vitamins.

The principal nutrients in vegetables are iron, vitamin A, vitamin C, and riboflavin. Vitamin A as such is not found in plants, but vegetables contain provitamin A, which is converted to vitamin A by your body. Dark-green and deep-yellow vegetables are top sources, especially spinach, broccoli, Swiss chard, kale, turnip greens, carrots, winter squash, cantaloupes, and pumpkins. Vitamin A helps promote growth and helps keep the linings of your mouth, nose, throat, and digestive tract in good condition.

Vitamin B is really a complex of nutrients, including riboflavin found mainly in leafy green vegetables, thiamin found in dried peas and beans, and niacin found in fresh peas and beans. Vitamin B is needed for maintaining healthy eyes, assisting cells to obtain energy from food, and keeping you calm and able to cope with daily activities.

Vitamin C helps hold body cells together and strengthens walls of blood vessels. Brussels sprouts, cabbage, collards, cantaloupes, turnip greens, and sweet peppers have this basic vitamin. Tomatoes do too. It is beneficial in helping heal wounds and building strong bones and teeth.

Some kids may not enjoy eating vegetables, but you can give veggies new flavors with herbs. Equally important, new vegetable varieties for the garden offer even better taste than store-bought veggies or old-time varieties. For example, snow peas let you eat peas and pods, a taste of oriental cooking. Many different tomatoes provide surprisingly different flavors. Try different tomato varieties and discover the truly different flavors.

Potatoes of different colors also have distinctive flavors and nourishment. Check plant catalogs for suppliers of seed potatoes for growing in your garden. Wood Prairie Farm, for example, offers 16 varieties of double-certified seed potatoes, including Red Cloud and Reddale with red skins, Yukon Gold and Carola with light yellow skins and honey-gold flesh, and All Blue with blue skin and flesh. They also offer heirloom Swedish Peanut Fingerling and Russian Banana Fingerling, both prized varieties for their culinary quality.

Other important nutrients such as iron, calcium, and protein are also found in fresh vegetables. Beans are one of the best sources of protein among vegetables, are available in a variety of shapes and sizes, and are a fine protein substitute for people who must restrict meat intake.

Soviet scientists discovered the amazing longevity of people in the Caucasus Mountains along the Black Sea, many reaching over 100 years old. One thing these people have in common is reliance on vegetables as the major part of their diet. About 70 percent of their caloric intake is of vegetable origin, mainly from beans, cabbage, celery, corn, lettuce, and spinach. Corn is part of every meal, often eaten with red pepper sauce. Green vegetables are a daily staple.

Studies in the Vilacamba area of the Ecuadorian Andes and Hunza region of Pakistan also reveal long-lived people who rely on mainly vegetable diets. They also work hard, so that shows the importance of daily exercise.

Enough about health. Fresh vegetables from the garden taste better than those you buy in the store. Prove it to yourself and family. Buy some supermarket vegetables. Cook them in one pot and your fresh-picked garden veggies in another. You'll be surprised at the difference in taste.

Commercial vegetable varieties are grown for their even maturity dates, ease of mechanical harvest, and ability to stand up well in packing and shipping to stores. In contrast, you have many more superior flavor varieties for your home garden, but they would not be satisfactory for mass harvest and shipping. Good for you. That's another reason you will enjoy tastier vegetables picked fresh and cooked right from the garden in your kitchen.

Another important asset is that plant breeders have been working hard to develop even tastier, more productive vegetable varieties resistant to diseases. As a home gardener, you have all the right ingredients to live better, more flavorful, healthier lives from your garden.

TEN FAVORITE VEGGIES

Annual surveys over the years reveal these ten vegetables as Americans' favorites to grow in their home gardens: tomatoes are first choice and are grown in almost every garden; beans come next, followed by sweet corn, cucumbers, peas, lettuce, radishes, squash, melons, and beets. Peppers rank high and might have been among the top ten if we counted those bought as transplants, not just seed packets.

Gardener surveys reveal that flavor is the most important reason for selecting a particular variety. Productivity and disease resistance are also key requirements. Another point is early harvest, especially in northern areas with short growing seasons. Plant breeders recognize and have responded to these gardener interests. You are the beneficiary, as you will see when you read mail order catalogs filled with awesome choices of vegetables to grow.

In this chapter, you'll find special emphasis on tomatoes. Many dozens of types—from giant to tiny salad varieties, sauce makers, and those with different colors—are available to grace your dinner table. You should try some of the newest varieties that offer colorful, flavorful surprises.

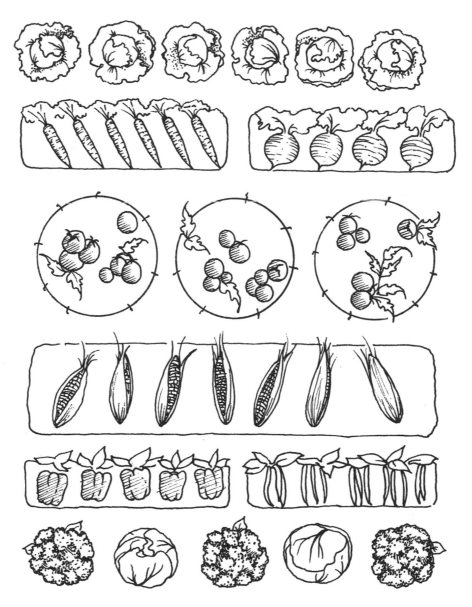

Use these designs to plot out your own vegetable garden.

Bush beans are very productive for the small space they require. Green beans are more popular than wax beans, but both are high in popularity. Pole beans are more productive and often better flavored than bush varieties, so they deserve a growing spot. You also can save space by growing up, getting triple or quadruple the harvest from pole beans than you can from bush beans, whether you grow snap, wax, or more exotic types for gourmet meals.

Sweet corn needs room. Happily, newer varieties require less space, produce more abundantly, and offer sugar-enhanced flavor that lasts longer. Short-season varieties let you pick early and replant the area for fall crops.

Cucumbers can be grown on fences, in wire hoops, or with other supports. These can replace early peas and also perform well in containers, since space-saver varieties are very prolific.

Lettuce deserves a new look. Many new varieties offer colorful and tasty additions to your salads. Leaf lettuce is one choice, but Bibb types and loose-leaf varieties provide a range of flavor, color, and texture options.

To help you have the most success, this chapter provides details of all these popular vegetables and a number of others. You'll find old-time favorites, including heirloom favorites, All America Selection winners, and the latest new hybrids.

There are many more varieties of each type of vegetable than I can possibly list here, so collect some of the best mail order catalogs and make your own decisions. Try some varieties this year, others next year, in comparison with your usual favorites to find those that please you and your family the most. Be aware when planting that the location for some annual vegetables should be changed each year, to avoid certain plant diseases or other problems.

For family fun with kids, make veggie row markers.

However, two basic perennial crops need a permanent place to set roots so they bear abundantly year after year: asparagus and rhubarb.

ASPARAGUS

This tasty vegetable deserves a place in every garden. An area 4 by 6 feet or 2 by 10 with full sun will provide an abundance of this treat. Asparagus will develop extensive roots, so it is vital to dig in deeply and prepare a rich, pliable soil in which they can grow deeply. Continuous mulching is important to control weeds and let stalks pop up where they will from the root system the plants build. Loams or sandy loams are best, since roots may extend 10 feet underground. If your soil is acid, lime it before you prepare the bed. Add humus and manure—the more you can add before planting, the better. Green manure is helpful to prepare the bed before planting asparagus. Plant a cover crop of rye, clover, vetch, or other green crop and till it under when mature. Clover, vetch, and soybeans have nitrogen-fixing bacteria in their roots to take nitrogen from the air, fix it on the roots, and put it into the soil when tilled under.

Recommended asparagus varieties include Mary Washington, Jersey Giant Hybrid, Jersey King, and Purple Passion, which is a European favorite. Washington varieties have disease-resistant properties and vigorous growth. Jersey King has high productivity and is longer lasting.

Your best bet is to purchase 1-year-old roots. You will get a light cutting the next year and regular harvests for years after. Follow this easy 1, 2, 3 planting procedure. (1) Spade or till deeply, at least 12 to preferably 18 inches deep. (2) Set root-stock crowns 6–10 inches deep, and make sure you spread roots well so they grow in all directions. Then add a few inches of soil over the crowns and tamp it down.

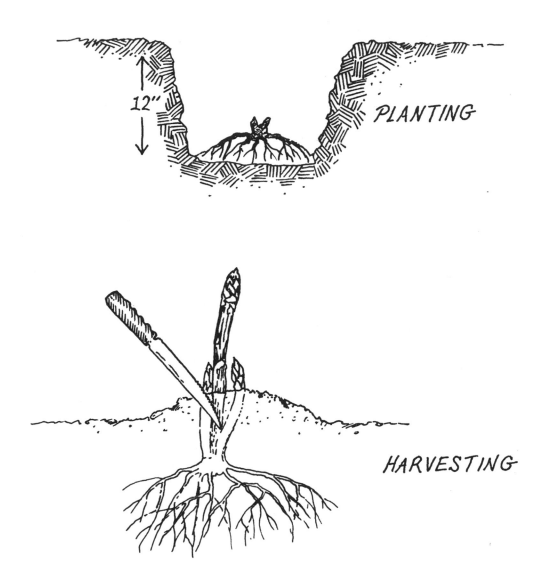

PLANTING

12"

HARVESTING

Every few weeks, add another 1–2 inches of soil until the bed is covered to the original soil level. (3) Keep your new bed well watered, mulched, and weed free.

Avoid the temptation to pick spears that appear the first season. The following spring, you'll see spears popping up magically overnight. Cut them with a knife or dandelion weeding tool. By July, stop cutting and let spears mature to their natural, fernlike growth. Keep the bed weeded and mulched. Add fertilizer in the fall, based on the amounts indicated on the package.

Cut spears only for a few weeks the second year. After that, your bed should produce prolifically year after year. Be patient. It does take deep planting and two years for an asparagus bed to set roots well. After that, they'll continue to produce their tastiest crops annually, providing you weed, mulch, and fertilize each year to maintain the bed.

RHUBARB

Rhubarb is another of those wonderful home garden plants that take time to establish but reward you deliciously. Just one plant provides you with the makings of rhubarb-strawberry pie, stewed rhubarb, and other treats. As with asparagus, take time to prepare the growing bed well, add compost to improve the soil, and this perennial will prosper. Old-time farm gardens always had a bed of asparagus and of rhubarb, which you can often see when you drive past abandoned farms in the countryside.

Just a few square feet will provide ample rhubarb for most families. With its classic large leaves, it is attractive in the corner of the yard or as a decorative border. The extra time you spend planting is amply repaid. Care is merely periodic mulching and a top dressing of fertilizer each spring. If space is tight, grow a clump in a barrel, using an enriched planting mix.

Rhubarb basically is a northern garden plant because it requires a dormant period in frozen ground to prosper. Recommended varieties are Cherry Red, which is red inside and out, juicy and sweet. Glaskins is a longtime, perpetual favorite. Valentine has dark-red stalks, grows fast, and is sweeter and needs less sugar in recipes than other varieties. Victoria is shorter but tasty too.

To plant, dig deeply and mix in as much leaf mold, humus, compost, and manure as you can put together. Remember, you only have to get it right at the start. Maintaining rhubarb is relatively easy. Follow the same basic steps for preparing asparagus beds. As you dig, mix soil ingredients well to create a favorable growing environment. Plant crowns from purchased plants as you would asparagus, described above. As with asparagus, hold off harvesting any rhubarb the first year. Let it set its roots well and deeply for years of harvest. Even the second year, only pull a few leaves to taste test your rhubarb. By the third and future years, the plants will produce abundantly.

To grow in a tub or barrel, mix two parts compost or humus, two parts manure or rotted leaves and manure, two parts peat moss, two parts garden soil, and a shovel full of sand. Put a 1-inch layer of gravel in the container, add a few inches of soil mix, then position the plant crown and fill with soil mix. Water well after planting and periodically as needed. Hold off picking for two years and then you'll have a portable rhubarb patch that gives you eating pleasure for years.

To harvest rhubarb, simply pull off the leafy stalks. They separate easily from the parent plant. Then, cut the leaves off and discard them. Read that again! Discard the leaves. Never ever use them, even for compost. Rhubarb leaves contain oxalic acid, which is a poison that can be fatal. The stalks are the only edible part of the rhubarb plant.

To cook rhubarb stalks, consult your cookbook. Strawberry-rhubarb pie is one of life's delights. As rhubarb prospers, harvest some stalks every few weeks, cut them into 1-inch pieces, and freeze them for future cooking. As a treat for dessert, simmer about a quart of rhubarb pieces in a double boiler and enjoy delicious stewed rhubarb in about 15 minutes. Stewed rhubarb is great by itself or over ice cream.

Few crops reward gardeners so abundantly for so many years. Rhubarb and asparagus are American traditions.

BOUNTIFUL BEANS

Beans, one of the most popular vegetables nationwide, have been cultivated for thousands of year. You may think of just a few, such as green beans or yellow wax beans, but your bean-growing horizon is far wider. Years before breeders developed stringless varieties, beans had fibrous strings along the seam of the pod and were aptly called stringbeans.

Calvin Keeney is hailed as the "father of the stringless bean" because he bred Burpee's Stringless Green Pod, which became the most popular variety until Tendergreen in 1925. Today, new varieties are introduced regularly that have great flavor plus disease resistance.

Bush beans are probably the most popular and certainly are easy to grow. So are their cousins, green pole beans. Kentucky Wonder remains one of America's most popular plant varieties, ever since it gained fame for Victory Gardens during World War II.

Today, beans are available in green, purple, and yellow colors. Bush beans grow on compact stems, while pole beans can climb up tepees and trellises. Few vegetables are as easy to grow and as versatile, which is why the National Garden Bureau designated 2003 as the Year of the Bean. Add their nutrients to the equation and you have a crop truly worthy of space in your garden. Beans contain fiber and a lot of protein, including the essential amino acid lysine. Most grains lack lysine, but when combined with beans they form a complete protein. Beans also provide folacin (folic acid) and some minerals, so they are indeed a healthful vegetable.

Types of Tasty Beans

All beans belong to the legume family. They have the ability to fix nitrogen in the soil and make that nutrient readily available to plants. According to the National Garden Bureau, there are three basic types of beans: snap, green shelling, and dry shell. Snap beans are named after the sound they make when you break off a piece of a pod. French beans are bush-type snap beans that produce very narrow, sometimes pencil-thin pods. Romano beans are thicker and flatter than other snap beans. Wax beans have yellow pods.

Bush snap beans take 45–55 days to bear a crop, depending on the variety. Pole snap beans produce large crops on tall plants and begin to bear in 60–70 days. For purple varieties, try Purple Teepee, Royal Burgundy, and Sequoia. Yellow varieties include Brittle Wax, Goldcrop, and Rocdor.

Lima beans, often called butter beans in the South, are shelled while the pods are green. They require somewhat warmer temperatures than snap beans to germinate well. Bush limas take 70–80 days to produce a crop, while pole limas need 80–95 days.

Some beans can be used in ornamental plantings. Old-fashioned scarlet runner beans have attractive red flowers and are edible when pods are young. Blue hyacinth beans produce striking, lilac-blue flowers followed by maroon bean pods. My friends at the National Garden Bureau remind me that they make an appealing, fast-growing cover for fences, trellises, and arbors.

Bush beans produce a lot of pods in a short time but take up more space in the garden than pole beans. Bush beans rarely have trouble with pests and diseases, mainly because they are not in the garden long enough to be bothered. After the plants have finished producing, simply dig up the stalks and plant a different crop or a fall crop of beans. Planting a different crop in that space helps you avoid bean disease problems that might occur.

For bush beans, try Blue Lake (which matures in 55 days), Kentucky Wonder, Festina (which resists common disease problems), and the violet-purple Royal Burgundy. More and more home gardeners favor heirloom varieties like Tenderpod and Greenpod. Executive is an All America Selection winner with Tendercrop parents. Greencrop is an All America Selection winner that is early maturing.

For yellow wax beans, Soleil is very flavorful and heavy yielding. Nugget is sturdy and has a rich buttery taste. Rocdor is excellent and handles heat as well as cold weather. Veteran gardeners also suggest Gold-Wax Improved, which matures in 50 days and has long, tasty, golden-yellow beans. Top Notch Golden is highly productive.

Pole beans offer growing ease and abundance. They climb up trellises or tepees to save space, and they continue to bear steadily through the summer. Better yet, pole beans are usually more prolific than bush beans. Kentucky Wonder is still a traditional favorite, and Blue Lake is popular. Kentucky Blue is an All America Selection winner. Fortex is another favorite. Among wax, Burpee Gold matures early. Romano pole beans have distinctive flavor worth trying and cooking.

Top lima beans include Eastland (a heavy yielder with excellent flavor), Fordhook 242, and Jackson Wonder (which features baby lima beans).

Bean Growing Tips

Beans are warm-season vegetables that prefer a light, well-drained soil with a pH between 6.0 and 6.8. Dig or till the soil 6–8 inches deep and incorporate organic matter, such as compost or dried manure. Bean lovers advise that you wait until all danger of frost has passed before planting. Sow beans 1 inch deep and space 1–2 inches apart, with rows 18 inches apart. To boost harvest, try repeated sowings every few weeks until 2 months before the average first fall frost in your area.

Pole beans are bountiful producers. Support bean vines with trellises or tepees on the north side of the vegetable garden so they don't block sun from other veggies. Sow six to eight seeds in a circle around each pole. Beans germinate in 6–10 days.

As Garden Bureau bean growers advise, when plants have two sets of true leaves, thin snap beans to stand 2–3 inches apart, limas 3–4 inches apart. Give beans ample water, at least 1 inch weekly. Water early so plant leaves dry before nightfall. As long as you incorporate nutrients into soil before planting, beans do not need extra fertilizing. Wax beans thrive with the same planting and cultivating.

For best taste, pick your snap beans young, about 4–5 inches long, and when seeds within the pods are just beginning to swell. Harvest lima beans when seeds are full size and pods look pudgy, but before pods begin to yellow. Shell just before cooking. Bush and even pole beans grow well in containers, outdoors or indoors, so give them a try that way too.

To benefit from the best bush or pole beans, check mail order catalogs for bean varieties resistant to diseases that can infest a planting. And look for those that offer most productivity and taste. If bean beetles are in your area, handpick or cover rows or apply pesticides as directed on packages.

Grow a Pole Bean Tepee

You can encourage kids to garden with a bean tepee, formed by fastening three long poles together at the top. Sow pole bean seeds around the tepee, leaving an opening between two of the poles. Beans will form a cool, dark tent where kids can hold "secret" meetings with friends. You can also add a cucumber vine to grow up a tepee or trellis and give children a chance to make some of their own pickles too.

BROCCOLI BASICS

This delicious and nutritious vegetable has been popular in Europe for generations and has gained favor nationwide here. Broccoli is prolific and hardy, withstands cold, and bears multiple crops when properly cultivated. If you pick side heads often, the plants bear longer. Read about the nutritional advantages of this veggie in cookbooks and you're sure to add it to your garden each year.

Broccoli is not temperamental. It does well in a variety of soils and temperatures. But it needs ample water weekly to sustain its high yields. Follow these proved tips from the National Garden Bureau. Start seeds indoors early, as you do tomatoes. Plant outdoors after frost has passed. You'll have ample seed in a packet, so plant spring and fall crops, since this plant thrives in cooler weather. Five plants will produce an ample supply for a family for weeks.

Packman Hybrid is a favorite extra early variety that does well in different climates and soils. Early Dividend produces many secondary stalks. Premium Crop is an All America Selection winner. Lucky Hybrid produces side shoots all season. Try also De Cicco types of Italian green sprouting broccoli that have a deep green color and lots of side sprouts. The fast-growing Green Comet hybrid, an All America Selection Gold Medal winner, is both heat and disease resistant.

Grow Better Broccoli

Prepare the soil well, adding fertilizer before tilling or digging. As you begin harvesting spring-planted broccoli, consider starting more seeds for fall-producing plants. Give plants ample room, about 12–20 inches apart in the row. When the first central head forms, cut and use it. Check plants daily, because side shoots produce smaller clusters that tend to flower quickly, which makes them bitter. Keep checking, and cut and freeze abundance if necessary. Like many plants, the more you cut, the more broccoli tends to produce more side growth. During this period, apply an inch of water weekly for tastiest crops.

BRUSSELS SPROUTS

This member of the cabbage family that looks like tiny cabbages is a nutritious veggie that deserves a try in home gardens. It likes the same soil conditions as broccoli and cabbage, as well as ample sun and water when it is setting its crop along the bottom of the stalk. Once you've tasted homegrown Brussels sprouts and shared them with friends, this vegetable should earn an annual space in your garden.

Note this harvesting tip: Pick only the lowest, earliest maturing heads when they look like small, firm cabbages. Then break off lower leaves below where you pick, but leave upper leaves on the plant to produce more tasty sprouts.

Recommended types include Jade Cross hybrid, which matures in about 80 days, bearing rich blue-green sprouts on 20-inch-tall plants. Diablo Hybrid is acclaimed as the tastiest by aficionados, and Oliver is an early type. Long Island Improved has round, dark-green, tight heads that actually seem to improve in flavor from early fall frost.

CHEERS FOR CABBAGE

Cabbage is a useful, multipurpose vegetable. You can enjoy it cooked, as in corned beef and cabbage or herb-flavored boiled cabbage. It also is great raw as coleslaw or to add zest to salads, and it can be made into sauerkraut. There are choice varieties and colors to whet the appetite. Happily, cabbage can handle cold weather. Covered with straw in the fall, it provides spring eating. One seed package provides many more plants than you need, so consider swapping varieties with neighboring gardeners.

Start cabbage indoors for earliest planting. The plants like good sun, well-drained loamy soil, and ample water as they set their heads. Since large, tasty heads are the goal, apply lots of nitrogen, which is the leaf-aiding nutrient. Till under 5–10 pounds of 10-10-10 fertilizer per 100 square feet in an area for cabbage, Brussels sprouts, and broccoli, or use the recommended amounts for the type of plant food you prefer.

For best crops, after plants have set roots well, plan to side dress with extra nitrogen, such as a 10-6-4. A cup for 15 feet should serve plants well. Be aware some varieties tend to split in hot weather. Check for varieties that tolerate different temperatures, and plant early, mid, and late varieties to extend your cabbage harvesting season.

Longtime garden experts note that some cabbage may be susceptible to root-knot disease. To avoid this threat, rotate other crops into that growing area for two years, but no relatives of cabbage such as broccoli, Brussels sprouts, collards, or cauliflower. Some insects seem to love cabbage, such as cabbage loopers. Best bet is to follow a simple pest control program and use one of the safer multipurpose pesticides if really needed to control pests.

Recommended varieties include the All America Selection winner Stonehead, a hybrid with 6-inch round heads and compact growth. Chieftan Savoy is another All America choice. Tendersweet is favored for making coleslaw. Megaton hybrid is mild, sweet, and about the size of a bowling ball. Good mini-cabbages include Alcosa, Gonzales, Red Express, and red Cairo Hybrid.

CHINESE CABBAGE TREATS

Oriental cooking has increased its popularity now that home gardeners can grow the right veggies for tasty stir-fry and other Asian-inspired meals.

Chinese cabbage, often called celery cabbage or wong bok, does well in home gardens. Actually these "greens" are more closely related to mustard. Recommended varieties include Minuet, a closed-head type; Greenwich, which has tall, flavorful heads that store well in the refrigerator; and Rubicon, with sweet, tangy, juicy flavor.

Chinese cabbage prefers rich, well-drained, moist soil. Because Chinese cabbage tends to generate seed stalks quickly in summer, spring and fall crops are advised. Follow the instructions for basic cabbage planting and cultivation.

CAULIFLOWER DELIGHTS

Varieties of this veggie for home gardens are far tastier than store-bought cauliflower. Check them out in mail order catalogs, especially the heirloom varieties, and give it a try. You will enjoy wonderful new flavors from the freshly picked crops.

Like cabbage, cauliflowers only produce one head per plant, so it pays to select the best new varieties and grow the plants to peak of perfection. Recommended varieties include Cassius Hybrid, called the best-tasting cauliflower in the world. Snow crown is the earliest heading. The All America Selection winner Snow King hybrid has a rich, creamy white heart and is heat tolerant. Cheddaris is a brilliant orange cauliflower.

Follow cabbage-growing procedures and the directions on seed packets. These veggies prefer nicely tilled, loamy soil with early fertilizer mixed in and as a side dressing as the heads begin to form. Once plants have set firm roots, thin to 8–12 inches apart, or more if growing largest headed types. Cauliflower is not quite as hardy as cabbage, and warm weather slows head formation, so plant early in spring and again in fall for best results. To achieve the whitest heads, tie the leaves over the head with string to help heads bleach.

You will need to sneak a peak to see if the head is ready. Seed packs give target maturity dates. When heads look full and bright, feel firm to the touch, and are just a bit below anticipated size, it's time to pick. For best flavor, cook immediately, and be prepared to be surprised how delicious homegrown cauliflowers can be. The taste is usually sweeter and tangier than most people have ever had.

COLLARDS DESERVE A TRY

This overlooked member of the cabbage clan deserves a try. Collards have been popular in the South for years, but new, northerly varieties will give you a surprise at dinner time. Follow cabbage-growing methods, but be sure to provide ample water as the plants mature to achieve the most succulent tastes. This nonheading member of the cabbage family produces tasty greens over a long period, even in poor soil.

Vates is a variety that grows upright, has dark-green leaves, and is vigorous and winter-hardy through the Mid-Atlantic states. Champion is a Vates type with long-standing ability and winter hardiness. Flash is dark-green leafed, vigorous, and high yielding. Give collards a chance and they may win your favor for a place every year in the garden and at mealtime. In northern areas, be sure you select hardier varieties.

COLORFUL CANTALOUPES AND OTHER MARVELOUS MELONS

Cantaloupes and other delicious, worthwhile melons all thrive under similar growing conditions. You'll find lots of tasty melons grouped together

here, and the National Garden Bureau website at www.ngb.org offers even more useful information so every home gardener can enjoy tastier melons for years to come. Today, although many tasty melons are available in supermarkets, they can't match the sweet taste of those special varieties you can grow from seed.

Melons are in the cucurbit or gourd family that includes cucumbers, pumpkins, and squash. As the National Garden Bureau notes, the Reticulatus group of melons, identifiable by its netted skin, is the most commonly grown and includes what we call muskmelons or cantaloupes. Also known as summer melons, they are aromatic when ripe. In contrast, melons in the Inodorous group do not have an aromatic smell. These smooth-skinned winter melons include the casaba, crenshaw, and honeydew.

If you fancy melons, you can expand your growing horizon with many types available through mail order catalogs. **Canary** melons have bright yellow rinds and a mild, juicy, cream-colored flesh. **Casabas** have a pointy end, a wrinkled yellow skin, and very sweet, very pale flesh. The French **Charentais** melons have a smooth, gray skin and orange flesh. **Crenshaws** have a slightly wrinkled green skin that turns yellow as it ripens, a spicy aroma, and pale orange flesh. **Persian** melons have a light brown netting over a dark-green skin that turns light green as the fruit ripens, and the flesh is a bright pink orange. Try some of these in the years ahead and you're sure to be tastefully delighted.

Begin with Melon Seeds

Melons are easy to grow from seed. The tastiest cantaloupe is Ambrosia, a truly gourmet treat with sweetest flavor and a gorgeous peach color, but it needs more time to mature than other varieties.

Earliqueen is extra early and super sweet, and Earligold is early and large fruited. Athena is delicious, durable, and disease tolerant. Gold Star by Harris is a deep-orange, juicy, heavy yielding type, and Superstar is perhaps the biggest.

For honeydew melons, try the early and flavorful Honey Pearl, or try Honey Orange, which has orange flesh that is tasty to the rind. Amy is an All America Selection winner of the canary type melons. Angel is a delightful Mediterranean melon. You can also try a Charentais such as French Orange or Savor, perhaps the sweetest. Among Asian melons, Sun Jewel is easy to grow and early. Arava is one of the first melons of the season, a Galia type with green flesh and ultra sweet.

If you garden in a mild-winter area, sow seeds directly in the garden at the same time as you plant tomatoes, which is after all danger of frost is past and the ground is warm and well dried from winter moisture. Melon lovers at the National Garden Bureau advise preparing a small hill of rich, improved, well-drained soil and planting 3–5 seeds 2 inches apart and about 1 inch deep. Water well. Once the emerging seedlings have two sets of true leaves, thin out the smaller or weaker plants and leave the two strongest to mature.

In cold-weather areas, it helps to plant melons through black plastic mulch. The dark plastic absorbs heat, warms the soil, conserves moisture as it controls weeds, and keeps fruit cleaner. Each fall, we spread compost and old leaves on the melon site and rototill about 8 inches deep. Then, we lay the black plastic over the future melon garden and weigh it down with old boards.

Come spring, when the soil temperature is above 60°F, you can start planting. Make 5-inch cross cuts at least 4 feet apart on 6-foot centers if you grow in rows. Or if you mix and match plants, allow at least 3 feet in all directions around the cross cuts in the plastic. Next, pull back the plastic where you made each cut, and form a hill of soil for your seeds. Because melons prefer richer soil, it pays to add lots of organic matter to that hill planting area. Then, plant seeds and they'll take root and grow. Thin to the strongest two seedlings when they are a few weeks old.

For colder northern areas, it pays to consider using transplants than directly seeding. Start melon

For vegetables that call for hill growing, plant seeds, cover with soil, and soon they'll begin to sprout and spread.

seeds indoors in peat pots filled with compost or potting mix about 15–18 days before planting time. Harden plants off for at least a week in a cooler indoor location before planting them outdoors. But remember, melons are cold sensitive, so pay attention to both the air and soil temperatures before transplanting. Be sure all danger of frost has passed.

When planting, always tear the peat pot down to its soil level and cover with garden soil. Otherwise the peat can wick moisture out of the soil. After planting, water well with your choice of a transplant nutrient solution to give melons a good start. Watch the weather. If frost or cold threatens, make a mini-greenhouse from a one-gallon, plastic milk jug by cutting off the bottom. Then set the jug over the hill, pressing it one-half inch into the ground for stability. During the day when the temperature goes up, remove the cap. You may only need to do this for a day or so until weather stays warm.

Melon Growing Tips

Melons need lots of water to give them their sweetest taste So it pays to provide at least 1 inch of water a week but 2 inches is better, especially as melons mature. Water melons in the morning, preferably at soil level using drip irrigation so the leaves can dry before evening to prevent fungal diseases. If faced with drought or water restrictions, be sure to provide critical water when the fruit starts setting.

Fertilize the plants every 2 to 3 weeks using an all-purpose fertilizer such as 5-5-5, and add several inches of compost monthly as a mulch.

Some gardeners worry when plants are due to begin making melons but they don't see any appearing. Not to worry. The earliest melon flowers are male, which bear pollen but cannot set fruit. Only the later female flowers develop into melons. Relax and let nature takes it course.

Several other points about melons are worth noting. Although they need ample moisture when setting fruit and it ripens, curiously the best and sweetest melons ripen when the weather is hot and dry. It pays to plant them in soil that is very well drained and with ample space for good air circulation around the entire vine. Sometimes melons don't meet our expectations and may not be as sweet as they should. This may be due to an abundance of rain in the 2–3 weeks prior to harvest. Melons need sufficient moisture while growing and fruiting, but prior to harvest, the best, sweetest flavor will occur if the plant is on the dry side. Cut back on watering the plant when you approach harvest, about 3 weeks prior to the main crop harvest.

Pick at Perfection

The biggest problem for novice melon growers is when to pick for peak taste. Most summer melons are fragrant when ripe. Sniff the skin. The aroma will signal when the melon is ripe for the picking. Another indicator is when the stem separates or slips easily from the vine. Cantaloupes are mature when the rind changes from green to tan-yellow between the veins.

Honeydew, crenshaw, and other winter melons are ready to harvest when they turn completely white or yellow and the blossom end is slightly soft to the touch. Since they do not slip, cut the melons from the vine. Once picked, they will continue to ripen for several days at room temperature.

Grow Strong Plants

It's a fact that insects prefer weak, sickly plants, so choose the best varieties, prepare and improve soil, and cultivate and fertilize well to produce strong, healthy plants and the tastiest delights you deserve.

Also, walk around your garden several times a week. Admire your plants, look at them carefully, and pay attention to the vines, leaves, flowers, and fruit. Look for any sign of pests or diseases. If you find a problem, try to identify the cause and if necessary fix the problem in the least toxic way possible.

Expert gardeners make this key point: "Prevention is the basic key to disease management, especially with melons." Be fastidious in fall cleanup. Get rid of all parts of the plants, leaving bare soil that you can mulch, fall till, or even plant with a cover crop for winter.

Whenever you spot any disease on plants, remove the infected part; remove and discard the mulch around the plant and replace it with fresh, clean mulch. Check with your local Cooperative Extension Service for advice on disease and pest management where you live, as it varies in different regions.

Consider Container Melons

Even if you don't have backyard room, you can grow some melons in containers. Compact new hybrids take little space but yield full-size, delicious melons. You'll find more details about container growing in chapter 15. Briefly, if you have a small, sunny space, select a large container—such as half of a whiskey barrel that has a drainage hole—and a compact melon variety. Fill the container with compost mixed with two handfuls of peat moss. Select a melon that grows only 3–4 feet and produces 4-inch fruits. Plant your seeds or seedlings and water regularly. You can train the vines up a trellis if you wish, supporting the fruit with nets made of old onion bags.

With thanks to fellow garden writer Cathy Wilkinson Barash and the National Garden Bureau for much of the information included here, melon

growing can be one of your tastiest projects every year.

CARE ABOUT CARROTS

Often gardeners overlook carrots because they are so inexpensive to buy in stores and are often considered "just carrots." If you don't try them in your garden, you'll never have a chance to savor that old-fashioned carrot flavor that commercial farms can't duplicate. Fact is, carrots can be uniquely flavorful, and you can grow long, medium, and short lengths, in colors ranging from orange to almost red, to perk up salads and add zest to cooked meals too.

Carrots need sandy loam to poke their tasty roots down deep and pack them with nutrients for you. Dig or rototill about 10–12 inches deep. You can use compost, peat moss, even construction sand to open up heavier soils for carrots and also other root crops that prefer sandy loam growing conditions. Fact is, a yard or so of sand on hand is useful around the garden in many ways. You can use it to loosen up heavier, clay soils as well as mix with compost to make planting mixes, cover tiny seeds in outdoor gardens, and improve drainage around home foundations.

Recommended carrot varieties include Goldinhart, a fine-grained, red-cored Chatenay type with deep outside and inside color, a small core, and sweetest flavor. It won applause from the Royal Horticultural Society. Nelson is rated the best tasting for earliest harvest, and Napoli also is a newer early type. Napa is a worldwide favorite. Scarlet Nantes is a short-topped variety with finely textured flesh that is nicely smooth. It does well in heavier soils. Ithaca Hybrid has long, tasty roots. For special carrot treats, try Short 'n Sweet, tiny and tasty. Pot o' Gold is the best for beta-carotene. Rainbo mix has white, cream, apricot, and orange carrots for colorful salads and dinners. Purple Haze is an All America Selection winner as a purple carrot. Look around and you'll find others worth trying too.

Once you have your land prepared, mix the tiny carrot seeds half and half with sand to assure more even seeding and avoid wasting seeds. You can grow carrots in the same spot year after year, so take time to prepare that area well. Review the soil improvement information in chapter 2 for more details. It pays to concentrate on building good tilth and rich soil to grow the best, tastiest, and sweetest carrots possible.

Carrot seed geminates well in early spring. Space rows 12 inches apart and sow seed lightly right near the surface. Barely cover it with fine soil and sand. Once seeds sprout, you'll see the too-thickly planted areas. Thin immediately. Give seedlings a few more weeks and thin again, leaving carrots 1–2 inches apart to mature properly. At this point and perhaps once more, thin tastefully: pull the tiny carrots that are growing too closely together and add them to your salad.

Plan succession seedling to assure yourself a long supply. Carrots will even take frosts; they go almost dormant in the ground, but they survive. Some gardeners pour hot water on the ground and pick carrots during winter. Carrots also store well in cold basements and similar areas to save refrigerator space.

As you enjoy carrots, continue your carrot soil improvement program. Add compost and humus and till it under. There is an alternative until you have soil well improved to a loose, friable condition. Select some of the best new short carrots that plant breeders have perfected. In fact, review the many different varieties that are now available and try them in your own comparison growing and taste tests. Share seeds with neighbors and try a Veggie Taste Test party during summer to evaluate different new varieties of all types of vegetables. That also gives you an opportunity to share and collect good growing tips from neighbors and fellow gardeners.

BEETS AND OTHER TASTY ROOT CROPS

In addition to carrots, the most commonly grown root crops are beets, parsnips, radishes, turnips, and rutabagas, but not all are popular. Because they all have similar cultural requirements and grow best in cool weather, you'll find them discussed together here, rather than individually in this chapter. All are relatively hardy and may be planted early in the spring. Some can be left in the garden until fall or even over winter. Parsnips actually improve in flavor when left in the ground during winter, as do some carrots. As tasty veggies, all have nutritive values. Also, beet and turnip greens are prized as cooked greens and can be collected while the plants are young.

Among the recommended beet varieties, Pacemaker III has excellent flavor. Bull's Blood is a dark, regal addition to gardens, with deep red tops for salads in addition to the red beets. Detroit Dark Red is still excellent, as is Red Ace Hybrid, probably the best flavored one. Golden is a gold-colored beet that doesn't bleed red when cut and cooked.

Parsnips are one of the few root crops that can be overwintered, and many believe this enhances eating quality. Try Improved Hollow Crown, an All America Selection winner. Gladiator germinates well and grows quickly, with tasty cream-colored roots. Cobham Improved Marrow is an outstanding late variety that thrives even in heavier soils. Lancer is good too. All parsnips are cold-hardy vegetables, delicious from late fall through early spring. Leave roots in the ground, pour on hot water in winter to soften the soil, and dig parsnip pleasure.

Good radishes include Cherriette, which is uniform, small, bright-red, and round to grow from spring to fall. Easter Egg is a fun mix for kids, with red, purple, and white radishes. White Icicle is a miniature daikon-type radish for salads. China Rose and Black Spanish are winter radishes. You can also try various Eastern radishes such as Shunkyo, a long pink one, and Miyasige, a fall-harvest, white-root type. D'Avignon is a traditional French radish.

Rutabagas are similar to turnips but do not become strong-flavored and fibrous when grown to a large size of up to 6 inches. Try American Purple or Gilfeather, which is perhaps sweetest. Marian has yellow flesh and purple tops. Joan has a mild flavor.

Turnips can be tasteful, not bitter, when you grow the right variety. Try Purple Top White Globe, a traditional old-time favorite. Newer Hakurei is delicious, with a fruity-sweet taste. Scarlet Queen produces beautiful red salad turnips. Golden Ball has an exceptional flavor and can grow 3–4 inches in diameter.

Turnips that you grow in your garden can be harvested at 2–4 inches in diameter, much smaller than one sees in supermarkets. They develop strong flavor if allowed to grow too large.

Root Crop Needs

My longtime friends at the National Garden Bureau emphasize that proper soil preparation is key to success with root crops. They grow best in a deep, loose soil that retains moisture yet is well-drained and lets their roots form properly. Root crops do not grow well in very acid soils. Take a soil sample for pH and nutrient analysis and apply fertilizer or lime as needs indicate.

Here are key nutrient facts. Nitrogen is important for beets, carrots, parsnips, and rutabagas, about three-quarters to 1 cup of urea per 100 square feet. Apply half during spring soil preparation. In midseason, apply the other half as a side dressing. For radishes and turnips, use about one-half cup urea per 100 square feet spread widely and tilled in before planting. Phosphorous and potash should be applied according to soil test recommendations. For most root crops, the optimum pH range is between 6 and 6.5. Liming will raise the pH of acid soils.

Soil improvement is discussed in chapter 2 but should be underlined here for root crops. Improve soil conditions by adding well-rotted manure or compost. Once you spread the needed spring fertilizer, deeply till the soil and smooth the surface to prepare a good seedbed.

Planting and Thinning

Root crops are usually grown by sowing seeds directly in the garden. Plant radishes and turnips beginning in mid-April for a spring crop, and again around August 1 for a fall crop. Start planting carrots and beets about mid-April and parsnips in early May. Rutabagas require a long growing season, so plant in May for a fall crop. Try double cropping with radishes and parsnips in the same row. Radishes will be ready to harvest in 3–5 weeks, opening up room for later-maturing parsnips. Double cropping, also called intercropping, lets you get more use out of the space in your garden.

It is important to thin root crops, especially to allow room for beets and turnips to develop properly. Save the seed packets and follow the directions for varieties you plant. Thin radishes as soon as they reach a small, edible size. If you wish to use the tops of beets for greens, simply delay thinning until the tops are a good size. Beets, parsnips, radishes, and turnips should be thinned to a 2-inch spacing and rutabagas to an 8-inch spacing.

Watch the Water

Proper watering makes the difference between good and poor production. Vegetables need at least 1 inch of water each week during the growing season. Always soak soil thoroughly when watering to promote good root development. Merely sprinkling just wets the soil surface and often promotes shallow root development and weed growth. That can increase your crop's susceptibility to hot weather and drought stress. For root crops in most soils, watering once a week is sufficient. In very sandy soils, more frequent watering is needed. Check 6 inches deep, and if it is dry, rewater sandy soil as needed.

Don't let weeds get a head start. Root crops grow slowly for the first few weeks after planting and can't compete with weeds. Pull out weeds, or use shallow cultivation to control weeds and keep the surface of the soil loose. Green Thumb Tip: It is always easier to pull, hoe, or cultivate early, when weeds are small. By July, uncontrolled weeds can be a major task. Roots of the root crops are very close to the surface of the soil, so cultivate just deeply enough to cut the weeds off below the surface.

Harvest Time Tips

Harvest beets and turnips when they reach a usable size. To insure best quality, pick when young and never allow them to become overgrown and tough. Spading soil next to the plants makes them easier to pull. Leave parsnips and rutabagas in the ground until late fall. Their roots can be 10–12 inches long. Spade or use a spading fork to open soil to avoid breaking these roots when harvesting. Radishes are usually ready in 3–5 weeks after planting. Pull them whenever you want some. They get bitter if left too long and become overgrown.

Potential Problems

All vegetables can be attacked by insects or diseases. Before you run for a sprayer, try to find out what problems you have. The County Extension Service has experts in every county in America, usually based at the county seat. Ask for help. Collect bugs and take them to be identified. Enroll in gardening classes. Consider working toward becoming a Master Gardener. Everything you learn will contribute to better gardening and more fun afield.

Some pests and symptoms to watch for include carrot root flies; the maggots feed on and destroy roots of many root crops. Flea beetles chew small, round holes in leaves and can spread disease and destroy the crop, especially when the plants are very young.

All tops with no roots or small roots is usually caused by planting too close or by not thinning. But excessive nitrogen fertilization also can contribute to extensive top growth at the expense of root growth.

In summary, root crops are the first and last vegetables to be harvested, and under proper storage conditions they will be available almost year round. They take up little space, which makes them ideal for small gardens. Even better, most root crops have no definite stage of maturity that must be reached before they are edible, which makes them ideal for short-season areas or unpredictable areas.

CRISP HOMEGROWN CELERY

Celery has a place in every garden to give you new flavor dimensions for salads. It doesn't take much room, fits in salads and soups, and is great as a snack too. One seed pack can grow more than a hundred plants, so it is probably wiser to buy started plants. Or you can start a lot of plants and swap with neighboring gardeners for other vegetable transplants.

Believe it or not, there are different nuances of flavor to different varieties of celery. Recommended are Utah 52-70, a tender, tasty new variety that is disease resistant. Conquistador is another top-tasting, Utah-type celery. Tango Hybrid is sweet and crunchy and a vigorous grower. Burpee's Fordhook celery is one of the finest flavored. Utah or Golden Crisp are good for fall planting.

Like lettuce, celery prefers cool weather and doesn't enjoy heat. Plant in early spring and in midseason for fall crops. Perhaps surprisingly, celery prefers rich, deep, moist soil. You can expand your carrot patch and interplant with celery. Fact is, they look good growing together and blend nicely in salads. Celery has tiny seeds, so consider mixing the seed half and half with sand to achieve proper dispersion when planting. Because celery is slow to sprout, soak the seed overnight—between two blotters is one good method—to help soften the seed coat for better germination. After planting, cover very lightly with sand or light soil and water well to encourage proper germination.

At first, celery seedlings look very tiny and weak, but with thinning they surprise you by how well they can set roots and grow. Thin within the first few weeks to leave sturdiest seedlings 6 inches apart. Each small plant will spread and become a mature, fully packed bunch of stalks. Because it is largely water, celery needs at least an inch each week so it can pull up nutrients from the soil to mature crisp and tasty.

Many gardeners prefer blanched celery. You can easily achieve this by mounding soil around your plants or along rows to get the whitish look around the base. Check periodically to be sure plants aren't rotting in wet weather. For finest flavor, pick stalks when they are white, pale green, or a bit darker. As with all veggies, test pick at different stages to get the feel of what time is best for harvesting.

SWEETER SWEET CORN

Sweet corn, or table corn, is one of America's all-time favorite veggies. Years ago there were few choices, mainly Golden Bantam and Country Gentleman. Today, sugar-enhanced sweet corn holds its sweetness much longer, and many varieties are available from different seed firms. In addition, plant breeders have perfected many new and delicious varieties. Even better, new varieties of sweet corn take much less space than just a few years ago. As you think about sweet corn, plan to set up your own taste tests. Plant breeders have achieved outstanding success in creating sweeter sweet corn. Read about them in mail order catalogs so you'll have the knowledge to select the varieties that will reward you best.

According to the National Garden Bureau, which celebrated the new millennium as the Year of the Sweet Corn, the favorite corn in the 1880s had white kernels. That changed in 1902 with the introduction of Golden Bantam, a Burpee variety that became a household name and changed the preference from white to yellow kernel corn.

Corn is one of the sweetest, most flavorful vegetables grown in any garden. If you wish to expand your horizons, you can grow popcorn varieties as well as Indian and ornamental corn for decorations. Indian corn kernels range from mahogany, red, yellow, and orange to deep blue, and combinations of these colors occur on one ear. Indian corn varieties can be harvested in 110 days. Just pull back the husks and allow them to dry. These ornamental types with their calico colors are used indoors or outside for Halloween and Thanksgiving decorations.

Popcorn is available in yellow, white, red, and glossy black kernels. High-yielding hybrids often bear two or three ears per stalk. The harvested popcorn ears need to be cured before popping by placing ears in a mesh bag or an open woven basket and storing in an airy, warm, dry attic or garage for 3 or 4 weeks to allow the outer shell of the kernels to harden. Then, shell by rubbing with both hands, or rub two cobs together, and store kernels in jars with airtight lids.

Today, there are three main types of sweet corn: normal sugar, sugar enhanced (SE), and supersweet. These terms refer to the sugar content and sweet flavor in the kernels when mature. For more details, visit the National Garden Bureau website at www.ngb.org. In normal sugar types, the sweet flavor is rapidly lost after harvest. In sugar enhanced and supersweet varieties, the sugar content is higher than in normal sugar corn at peak maturity, and the sweet flavor lasts longer after harvest. Sugar enhanced types have increased in popularity among home gardeners because they combine sweet flavor with ease of growing.

Happily for us today, there are hybrids that combine two or three types of sweet corn. In 2000, an All America Selection winner was Indian Summer, a supersweet with multicolored kernels in yellow, white, red, and purple. Old-time Country Gentleman and Golden Bantam are still available. Today, it is worth the taste to grow these newer, supersweet varieties. Silver Queen is probably the most popular white sweet corn in America. Early Sunglow is an early golden. But if you want the sweetest corn, grow the newer types for truly tastier eating.

Among new genetically sweeter sweet corns, consider these among SE hybrids: Bodacious and Sugar Buns for yellow, and Silver King or early Silver Princess for white varieties. Among Super Sweet hybrids, try Butterfruit original, very early and extra sweet and Honey 'N Pearl, a bicolor All America Selection winner. Xtra Tender varieties are also worth trial growing. Triplesweet hybrids include Honey Select 2001, an All America Selection winner, and Avalon, the first white triplesweet type. There are many more coming along, so check the latest mail order catalogs and do some comparison tests to find the corn your family likes best.

The National Garden Bureau experts have provided some simple rules to follow to grow a bumper crop of sweet corn. I've followed their tips for years and thank them for ongoing advice for home gardeners. As the NGB advices, site selection, soil nutrients, and water are very important to grow a bounty of fresh corn on the cob. To begin, select a site on the north side of your garden. Corn plants are tall, so if planted on the east or west side, they will cast shadows on the other garden plants and decrease plant production. All your vegetable plants need maximum sunlight.

Prepare Corn Garden Soil

Average soil will support sweet corn, but you'll have better results if you improve the soil. Veteran corn gardeners recommend planting a green manure in the fall and tilling it under in the spring. Next, incorporate compost or manure to a depth of 12 inches or add 1 pound of 5-10-10 or 10-10-10 fertilizer, bonemeal, or wood ash per 25-foot row.

Corn can be grown in two basic ways, in blocks or in hills. If space is not a problem, plant rows of corn in blocks of a minimum of four rows, about 2.5 or 3 feet apart. Rows can be as long as you wish. To ensure adequate pollination, sow all corn seed at the same time. For small plantings of sweet corn, a hill system is recommended. Hills are groups of four or five seeds sown in a circle, with 2 inches between seeds. Space the hills 2–3 feet apart. When the seedlings are established, thin each hill to two or three plants, but be sure for adequate pollination to have a minimum of 12–24 corn plants.

Although sweet corn prefers well-tilled, reasonably fertile, loamy soil, it can produce in lesser quality ground if you add fertilizer before tilling and then side dress during the growing season. Don't get too anxious. If spring soil is too wet, it may rot the seeds. Be patient. You can enjoy early corn by selecting early varieties. Then, stretch your season by planting mid and late maturing types too.

In rows, sow seeds an inch and a quarter deep and 4–6 inches apart. Most supersweet varieties will not germinate well in cool soils. Soil temperatures should be at least 65–70°F to achieve optimum germination. When the seedlings are 4 inches tall, thin them to 8–10 inches apart. Be uncompromising when thinning. If plants are too close, yields will be reduced.

Yes, sweet corn can be grown in large tubs for a patio container crop. Choose a large container, 2–3 feet deep, to be able to maintain soil moisture levels. Place container in full sun. Sow two to four seeds in clusters, 6 inches apart. Thin seedlings to the most vigorous, keeping one plant for every 6 inches in the container. Maintain high nutrient levels and water frequently, as soil will probably dry quickly in the container. To ensure proper pollination, shake the stalk each day for several days, allowing pollen to fall into the silks. Continue watering and fertilizing as ears fill out.

Good Growing Tips

Once planted, corn needs ample watering. One key is that when watering, irrigate the soil rather than using overhead sprinklers. Sweet corn is pollinated as pollen drifts from the tassel to the silk. If tassels and pollen are wet, pollen won't leave the tassel or will be washed away.

It is critical to water sweet corn just before the appearance of the silk and a couple of weeks after the silks turn brown during the kernel-filling state. Deep watering is always better than shallow for all except sandy soils. You can expect to begin picking in 9–15 weeks, depending on the variety. For optimum growth and production, keep the sweet corn rows or hills weeded.

Another growing point: Sweet corn is a heavy feeder and will quickly deplete soil nutrients. Additional fertilizer or compost is needed when stalks are 8 inches tall and again when the tassels appear. Check the amounts recommended for the type of fertilizer you buy.

Solve Growing Problems

Corn borers can be a problem. Look for a small pile of sawdust-like matter near a small hole on the stalk beneath the tassel. The worm will crawl down and eat its way into the ear if not removed. Corn earworm is another bother. This pest lays eggs on the silks, and larvae of the moth eat their way through the ear of corn. Research has shown that the earlier in the season the corn is planted, the less severe earworm damage is, and that corn earworms are less of a problem in areas where the winter temperatures fall below 0°F. Otherwise you might use appropriate pesticides for control.

Raccoons and deer may raid corn plantings. Veteran gardeners have found a curious solution. To discourage both deer and raccoons, hang half a bar of Dial soap on stakes, allowing the soap to dangle 6 inches above the ground. Place the stakes 4 feet apart, all around the perimeter of the block of corn, and intersperse between the rows. Nobody knows why this seems to work, but it has proved useful, so it is included here to help you beat other animals to your sweet corn crop.

Pick When Perfect

When to pick for sweetest taste is always a question for gardeners. With corn, wait until ears are firm to the grasp and silk has begun to dry in a gold to dark mellow brown. Sneak a peak. Pull the husk back a bit. If kernels are full to the end of the ear, the corn is ready to pick. Corn is best tasting if cooked right after picking. The new supersweet varieties hold their sweetness in storage for a day or so, but veteran gardeners say they prefer to eat corn as soon after picking as possible for greatest flavor rewards.

Cultivate cucumbers for salads or pickle making. (A) Plant seeds in a hill, and mulch to prevent weeds. (B) Pick cukes as they mature and the plant will continue to produce more.

CUCUMBERS

Cucumbers for salads or pickling are one of the most popular veggie crops today and among America's top ten. As vine crops they require space, but you have two options. You can train vines up wire or fabric fences or on a trellis, or you can select one of the tasty new bush varieties that even produce abundantly in containers. You can enjoy many types, from small gherkin to long slicing varieties to suit your taste.

Cucumbers are a subtropical crop needing long warm days, lots of sunshine, and mild nights. Plant breeders produced new varieties with much shorter growing seasons for northern areas. Cukes thrive at relatively high temperatures, 65–75°F and won't tolerate a frost. To get the best results, start cucumbers indoors and transplant outdoors when all frost danger has passed.

Recommended varieties for slicing and salads include Straight 8 and Park's Whopper, plus Diva and Sweet Success Hybrid, both All America Selection winners. Eureka grows in almost any condition. For pickling, try Alibi for sweet gherkins. Clinton yields well and resists diseases, and Northern Pickling is a high yielding, early variety. Space-saving Bushmaster is good for container gardening. More new, excellent hybrids are available too for fresh use and pickling.

Some other useful cukes include heavy yielding Straight Eight, Spacemaster for big fruits in small spaces with mosaic and scab resistance, and Sweet

Slice Burpless, good for the digestion if cucumbers give you problems. Also check out Salad Bush Hybrid, Bush Champion, and Midget Bush Pickle.

Happily, cucumbers can be grown successfully in many types of soils, even poorer types. However, they prefer loamy soil that is loose, well drained, and has ample organic matter and plant nutrients. To get peak production, incorporate well-rotted manure or compost into the growing area before planting. Cukes prefer a soil pH between 6.0 and 7.0. It is best to add lime and fertilizer based on soil test results. Generally, you should add a complete 5-10-10 fertilizer according to label directions before planting. Then, about one week after blossoms appear, use a high nitrogen fertilizer to side dress the hills and again 3 or 4 weeks later. Do not overfertilize, as this encourages vine growth and retards fruiting.

For earliest cukes, preplant seeds indoors 10–14 days before anticipated outdoor planting after danger of frost is gone. You can also direct seed using a traditional hill system, with four or five seeds in hills spaced 4–5 feet apart. Using black plastic as mulch warms soil well, smothers weeds, and holds in needed soil moisture. Otherwise, conventional organic mulches can be worthwhile after transplanting or direct seeding outdoors.

Pests can attack cukes, including cucumber beetles, aphids, mites, and pickle worms. Diseases, some brought by insects, include bacterial wilt, anthracnose, powdery and downy mildew, and leaf spot. You can keep problems under control with careful use of combination pesticides. Newer varieties have built-in disease resistance and are worth trying.

Most cukes are ready for picking 50–70 days after planting, depending on variety and intended use. Never let cukes reach the yellowish stage, because they get bitter. Cut the stem one-quarter inch above the fruit and harvest regularly to encourage continued fruit production.

EGGPLANT WONDERS

Although favored in Asian and Greek gardens and cuisine, eggplant has only recently gained favor in America. It is worth trying one or two types, and you may then be certain to include these unique veggies every year.

Eggplant is very tender, so it requires a long, warm season to grow well. Plants are killed by light frost and injured by long periods of chilly, frostless weather, so they should never be set outdoors until all danger of frost has passed. Eggplant also needs some special attention with lime and fertilizer applied to your growing ground, based on a soil test, before planting. As with other tender crops, applying 2 pounds each of actual nitrogen, phosphorus, and potash per 1,000 square feet of garden space is adequate. Eggplant fanciers say that an additional 1 pound of actual nitrogen per 1,000 square feet after fruit has begun setting may help maintain plant development. Soil pH should be between 6.0 and 6.8.

With tender plants, plastic mulch is useful to help warm the soil, conserve moisture, and control weeds. It pays to start seedling indoors as you would other tender plants and set outside when all danger of frost is gone. Space eggplants 18 inches apart. Smaller varieties can be placed closer. Consider side dressing with a reliable fertilizer to help plants produce more fruits through the entire summer.

You have a wide choice of shapes, sizes, colors, and even tastes. Some recommended eggplant varieties for oval or elongated types are Burpee Hybrid, Park's Whopper, and Black Beauty. For a long, slim shape, try Machiaw. If you like white-skinned and oval types, there is Casper and Easter Egg varieties.

Check catalogs and you'll find many more types. Try two different varieties a year and get friends to try others to swap around. Those who love eggplant vow that once you try them, eggplants will be a must-plant veggie in your garden.

Some insect pests of eggplant include flea beetles, Colorado potato beetles, aphids, and spider mites. Bacillus thuringiensis (Bt) insecticides will control small larvae and are very safe to use. Veteran growers also suggest safer pesticides like Sevin and malathion. They also suggest a 4-year rotation with nonrelated crops and disease-free varieties to thwart diseases such as Verticillium wilt. Avoid tomatoes, potatoes, and peppers in rotation with eggplant. For specific help to control pests, contact your County Extension agent.

Eggplant fruits are edible from the time they are one-third grown until ripe. You can cut fruits over an extended period by removing them when they are well colored. With adequate soil fertility and water, you can encourage more fruits to form.

LET'S GROW LETTUCE

You have an amazingly wide range of lettuce varieties for tastier salad making. Select from various head types and colors, from light to dark green and red leafed too. There are four basic kinds of lettuce: crisphead (iceberg types), butterhead (Bibb and buttercrunch types), looseleaf, and romaine or cos. All are easily grown, vital for salads, and respond to cultivation mainly as spring and fall cool-weather crops. New improved varieties resist bolting to seed heads, so try some of them as featured in garden catalogs. You'll find details about growing lettuce and related green salad fixin's here. Because of changing dining tastes, there have been changes in garden crops too. Likeable as lettuces are, blends of "salad greens" are gaining wide popularity.

In recent years, mesclun has become a major salad trend across America. Because of its ongoing popularity, it rates space here and is well worth trying in your garden. These so-called designer greens are the rage for health-conscious Americans. The leafy mixes known as mesclun are not only low in calories and high in nutrition but also are very tasty.

Mesclun, a comparatively recent import from France, refers to mixes of tender young lettuces and other greens. The Provençal tradition calls for chervil, arugula, lettuce, and endive in precise proportions. But from 8 to 16 or more different plants may be used to meet our American tastes. American mescluns may include lettuces, arugula, endives, mustards, purslane, chicory, cresses, parsleys, fennels, escarole, and tender wild greens as well. Lettuces are most common in the milder blends. Piquant, peppery mescluns include such things as sharp arugula, tangy mustards, spicy cresses, and zesty chicory.

Some mescluns may include varieties of greens that are comparatively unknown to American gardeners. Look for mizuna, a delicate, leafy green from Japan, and tat-soi, another Asian green with sweet dark leaves. Cultivated French purslane, a succulent relative of our well-known garden weed, is a choice European salad ingredient that has tart, lemony leaves which are a rich source of vitamin E

If space is scarce, consider growing veggies in a pyramid garden.

plus Omega-3 fatty acids, said to reduce the risk of heart disease.

Piquant and mild are the two main divisions of mesclun. The National Garden Bureau recommends planting piquant and milder mescluns in separate wide rows, then harvesting separately and mixing in proportions to suit the occasion, the meal, and your personal taste. Mesclun seeds are blended to many tastes and appropriately called by such names as spring salad, stir-fry greens, piquant mix, and Provençal. Look through different seed catalogs and you'll find a variety of mixtures worth a try.

Although ingredients in mesclun are varied, all mescluns are noted for their tasty combinations of flavors, colors, and textures, typically including a rainbow of greens from light green to deep emerald, from deep reddish green to bronzy red to lime. Also consider using edible flowers or petals, including bachelor's buttons, calendulas, chive blossoms, marigolds, nasturtiums, and violets, as part of your salad fixins'.

Easiest to grow are the looseleaf lettuce varieties, which are the backbone of most mescluns. A favored old variety that is quite heat resistant is Oakleaf, with handsome green leaves. Prizehead is a reddish-green variety known for crisp sweetness. Black Seeded Simpson is another old-timer, a fast-growing green leaf lettuce for spring and fall crops. Other varieties include the old-fashioned Red Oakleaf, which will be as red as possible when grown in full sun. Red Sails, an All America Selection winner, is a compact looseleaf with mild flavor and handsome reddish leaves. Another good red-green variety is Red Salad Bowl, an Oakleaf type that is bolt-resistant. Check out other types of lettuce and try them to provide tasteful contrasts of color, leaf form, and crispness.

Other components commonly blended in mescluns are chicory and its close relative, endive.

Best known among chicories is radicchio, with red foliage swirled with pale green and white. Dandelion greens are another likely addition to mescluns.

Other greens are often watercress, arugula, kale, and mustards. Parsley and fennel may be components too. These are key ingredients. Friends at the National Garden Bureau suggest other greens such as young leaves of spinach and chard plus purslane. Again with thanks to these experts, I've compiled their best growing tips here for you.

Lettuce and Mesclun Growing Tips

Lettuces and mesclun mixes grow best in soil that is rich and loamy and has a loose structure. Soils should be well drained with a pH slightly acid to neutral, between 6.0 and 6.5. Most mixes prefer cool, mild weather and sun to partial shade. For protection during hot weather, choose a site shaded from afternoon sun.

Lettuces and leafy greens of mesclun are shallow rooted. They benefit from an inch or so of fine organic fertilizer or compost worked into the top few inches of soil before planting. After true leaves are growing, an additional dressing of finely textured compost or organic fertilizer will encourage vigorous growth.

Don't just focus on the vegetable garden to grow mesclun. It can be used in ornamental gardens as well. Leaves offer a range of green shades and textures. The National Garden Bureau notes that mesclun makes a handsome addition to an herb garden either as a border or when broadcast in a well-defined area.

And yes, mesclun grows well in containers, making the leafy blends ideal for patio or terrace plantings in tubs and other containers. Once you have grown mesclun, you will quickly appreciate its ornamental assets. Then, let your imagination be your guide in site selection around your property. Care for this simple but elegant short-lived crop is just as easy in ornamental beds or containers as it is in vegetable gardens.

Mesclun rewards you faster than most vegetable crops. Perhaps in today's busy society, that factor accounts for the rapid rise in popularity. Just sow seeds and begin to harvest baby leaves in 2–5 weeks, depending on the season, condition of soil, and temperature.

Lettuce and the other leafy greens of mesclun mixes grow swiftly, so plan to make successive plantings throughout the growing season. If you plant mesclun seed mixes every 10 days to 2 weeks from spring through fall, you'll have mesclun for salads and stir-fry dishes all season long. Check more details at the National Garden Bureau website, always a worthwhile, detailed resource for home gardeners.

Lettuce is a cool-weather crop, so plant indoors early, then transplant outdoors when soil is warm, usually safe after Memorial Day, and again in late summer for a fall crop. Although lettuces will grow at their best when temperatures are in the 60s, you can get good early growth by providing afternoon shade and constant soil moisture. Veteran gardeners report that even in regions with long, cold winters, you can lengthen the growing season practically all year with grow lights, greenhouses, cold frames, row covers, and other devices.

Mescluns will germinate in temperatures even as low as 40°F, according to the National Garden Bureau. To get started, plant mesclun seed about 1–2 weeks before the last frost date. Check with your local Master Gardener or County Extension agents to see what that date is in your region. Another way to know when to sow mescluns is to monitor soil temperature. When soil temperature at a depth of 2–3 inches is between 32 and 40°F, you can plant mesclun seed as well as spinach, cabbage, carrots, and radishes.

After planting, keep the bed moist but not soggy. Packets say seed will germinate in 6–14 days under cool soil conditions. Seeds will germinate in only 3 or 4 days when sown in the late summer with day temperatures about 85°F and night temperatures about 65°F. A warning: if night temperatures are 80°F or above, do not sow mesclun seed, because that is too hot for germination. Wait until day and night temperatures decline.

Because many mescluns are blends of several kinds of seeds, gently shake the seed package to mix the seeds before sowing. Make a furrow one-quarter inch deep, sow seed, then cover with light soil or sand. If you sow wide rows or areas, just scatter seeds and cover with about one-quarter inch of fine soil or compost. Keep seeded areas moist.

Pick Your Pleasure

Pick mesclun when the leaves are small, young, and tender. Therefore soil preparation prior to planting is perhaps the most important factor. A constant supply of soil moisture is extremely important when growing salad crops, including mesclun mixes. It is very important to time supplemental waterings so that the soil stays constantly moist but not soggy.

With mesclun, early harvesting is also thinning. Since first picking takes place when plants are young, you don't have to thin crowded seedlings as you might when growing lettuces and other greens in the usual way. Instead, begin cutting the leaves as soon as the plants are about 2 inches tall.

National Garden Bureau experts explain that mesclun is at its crispy peak when picked early in the morning before the sun is strong. Simply use scissors to clip mesclun greens, beginning when they are only a couple of inches high. Never let it get more than 6 inches tall. Regularly harvesting will encourage your crop to continue to grow. Since some of the greens grow more quickly than others, the exact proportions of your mesclun salads will vary from cutting to cutting. Harvest the mild and piquant mescluns separately and then blend according to taste in the kitchen or even at the table. Most Americans prefer using mild, light dressings on mescluns so as not to hide the delicate flavors of the greens.

Some seed houses mix the seeds according to the season rather than the flavor. Thus, there may be mesclun mixes for hot weather, for mild seasons, and for cool seasons. Study the different catalogs to see which you prefer, according to Barbara Perry Lawton, who has done extensive research about mesclun. Other experts who provided guidance for this section include Beth Benjamin, Shepherd's Garden Seeds; Rose Marie Nichols McGee, Nichols Garden Nursery; and Shepherd Ogden, Cook's Garden. All of those companies offer mesclun mixes and are listed in chapter 18 of this book.

APPEALING ONIONS

Onions are members of the allium family, related to garlic, chives, leeks, and shallots. You can try different types to add new flavors to meals. Check mail order catalogs and you'll be amazed at the different types of onions available. Surprisingly, they provide distinctively different tastes.

Onions adapt well to the home garden and occupy little space. They do best in a fertile, well-drained soil that is well supplied with organic matter. Because onions are shallow rooted, they require frequent watering. When properly cured and stored, some onion varieties will keep until spring.

Among the best, try Walla Walla Sweet, a Vidalia type. Yellow Granex is a sweet Georgia Vidalia type that keeps well. Olympic is one of the earliest to mature from seed. Copra is a top storage onion. For red onions, try big, early Mars and Redwing, which stores well, and red Burgermaster for salads. While searching out the best onions, review bunching onion varieties, shallots, and related veggies to perk up meals. If you haven't tried some of these offshoots in the onion family, give them a field test and taste trial this year.

To produce the best onions abundantly, build a productive soil by adding several bushels of organic matter to boost texture and then follow fertilizing recommendations based on a soil test to nourish them well. Choose a location with at least 6 hours of direct sunlight. All day sun is even better.

Planting Methods

You can start onions in three ways: from sets, by direct seeding, or by transplanting. Planting onion sets is the most popular way to grow them, but you have wider variety choice from seeds started indoors to transplant outdoors. Onion sets you buy are about marble size and were grown from seed last year. They are available for white, yellow, and sometimes red onions from mail order catalogs and garden centers.

Divide sets into those larger than a dime and those smaller. Plant larger sets for early onions and smaller ones with adequate spacing to produce bigger onions later. Sets will tolerate light frost, so you can plant them outdoors when temperatures reach 48°F. Plant them pointy end up, about 2 inches deep. Plant the biggest sets for early onions almost touching. Space smaller ones 3–4 inches apart for your fall crop. Firm soil around the sets. If you want onions for winter storage, you'll need to plant seedling onions, because onions from sets don't store as long as the others. You also have a wider variety choice from seeds, which also cost less.

Schedule indoor onion seeding in flats or peat pots 8–12 weeks before outdoor transplanting, which would be in February to transplant outside in May. Buy only as much seed as you will use this year. Onion seeds don't remain viable for much over a year. When you select varieties, be aware day length is important. In northern long-day areas, you need to buy long-day onion seeds. Southern gardeners should order short-day onions. Long-day varieties start to bulb when day lengths are about 14–16 hours. According to National Garden Bureau authorities, onion seedlings will form bulbs too early if exposed to long days at any time during their development. You will not get anything bigger than sets.

Plant onion seeds between one-quarter and one-half inch deep in a starting mixture in a flat or seed starter unit. Plant in a deep flat, 4–6 inches, or other container. Keep tops trimmed 3–4 inches tall and water regularly. Like tomatoes, onion seedlings need to be hardened off before transplanting outside, after frost danger has passed. After gradually exposing them to cooler days and bringing indoors at night for a week or so, plant seedlings in their garden spot. Space them 4 inches apart and deeply enough to catch in the soil. As they mature, onions will appear to sit on top of the soil.

Keep them well watered with an inch a week, especially when bulbs start to swell. For best onions, incorporate fertilizer based on a soil test before planting. A side dressing again when leaves are 6 inches tall and again when bulbs begin to swell produces best growth.

You can plant onion seeds directly in the garden, but seedlings and sets work better for most gardeners. However, direct seeding is worth a try. Plant seeds in well-drained, prepared soil in a sunny location. Cover seeds with one-half inch of soil or sand, and water regularly.

Onions have few serious growing problems, but onion maggot and thrips may occur. A single onion maggot will ruin a bulb. If found, you can treat the soil with diazinon prior to planting, according to label directions. Thrips are tiny; during infestations, leaves will take on a silvery appearance. You can control them with diazinon or malathion as directed on the labels. Onion diseases should not present a problem, but for any concerns, check with your local garden center or Cooperative Extension office for recommended treatments.

Pick for Taste

You can pick onions at any stage. Begin picking when the white portion is pencil thick, then pick more as they grow, and let some grow to full maturity. That way you get to taste test new varieties through the season. Keep taste test notes, as you should with all veggies, so in future years you can plant those that please.

For early treats, pick immature bulb-forming onions as you thin your planting. Generally, onions are ready when about half of the tops have fallen over and bulbs have developed a papery skin. Select most mature bulbs, pull them, and allow them to fully cure in a warm, airy place like a garage for a week or two. You can also hang them to dry in clusters and store them by tying tops together or putting in old mesh bags. Onions will last for months, depending on variety, in cool, dry storage. Check storage details on the seed packages you saved or in catalogs. Don't let onions freeze in storage, but keep them cool, because they may start to sprout at temperatures over 40°F.

GET TO LIKE LEEKS

Leeks are another tasty treat in the onion family and have a mild onion flavor. Leek soup is a gourmet feast in Europe, and you can enjoy them in many ways here, including in casseroles and quiche. Leeks look like overgrown green onions with tall, flat, and folded leaves. Plants grow 2–3 feet in height. The stem, which is usually 6–10 inches long and up to 2 inches in diameter, depending on variety, is eaten, and leaves can be too.

Recommended varieties include Giant Musselburgh, a favored heirloom variety which is widely available. Blue Solaise can overwinter, and Lancelot is virus tolerant and bolt resistant.

Leeks need a long growing season of about 120–150 days and about 8 hours of bright sunlight daily. They prefer slightly acid soil, with a pH between 6.0 and 6.8, but will grow well in even a slightly alkaline soil. You should start them indoors as you do onions and transplant outdoors when they are about 10 weeks old. Leeks also need to be hardened off for several days before final transplant to your garden when daytime temperatures are at least 45°F.

Set plants 2–6 inches apart with 15–20 inches between rows. To achieve long white stems, plant leeks in furrows or hill them. As plants develop, add soil or mulch along stems up to the leaves during the growing season. Leeks prosper from fertilizer. Experts recommended a transplant solution of half-strength 10-10-10 balanced fertilizer along rows when planting and a side dressing with a balanced 10-10-10 at a rate of 1 cup per 10-foot row by midseason for continued good growth.. Mulch or clean cultivate, being careful not to damage their shallow roots. Water leeks well every week for peak growth and flavor.

Unlike onions and shallots, leek tops do not die back as the crop matures, and the top growth, called the flag, should be dark blue-green. When leek stems are larger than 1 inch in diameter, they are near picking time. Harvest leeks by gently twisting and pulling them up or digging. Because leeks are fairly frost tolerant, you can delay harvest until after the first few light frosts.

OTHER ONION-LIKE CROPS

Green onions may be of any onion variety that are pulled before they bulb. You may also try bunching onions such as Beltsville Bunching and Evergreen. Japanese or Welsh bunching onions are hardy perennials that don't bulb, but do form clumps to be thinned by pulling and have the advantage of being available from early spring to late fall.

You might experiment with perennial or multiplier onions or Egyptian walking onions. These increase by producing new bulbs in a clump. Walking onions send up a flower stalk that bears marble-sized bulbs at the top; then from weight, the flower stalk collapses and little bulbs take root where they land, hence the term "walking."

Chives are hardy perennials that are grown from seed or plants. They are featured in chapter 5, which covers herbs. The leaves are tasty in salads and on potatoes and other food. Once planted, they grow for years, and you must divide the clumps to keep them under control.

Garlic has a bulb composed of about ten cloves that are arranged inside a membrane. You can plant the cloves in August or September so they get some root growth. They like the same basic culture as onions. After the tops die down next summer, harvest the bulbs, cure, and store like onions.

Shallots have a milder flavor than onions and thrive with similar cultivation. Plant bulbs in early spring and cut at the ground level to use greens in summer. Uncut plants will form many bulbs attached together in a clump, so you can harvest them and separate the bulbs for use or storage in fall.

PEAS PLEASE

Peas are pleasers, especially since they can be the earliest vegetable from your garden. Peas actually seem to love cold weather more than gardeners do. They deserve a place in every garden, because nothing beats fresh pea flavor.

Pea vines have small white or purple flowers, dainty-looking but strong tendrils, and bright-green drooping pods. They are hardy, vigorous, and full of good things such as flavor, healthy fiber, vitamins, and minerals. Better yet, pea plants come in sizes suitable for any garden, from a diminutive 12 inches tall to a 5-foot vine. They require little attention after you sow them, except to pick their bounty. The National Garden Bureau website at www.ngb.org has lots of helpful information on the pea, its history, and how to grow and harvest your own crop most successfully.

There are three types of peas. The difference is in the way you eat them. There are shelling peas, snow peas, and snap peas. Snow peas have flat, edible pods. Snap peas, such as the original Sugar Snap, may be the result of a fortuitous, natural cross between snow peas and shelling peas. Allow shelling peas to fully ripen in the pod. Then, open the pods and remove and cook the peas. Snow peas are harvested when the peas inside the pod are immature; the entire pea pod is eaten, either raw or cooked or stir fried. Mammoth Melting Sugar is a popular old-fashioned variety with wilt resistance that produces sugar-sweet pods in 72 days. Snap peas can be harvested when the peas are immature, like the snow pea, and are eaten raw or cooked.

The snap edible-podded pea is the most versatile. If the immature pods are left on the vine and peas form inside, the pod can be harvested and the peas shelled. In spite of its maturity, the pod is still tender and tasty, so the entire pod and peas can be eaten. Take your pick, order your seeds, and let peas please you. It pays to plant early, mid, and later varieties to extend your good dining time.

Recommended shelling peas include Dakota, an extra early variety, and Eclipse, which holds its sweetness from extra sugar content. Dwarf White Sugar produces heavy harvests on compact vines. Paso has heavy yields, and Mr. Big is an All America Selection winner with supersweet flavor and disease resistance.

For sweet snap peas, Super Sugar Snap is an All America delight that resists diseases. Sugar Lace II and Sugar Sprint also are excellent. Oregon Giant is the first sweet, large-podded snow pea. Snow or sugar peas are perfect for stir-fry meals using pods with the peas in them.

Pick Your Pea Spot

All three pea types need the same growing conditions. Select a site that receives at least 6 hours of direct sun daily. Peas prefer full, unobstructed sun, but in the deep South, they like some shade from the midday sun. All types of peas grow well in almost any kind of soil, but they thrive best in a fertile, somewhat sandy soil with good drainage and a neutral or slightly alkaline pH. Add lime if your soil has a low pH. You can easily improve the soil before planting by digging or tilling to a depth of 6 or 8 inches and incorporating organic matter such as compost or dried manure. Remember that nitrogen is a leaf-feeding nutrient, and too much may encourage more leaf production than pods.

Peas, like beans, are legumes that have the ability to fix nitrogen from the air into the soil, which makes that important nutrient readily available to other plants. Nodules on plant roots, with the help of a bacterium that lives in the nodules, "fix" the nitrogen and store any excess nitrogen. As roots decay, they release it into the soil, which benefits plants nearby. Because pea plants also produce long root systems, they help open soil as they reach out for moisture. Spent plants decompose into organic matter to further enrich the soil. At the end of the season, you can dig the plants into the soil to improve it, a nice bonus from peas.

Pea Growing Tips

Because peas are frost tolerant and germinate well in cool weather and soil, you should plant seeds directly into prepared garden soil in early spring as soon as you can work the ground. Count back 4–6 weeks from the last expected frost, which in most areas means on or close to St. Patrick's Day in March. In hardiness zones 8 and warmer, where early heat tends to make growing peas difficult, sow seeds in early fall for a winter crop.

Follow these basics from National Garden Bureau experts. Plant dwarf and semi-dwarf peas 1–2 inches deep in wide beds. For double rows, allow 3–4 inches between the pair of rows. Set pea fencing or brush between the plantings, and leave 2 feet between each double row. To make picking easier in wide beds or single rows, place brush from your shrub or tree prunings amid the planting to provide support for the vines. Plant seeds of taller varieties 1–2 inches apart along a trellis or next to the wire fence you use to enclose your garden. It helps when you plant peas to sprinkle an inoculant in the rows to help increase the natural nitrogen-fixing ability and growth. Inoculants are available at garden centers and from mail order companies.

Cover seeds with soil, and water well. You'll likely see germination in 7–10 days. Don't worry about thinning. Lush growth shades the soil, which helps prevent weeds from germinating and keeps ground cool. You may want to help vines twine their tendrils around the support by guiding and tying the young stems at first.

To assure yourself of tasty dining for many weeks, plant a succession of peas every few weeks until the middle of May. Or plant early, midseason, and late varieties all at once. Peas enjoy cooler growing conditions, so a mulch helps maintain a cool, moist soil. Compost, straw, and grass clippings work well. Use a mower to chop up old leaves before applying.

Peas don't require much fertilizer. If you fertilize, do so sparingly and be sure to use a fertilizer low in nitrogen so you don't encourage excess leaf growth. Peas do like water, so be sure to supply an inch of water weekly. Water deeply, preferably with a soaker hose or drip irrigation system. Plants need water especially when flowering and producing pods.

Few pests bother peas, except for aphids, which you can wash off with a hose, or apply appropriate insecticidal soap or spray. To avoid diseases, select disease-resistant varieties. Another way to thwart problems is to rotate areas for growing peas, plant early, pull up old vines, and plant more later for fall crops. To insure time to pick peas, look at the days to maturity on the seed packet and count backward from the average first frost date in your area. That should let you harvest before a hard freeze kills the plants.

Pots of Pleasing Peas

Peas respond to container growing nicely. Use a half-barrel filled with growing mix, plant your peas, provide a wire hoop support, and you'll have pleasing peas growing on a deck, terrace, or patio.

The 1984 All America Selection winner Sugar Ann is a short, bushy plant bred for containers. This edible-podded snap pea is early, ready in about 56 days. Try a selection of early, midseason, and late varieties to extend the harvest. Mulch with a layer of compost or wood chips, and water when the soil dries to a depth of 2–3 inches. Fertilize the container once or twice with a low-nitrogen fertilizer. As peas stop bearing, use the container for other plants.

Pick the Right Picking Time

You can tell when peas are ready by color and touch. For shelling peas, look for nicely rounded, bright-green pods that feel velvety and show the peas just beginning to swell. For snow peas, harvest before the peas begin to fill the pod. Pick snap peas anytime, because pods of snap peas remain edible whether immature or mature when seeds fill out the pods and reach full flavor.

Pick carefully. Grasp the vine in one hand and pinch the pod off with the other. Harvest frequently, such as every other day when the crop begins maturing. This keeps vines producing new pods for larger yields.

The National Garden Bureau provided good information for this discussion of peas, and veteran gardeners and pea experts who shared their knowledge about this tasty crop include Eleanore Lewis, Dan Croker, and David Webster of Seminis Vegetable Seeds and Mark Mason of Syngenta Seeds, Inc.

POPULAR PEPPERS

Peppers are heat-loving vegetables that require a long, frost-free season. Curiously, they aren't related to the spice, pepper. Instead, they are close relatives of tomatoes and potatoes. You can pick your pleasure from two groups of peppers, sweet and hot.

The sweet or mild category includes bell, sweet cherry, pimiento, and sweet banana peppers. They're colorful, ranging from green, red, yellow, and orange to purple and brown. Jalapeño, serrano, cayenne, chili, and hot cherry are examples of hot peppers, which can be red, green, or yellow. Color has nothing to do with their heat.

Today, garden centers stock a plentiful supply of both hot and sweet peppers. However, there are so many special varieties, you'll enjoy trying others that can be started easily from seed indoors. There are lots of seeds in each package, so share or save them. Kept cool and dry, a packet of pepper seeds can last several years.

You can buy seedlings and plant them outdoors when all danger of frost has passed, as you would plant other sensitive vegetables. Because your options for exceptional new flavors are so enticing, it pays to start seeds indoors about 8 weeks before you plan to transplant outside. Peppers need warm soil, at least 65°F, so wait until at least 2 weeks after the last frost date before planting them outdoors.

Among sweet peppers, Ace is a dependable early bell type. Red Knight has disease resistance in a compact plant. A perennial favorite, California Wonder is great for stuffing. For color, try Islander, with its lavender fruits, or Sweet Chocolate, a brown pepper. Ethnic types include Hungarian, Italian, and Romanian.

To grow hotter for stir-fry meals, try Habañero, a fiery hot orange pepper, or Hungarian Hot Wax. For southwestern-style meals, Serrano Del Sol is hot and flavorful. Johnny's Selected Seeds offers a salsa garden collection of pepper, tomato, tomatillo, and cilantro seeds.

For drying peppers, you have a range, from Joe's Long Cayenne to Early Jalapeño. There are even ornamental peppers to decorate your garden and provide nice spicy fruits too. As America's culinary tastes have changed, so have the pepper varieties being offered by mail order firms. From sweet to colorful to hot, they hit the spot.

Use a planting tray, special flat, or peat pots. Plant seeds only one-quarter inch deep in a sterile soilless planting mix. Then, lightly dust the top of them with milled sphagnum moss or planting mixture. When the seeds sprout, move them into a brightly lighted, warm location near a window. Germination normally occurs in about 10 days. Peppers require a lot of moisture during this early stage, so water frequently, but don't let the soil become waterlogged. When seedlings need transplanting, move them into larger containers until you move them outdoors. By using peat pots, you let the seedling grow to their proper outdoor transplanting size in the pots, which you then bury in the garden and let plant roots grow through the walls.

Peppers, like tomatoes, need hardening off. When seedlings are about 5 inches tall and 6–8 weeks old, put plants outside in a place where they'll receive half-day sun and protection from wind. Gradually expose them to more sun over the next 7–10 days, but be sure to bring them indoors each night if temperatures approach freezing.

Peppers do best in an area with full sun. Wait until all danger of frost has passed and the soil has warmed. Space hot pepper plants 12–15 inches apart and sweet or bell peppers 15–18 inches apart because they usually grow into bigger plants. Figure on about 75 days from transplanting to picking your first pepper.

Cutworms seem to like pepper plants as much as tomato plants. Nasty cutworm caterpillars emerge from the soil at night, crawl up the stems about an inch, then chew through the stems, leaving tops uneaten. Seldom seen, they are grayish black or brown and curl up into a "C" when exposed to light. Thwart them by wrapping the lower two inches of each stem with aluminum foil or a double thickness of paper tucked into the soil. Tuna or small mushroom or sauerkraut cans opened on each end also work. Simply press the can down about an inch into the soil around each plant.

Peppers prosper with fertilizing. Try a teaspoon of granular 5-10-10 around each pepper plant at planting and again when blossoms set. Veteran pepper fanciers suggest spraying plants with 1 teaspoon Epsom salts dissolved in a quart of water at blossom time and 10 days later. They say extra magnesium helps the peppers set fruit.

Mulch your peppers with straw, grass clippings, or other organic mulches to retain soil moisture and reduce weeds. Black plastic mulch has been found to increase pepper yields, probably because it absorbs heat and helps plants grow by stopping weed competition. Taller peppers such as bell and banana peppers benefit from wire tomato cages that reduce damage from heavy rains and winds.

Pick Perfect Peppers

Don't worry if some of your peppers don't turn red right away. Green bell peppers are actually immature red peppers; they'll turn red if left on the plant to ripen. Pick them any time after they're 3–4 inches long. Use red peppers soon after picking because they are more mature and deteriorate more rapidly than green peppers.

For hot peppers, you'll need to learn picking time from experience. Generally, pick hot peppers once they're large enough to use. Frequent harvesting encourages more to grow. Cut the fruit from the plant rather than tearing it, which could uproot plants. Wear garden gloves, and keep your hands and peppers away from your eyes so the capsaicin oil that makes peppers hot doesn't get into your eyes. My trusted sources at the National Garden Bureau remind me that a hot pepper's pungency depends on the amount of capsaicin oil it contains. That oil is most concentrated in the seeds and membranes inside the fruit. Hot peppers become hotter as they mature. Because peppers are frost sensitive, pick all peppers, regardless of size, before fall frost hits.

Keep Peppers Healthy

Temperature changes can cause blossom drop above 90, and nighttime temperatures below 60 or above 75 may also cause blossom drop. Normally, plants will produce more flowers when temperatures are moderate. Blossom end rot is a water stress problem that appears as a tan, leathery patch at the tip of the fruit. Cut away the leathery patch and eat the rest of the fruit. Uneven watering causes moisture stress problems, so water soil regularly to a depth of 6 inches, but don't use overhead sprinklers. Splashing water can spread diseases from soil to the plants or from leaf to leaf. Water around plants with soaker hoses or drip irrigation systems. That's a good idea in general to avoid spreading plant diseases such as mildew, rust, and fungus problems.

Occasionally, aphids feed on peppers and can transmit cucumber mosaic virus. Cover squares of cardboard with aluminum foil and place these reflectors on the ground beneath young plants. Organic gardeners believe the reflected light discourages aphids from landing on plants. You can also wash aphids away with a garden hose or apply insecticidal soap according to directions.

POTATO POINTERS

Today, potatoes are so common, they are taken for granted, but they offer many tasteful treats and even colors for home gardeners to enjoy. Potatoes also provide 13 essential vitamins and minerals. The average potato provides 40 percent of the recommended daily allowance for vitamin C, has 3 grams of protein, is an excellent source of dietary fiber, and furnishes other essential vitamins and minerals, and all with no fat.

Potatoes are very productive: a 100-foot row can yield more than 200 pounds of potatoes. To get the best results, it pays to use high-quality, certified seed, and pay attention to basic cultivation requirements. Many varieties are available in mail order catalogs. Select varieties that suit both your culinary needs and your local growing conditions. Early varieties provide new potatoes by early July. Later maturing varieties take about 100 days from emergence to produce a crop with an acceptable yield.

Recommended varieties include Superior, an early and ideal potato for home gardeners, with high yield, flavor, and even scab resistance. Caribe is a very early potato that does well in a variety of soils and stores well too. The popular Yukon Gold has yellow flesh with long storage life. Gold Rush is an early, flavorful russet. Kennebec is an all-purpose potato. For colorful treats you can grow All Blue, with solid, deep-blue flesh, and All Red, a cranberry color, or Red Cloud. Russian Banana is a long, slender, deliciously flavored variety.

Planting and Growing Tips

Prepare your planting area by deep tilling, because potatoes form underground. They prefer a sandy to sandy loam soil. Till the soil to a depth of 16 inches and pre-irrigate the soil until moist. It pays to fertilize for highest productivity. Place fertilizer in a band about 6–7 inches deep and to the side of the seed in the bed. Potato-growing veterans suggest a complete fertilizer like 20-20-20. Some suggest applying half the fertilizer at planting and the other half in late June. Keep an eye on your plants, and if they appear to be yellowing at midseason, apply nitrogen to the sides of the hills or add it with the irrigation water. Be careful not to apply too much nitrogen that feeds vegetative growth rather then building good-size tubers. If you prefer organic manure, it is best to add it the year before planting potatoes and be sure it is well aged. Manure may promote common scab on new tubers.

Best way to grow potatoes is by vegetative propagation, using whole tubers or cut seed pieces from tubers. Whole tubers should weigh 2 ounces or more for best results. If using cut seed pieces from larger tubers, each piece should have two to three eyes and weigh about 2.5 ounces. Plant cut seed immediately if soil conditions and temperature are ideal. About 15 pounds of seed will plant about 100 feet of row.

Buy only certified potatoes that have been inspected for disease and quality. Never use potatoes from supermarket stores. Most have been treated with a sprout that prevents tubers from sprouting and forming a healthy plant. Mail order firms and reliable garden centers provide quality seed potatoes from the key varieties you want. In fact, you have so many varieties available today, potato growing is a wonderful new pleasure in gardening.

Timing is key. Plant potatoes up to 2 weeks earlier than the average date of the last spring frost if soil temperature is 45°F or warmer. Place seed pieces 10–12 inches apart at a depth of about 4 inches in rows 30–36 inches apart. Hills may be formed at the time of planting or in the following four weeks. Hilling, by pulling up soil around the plants, provides more space for the developing tubers to grow. It is a good idea to rotate garden areas for potato production to avoid disease and insect problems.

Once you have planted, keep soil moist but not wet. Potatoes require abundant oxygen and will not thrive in compacted soils. Curiously, potatoes have a shallow root system, and moisture is taken up from the top foot of soil. Be especially careful to avoid overwatering during the first weeks after planting. Then, when plants emerge, irrigate every 3–5 days. Thoroughly wet soil to a depth of about 2 feet. Don't stress potatoes with excess water, which is revealed by wilting and dark gray-green foliage. Potatoes need maximum water during vine growth and then during early tuber development. To prevent rotting maturing tubers, reduce watering when vine death begins.

Lightly till or hoe to control weeds in your potato area. After plants reach 8–10 inches tall, avoid cultivation to prevent root damage that could reduce yield.

Potatoes are sometimes attacked by insects such as aphids, flea beetles, psyllids, and Colorado potato beetles, so it is best to use an insecticidal soap or control insect pests with approved insecticides. Actually, many diseases can be avoided by using certified seed. If diseases appear, check with your County Extension agent for the latest approved control methods. Always read and carefully follow all label directions when using pesticides. And keep the bottles away from children.

Potato Picking Pointers

Potato plants die before you harvest the crop. They usually mature and begin to die about 70–100 days after planting, depending on the variety. As they mature, they use less water. To promote proper skin set, leave tubers in the ground for 10–21 days following vine death. This practice reduces bruising during harvest and permits better storage. However, "new" potatoes should be harvested when vines are still lush and green. Pick portions carefully, because skins of these small tubers are fragile and the tubers dry out if not used immediately.

To savor potatoes, store them in a cool, dark, humid area that has ample air circulation. After harvest, cure tubers at 50–60°F for 2–3 weeks, then reduce to the desired storage temperature, about 38–45°F and 90 percent humidity. Following this system, tubers will not sprout for about 3 months.

PRIZE PUMPKINS

Pumpkins are a type of squash native to the New World. To grow pumpkins, follow the directions for growing squash, from preparing soil to planting seed. To grow giant, prize-winning, super pumpkins, start with seeds from the varieties that can become the biggest in town. Dill's Atlantic Giant is the granddaddy of big pumpkins that can weigh more than 800 pounds; it holds the world's record at 1,385 pounds. Prizewinner and Big Moon are other mighty-size contenders.

Tiny pumpkins, 3–4 inches across, are fun for holiday decorations. Wee-B-Little, Jack Be Little, Baby Pam, and white Baby Boo are delights. Howden is the traditional Jack o' Lantern type but other varieties offer promise, such as Lumina, Tom Fox, and Big Rock for Halloween carving fun.

For that Charlie Brown giant pumpkin, David A. Mangione of the Pickaway County Extension in Ohio suggests ordering Prizewinner or Dill's Giant, varieties that have the genetics to attain the largest size. According to Mangione, always apply lime and fertilizers based on soil testing to provide adequate nutrients throughout the growing season that will ensure healthy, vigorous vines bearing large pumpkins. Granular fertilizers should be applied as a broadcast application over the soil surface

and incorporated into the soil 4–6 inches deep a few days ahead of setting out your transplants. Giant pumpkin vines require approximately 2 pounds nitrogen, 3 pounds phosphorous, and 6 pounds potash per 1,000 square feet of growing space. He urges addition of organic matter and manure if available to build good soil tilth. (You'll find more details on that in chapter 2 of this book.)

Next, adopt a foliar fertilizer feeding program after pollination and fruit set has occurred. There are several foliar fertilizers available at garden centers and chain stores. Be sure to follow label directions and continue application throughout the growing season.

To grow giant pumpkins, you need to start early. Sow seeds individually indoors in peat pots about the end of April, using a well-balanced potting medium. Plants are ready for transplanting when the first true leaf is fully expanded. This is usually 10–14 days after seeding. Transplants can be protected from late spring frost using a floating row cover or hot cap. Save extra plants indoors in case frost kills those you planted outdoors.

Allow each plant approximately 200 square feet for vine growth to produce giant pumpkins. They need long hours of sunlight, and good drainage. Remember, pumpkins are shallow rooted, so provide at least 1 inch of water per week and more water during hot, dry, windy summer days. Trickle irrigation is best, but soaker hoses also work well. If you water by hand, do it in the morning so foliage dries to avoid disease problems.

Hand weed early or mulch around those selected, key plants. Later, large leaves on vines cover the ground and shade out most weeds. Plastic mulches also are effective for controlling weeds; they also warm the soil and maintain good moisture levels. If you don't use plastic, do apply mulch around plants, David Mangione suggests, to improve soil, thwart weeds, and hold in soil moisture. With organic mulches, he notes that it helps to add additional nitrogen so mulches decay properly. He suggests mixing 1 tablespoon of ammonium sulfate, calcium nitrate, or nitrate of soda per 1 bushel of mulch. Then, apply once or twice during the early growing season.

Here's another tip from Mangione. Use windbreaks to protect young plants that are not fully rooted until late June, when side runners are 3–4 feet long. A snow fence or woven wire with burlap makes an excellent windbreak. Also, cover vines at each node with soil to promote secondary root development.

Remove all but four to six pumpkins per plant. Once they reach volleyball size, trim back to one pumpkin. By reducing competition for nutrients, the better the chance of achieving a giant-size pumpkin. Training vines and root pruning also are important to prevent stem breakage and splitting. Keep watch, and water to promote steady growth. Read some prize pumpkin growing tips on the Internet and adopt the tips that you think would work for you.

Although pumpkins love sun, they also need shade as fruit matures. A shade made from burlap or other lightweight material will prevent premature hardening of the outer skin and allow the pumpkin to reach its full potential, Mangione explains. In fall, cover pumpkins during a light frost, and avoid leaving them exposed during a hard freeze to prevent softening. When your pumpkin or pumpkins have a deep, solid color and the rind is hard, it's time to pick. Watch your back. Get help to move your prize pumpkins into a garage or storage area to await exhibition at county fairs or garden shows. Good luck on bringing home a prize.

SURPRISING SPINACH

Spinach is enjoying a remarkable growth in popularity, perhaps because Americans are more health conscious and focused on vegetables that are nutritious as well as tasteful. Fact is, this veggie contains more than just iron. It has large amounts of vitamins A and C, thiamin, potassium, and folic acid, one of the B complex vitamins. Dark-green leafy vegetables, like spinach, contain lutein and zeaxanthin, which are carotenoids that help your eyes stay healthy as you age by preventing macular degeneration and cataracts. Better eating means paying attention to foods that keep us healthier, and you get that in a decorative vegetable that tastes great whether you eat it raw in salads or cooked in various recipes.

The National Garden Bureau website at www.ngb.org provides lots of information about spinach, which has varying leaf shapes and textures. Smooth-leaf spinach produces light- to dark-green leaves with an oblong shape. The leaves of savoy spinach are thicker, rounder, usually darker green, and range from very to somewhat crinkled. Smooth-leaf types are easier to wash clean.

Top varieties include the highly productive Oriental Giant for early spring or fall. Teton grows well in spring, summer, and fall. Hector is mild and tender for salads. Green, a hybrid, bears productively, and Tyee is the most bolt-resistant savoy-type spinach. One of the most popular hybrids, Melody, is a savoy hybrid that grows very fast, is slow to bolt in hot weather, and does well as both a spring and fall crop.

As you expand your taste buds, you can replace cool-season spinach in warm weather with Malabar spinach and New Zealand spinach. Those both taste similar to true spinach but are in completely different families. Because Malabar spinach is a vining plant, which grows quickly to about 20 feet, you need to start seeds indoors in northern regions. New Zealand spinach is a shrubby plant with difficult seeds, so it helps to soak seeds overnight before planting.

Basic spinach is a cool-weather crop. In warmer weather, many varieties tend to bolt to seed, and that means they lose their flavor. The cooler, shorter days of spring and fall are the best times to grow spinach. As you plan, note that from sowing to harvest is from 30–45 days. Therefore, sow seeds in spring as soon as the soil in the garden is workable, which can be as early as February, depending on your hardiness zone.

Spinach doesn't need to get a jump on the growing season by being started indoors but experts with the National Garden Bureau recommend sowing seeds indoors for a few good reasons. As a truly decorative leafy plant, it is easier to incorporate spinach in a flower garden if you set out transplants instead of using seeds. Also, for a fall harvest, you need to sow near the beginning of August, which is very hot in most areas. Starting spinach seeds indoors provides them with cooler temperatures for better germination.

Spinach Seeding Tips

Start seeds about 3 weeks before outdoor transplanting time in flats or individual pots. Peat pots offer a definite advantage because they go right in the ground with the seedlings and biodegrade there as roots grow through them. Follow the tips for starting plants in chapter 14 and you'll have hardy seedlings ready for outdoor transplanting when you want them. Insert seedlings into the ground at the same level they were growing in the flat, or plant the peat pot flush and completely cover the rims, spacing about 6–8 inches apart, and water well.

If you prefer direct planting, prepare the soil first. Dig or till to a depth of 6–8 inches, incorporating available organic matter such as compost or dried manure. Spinach prefers a light, rather sandy soil with a pH between 6.5 and 7.5. If your soil pH

is below 6, add lime at the recommended rate to raise the pH. Remember that lime reacts slowly, so it may take more than one growing season to raise the soil pH.

If you enjoy spinach, plan to sow a little every 7–10 days in spring. Most varieties take 4–6 weeks to mature, but you can harvest younger leaves as you please.

Outdoors, plant in rows 12–15 inches apart or scatter in an area for broadcast growing. Cover seeds with one-quarter to one-half inch of soil, sand, or compost, then firm it down and water well. When tiny plants have a few true leaves, thin them according to your seed packet directions, usually spacing them 6–8 inches apart.

Spinach is a heavy feeder and needs a lot of nitrogen to produce abundant leafy yields. Provide initial fertilizer by incorporating a fertilizer into the soil before planting. Then feed the plants after you thin them and again in a couple of weeks by side dressing using amounts recommended for the type of plant food you buy. Spinach has shallow roots, so cultivate lightly to remove weeds. Because you want tasty, succulent leaves, water frequently to keep up with the fast growth of these plants.

Enjoy a fall crop too. Spinach is one of many vegetables you can grow for a fall harvest. In the beginning of August, plant seeds outdoors or start them indoors. Keep soil evenly moist, and water the plants regularly. Good varieties for fall crops include the hybrids Avon, Indian Summer, Melody, and Tyee.

Spinach is especially cold hardy, so it may overwinter in your garden. Try planting some seeds or transplants in September and even up to November in southern regions. If weather stays mild, you may enjoy tasty spinach at Thanksgiving or even later. In fact, test your skill. When the ground freezes, cover spinach plants in the open garden with a row cover or a mulch of hay. As temperatures warm up in early spring, uncover the plants and care for them as you would any spring crop. Water and fertilize. Overwintered plants tend to be larger, with more spread, than those started in spring. Try cold-resistant Savoy and Tyee for winter crops.

Pick your spinach pleasure as you do leaf lettuce by cutting individual outer leaves or by using the whole plant. By judiciously picking a few leaves for salads or cooking, you leave the plant to continue growing for longer harvest. If you cut an entire plant, do it about an inch above the crown, where leaves join roots. That encourages the plant to put out new leaves for an extended harvest.

A final thought about kids. Children may reject spinach, but you can entice them to try this highly nutritious veggie. Help them to grow their own, either in their very own part of a main garden or in a couple of containers. Homegrown, freshly picked spinach tastes far better than store-bought, packaged spinach. Then, let kids mix their own blend of green and red-leaf lettuces with smooth and savoy spinach. Fact is, fresh, uncooked spinach often goes over better than cooked, so try a few leaves in your regular salad as a taste test. And try adding a few chopped leaves to soups just before serving.

Container Pointers

Spinach will thrive in containers. Try some in 6-inch to 12-inch containers or even mixed with flowers in windowboxes. Combine with annuals such as petunias or marigolds or herbs that can survive in fairly moist soil. Position spinach plants far enough apart so you can add small transplants of summer blooming flowers, which will take over as your spinach harvest comes to an end. Smaller spinach varieties, such as Baby's Leaf Hybrid and Melody, are good in containers.

To avoid problems of mildew and other plant diseases, rotate your plantings each year, and don't sow spinach in the same row or bed every year. If you or neighbors have had disease problems, try resistant varieties such as Melody, Nordic IV, Olympia, and Tyee.

SQUASH GROWING FUN

Squash of all types have gained popularity in the past few decades. Today they are favored in many recipes. Use these helpful growing ideas and tips for the most common types of squash, both summer ones and those to save for fall and winter eating.

Summer squash need warm weather and can produce overabundantly in a relatively short season. Winter squash can be conveniently stored for use through the winter. Basically, squash produce maximum growth, yield, and quality when days are warm and sunny and the season is long. Summer squash usually require 50–65 days for first production. Because squash can be cold sensitive, delay planting until a week after the average last spring frost date for your area, but if weather is chilly or windy, delay longer. Ideally, soil temperature at a 2-inch depth should be 60°F.

To get a deserved jump on spring, you can start seedlings indoors and transplant to the garden when the weather warms. Squash plants can't take much root disturbance, so the preferred method is to start seedlings in peat pots that you can simply plant in the ground. The plant roots will grow through as the peat decomposes.

Recommended summer squash varieties include buttery-flavored Yellow Crookneck, which yields over a long period, and Butterstick, a vigorous bush-type squash. You also can try Pattypan or scallop types such as Sunburst Hybrid, an All America Selection winner. Zucchini squash are

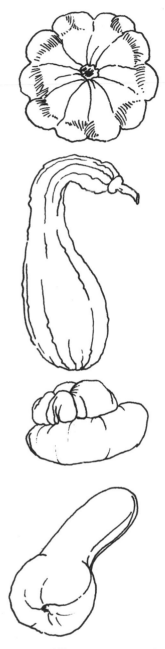

There are many different varieties of squash.

squash, the winter type is harvested and eaten in the mature fruit stage, when the seeds within have matured and the rind has hardened. At maturity, most winter squash varieties can be stored throughout most of the winter. Favored varieties are adapted to a wide variety of conditions but as vining plants require considerable growing space. However, you can adopt bush and semi-vining types for smaller gardens.

For Acorn types that mature in 80–100 days, consider Cream of the Crop, an All America Selection winner with creamy smooth, tasty flesh. Ebony is early with flaky flesh texture. Swan White has creamy white skin, pale yellow flesh, and is smooth and delicate. Table Ace is a semi-bush type with black fruit and excellent, low-fiber flesh. Squash lovers also suggest Table King, a compact bush type.

Delicata, also known as sweet potato squash, has a long cylindrical shape and cream color. Honey Boat, shaped like Delicata, has tan background with very sweet flesh. Sugar Loaf is elongated oval and very sweet.

For Spaghetti squash, try Orangetti, a hybrid semi-bush plant, high in carotene. Pasta has a yellowish cream fruit. Tivoli is an All America Selection winner, and Vegetable Spaghetti is a good keeper.

Among Butternut squash, fanciers suggest Butterbush, with a bush habit, for early, 1–2 pound fruit. Early Butternut, a hybrid All America Selection winner, matures early with high yield. There are many others in mail order catalogs, including Ponca, Puritan, Ultra, and Zenith. Also check out other winter squash varieties, from old-time favorites to new introductions, and try a few. You'll be surprised by the tastes they provide for your meals.

prolific producers. Varieties include Spineless Beauty, Raven, and Revenue, a virus-tolerant type. Costata Romanesco is one of the best tasting, according to squash lovers.

Winter Squash Notes

Winter squash is a warm-season vegetable that can be grown in most of our country. Unlike summer

Squash Planting

Before tilling, prefeed the ground with 2 pounds of urea and 2 pounds of triple superphosphate, both of which contain about 46 percent active ingredients, per 1,000 square feet, and till under into the top 4 inches of soil prior to planting. Organic gardeners say they prefer using 2 bushels of manure, 1 cup of bonemeal, and 1 cup of dried blood per 100 square feet but usually prefer to work it in around the growing hills rather than spread over the whole area.

Squash are best planted in hills or mounds so excess water drains away from the seedlings. Plant five or six seeds in circles 4–6 feet apart. Cover seeds with about 1 inch of soil. When the young plants are well-established, thin to the best two or three plants per hill. For semi-vining varieties, thin to the best two plants per hill. Thin bush varieties to one plant every 3 feet.

If your soil is moist, no further watering should be done until seedlings emerge. As the plants grow and weather warms up, add more water, and consider mulching around the plants to control weeds and retain soil moisture.

As squash plants near maturity, they'll have spread out widely and may need an inch plus of water per week to really prosper. Squash authorities believe it is better to irrigate thoroughly every 5–8 days than to sprinkle lightly every day. If plants seem to wilt, try more water.

Watch for Pests

Squash in general are attacked by a number of insects. Insecticidal soap is the least toxic and most environmental friendly control. Many veteran gardeners rely on a balanced pesticide that controls a variety of the insect enemies. Before using pesticides, try to positively identify the target pest and get advice from local garden center experts or County Extension agents. They usually are tuned in to local pest problems and have solutions at hand.

Be sure to follow label instructions for the pesticide used.

Diseases can strike squash too. Assess the situation, and try simple remedies first. If only a few leaves are affected, remove them. If the problem gets worse, then chemical control may be in order. Always remember that weeds often are first hosts to insect pests and diseases, so mulch to stop them, and pull weeds when young or till and hoe during the season to stop weeds from hosting problems, as well as stealing soil nutrients and water.

Fruiting Time Tips

Most squash varieties produce several male flowers before female flowers appear and fruits are set. If female flowers are produced but you notice poor fruit set, there may be growing fruits already on the plant that will inhibit further fruit set until they mature or are harvested. But remember, these plants depend on insects, mainly honeybees, for pollination. If insect activity is very low, fruits may not set due to lack of pollination. That can happen in wet weather when bees stay in the hive. Sooner or later, pollination does get done.

Pick Squash Right

It is best to harvest summer squash as immature fruit. Tender squash has superior flavor. Actual time of harvesting depends on fruit size. Pick summer squash when fruits are about 6 inches long. Harvest often and thoroughly, especially with fruits such as crookneck summer and zucchini squash. Only a few hills can produce bushels of fruits during the whole summer.

Winter squash and pumpkins should be harvested when mature. The skin will harden to protect the meat and keep the interior useful in storage for cooking later. Mature fall and winter squash can be stored most of the winter if protected from freezing. They make great eating and supply their wonderfully nutritious orange vegetable for balanced diets.

SWEET SWEET POTATOES

No doubt, sweet potatoes are more important in warmer areas than are white potatos, because they thrive in a hot, moist climate, while white potatoes require a cool climate. Northern gardeners prefer the dry-fleshed varieties of sweet potato, such as Big Stem Jersey and Little Stem Jersey. For southern gardens, growers seem to prefer the moist-fleshed varieties, such as Porto Rico and Nancy Hall. These softer varieties are erroneously called yams in the United States, but the yam is an entirely different plant.

The flesh of most sweet potato varieties is white, but in the United States we prefer yellow or orange-fleshed varieties because of their valuable carotene content. Skin colors range from nearly white through shades of buff to brown, from pink to copper, and even magenta and purple.

The sweet potato is a tender, warm-weather vegetable that needs a long growing season to mature. The plants grow as trailing vines that quickly cover the garden ground and root at their nodes. Bush varieties with shorter vines for small gardens have become available.

Sweet potato authorities recommend several varieties. Beauregard has dark-orange flesh; Bush Porto Rico is compact, with copper skin, orange flesh, and big yields. Centennial is a good keeper and resists diseases. Jewell is an excellent keeper.

Best way to plant is to use transplant slips as soon as soil warms up after the last frost. Be sure to buy plants grown from certified disease-free roots. Set transplants 12–18 inches apart, preferably on a raised ridge about 8 inches high. Experts explain that a ridge dries better and warms earlier than an unridged area. Black plastic mulch stores the sun's heat, which encourages plant growth. Because most varieties spread, allow 3–4 feet between rows.

Once the vines spread over the ground, little weeding is needed. Water periodically, especially during dry periods, but avoid watering during the last 3–4 weeks before harvest to protect developing roots. You can do some harvest in summer by digging into the side of the ridge, carefully removing a few small tubers while leaving the plant in place. Before expected first frost, dig the main crop with a spading fork. Be careful not to bruise or damage the roots. Where possible, allow sweet potatoes to dry on the ground for 2–4 hours. Then move to a warm room for curing at 70°F or warmer and at high humidity for 10–14 days. Finally, move into a cooler area of 50–60°F for storage.

CLASSIC SWISS CHARD

Swiss chard isn't a leafy vegetable; it is really a beet that has been chosen for leaf production at the expense of storage root formation. Chard goes by many names, including Swiss chard, leaf beet, and spinach beet. It is a beautiful, large-leaf vegetable with wide flat stems resembling celery.

These flavorful plants yield fresh white, yellow, or red leaf stalks that add attractive ornamental color to the vegetable garden. Choices of red midrib varieties include Burgundy, Rhubarb, and Ruby. White midrib types include Fordhook Giant, Geneva, and Winter King. Rainbow is a red, white, and yellow mixed midrib variety.

Chard packs a huge amount of vitamin A and is naturally high in sodium. Chard is also surprisingly high in other minerals, including calcium, iron, magnesium, phosphorus, and potassium.

Swiss chard should be directly seeded in your garden in early spring. Plant seeds up to three-quarters of an inch deep, about eight or ten seeds per foot of row. When they have true leaves, thin seedlings to 4–6 inches apart. An alternative method is to thin the seedlings to 2–3 inches apart, and when they are large enough for greens, about 6–8 inches tall, harvest the excess plants whole, leaving a final spacing of 9–12 inches between plants. For tastiest leafy chard, be sure to give them ample water, 1 inch a week to have the most succulent leaves.

If you like spinach, you will adore chard. The flavor is mild yet earthy and sweet, with slightly bitter undertones. Chard should be harvested while the leaves are young and tender. Chard is extremely perishable, so keep refrigerator storage time to a minimum.

TERRIFIC TOMATOES

Tomatoes are America's favorite vegetable, and thousands of hybrid varieties have been introduced. Besides better taste, major achievements have been the multiple disease tolerances bred into tomatoes. Today, many tolerate diseases such as fusarium wilt or root-knot nematodes, and there is less need for fungicides or pesticides to kill insects that spread diseases. Visit the National Garden Bureau website at www.ngb.org for good information about growing tomatoes, as well as their interesting history. My thanks to their tomato growing experts for these culture tips I gladly share with all readers of this book as well as my newspaper columns and magazine feature articles.

Tomatoes come in a surprising range of sizes, colors, shapes, and tastes. The three ways to classify tomatoes are fruit shape, earliness to mature, and

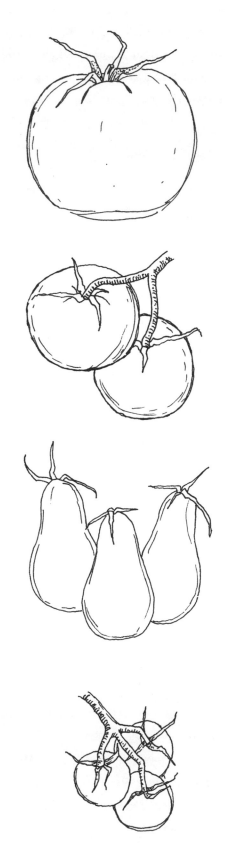

You can grow many types of tomatoes: pear shaped, cherry, plum, and in clusters of the tiniest yet very tasty grape-sized tomatoes.

color. From smallest to largest, the major shapes are grape, cherry, plum, pear, standard, and beefsteak. Cherry and grape tomatoes are produced in grapelike clusters. Plum and pear tomatoes have meaty interiors, thick fruit walls, and less gel than others. Standard tomatoes are round and weigh 4–8 ounces, while beefsteaks can be 2 pounds or more.

Tomatoes also are categorized by maturity date, which means the number of days from planting outdoors to expected ripe fruit. To extend enjoyment, you can grow early, midseason, and late maturing tomatoes. Early ones ripen in 55–65 days from transplanting, midseason in 66–80 days, and late types in more than 80 days. You have a wide range of colors too. Check mail order catalogs and you'll find tomatoes from creamy white through lime green to pink, yellow, golden, orange, and red. Pink, yellow, and orange tomatoes are milder tasting than most red varieties.

Types of Tomatoes

You can grow determinate or indeterminate tomatoes, and even semi-determinate types. Indeterminate growth means varieties grow, blossom, and produce tomatoes throughout the growing season until killed by frost. Continuous growth produces many main stems that produce fruit. Because of their abundant growth, it is best to support the plants with wire hoops or stakes. It pays to remove all but two growing stems and loosely tie the stems to the stake. You can prune indeterminate plants to force larger tomatoes, or just let them produce many fruits. To prune, use your fingers to pinch out sucker shoots that develop between the main stem and a branch.

Determinate tomatoes are relatively compact, full, and bushy plants that reach a predetermined height, flower, set fruit, and ripen in a short time, so that the main harvest is concentrated into a few weeks. Determinate tomatoes may be ideal if you wish to can or preserve the fresh tomato harvest. Semi-determinate varieties produce a bushy plant that will set and ripen fruit over a longer period of time than a normal determinate. It is best not to prune determinate or semi-determinate plants. Just place a wire cage around young plants and let them grow to maturity inside the cage.

The best cherry tomato varieties include Jolly Hybrid, an All America Selection winner with high-yielding vines, and Supersweet 100 Hybrid, sweet as its name implies and disease resistant. Gold Nugget is a small yellow type. Sweet Million, Early Cherry, and Tumbling Tom are other favorites. For grape types, try Ildi, with dozens of yummy yellow fruits per bunch, as well as Juliet Hybrid and Sugary, both super-sweet All America Selections that yield abundantly.

For standard tomatoes, Early Girl is widely adapted, and the fruits are 4–5 ounces. First Lady II is early, flavorful, and productive. Northern Delight, bred for northern gardens, produces a sweet early crop. Stupice also is a cold-tolerant variety. Key main-season tomatoes include Big Beef Hybrid, Beefmaster, and Better Boy Hybrid. For containers, try Container Choice Hybrid and other space savers in mail order catalogs. Look for plants with compact, bushy growth but high, tasty yields.

For more exotic tomatoes for paste and special recipes, La Rosa has a deep red color and thick flesh. Red Agate and Sanarzano are both good. You can also have fun with Striped German, Green Zebra, Black Prince, and other more exotic colors, shapes, and sizes, including Yellow Pear and Red Pear varieties. Try something different with tomatoes and surprise your family and friends. All have wonderful, distinctive tastes.

Seed Offers Tastier Choices

Starting tomato plants from seed allows you a wider choice of tomato varieties than if purchased as bedding plants. Start tomato seed indoors 6–12 weeks before the last expected frost date. Most varieties germinate in 5–12 days. For maximum germination, soil temperature needs to be warm, about 70–75°F.

Place a prepared, sterile germination mix in seed flats or individual containers with holes for drainage. Water the mix thoroughly and allow to drain. Sow seeds and cover lightly with the planting mix. Mist the top and cover with newspaper or plastic to prevent it from drying out. Keep in a warm place, and check daily for germination. When seeds have sprouted, remove the cover and place in a sunny location. Keep seedlings warm, and water regularly.

After a week or two, transplant young plants into 2-inch individual peat pots filled with a sterile, soilless growing mix. Disturb the roots as little as possible. With tomatoes, you can plant seedlings deep, to the first leaf set. Roots will develop along the buried main stem.

Young tomatoes love sun, so provide as much direct sunlight as possible; up to 12 hours of light is desirable at this stage. Using artificial grow lights to supplement the natural sunlight is worthwhile. The plants may stretch or get leggy if they do not receive enough direct sunlight. No problem. When planting seedlings outdoors, burying part of the stem helps them set more roots faster.

Planting Tips

Tomatoes especially benefit from hardening off. Young plants are tender and need to be exposed gradually to the harsh outdoor climate, even after frost is well past. Put plants outside in a protected area where they will receive full sun, but out of the wind. At night, move plants inside and continue this routine for 3 or 4 days. Day and night temperatures should be increasing, but if it drops to 50°F, move plants inside. After 4 days, allow plants to be outside all day and night. After being outside for a week or two, the plants should be hardened off and ready to transplant.

Remember two key points: Tomatoes need as much direct sunlight as possible to produce the highest yield. Because they are native to the tropics, tomatoes require warm, 70°F temperatures for good growth.

In northern gardens, if seedlings have grown tall and leggy, just dig a deeper hole and bury the plant to the first pair of leaves. However, deep planting is not recommended for southern gardeners, due to fungal rot attacking young stems.

Some gardeners prefer the trench method of planting. Dig a long, shallow hole and lay the seedling horizontally into the trench. Pinch leaves off the stem and allow the top 2–3 inches of stem to lead out of the trench. Firm soil on the trench, and push a bit of soil under the top stem. This stem will grow up toward the sun, but because most of the stem is buried, the newly developing roots and surrounding soil will warm up relatively quickly. This method speeds up tomato plant growth for gardeners living in a short growing season.

Be sure to water deeply to encourage deep root growth. Continue watering lightly each day if it does not rain. After about 2 weeks of regular watering, your plants should be established and you can decrease watering. Established tomato plants need about 1 inch of water per week from rain or irrigation. As they set fruit, be certain they get at least that amount to develop tastiest fruits.

Even after frost time has passed, night temperatures may be cool. Veteran tomato growers who live in short growing areas use a cloche or hot cap to protect the newly transplanted tomatoes from freezing if night temperatures drop. Tomato plants will probably die if exposed to 32°F without protection. Row covers are readily available. You can save gallon plastic milk jugs, cut off the bottoms, and use them as individual protectors over seedlings for a week or so, but be sure to remove each morning so you don't overheat tender plants.

Feed Tomatoes So They Prosper

Tomatoes need nutrients to produce abundant crops and tastiest fruits. Specifically, they require phosphorus, nitrogen, potash, and minor elements. Water-soluble fertilizers have become popular and can be used when watering tomatoes. There are pelleted and granular forms you can add to the soil before planting. Easiest to use is a timed release fertilizer applied when planting that continues to feed plants over several months.

Whatever kind of fertilizer you prefer, always follow directions on the label. Don't overfertilize or use a mixed fertilizer with high nitrogen, because you end up with lush, tropical plants but little fruit set. Another key point is to select a fertilizer that contains more phosphorus (P) than nitrogen (N) or potassium (K), because phosphorus promotes flowering and fruit set.

Tasty Container Tomatoes

New hybrid tomatoes have been designed for container gardening, so if you don't have a backyard, you can still enjoy delicious tomatoes all summer long. Key is selecting a compact bush variety. Cherry tomatoes do well in containers. Your container should be at least a foot deep with drainage holes on the bottom. Fill it with a sterile growing mix. Plant as you would outdoors, and keep plants evenly watered without overwatering. Use a dolly so you can roll the heavy containers around, to give the plants as much direct sunlight as possible. Low light levels result in leggy plants that produce fruits but fewer of them.

Container plants need close attention to water, because they tend to dry out fast. They also need your loving care to feed them properly. A water-soluble fertilizer lets you do this weekly. Keep in mind that nutrients tend to leach out of pots faster than in garden soil. Water often during dry weather, possibly three or four times weekly as needed.

Solving Problems

Tomatoes are fairly easy to grow without serious problems, especially when you select new disease-resistant hybrids that also have top taste. However, some problems deserve attention. Be observant. Examine leaves regularly to detect any difference in leaf color, size, or shape. Holes in leaves usually indicate insects. Huge tomato hornworms can be bothersome, but they can be handpicked and destroyed. If a problem develops, take a sample of the leaf or fruit to your local Cooperative Extension agent for assistance. The National Garden Bureau and veteran tomato growers recommend rotating tomatoes and other crops in your garden to reduce diseases. In general, except for carrots and perennials such as asparagus and rhubarb, do not grow the same crop in the same place year after year.

When considering varieties to grow, you'll notice the letters V, F, N, or TMV on the packet or in the description. These letters mean the plant is genetically tolerant of the following diseases or virus.

Verticillium wilt (V) is caused by a soil-borne fungus. Symptoms are wilting of older leaf tips, yellowing and browning of leaves in a V-shaped pattern, and leaf drop beginning with the older foliage. Cool weather conditions encourage this disease, which is common in soil.

Fusarium Wilt (F) is a soil-borne fungal disease that commonly occurs when soil is above 75°F. Light sandy soils are most susceptible, and soils with low pH. Symptoms are yellowing, curving, and dying leaves producing stunted plants and fruits.

Nematodes (N) are microscopic worms living in the soil. Some nematodes are good, some bad. The bad ones include root-knot nematodes that cause plants to wilt or portions of plants to die back. You can identify this suspected problem by examining the roots of the plant. The roots will have growths or galls on them, which means root-knot nematodes are the problem.

Tobacco mosaic virus (TMV) is one of the most widespread viruses affecting tomatoes. Weeds harbor the virus. Insects feeding on the weeds transmit the virus to the plant, turning leaves dark or light green, possibly even a mottled yellow appearance. Yes it can be caused by people who smoke cigarettes while handling plants.

Unfortunately, there is no cure for these four problems. If you suspect any of these, the plants should be destroyed and never used for compost. Luckily, the easiest way to avoid such problems is to grow tomato varieties that have disease or virus resistance.

Tomatoes also are subject to three fruit disorders: blossom end rot, cracking or catfacing, and sunscald. Blossom end rot begins with tan lesions on the blossom end of the tomato, which enlarge and become dark sunken areas. It begins when fruit are about half developed and usually appears during periods of high growth or when soil moisture is al-ternately high or low. To help control this rot, try adding calcium soil amendments, water during dry weather, and use a mulch to maintain more uniform soil moisture.

Cracking usually occurs near the fruit stem, while catfacing occurs near the blossom end. Experts believe these problems are caused by conditions such as fast growth caused by high temperatures and moisture levels, initial fruit growth during a dry spell followed by heavy rain or watering, or excessive swings in day and night temperatures. To avoid the problem, select newer varieties such as Big Beef and others that are resistant to cracking and catfacing.

Sunscald is caused by the sun burning the tomato skin, producing white, shiny blisters. Normally, leaf cover keeps the tomatoes in the shade. Sunscald can occur due to excessive pruning, insect damage to leaves, or foliage disease causing leaf loss. Look for varieties that are more tolerant or resistant to these disorders, and consider growing All America Selection winners. They have been tested and proved better than usual varieties in nationwide trials.

Pick at Perfection Time

For fullest tomato flavor, allow the fruit to fully ripen on the plant. Wait until it is deep red, or whatever the final color is to be. With tomatoes, no additional sugars go into the fruit after harvest. To pick tomatoes, gently hold the tomato and twist it so the stem separates from the vine. Forget about refrigerating tomatoes. They are best stored at room temperature and will keep on a kitchen counter for a week or more, depending on the variety.

Frosts will destroy tomatoes, so when frost is predicted, harvest all green tomatoes and place them on a windowsill for future use. Most will gradually turn red and have fair tomato flavor. Placing unripe tomatoes in a closed paper bag will hasten the ripening process. Green tomatoes also offer you that delicious cooking option, fried green tomatoes in olive oil, a fall treat for many gardeners.

As you prove every year the great taste of vine-ripe tomatoes from your home garden, you'll be tempted to try ever more flavorful, new, and even exotic varieties. If you need more convincing, consider the nutritional facts. A fresh, raw tomato contains an exceptional amount of vitamin A as well as vitamin C, potassium, and calcium. Tomatoes also contain lycopene, which contributes to preventing certain types of cancers, including prostate cancer. The National Garden Bureau adds this thought worth sharing with all: "To offer the best, most nutritious food, grow your own tomatoes and eat them fresh from your garden."

One final tomato thought for those who think big. If it's record-setting size you're looking for, the Totally Tomatoes catalog listed the following as the largest red tomato cultivars, in descending order: Burpee Delicious, Burpee Supersteak Hybrid, Beefmaster Hybrid, Burpee Super Beefsteak, Dinner Plate, Ponderosa Red, Goliath Hybrid, Big Beef Hybrid, Better Boy Hybrid, Abraham Lincoln Original, Burpee Big Boy Hybrid, and Park's OG 50 Whopper Hybrid. Most fruits of Burpee Delicious weigh over 1 pound, and many are 2–3 pounds, but it holds the world's record of 7 pounds, 14 ounces! For a free catalog, contact Totally Tomatoes, P.O. Box 1626, Augusta, GA 30903.

WATERMELONS

Most watermelons need a long growing season of at least 80 days and warm ground for seeds to germinate and grow productively. But today we have a wide choice of delicious fine varieties even for short growing seasons. Soil should be 70°F or warmer at planting time. Hold off until it is. Plant seeds 1 inch deep, and keep well watered until they germinate. It pays to warm the soil with a covering of black plastic mulch. Then cut slits through and plant your watermelons.

To gain time, plan to start seeds in peat pots or special planters indoors 2 or 3 weeks before they are to be set out in the garden. You should not start seeds any earlier, because large watermelon seedlings transplant poorly. Sow three or four seeds about half an inch deep in 3–4 inch peat pots or large cell packs. After they sprout, thin to the best single plant. To encourage proper growth, be sure the area is warm, day and night, and close to 80°F if possible. It pays to use a seedling heat mat under your starting containers.

Give Plants Ample Room

Watermelons need room to roam. Vines can reach 20 feet in length. Prepare soil by adding organic matter such as compost or composted cow manure. You also can add a balanced fertilizer that is high in nitrogen to give plants sufficient nourishment. When soil has thoroughly warmed up, transplant to the outdoor garden. By starting early indoors, you will give the watermelons extra time to grow and mature.

Or you can sow eight to ten seeds in a hill, 1 inch deep into the soil, spacing hills 3–4 feet apart, with at least 8 feet between rows. Thin plants to the three best in each hill, and keep weeds under control by shallow hoeing or with mulch or light tilling. Because watermelon plants have moderately deep roots, watering is seldom necessary unless the weather is really dry. Feed by side dressing with half

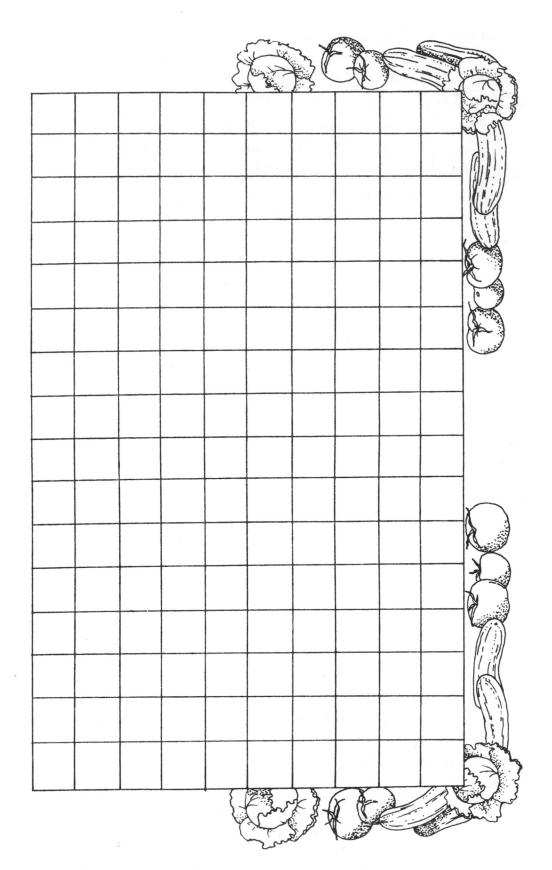

Map out your vegetable garden by using this chart. Enlarge as you wish.

a cup of balanced fertilizer such as 5-10-5 as vines are half-grown, and then apply another fertilizer application after melons are set. Withhold water as melons mature to improve their sweetness. Watch for pests such as cucumber beetles and vine borers. Two materials work well: an insecticide such as Sevin and organic Bacillus thuringiensis (Bt).

How do you know when a watermelon is perfectly ripe? Here are tips from experts. Watch the tendril closest to the melon stem, which is a modified leaf or stem in the shape of a slender spiral. When it turns brown and dries up, the melon is ripe. However, with some watermelon varieties, the tendril dries and drops off more than a week before the melon is fully ripe. Other veteran growers advise that the surest sign of ripeness is the color of the bottom spot, where the melon sits on the ground. Coming to maturity, this spot turns from almost white to a rich yellow. Another guide is that watermelons lose the powdery or slick appearance on the top and take on a dull look when fully ripe. Give yourself a few tests and you'll get the feel of picking watermelons and other melons at the best tasting time.

Good growing for tastier living!

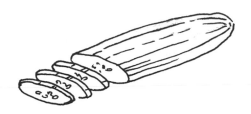

7

ENJOY LOVELIER LANDSCAPES

You can create the loveliest landscapes you want and enjoy outdoor living for many years amid scenes of fragrant and blooming beauty. With some basic planning, you can design appealing gardens that showcase your home in the neighborhood, give you visual delights from spring to fall, and in the process boost your property values too.

Plants are an indispensable resource and essential part of our environment, according to the Associated Landscape Contractors of America. Here are key points to consider as you think about improving your own home landscape, with the help of a professional or by yourself.

Landscaping can add up to 20 percent to a home's value, increasing your property value as you enjoy the beauty plants provide. Landscaping also can reduce air conditioning costs by up to 50 percent, as trees shade homes and also reduce noise up to 50 percent, according to traffic studies.

A tree removes carbon dioxide and releases enough oxygen for a family of four to breathe for a day. Fact is, a single tree can provide up to $300 a year in air conditioning, pollution reduction, and erosion and storm water control, as well as providing wildlife shelter. In addition, an acre of trees can remove 13 tons of dust and potentially harmful gases from the environment each year. And landscape plants control runoff, slowing erosion and allowing water to be absorbed by the soil. The benefits are there, just for your efforts to dig in and improve your home grounds.

Take a walk around your property today with a notebook and pencil in hand. Make notes and sketches of your present gardens and landscape features. Draw in buildings and property lines. Save those sketches so you can draw another design, adding the new features of trees, shrubs, beds, and borders and whatever else you wish to upscale your outdoor environment.

Now, walk around your property with some colorful mail order catalogs in hand. Envision where some of those delightful flowering trees and shrubs would give you blooming vistas. Think where some trees would provide shady areas. Pick the best sunny spot for a productive vegetable garden. Plan a kitchen herb garden.

Admire the plants in the catalogs and plan to enjoy flower beds and borders that will give you colorful delight and add other lasting values to your home. Most of us garden for pleasure and want to enjoy our careful landscape creations for many years to come. Think about some fruitful plants,

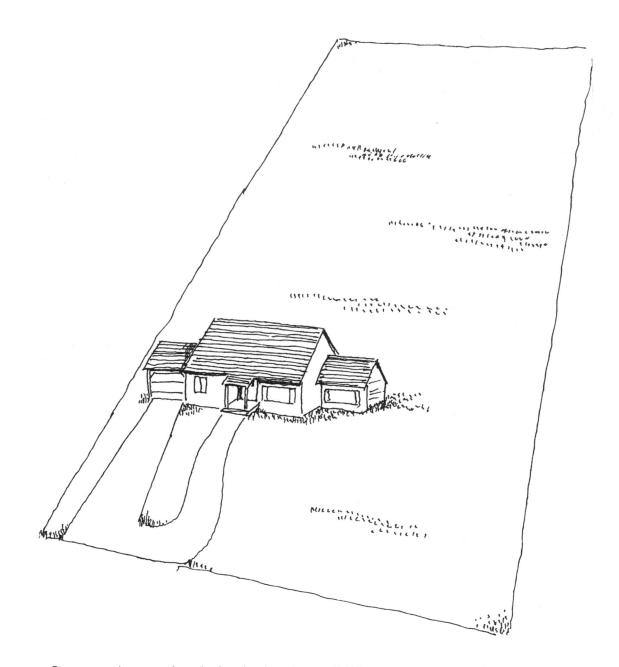

Picture your home as if you had no landscaping at all. What improvements would you like to see?

from berries to fruit trees. Decide on what projects should come first, and set your priorities for landscape improvement projects.

The next step is to drive around your town and take part in annual garden tours. Make mental and written notes of the landscape designs and gardens that you like most. Ask questions. Gardeners are rightfully proud of their gardens and usually

pleased to answer questions. Make friends with good neighborhood gardeners and join a local club. Often speakers provide abundant knowledge about plants that fit best into your area and growing conditions. Contact your county agricultural agent or the Cooperative Extension agent who serves gardeners in your county and has access to the top horticulturists in your state at your state agricultural

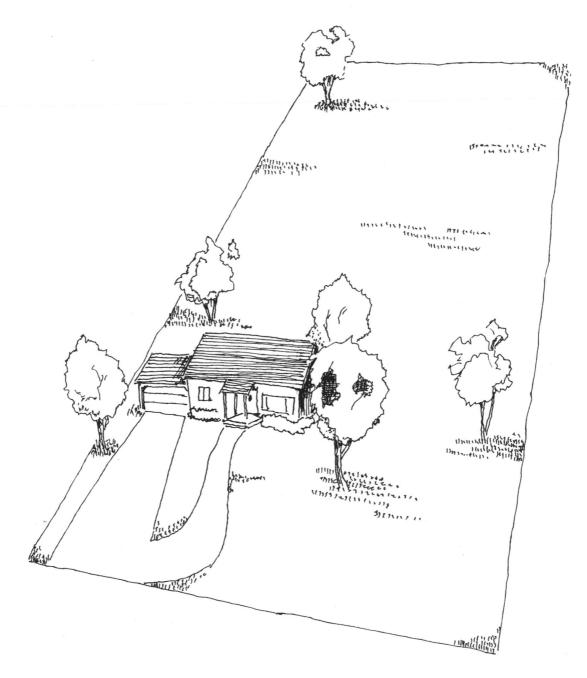

Plot and draw trees and shrubs as you plan your own home landscape improvements.

college. They have the latest knowledge of best gardening techniques plus lists of plants that thrive in your area. Annual open houses let you learn much more about gardening in your locale.

Take a good look at your home from the street as friends and visitors see it. Consider how to make that first view of your home more appealing. When you drive home at night, think how some beds and

borders, a flowering shrub, or accent plants might make your land sparkle. Make notes, save garden catalogs, and read about the many plants available for your landscape.

Look out windows of rooms where you spend the most time—the kitchen and family room perhaps. Envision what blooming beauty scenes you wish to see from inside your house. Read catalogs to

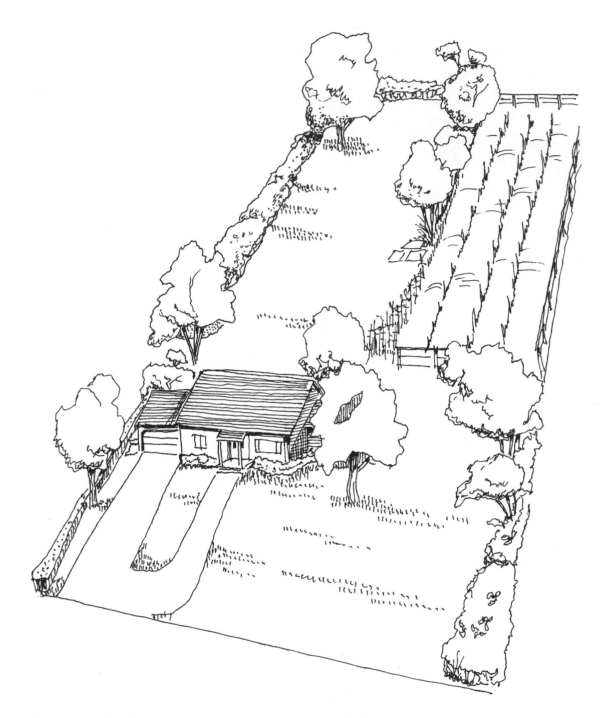

Finally, add other elements to your garden plan and get ready to dig in and plant the lovely plantscape your home deserves.

find those plants that will provide colorful views from early spring through summer into the fall. That way, you'll be able to create a landscape plan that you can make come alive by planting the appropriate plants in your home grounds.

At some point, find a quiet corner, take pencil in hand, and begin drawing your own design. True, you can hire a landscape designer or architect, but most gardeners realize doing the designs themselves is more fun and lets them express their own visions

CHAPTER 7

Consider the different shapes of trees and decide which would look best on your grounds.

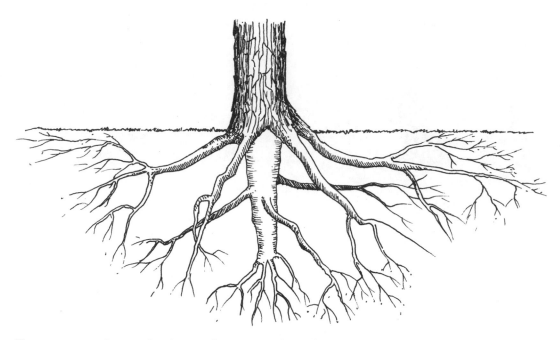

Tree roots grow deep and wide over the years, so keep that in mind when you are deciding where to place your trees.

better. Catalogs give you the colorful photos to see how many different shrubs, trees, and flowers will look when mature. That makes it easier to picture your future plantscapes.

As you envision your future plantings, focus on these ten tips from landscape pros.

1. Make walkways 5 feet wide.
2. Use horizontally branched trees for canopies and screening.
3. Select plants for what they do, not what they are.
4. Use outdoor color schemes that complement your interior colors.
5. Use plants in odd numbers: 1, 3, 5, 7. . . . Seems odd, but it works well.
6. Choose materials and forms that match or complement your home's architecture.
7. Set moods with the dynamic elements of lighting and water.
8. Create separate spaces for separate functions.
9. Plan for bold masses of color in your beds instead of sporadic planting between shrubs.
10. Consider dramatic specimen plants for special eye appeal.

A major consideration in selecting plants for your area must be those that will not only survive in that climate but also perform to their peak growth and display. Thanks to years of research, the U.S. Department of Agriculture has produced a list of "Indicator Plants" for the different hardiness zones in our country. These are often referred to as horticultural zones. Sometimes plants you may love just won't fit and grow well where you live because of climate, prevailing winds, or soil conditions. You'll find that list of plants later in this chapter. Local garden centers and nurseries can advise about best plants from the list of those you prefer. Also, catalogs provide details about hardiness and required growing conditions.

Be aware that landscaping also can save energy and consequently money. By planting trees, shrubs, and hedges, you can reduce heating and cooling costs. For example, good tree and shrub barriers stop winds from beating against your home and sucking out heat. The Department of Energy says that proper placement of just three trees will save between $100 and $250 per year in energy costs. Reports from other sources reveal that carefully placed trees can save up to 25 percent of energy costs for heating and cooling. Consider that deciduous trees shade your home in hot summer weather and cool it, then drop leaves so the sun warms your home in winter. Coniferous trees provide windbreaks and shade too. Many homes in the west use windbreaks of trees to stop cold winds from hitting homes.

The Associated Landscape Contractors of America reports that the proper placement of shrubs and trees around your home or office can reduce utility bills and conserve energy while creating a healthy environment. During summer months, one large tree can absorb as much heat as several window air conditioners and can lower temperatures by 10 degrees.

In climates with cold winters, your goal is to block the winter wind with trees and shrubs while capturing the winter sun's solar heat. In warmer climates, your goal is to block the summer sun while channeling in the summer breezes. In temperate climates, both strategies are employed. For example, a dense row of evergreens to the north and northwest works effectively for extreme and temperate climates. Deciduous trees and shrubs should be planted to the east and west. A semicircular row of deciduous trees and shrubs planted from southeast to southwest, with a break to the south, will funnel in summer breezes.

There are three ways in which trees and shrubs cool the air: by providing shade from solar radiation, by cutting wind speed, and by reducing air temperature through evaporation and transpiration. They also absorb heat, thus reducing the need for air conditioning and allowing for less carbon dioxide to be emitted from electric generating facilities. Not only do plants absorb pollutants and block noise levels, but they do it very well. For instance, a cypress hedge planted 2 feet thick along the front of a property can reduce street noise by five decibels.

Think about walking in a forest or park where the trees keep you cool. Both the shade and transpiration from trees reduce surrounding air temperatures as much as 20 degrees. Cool air settles and tree leaves shade the ground area. Berkeley Labs discovered that summer daytime air temps can be 3–6 degrees cooler in tree-shaded neighborhoods.

As you think more about improving your landscape, you may wish to get additional details about landscape contractors. The organization offers a free copy of *Landscaping: It Works for Everyone*. Just send a business-size, self-addressed, stamped envelope to the Associated Landscape Contractors of America, Attn: Landscaping Brochure, 150 Elden Street, Suite 270, Herndon, VA 20170.

Millions of Americans move each year for business or other reasons. Even if you plan to stay rooted where you live and enjoy your home landscapes, it is nice to know that improving landscaping has rewards beyond just the appeal of the plants and the look they impart to your home grounds.

Trees deserve praise and space around your home. The National Academy of Sciences estimates that urban America has 100 million potential "tree spaces," those locations where trees could be planted. The academy estimates that filling these spaces with trees that lighten dark, urban surfaces could result in annual energy savings of 25 percent of the 200 billion kilowatt-hours consumed every year by air conditioners in the United States.

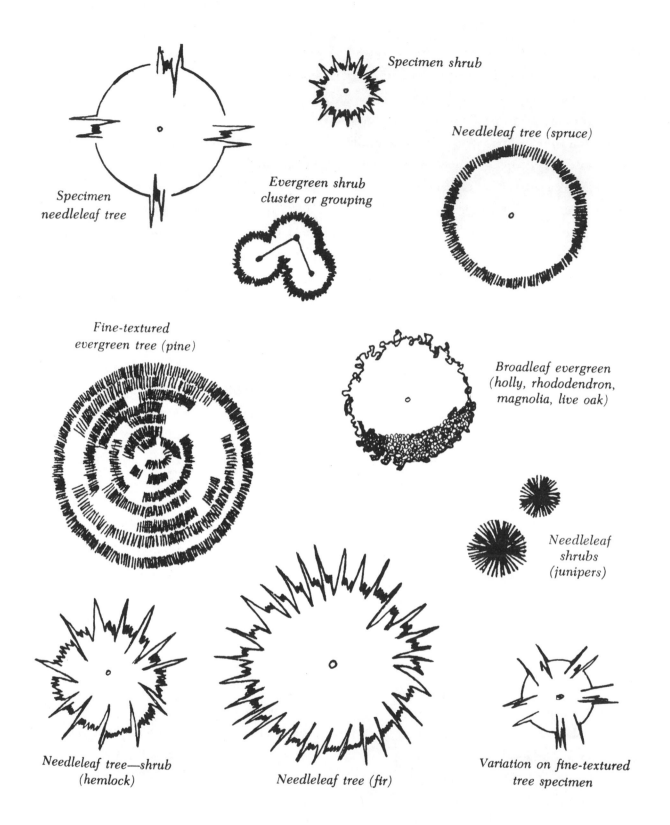

Specimen shrub

Needleleaf tree (spruce)

Specimen
needleleaf tree

Evergreen shrub
cluster or grouping

Fine-textured
evergreen tree (pine)

Broadleaf evergreen
(holly, rhododendron,
magnolia, live oak)

Needleleaf
shrubs
(junipers)

Needleleaf tree—shrub
(hemlock)

Needleleaf tree (fir)

Variation on fine-textured
tree specimen

Copy and use these illustrations of evergreen trees as you design your landscape.

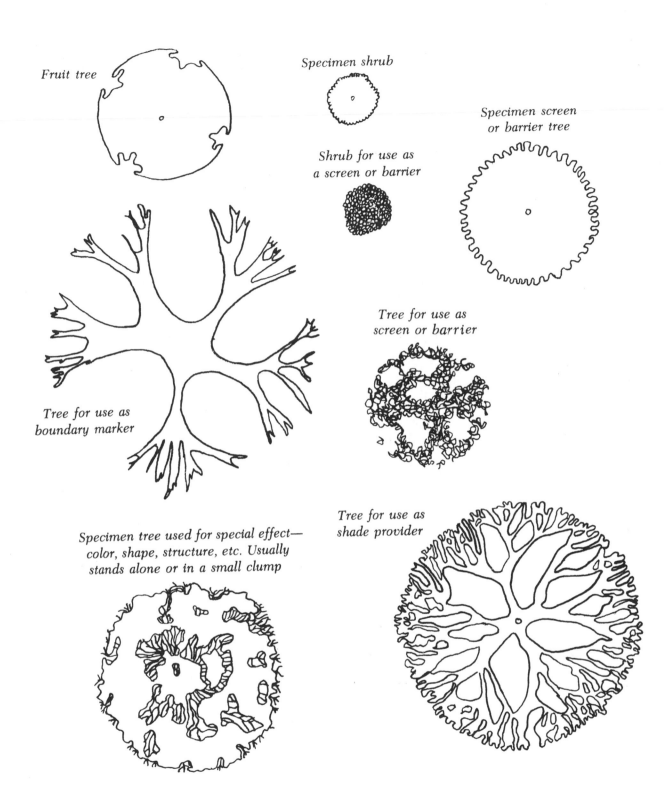

Fruit tree

Specimen shrub

Specimen screen
or barrier tree

Shrub for use as
a screen or barrier

Tree for use as
boundary marker

Tree for use as
screen or barrier

Tree for use as
shade provider

Specimen tree used for special effect—
color, shape, structure, etc. Usually
stands alone or in a small clump

Copy and use these illustrations of deciduous trees as you design your landscape.

Attractive landscaping also can increase market value of a home up to 10 percent, according to recent real estate surveys. For reasonable cost, you can create strong visual appeal that beckons home buyers and sets a warm mood. You get to enjoy appealing landscaping as it grows in size and adds even more value to your property. Realtors will tell you that renovating kitchens and baths is important, but just $1,000 or so spent on upgrading your landscaping pays dividends. That value grows bigger and better every year, naturally.

Realtors report that 90 percent of home shoppers don't even want to see a home if it doesn't please them as they drive up to it. They urge people to plan ahead to give their homes "curb appeal" with attractive landscapes. Not only do you get to enjoy your more appealing home when you drive up, but it pleases neighbors and greets friends pleasantly too.

Flowers blooming in the garden and cut flowers scenting the house when guests visit is an important point in presenting a home's best face. Research has demonstrated that homes in neighborhoods with overall excellent landscaping sell for about 7 to 10 percent more than similar homes in other neighborhoods. Fact is, all things being equal, improving the quality of a home's landscaping can boost resale prices as much as 10 percent. Home owners who have upgraded their landscape quality from good to excellent have been rewarded by 4–5 percent in increased resale prices in neighborhoods where other homes have excellent landscaping.

Happily, attractive landscaping is easier than most people think. Just a few trees can be a good starting point. Then, focus on perennials and bulbs that provide beauty from spring through summer and return to reward you every year. You'll find perennials detailed in chapter 8 and bulbs in chapter 9. The best part is beauty that grows again each year. Planting perennials and bulbs, plus trees and shrubs, should be first focus in any landscaping and gardening plan. Focus on that key word, *landscaping*. Actually, I prefer the word *plantscaping*.

Take another look at how your house looks from a distance and as you approach your front door. To improve overall appearance, it pays to plant attractive shrubs along the front. Flowering shrubs offer spring and summer beauty. Use multi-purpose trees and shrubs that have blooms in spring and colorful fruits or berries in the fall. These will frame and showcase your house and gardens. Local landscapers can suggest attractive plants to enhance the overview of your property. Cultivate local garden experts and sources, especially at nurseries and private garden centers. They have the experience to know which plants grow best in your area.

As you upscale your plantscape, focus on your entryway. Appealing shrubs and flowers say welcome. Crocus, daffodils, hyacinths, tulips, and lilies give you color and beauty from earliest spring through summer. Use perennial flowers. Once planted they bloom every year with minimal care. That's a big plus. By selecting those that bloom early, in summer, and into fall, you can have colorful gardens of blooming beauty month after month. Mail order catalogs provide excellent specimens in color so you can choose those that appeal and add to your home grounds year by year. Annuals are nice for fill in, but perennials give you the opportunity to build a long-range landscape look that has deep, lasting roots.

Colorful landscapes are a welcome delight. Multipurpose trees and shrubs provide double rewards from blooms in the spring to fall berries or attractive foliage color. Check local nurseries for the brightest colors of trees. The brilliance of a tree's foliage is retained throughout that tree's life, so select the brightest to plant in your grounds.

Here's a color checklist from landscape experts. To have vivid colors, plant sugar maples, which have red, orange, and yellow fall foliage. Use scarlet oak and sassafras for orange to scarlet. Red maples are crimson, and sweet gum is scarlet to burgundy. To have yellow colors try aspen, birch, beech, poplar, and Norway maples. For browns and oranges, plant oaks and horse chestnut trees.

As you plan, keep in mind that trees and shrubs can save you energy money too. Research reveals that cities can be 5–10 degrees warmer than suburbs because of the urban "heat island" effect. That is caused by heat-absorbing surfaces such as roads, buildings, and driveways. Just walk city streets to experience it. Consider that about 8 percent of current electricity demand for air conditioning is needed to compensate for this heat island effect.

Trees truly are nature's air conditioners. Roof and wall temperatures are reduced by 8–15 degrees when shaded by trees. Trees also give off tremendous amounts of water daily to cool surrounding areas and also can funnel breezes to your home grounds. Firs, cedars, and pines have the advantage of reducing winter winds. Experiments in the Midwest revealed that shelter belts of trees are worthwhile. In one test, a shelter belt on three sides of a house accounted for a 70 percent reduction in wind and 40 percent savings in fuel. Because most winds come from northern or northwesterly directions, windbreaks of trees on north and west sides make sense.

Trees also reduce noise. Research reveals they break up street and traffic sounds, so plan a buffer of trees along roadways. Even shrubs help. Dense rows of trees and shrubs reduce noise pollution by many decibels. Trees along a busy highway can reduce noise penetrating to surrounding areas by as much as 60 percent. They do more. In addition to absorbing carbon dioxide and giving us valuable oxygen, trees also clean the air of soot. Then, rains wash these residues off leaves back to the ground. You also can achieve greater privacy in this hectic world with more foliage around you. Shrubs and trees can screen out unsightly views of street, stores, and traffic and their sounds.

Think tastefully when you redo landscapes. Just a few bushes or rows of blackberries, blueberries, and raspberries are attractive and provide fruit for your table. A few fruit trees brighten spring with blooms and enrich your life with delicious apples, cherries, peaches, pears, or plums as you wish.

You can consult with or hire a landscape contractor. Some not only design home plantscapes but also install and maintain home grounds for their clients. Actually, you may wish to help with the design, tapping the talents of an expert and even contracting to have much of the planting done. Some like to contract lawn mowing and pruning but like to tend their veggies, herbs, fruits, and flowers themselves.

Professional landscape contractors should be certified and licensed as well as insured. Ask about guarantees, especially coverage of new and more expensive trees and plants. Get references about their recent jobs and look them over. Be sure to get a written plan and plant material list with all costs detailed and a timetable and terms of payment indicated. There are many honest, reliable contractors serving home owners, but there also are those with poor credentials and reputations. For your own protection, investigate the credentials of the one you may wish to hire. Then, be specific about what you want them to do and what you intend to do yourself, on a given project or ongoing basis.

BASE PLANS FOR BETTER LANDSCAPES

Whether you hire a contractor for most of your landscape design and planting or not, here are the basic steps to achieve a more attractive home land-scape. First, develop a list of existing and desired outdoor features. Collect mail order catalogs so you have pictures of shrubs and trees as they will look at maturity. That is an important guide in deciding what you want and what will fit where in your grounds, in a few years and to maturity too.

Next, draw a base plan. Outline existing major landscape features in general. Indicate which plants may not be desired and should be removed. Often,

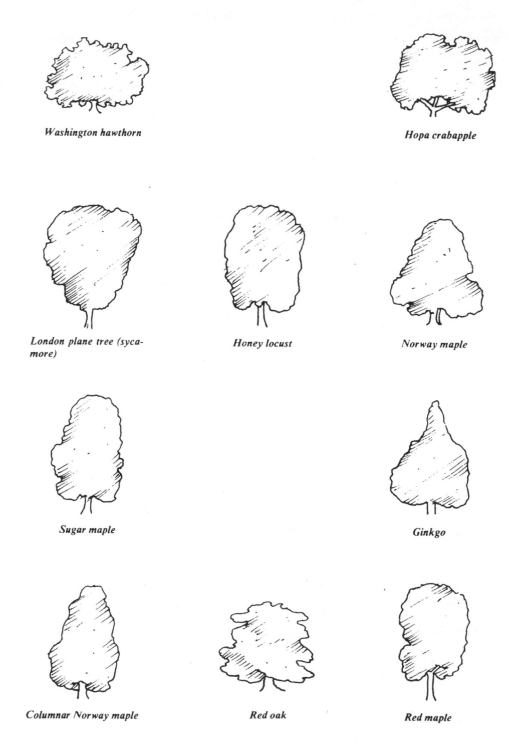

Washington hawthorn

Hopa crabapple

London plane tree (syca-more)

Honey locust

Norway maple

Sugar maple

Ginkgo

Columnar Norway maple

Red oak

Red maple

These are the ten best trees for city streets.

older homes have overgrown shrubs that need only careful and sometimes severe pruning to bring them back to their most beautiful appearance.

Position on paper the desired features in their proper areas. As you do, you'll again realize how much easier it is to revise a paper plan than digging up and transplanting actual plants. Copy the line drawings in this chapter and use them to make your own landscape designs. Note the illustrations that show typical sizes, shapes, and the look of trees at maturity. You'll also find lists of the best trees for city streets.

Plot your finished landscape plan on paper so it can serve as a guide. Move line drawings around. Consult mail order catalogs to determine the mature width and height of shrubs and trees. Some grow faster and others require years to mature. Take those facts into consideration as you plan. Sometimes it pays to have additional plants for a few years and remove them as the more appealing, desired shrubs or trees mature. Take time to plan on paper to achieve that happier, more attractive outdoor environment you deserve.

Design your outdoor living area to suit your family needs and lifestyle. You may want to include a patio for entertaining, a children's play area, a sports area, flower gardens for cutting, vegetable and herb gardens, and fruitful plots too. As you plan, walk your home grounds at different times of the day. Be sure that the sun reaches areas where you would like to have flowers, vegetables, and fruits and will shine there long enough each day to satisfy those plants' needs. Some plants need hours of sunlight. Others can prosper with limited shade. Gather information about best plants for sun, shade, moist, or dry areas. It is easier to match plants to the growing conditions and environment than change the ground. However, chapter 2 tells you how you can improve your soil.

Think about other outdoor living opportunities. How about a deck to expand your home space and provide space for entertaining. What about views from windows overlooking your grounds? Special landscape efforts to beautify areas you see from your kitchen or dining room let you enjoy blooming beauty while busy indoors.

Birds delight us with their songs and antics, and children love to watch birds, especially those that nest nearby and feed their young. Select trees that attract songbirds and provide wildlife habitats. Local garden centers and nurseries offer many, including aromatic sumac, bayberry, firethorn, bittersweet, holly, and American cranberry bush. These shrubs look great and offer abundant food for birds. Consider living screens of multiflora roses, mulberries, and even blackberries for property borders or to hide unattractive areas such as compost piles or neighboring yards.

Think about specimen tree plantings or groupings. Good trees include autumn olive, mountain ash, ornamental crabapples of all types, and dogwoods. Hawthorn is our favorite for hardiness, blooms, and fall berries. Ornamental crabapples bear white, pink, or reddish blooms and bright berry crops in fall.

As fall foliage glows, visit your local nursery to identify the most colorful autumn accents for your landscape. You'll discover a wide range of deciduous shrubs and trees that delight the eye with colorful leaves or bright fall berries for birds. Look closely at trees of the same variety that have brighter foliage. They'll have that same more vivid color throughout their lifetime, because these trees have their own specific genetic makeup. Select the most colorful for your home grounds.

Foliage brilliance changes each year and is improved by ideal weather conditions, cool nights, and warm sunny days. Intensity of light also can

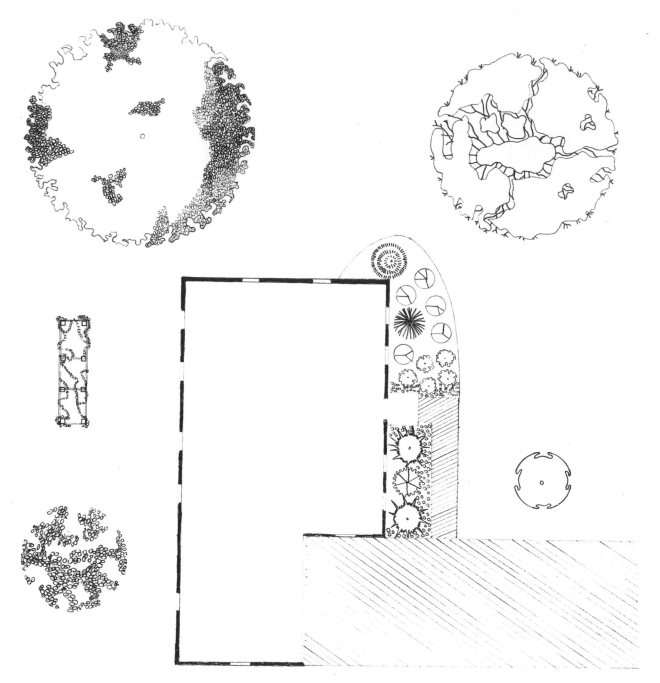

Here's one example of a home landscape.

intensify reds and purples. If fall days are often overcast, you'll see more oranges and yellows in foliage. Frost actually has almost nothing to do with autumn colors. In fall, cells at the base of a leaf stem begin to harden. Photosynthesis slows and stops. Green chlorophyll that colors summer leaves van-ishes. Actually, the green masked the other colors within the leaves all summer. Now, they come out to turn leaves those glorious fall colors people love.

Many shrubs as well as trees offer multiseason beauty: blooms in the spring, and yellow, gold, or scarlet foliage for weeks of autumn beauty before

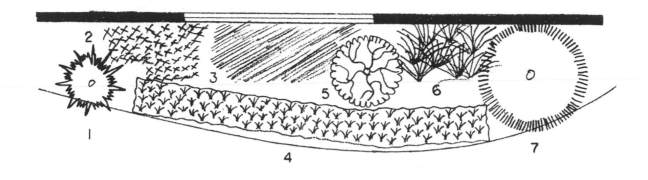

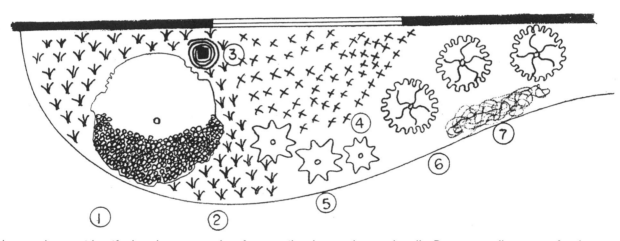

Use numbers to identify the plants you select from mail order catalogs or locally. Be sure to allow room for them to mature.

leaves fall. Take a drive around your area. Look for the best fall displays and plan to adopt some of the plants to improve your own home grounds. Norway maples are hardy, excellent shade trees that turn bright yellow in fall. Red maples bear reddish blossoms in spring, scarlet leaves in fall. Sugar maples may range from bright yellow to orange and reddish. Honey locusts have thin, airy foliage that provides light shade and yellow fall foliage.

Birch, beech, poplar, and aspen also turn yellow. Sassafras turns orange to scarlet. Dogwoods turn crimson, and sweet gum turns scarlet. Red oaks are the fastest growing oaks with deep-red fall color. Washington Hawthorne has dense, shiny fo-

liage and white flowers each spring. By fall, orange leaves are complemented with small red fruit that birds enjoy. Hopa crabapple grows only 20 feet tall and has rose flowers in spring and small red fruits in autumn.

Another sweet delight to consider is the delicious fragrance of different types of flowers. Too often this joy is overlooked as we choose flowers and shrubs for color, display, and other purposes. You'll find recommendations for perennials in chapter 8 and annuals in chapter 11. Hyacinths, for example, are noted for their fragrance, especially the larger hybrid types. You have a wide choice of many other fragrant plants, from lily of the valley to

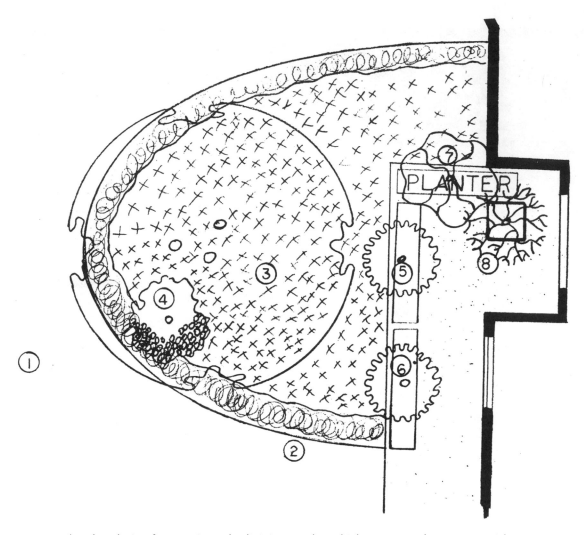

Another design for a patio and adjoining garden which you can adapt as you wish.

lilac, from clematis to various lilies, from old-time roses to viburnum.

When planting for fragrance, concentrate the most fragrant plants near areas where you are likely to spend time outdoors; especially in early morning or evening when most fragrant plants are at their peak. Paths, walkways, outdoor dining areas, or quiet sitting nooks are ideal spots. Site plants upwind so their perfume drifts with the breeze where you want it.

Other top flowers for fragrant gardens from seeds, according to my good horticulturist friend Lynn Harris, include carnations, various pinks, mignonette, lavender, fragrant nicotiana, almost all stocks, sweet pea, violas, plus ornamental basil and rosemary. You can also plant biennials such as dame's rocket, sweet William, and English wallflower. Two of my favorite catalogs for beautiful, dramatic, and fragrant plants are Park Seeds, 1 Parkton Ave., Greenwood, SC 29647, telephone: 864-223-7333, and Wayside Gardens, Hodges, SC 29695, telephone: 800-845-1124.

KEY POINTS

As you focus on your landscape horizons, keep these key points in mind. Sketch a plan that includes property lines, buildings and their dimensions, plus major existing trees and structures. Always measure property lines and boundaries to avoid planting valued trees or plants on a neighbor's land. Check with local utilities, especially in cities and new suburban areas, to locate and mark utilities, both above and below ground. There is nothing worse than planning for a new tree but hitting a power, water, sewer, or gas line when you dig. Some of these accidents can be fatal. Be sure your contractor checks for dangerous buried electrical and gas lines. In many states, it is the law.

Plants grow, but many of us may overlook that fact of plant life. Determine how tall your trees will grow so they don't send branches into overhead electric lines, including cables to your home. Also know mature breadth or circumference of your trees, so you don't plant too close to buildings. Trees can rub against your house, scraping off paint or causing other problems.

Sketch in the approximate locations of major landscape areas. If you want a deck or patio some day, outline it. Look thoughtfully at your public area and think about the way your home looks to friends, neighbors, guests, and passersby. Does it showcase your gardening ability and present your home in the best way?

As you plan, also consider the play or entertaining area behind your home. Living hedges, shrubs, and fences work well to screen out unpleasant sights. Thorny berry bushes make a useful property border to discourage wandering cats and dogs. Sometimes you and your neighbor can plant a fruitful or flowering hedge together and share the bounty of berries or blooms for cut flowers.

Next step as you set your landscape improvement priorities is to drive up to your house and look at its setting carefully. That is your landscape face to the public that everyone sees first before they knock on your door. Is it as appealing, friendly, and attractive as you would like it to be? Does it set your house off as one that welcomes friends and guests. If you think your curbside face needs improving, give it a top priority. That way, every time you return home, that glowing face of landscape beauty will greet you, and all who come to visit you as well.

Another key point is that landscaping should blend your home into the surrounding area so it looks natural and comfortable. You can accomplish this by softening strong vertical lines of the house with trees and shrubs. Trees can frame a house and add depth to it. Low-built homes look best with small or medium-size trees that won't outgrow and dwarf the house. Bedded shrubs and border plantings can create a transition from open lawn areas to your house itself.

Your doorway is the focal point for your public area planting. Plants should lead a visitor's eye to the entrance. You can accomplish this by positioning larger plants at the corners of the house and tapering off to smaller plants toward the door. Taller trees can be used to break the roof line, or in the private backyard area, provide a natural, softer backdrop to your house when viewed from the street. You'll find examples of designs that illustrate these points in this chapter.

Next, think about how much time you spend outdoors. Ask yourself how you want to decorate your entertaining and living area with plants. Should it be combined with a children's play area where you can watch them amid the gardens you create, and encourage their interest in gardening too? You can use hedges and shrubs to provide privacy. There are fast-growing privet hedges and more ornamental flowering shrubs that let you create areas of privacy, solitude, and even prayerful meditation. Local landscapers, established garden centers, and nurseries have details about the best, most suitable shrubs and trees for your area. They know your soil, climate, and growing conditions. Tap their knowledge and buy your basic landscape needs, trees, and shrubs locally if possible. That gives you a useful connection for resources and answers to your questions over the years.

The advice that follows has been generously given by garden designers and landscape horticulturalists alike. As we realize, there are many different sizes, shapes, and designs of homes that call for different approaches in landscaping. This chapter isn't intended to be a complete landscaping guide, but key points offered by veteran landscape specialists and designers can help.

You'll find some illustrations too that focus on the types of homes described here. A long, low house calls for careful long-range planning. In a modern contemporary home, taller trees in the backyard and rear of the property provide a natural display of foliage to break up the long, low roof line. Think about hemlocks, which grow tall and

somewhat pyramidal, to break up and soften lines. They can be pruned periodically. Junipers work as part of the front shrub plantings, as do yews, spreading or upright.

Flowering trees such as almond, hawthorn, and crabapple on the lawn provide delightful blooms in spring and berries in fall. If you have a slope, don't despair. A firethorn will thrive at the side of the drive and can be trained to reach over the garage door. Holly, yew, or mugho pine can be used at the doorway with a grouping of shrubs, including pyramidal yews, at the corner of the home. Upright taller arborvitae and cedars can be used at the lower driveway level, or use medium-size deciduous trees instead. If you have steep slopes from drive to front door, consider a rock garden or several terraces. An alternative could be ground covers like myrtle that hold soil and reduce mowing chores.

Smaller homes can look poorly without landscaping. Take heart. You can create a well-loved look with a few trees and shrubs that won't strain

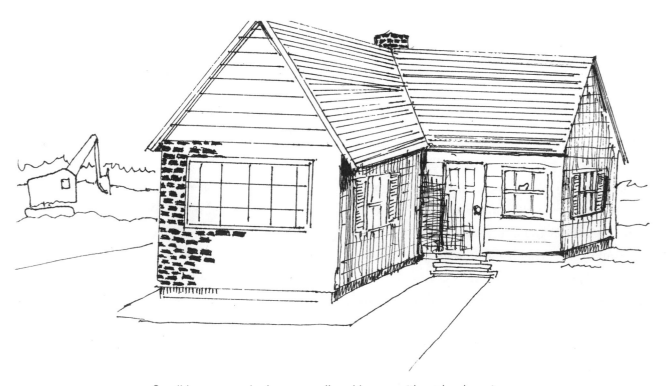

Small homes can look very small and barren without landscaping.

By adding shrubs, trees, and other decorative plants, you can begin to develop a much more attractive home—even on a low budget.

your budget. Even the smallest houses are brightened with that simple, effective, easy-to-tend, and ages-old garden device, the windowbox. They are a colorful and worthwhile addition to American homes.

Trees at the corner of a home seem to extend the size of the house while giving it a nicely landscaped look. Lower shrubs beneath windows draw the eye to the entrance. A corner planting from a house, with a taller framing tree, helps expand the length of your house in a visual way. Lower-growing shrubs and flowers can be extended from house to lawn trees to tie plantings together.

Avoid planting tall shrubs that will grow up to hide your home. Note well that, in all landscaping,

some shrubs require regular pruning. Actually, most plants thrive with pruning and can use it yearly. However, some shrubs are naturally dwarf in growth habit. In today's busy world, low-maintenance landscaping is more than a desired goal; it is a necessity.

Another key tip is not to overcrowd a landscape plan. A few well-chosen trees and shrubs will improve a home's appearance. It is far better to underplant than create a plant jungle that hides the beauty of your home. Trees and shrubs grow all around, not just upward. Plant them far enough from your foundation so painting and building maintenance can be accomplished properly and easily.

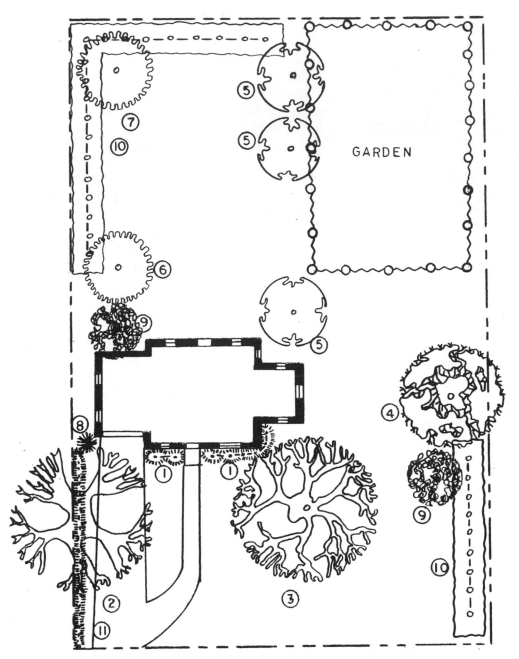

Here's an example of how we planned one of our homes. It took some years to afford all the trees and plants, but over time, new plants complemented those already on the property to give us an appealing front walk, backyard sitting and play area, plus veggie and herb garden. Along part of the back, we had a living fruitful planting.

Shape also is important in landscape design. You'll find tree shape illustrations in this chapter and will see that some trees are round, others oval, pyramidal, or weeping. Naturally, you will select those that appeal to you. Avoid a "plant collection" look with all individual types. It is better to use a few of each to achieve pleasing balance with variations in form, texture, shape, and growth habit. Try to strike a balance where possible. Specimen trees have their place for their special significance, so give

An end or corner planting with a taller framing tree extends the V form of visual focus well beyond the house for an appealing look.

A tall house may need a more massive corner planting and also a large framing tree to give the house the best display appearance.

You can vary trees with different form, shape, and texture for added appeal, combining evergreen and deciduous trees with shrubs and flower beds for a long, low house.

Just a few trees and shrubs greatly enhance a home's appearance. Don't overcrowd your landscape.

Trees at the end of a small home appear to extend its size.

them a place where they can be showcased by themselves.

Let your growing knowledge of gardening be your guide as you shop for trees. There are many types of oaks, from pin oaks that prefer moist soil and thrive in it, to red, black, and white oaks. There are red and white cedars and related arborvitae that perform well. Different poplars and aspens may prove best for your area. Your choice of pines ranges from the various east coast types to bigger western ones. America is a giant country with many different horticultural zones. Therefore, you are well advised to consult with local nurseries to determine which species will do best and prosper in your locality.

By varying types of trees with their own forms, shapes, and textures you can produce an extra special look. Evergreen and deciduous trees combined with shrubs that have varying growing habits and shapes, different leaf colors, textures and patterns, can give a pleasing look to a long, low ranch home. A taller home usually needs a more massive corner planting. A large framing tree can dramatize the home.

Also, keep in mind that your landscaping should reflect your personality and your garden viewpoint.

INDICATOR PLANT GUIDELINES

Learn about the best plants for the conditions that exist on your property. Some plants like it hot; others prefer cooler weather. Some can withstand stark, frigid northern winters. Local nurseries can advise you which survive and thrive in your area. Unfortunately, your favorite tree or shrub from living in another part of the country may not survive where you live now. Instead, keep it treasured in memory.

Happily, the National Arboretum of the U.S. Department of Agriculture, in cooperation with the American Horticultural Society, has developed excellent plant guidelines. Their list of "indicator plants" serves as a handy reference to typical plants that thrive in the various horticultural zones. The Superintendent of Documents in Washington, D.C., offers a colorful horticultural zone map with details of tree and shrub groups that thrive in the respective zones. Local plant suppliers can add to

Houses with slopes need special attention. Plan carefully to break up harsh lines.

the basic list, based on their experience in your particular area.

The map on the first page of this book details the expected minimum temperatures in most of the important continental areas of the United States. It is a guide, and local conditions may vary. The indicator plants are based on proven facts as they apply to each zone, but there may be islands of variation within the zones. Map zones and indicator plant lists have been most useful in determining minimum temperature survival of plants in specific areas.

You can improve soil condition, fertility, water, and cultural methods, but you still are confined by the normal weather where you live. With those cautions in mind, here is the Indicator Plant List for your reference, thanks to the USDA.

Common plant names are followed by their botanical names in parentheses.

Zone 1 (Below -50°F)
Dwarf birch (*Betula glandulosa*)

Crowberry (*Empetrum nigum*)

Quaken aspen (*Populus tremuloides*)

Pennsylvania cinquefoil (*Rotentilla pennsylvanica*)

Lapland rhododendron (*Rhododendron lapponicum*)

Netleaf willow (*Salix reticulata*)

Zone 2 (-50 to -40°F)
Paper birch (*Betula papyrifera*)

Bunchberry dogwood (*Cornus canadensis*)

Silverberry (*Elaeagnus commutata*)

Eastern larch (*Larix laricina*)

Bush cinquefoil (*Potentilla fruitcosa*)

American cranberry bush (*Viburnum trilobum*)

Zone 3 (-40 to -30°F)

Japanese barberry (*Berberis thunbergii*)

Russian olive (*Elaeagnus augustifolia*)

Common juniper (*Juniperus communis*)

Tartarian honeysuckle (*Lonicera tatarica*)

Siberian crabapple (*Malus baccata*)

American arborvitae (*Thuja occidentalis*)

Zone 4 (-30 to -20°F)

Sugar maple (*Acer saccharum*)

Panicle hydrangea (*Hydrangea paniculata*)

Chinese juniper (*Juniperus chinensis*)

Amur River privet (*Ligustrum amurense*)

Virginia creeper (*Parthenocissus quinquefolia*)

Vanhoutte spirea (*Spiraea vanhouttei*)

Zone 5 (-20 to -10°F)

Flowering dogwood (*Cornus florida*)

Slender deutzia (*Deutzia gracilis*)

Common privet (*Ligustrum vulgare*)

Boston ivy (*Parthenocissus tricuspidata*)

Japanese rose (*Rosa multiflora*)

Japense yew (*Taxus cuspidata*)

Zone 6 (-10 to 0°F)

Japanese maple (*Acer palmatum*)

Common box (*Buxus sempervirens*)

Winter creeper (*Euonymus fortunei*)

English ivy (*Hedera helix*)

American holly (*Ilex opaca*)

California privet (*Ligustrum ovalifolium*)

Zone 7 (0 to 10°F)

Bigleaf maple (*Acer macrophyllum*)

Kurume azaleas (*Azalea Kurume* hybrids)

Atlas cedar (*Cedar atlantica*)

Small-leaf cotoneaster (*Cotoneaster microphylla*)

English holly (*Ilex aquifolium*)

English yew (*Taxus baccata*)

Zone 8 (10 to 20°F)

Strawberry tree (*Arbutus unedo*)

Mexican orange (*Choisya tenata*)

New Zealand daisy bush (*Olearia haastii*)

Japanese pittosporum (*Pittosporum tobira*)

Cherry laurel (*Prunus laurocerasus*)

Laurustinus (*Viburnum tinus*)

Zone 9 (20 to 30°F)

Asparagus fern (*Asparagus plumosus*)

Tasmanian blue gum (*Eucalyptus globulus*)

Bush cherry (*Eugenia paniculata*)

Fuchsia (*Fuchsia* hybrids)

Silk oak (*Grevillea robusta*)

California pepper tree (*Schinus molle*)

Zone 10 (30 to 40°F)

Bougainvillea (*Bougainvillea spectabilis*)

Golden shower (*Cassia fistula*)

Lemon eucalyptus (*Eucalyptus citriodora*)

Rubber plant (*Ficus elastica*)

Banana (*Musa ensete*)

Royal palm (*Roystonea regia*)

HOW TO PLANT A TREE

At last, the tips you need to dig in and plant a tree or shrub. You can get excellent brochures from various Cooperative Extension offices and agricultural colleges. They are useful to have on hand because they focus on environmental and growing conditions in your home area. Use these basics as your foundation guide.

Proper placement of trees is critical for your enjoyment and their long-term survival. Check with local authorities about regulations pertaining to placement of trees. Some communities have ordinances restricting placement of trees within a specified distance of a street, sidewalk, streetlight, or other utilities.

As noted earlier, consider the tree's ultimate size. When the tree nears maturity, will it be too near your house or other structures? Be considerate of your neighbors too. Perhaps an evergreen tree planted on your north side will block the winter sun from your nextdoor neighbor. Before planting, consider how large a tree will grow in a few years. Will it shade your vegetable and flower gardens? Most vegetables and many flowers require considerable amounts of sun. If you intend to grow these plants, consider how the placement of trees will affect these gardens. Look up to see if a new tree may cause problems for overhead cable or telephone lines.

Remember that a properly planted and maintained tree will grow faster and live longer than one that is incorrectly planted. You can plant trees almost any time of the year as long as the ground is not frozen. Late summer or early fall is the optimum time in many areas to give the tree a chance to establish new roots before winter arrives and the ground freezes. Then, when spring arrives, your tree is ready to grow. Second choice for planting is late winter or early spring. Planting in frozen soil during the winter is difficult and tough on tree roots. When the tree is dormant and the ground is frozen, there is no opportunity for the growth of new roots. Avoid planting in hot summer weather.

The next point to consider is whether your trees are container grown, balled and burlapped, or bare root. Container grown are the easiest to plant successfully in any season, including summer, because little damage is done to the roots as the plant is transferred to the soil. Container-grown trees range from small plants in gallon pots up to large trees in huge pots. Balled and burlapped plants fre-

quently have been dug from a nursery, then wrapped in burlap, thus giving roots an opportunity to regenerate. Balled and burlapped plants can be quite large.

Bare-root trees are usually young, smaller plants and are usually offered by mail order firms. You can find more varieties and types of trees from such firms than you can at your local garden center, but you must plant them as soon as they arrive. Predigging their location is one way to prepare for their arrival. There is no soil on the roots, which are dormant, so you must keep roots moist and plant as soon as possible on arrival.

Whichever type of tree you buy, be sure to carefully follow the planting instructions that come with it. Some basic tree planting tips follow.

The vital first step before digging is to call your local utility companies to identify the location of any underground lines. It helps to draw the underground utility lines on the plan you created of your home grounds for future reference.

Next, dig a hole twice as wide and slightly shallower than the root ball. Roughen the sides and bottom of the hole with a pick or shovel so that roots can penetrate the soil. It pays to dig a larger hole so tender young roots can make their way into

Dig deeply to give trees the room they need to set roots, spread well, and reward you with good growth.

the ground readily, especially if you have heavy clay soil below the surface.

If you have a container grown tree, gently remove the tree from its container. Best way to do this is to lay the tree on its side with the root end near the planting hole and gently tap or hit the bottom and sides of the container until the root ball is loosened. If roots are growing in a circular pattern around the root ball, slice through the roots on a couple of sides of the root ball.

If trees are wrapped in burlap, remove the string or wire that holds the burlap to the root crown. It is not necessary to completely remove the burlap, but be sure to tuck it underground where it will rot in the soil. With plastic-wrapped plants, remove the plastic completely. Gently separate circling roots on the root ball. Shorten exceptionally long roots, and position the shortened roots downward and outward as you plant. Remember that root tips die quickly when exposed to light and air, so keep them moist and don't waste time as you plant.

Next, place the root ball in the hole. Leave the top of the root ball, that point where the roots end and the trunk begins, at one-half to 1 inch above the surrounding soil. Be sure not to cover it unless roots are exposed. For bare root plants, make a mound of soil in the middle of the hole and spread plant roots out evenly over that mound.

The key point is not to set trees too deep. As you add soil to fill in around the tree, lightly tamp the soil to reduce air pockets. Then, add water to help settle the soil. Form a temporary water basin around the base of the tree to encourage water penetration, and water thoroughly after planting. A tree with a dry root ball cannot absorb water. Therefore, if the root ball is extremely dry, use a soaker hose or allow water to trickle into the soil by placing the hose at the trunk of the tree.

There's more to ensure your trees get their deserved good start and a firm, long-lasting roothold. Mulch around the tree. A 3-foot diameter circle of mulch is common. Many materials are available, but peat moss, rotted wood chips, and compost are useful. Mulch stops weeds from competing and also reminds you to avoid mowing too closely, which might knick the bark and harm the new tree.

Depending on the size of your new tree and the site conditions, you may wish to stake it until it sets its roots firmly. Staking with tall or low supports connected to the tree should allow for some movement of the tree. If using wire, use cut pieces of hose so the wires don't harm the bark. After trees are established, remove all support wires.

Once you have planted your tree, remember to water it every week, especially in dry weather. In fact, for the first year or two, especially after a week or so of especially hot or dry weather, watch your trees closely for signs of moisture stress. If you see leaf wilting or soil that has become hard and caked, water trees well and slowly enough to allow the water to soak in to encourage deep root growth. Keep the area under the trees mulched.

If you are planting evergreen trees, some may need protection against winter sun and wind. A thorough watering in the fall before the ground freezes is recommended. Spray solutions are available to help prevent drying of foliage during the winter. These antidesiccant sprays are available at garden centers. They are especially useful on broad-leaved shrubs such as rhododendrons to prevent dehydration. By spring, these coatings break down and fall off naturally.

Fertilization is usually not needed for newly planted trees. Depending on soil and growing conditions, fertilizer may be beneficial at a later time. Some mail order firms suggest using their tree pep pellets when planting, and that's fine, but they

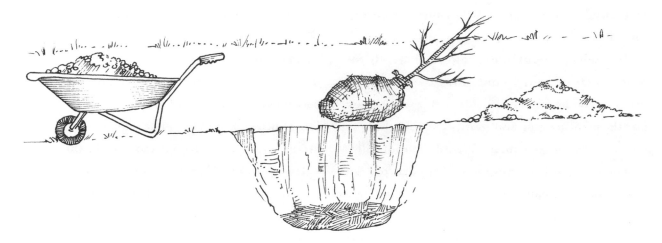

Put loose soil at bottom of hole and mix peat or compost with topsoil so your new tree gets a well-deserved good start.

generally are not needed, especially for container-grown trees and shrubs.

Rodents and rabbits can harm newly planted trees. So can you with weed whackers and lawn mowers if not careful. Mice and rabbits may girdle small trees by chewing away bark at snow level. Since the tissues that transport nutrients in the tree are located just under the bark, a girdled tree often dies in the spring when growth resumes. Plastic tree guards are an inexpensive and easy control method. Mulching around new trees also reminds you to avoid damage with lawn mowers.

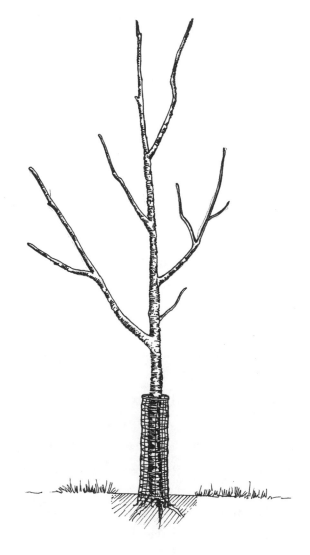

Consider a windscreen to protect newly planted trees during their first season.

Use wire or other protection around newly planted trees to stop mice and other pests from eating the bark.

Another consideration is pruning, which applies more to mature trees that may tend to overgrow, especially near homes. Usually, pruning is not needed on newly planted trees. As the tree grows, just prune lower branches to provide clearance above the ground and to remove dead or damaged limbs or suckers that sprout from the trunk. Larger trees, especially fruit trees, may need pruning to allow more light to enter the canopy. Small branches can be removed easily with pruners. Large branches should be removed with a pruning saw. Cuts should be vertical to allow the tree to heal quickly without the use of sealants. Do major pruning in late winter or early spring when the tree is more likely to "bleed" as sap is rising through the plant, which will help prevent invasion by many disease organisms. You may wish to contact a professional to do major pruning or tree removal.

Plan your lovelier landscape today. Then dig in and enjoy the beauty you create.

8

PLAN PERENNIAL BEAUTY

Millions of gardeners bet on perennials as some of the most rewarding of all garden plants, indeed the backbone of the flower garden. Perennial popularity continues to grow as more gardeners discover hundreds of types and varieties with a wide range of colors, sizes, forms, and blooming times. Even better, there are perennials suitable for almost any spot in the garden—as tall flowering backgrounds, for dazzling displays in the sunniest part, and as low-growing perennials that brighten dark, shady areas.

The best bet is to look over your entire home grounds, see where you may need some colorful accents, and then thumb through the dramatic color photos in mail order catalogs. It may help if you make a drawing of where you want which glorious new perennials to grace your landscape and brighten your views. With a bit of careful planning and preparation, your perennial garden will produce amazing results from a relatively small financial investment. Once well rooted, perennials reward you with blazes of color year after blooming year. By carefully selecting different varieties, you can have welcome blooms from spring into late fall.

Remember, most perennials need at least 1 square foot of garden space per plant. Also, plants look better in groups of 3, 5, or 7 rather than as a single plant.

Underline this next point as you grow in knowledge with your garden: *keep a record*. On a plan of your home grounds, mark which plants are in which area, especially those you must dig up in fall. Label those plants too, so you know what variety the bulbs, roots, or rhizomes are and where they should be replanted come spring. Buy some plastic, wood, or metal plant labels to identify newly planted perennials. Some perennials take time to sprout and mature, and some don't bloom the first year. Labels let you know who's who and which you want to keep or replace.

Veteran gardeners sing the praises of certain perennials, and you'll find details about America's favorite perennials in the first part of this chapter. It seems logical to provide more information about those that have rightly gained fame as long-standing favorites. Later in the chapter, you'll find briefer details of other popular perennials, with culture tips too, and general directions for growing perennials to perfection. In this way, you have a handy guide to the favorites and most popular perennials that do best in gardens nationwide. So many perennials can be grown in this country, there is no space in this book to include all of them. Fortunately, you can get details about others in mail order catalogs that provide culture tips with plant and variety listings. A list of catalogs and other sources is included in chapter 18 of this book.

But to get you started, here are America's favorite perennials with some cultural directions and top recommended varieties to consider for your permanent plantings.

BEGONIAS

The begonia family is a large, varied, and curious one with members originating in China, India, South Africa, and South America. No one can resist these flowering treasures. From the first of summer to the first frost, begonias add consistent color and beauty to your garden. More gardeners have discovered them, which has led to more varieties being made available in stores and mail order catalogs.

Tuberous begonias lend a sumptuous air to gardens with blooms so full and lush they appear almost artificial. They may seem hard to grow well, but don't be fooled. Begonias respond happily to your basic tender loving care. They are ideal for spots with light to medium shade, and they provide rich and complex colors as a feast for the eyes. Try them in containers or near your patio to relish the incredible season-long show.

To help you savor these colorful treasures, veteran fanciers and members of the American Begonia Society provide ideas and advice. Visit their site at www.begonias.org. The purpose of that national group is to stimulate and promote interest in begonias, to encourage introduction and development of new types of these plants, and to gather and publish information about the kinds as well as propagation and culture of begonias and compan-

ion plants. As avid fanciers, they also want to expand contact among all who love and grow begonias.

Basics first. There are cane-stemmed begonias that grow bamboo-like tall stems and large airy flower clusters. Shrublike types grow upright on branching stems. Rhizomatus are easy-care begonias with interesting leaves, and semperflorens are also fairly well known. Tuberous with their show-stopping flowers are legendary. You can grow them well yourself. Rex have gloriously colorful leaves that can be grown indoors or out. Trailing scandent begonias, like vines, grow up or down.

Begonia supporters point out that their favorite flowers are easy to grow, do well in shade, need moderate care, and will reward you with a lovely display of blooms all summer long. Tuberous begonias provide shades of white, pink, red, yellow, orange, and salmon as well as bicolors on usually double flowers that may be 6 inches or more in diameter. Plants generally grow 12–18 inches tall. Depending on the variety, plants may have camellia, ruffled camellia, or rosebud-type flowers.

Tuberous begonias do best in a location that has partial to full shade and well-drained soil. That's great. You can have blooming beauty to brighten shady spots. They also are excellent in containers for portable color displays. If you haven't tried a few, do so this year and be surprised at how enthusiastic you and your family may become.

Begonias like fertile soil, so add organic matter such as peat moss or compost into the upper 8–10 inches, and add fertilizer at rates indicated by a soil test. If you didn't do a soil test yet, mix in 10-10-10 or another general-purpose fertilizer at the rate of 1 pound per 100 square feet before planting. Then, during the growing season, plan to fertilize them with a surface application of 1 pound per 100 square feet about once a month.

Buy only high-quality, firm tubers you can start early indoors, about a month before the frost-free date for your area. Plant in flats or pots filled with a basic commercial planting mixture that includes moist peat moss and perlite. Be sure the depressed side of the tuber faces up. Tubers should be sprouted at 70°F, in the dark.

As soon as shoots develop, cover tubers with more peat moss and move them to a bright location. Wait until all danger of frost has passed before transplanting outdoors. When planting in your garden, place the tubers just slightly below the soil line, because they rot easily when planted too deep. Space plants 18 inches apart so they fill out properly. To avoid damaging their fibrous roots, don't cultivate around the root system.

Water whenever the soil begins to dry. Be especially careful, because tubers will rot if they are overwatered. Water in the morning so foliage dries, to avoid the chance of disease on the leaves. By following these steps from begonia lovers, you too can enjoy the spectacular displays these plants provide.

Come fall, after first frost, dig up the tubers and remove the foliage. Dry tubers for a few days, then store in dry peat moss or sawdust in a paper bag at about 50°F until ready to start them again for another year's delights.

Some fine tuberous begonias include Hanging Sensations hybrids in pink red, rose, and yellow, and Park's Whopper, with blooms 8 inches wide. There isn't room in this book to cover all other types of begonias or their culture as house plants. However, you can find details about them from the American Begonia Society, P.O. Box 471651, San Francisco, CA 94147-1651.

CANNAS

Originally from the West Indies and South America, cannas are one of the showiest summer displays you can grow. These are truly lush tropical plants that produce large and often colorful leaves, tall flower stalks, and vibrant blossoms. Because they tolerate moist soils, cannas can be planted along ponds or in a wet spot in the yard.

Cannas are hardy to zone 7, but even in the North, cannas can fit in. Just dig up the rhizomes and store them at the end of the fall season, then replant in spring for a tropical garden corner. Another plus, cannas aren't fussy about soil type, but they prefer a sunny spot and lots of water.

Look through catalogs and select the bright, bold-leafed cannas to try. They offer red, pink, yellow, orange, and cream flowers and even more dwarf forms to fit small gardens better. Other varieties can grow 3–8 feet tall. Fact is, some giant cannas such as Wyoming and Red King Humbert get tall so quickly, they are extremely useful as a temporary screen or garden area divider. New varieties have a dwarf growth habit to fit with other perennials and in containers too.

Start canna rhizomes indoors by mid-March for outdoor transplanting after frost, usually after Memorial Day in most northern areas. Prepare your planting site with composted humus, peat moss, or rotted manure to improve the soil. Space most 18–24 inches and water thoroughly. As shoots emerge, apply 5-10-5 or 5-10-10 fertilizer at the rate of 3–4 pounds per 100 square feet, or as your fertilizer package directs. Keep plants watered during summer so they don't dry out. Deadheading encourages more blooms. When frost blackens the plants, simply dig them up, cut off foliage, leaving an inch on the rhizomes, dry them, and store in a cool, dark place.

Good dwarf varieties include Maudie Malcolm, the earliest and a long bloomer, and Wyoming Dwarf, a deep gold with an orange eye and a height of 2 feet. Kankok has pinstriped foliage. Lucifer is small for limited space. For tall, try Tropical Sunrise and Reinne Charlotte. You can also try growing cannas from seeds offered in catalogs that yield dwarf plants with rose, red, salmon, and yellow blooms in about 90 days.

CHRYSANTHEMUMS

Chrysanthemums are the undisputed favorite fall flower. Hybridizers around the world have developed a wide range of floral shapes, sizes, and colors, including various shades of pink, purple, red, yellow, bronze, orange, and white. As a landscaping plant, mums make a beautiful display for the home garden. They can showcase an entrance way, sparkle in a bed or border, and provide cut flowers. The National Chrysanthemum Society is dedicated to researching, teaching, and disseminating procedures for the propagation and cultivation of chrysanthemums, as well as promoting a wider interest in growing them. Details are available from the society's secretary, Galen Goss, 10107 Homar Pond Dr., Fairfax Station, VA 22039. Or visit their website at www.mums.org.

For dynamic fall color, the chrysanthemum undoubtedly is one of the most exciting flowers that can be grown in the home landscape. Garden mums require a minimum amount of care and do well even under adverse conditions. And hundreds of cultivars are available. For greater appeal, consider various types such as singles, anemones, decoratives, pompons, spoons, spiders, and standards. Be careful when you see a mum described as "hardy," because not all mums are hardy in all parts of the country. In years past, mums were promoted for fall planting. Many didn't overwinter. Today you can buy prestarted mums in pots for spring planting so they set sturdy root systems. You also can buy started plants by mail order or plant from seeds in spring.

Mums prefer a sunny location and well-drained soil. Most should be spaced 18–24 inches apart, but vigorous, larger growing cultivars need 30–36 inches to let plants develop to their maximum for best floral show. Set transplants or remove potted mums and set in ground the same depth they were growing in containers.

To promote the most profuse flowering, apply a complete dry fertilizer such as 5-10-5 or equivalent at the rate of 2–3 pounds per 100 square feet of bed. Always water dry fertilizer into the ground after it is applied. Soluble fertilizers such as 15-30-15, or even 20-20-20, are satisfactory to use by following the application directions on the package. In summer, pinch plants back to produce compact plants with more flowers. Simply remove the top growth by pinching shoots off between your thumb and forefinger, leaving two or three leaves on the shoot whenever it becomes 3–4 inches long. Do this when fertilizing, usually once a month from May to July. Make the last pinch no later than August 1 so you don't eliminate desired flower buds from the plants.

Keep weeds under control by cultivation or, better yet, with mulch so your plants don't compete for moisture and nutrients. Mums respond to ample water, so apply enough water to soak the soil to a depth of 4–6 inches. Soaker hoses are good investments for use in all parts of your perennial gardens, and a timer is a big help too. Mums have few insect or disease problems, but when they do, check with your county Cooperative Extension agent for the best control methods recommended in your area.

Follow these steps to help mums survive in colder temperatures. When frost kills the tops, cut off the dead stems and remove. In a northern area, add about 3–4 inches of mulch over the mums for winter, and remove mulch by spring. That often helps them come through and grow again.

Some recommended cultivars in white include Encore, Nicole, and Tolima. For yellow, try Goldmine and Target. Naomi and Sundoro are both pink. Also try red Remarkable and bronze Grace or Triumph.

DAHLIAS

The dahlia is the national flower of Mexico, which is logical since that glorious flower originated in the mountains of Mexico and Guatemala. With thanks to the American Dahlia Society and dahlia lovers too, here are ways you can enjoy these dramatic floral wonders.

Dahlias, *Dahlia variabilis*, are a popular addition to the landscape. They grow to heights of 1–6 feet and their flowers offer a variety of shapes and sizes, reaching 2–12 inches. Their color range includes orange, pink, purple, red, scarlet, yellow, and white. Some flowers are striped or tipped with a different color. Dahlias begin blooming in early summer and continue to frost. There are 18 classifications of form with such descriptives as semi-cactus, laciniated, waterlily, and collarette. In addition, there are 15 different colors and combinations, ranging from yellow and orange to red, flame, and variegated. Pick your pleasure and grow them well.

Dahlias can be started indoors in individual pots with damp peat moss and vermiculite. They also can be planted directly in the desired outdoor location, but because they are weather sensitive, plant or transplant outdoors only when danger of frost has passed. Dahlias prefer sunny areas with well-drained, sandy soil and a pH of about 6.5. Dig deeply, 10–12 inches, and improve the soil with compost. Replace about half the soil and place the tubers flat, cover with the remaining soil, and tamp lightly. Space tubers 12–36 inches apart, depending on variety. Plant dahlias so crowns are just above soil level. Water after planting and again when shoots appear. Dahlias tend to have shallow roots, so be careful when cultivating. About the end of June, mulch plants with compost, aged manure, peat, or straw, and water regularly if rain is insufficient, but avoid wetting foliage.

For best blooming results, dahlias require a rich soil and feeding. Mix a commercial fertilizer low in nitrogen, such as a 5-20-20, into the soil a month before planting. Some veteran dahlia growers suggest adding 2–4 inches of organic matter such as compost or well-aged manure and 2–4 pounds of 8-8-8 or 10-10-10 per 100 square feet before planting. As plants grow, provide a monthly feeding. If using a granular fertilizer, water it thoroughly after application. Prize-winning growers have suggested fertilizing monthly with a water-soluble fertilizer or a granular, using 2–3 pounds of 5-10-10 or 10-10-10 per 100 square feet in July. That is 2–3 tablespoons per square foot. Excessive nitrogen can result in foliage production at the expense of flower production. A second application of fertilizer may be needed for sandy soil or during rainy seasons. Do not fertilize dahlias after mid-August.

To achieve larger and more flowers during the season, pinch and disbud dahlias. Note that buds tend to grow in threes—two on the sides, and a top one—so remove the side buds to let the central bud develop into a large bloom. When the plants reach a height of 3–4 inches, pinch the terminal bud just above the second pair of leaves to produce two main stems. This keeps plants more compact and encourages more stems for blooms. An exception is Royal Dahlias, which do not require pinching. Watch for blooms to mature, and cut flowers when fully opened. Cut them in the early morning for the longest-lasting cut flowers. As soon as you cut blooms, plunge their stems into water.

Dig up dahlia tubers before winter freeze, after frost kills the foliage. Cut the stalk approximately 6 inches above the tuber, and mark the tubers with tags to identify their names. Let tubers dry thoroughly and then pack them carefully in dry sand, peat moss, or sawdust and store in a cool, dry place at 40–45°F. Check tubers in a few weeks and again in January for signs of shriveling, and add a small amount of moisture if shriveling has occurred. Dahlias can be temperamental, so don't expect 100 percent survival.

Come spring, separate the tubers from the stalks, leaving 1 inch of stalk attached to each tuber, which must have an eye or bud to bloom. Take tubers out of storage in March or April, locate eyes on each, and with a sharp knife divide tubers with a portion of crown attached so that each piece has its own eye. You can then pot them individually to have well-started plants for a longer blooming season outdoors, but always wait until frost danger has passed.

Some pests include aphids and slugs early, and mites in mid to late summer. Thrips, earwigs, caterpillars, and wasps may occasionally attack too. Ask your Cooperative Extension agent for the latest recommended controls. Destroy any diseased plants with abnormal or deformed crowns.

Some glorious varieties are Tahiti Sunrise, with 6-inch bicolor blooms; Purple Taiheijo, the biggest, with 12-inch flowers on compact plants; Hawaii, with tricolored 8-inch flowers; Bodacious, with bold, flame-colored 10-inch blooms; and Margaret Ellen, with white and rose blooms. There are many more, so check around and try some. To learn much more about dahlias, contact the American Dahlia Society through Alan A. Fisher, ADS Membership, 1 Rock Falls Ct., Rockville, MD 20854, telephone: 301-424-6641. His e-mail address is AFisherADS@yahoo.com.

DAYLILIES

Daylilies (*Hemerocallis*) are a hardy, versatile perennial for gardeners nationwide. Each flower lasts only one day. Fortunately there are many flower buds on each daylily flower stalk, and many stalks in each clump of plants, so most daylilies flower for several colorful weeks.

Daylilies are a common sight today because they are so easy to grow, have few insect and disease problems, and are available in many colors. In addition, they tolerate heat, drought, salt, compacted soil, and various pH levels, according to the American Hemerocallis Society, a nonprofit, educational group devoted to the promotion, propagation, and advancement of daylilies. They say a daylily is available for almost any landscape condition.

Hybridizers have made great improvements in daylilies, providing colors ranging from pastels, yellow, orange, pink, vivid red, crimson, purple, nearly true-blue, and dramatic blends. Scan mail order catalogs and you'll discover a new world of delightful daylilies to beautify your home grounds.

Most daylilies prefer full sun but will tolerate partial shade with a minimum of 6 hours of direct sun per day. Fact is, light-colored cultivars need full sun to bring out their colors. However, many red and purple cultivars benefit from partial shade. Reblooming daylilies, those that flower more than once during the season, are available. Some flower in the spring and then rebloom in the fall. Others have a succession of bloom periods that offer flowers over several months.

Another advantage is that daylilies grow well in any good garden soil, even clay soil if you improve it with peat moss and sand to make it more friable. Sandy soil should be improved with compost and peat moss for best growing conditions. These plants also like moist but well-drained soil so they can spread naturally. Longtime growers praise daylilies as rugged, vigorous plants that will bloom well for years with little or no care even in poorer soils.

Daylilies are rugged, adaptable, vigorous perennials that endure in a garden for many years. They are good as ground covers planted in masses or on slopes where you can't mow. They will form dense mats in a few years.

Plant daylilies whenever you can work the soil. Till deeply to give their roots room to roam. Dig a hole large enough for roots without bending them. Cover with soil, firm, and water well after planting and each week. Daylilies spread, so dividing is helpful. Dig the entire overgrown plant in early spring and gently pull the fans apart. Cut foliage, leaving only 5–6 inches. Replant so the crown where the root and stems meet is 1 inch below the ground level. Water thoroughly and each week so roots reset well. Mulching after planting stops weed competition, but as plants spread, they fill in their area without much extra care. Because they are vigorous growers, expect to divide plants every 3 or 4 years. Few insects seem to bother daylilies, but if aphids and thrips appear on flower buds, use insecticidal soap or materials recommended by Cooperative Extension agents for your area. Daylilies can benefit from light fertilizer applications that promote better blooming.

Try Sue Rothbauer, a fragrant rebloomer. Bold Tiger is heavily ruffled, and Sunday Gloves and South Seas flower in profusion. Stella d'Ora is low and prolific. You will find many attractive old-timers in catalogs, as well as new, dramatic varieties introduced annually, so see what appeals. Other useful information is available from the American Hemerocallis Society: www.daylilies.org.

GLADIOLUS

The gladiolus is often called the Sword Lily because of the shape of its leaves. There are about 4,000 different gladiolus cultivars, hybrids of gladiolus species that vary in size from floral giants more than 5 feet tall with 6-inch florets to miniatures that have florets under 2.5 inches across. Glads can be found in almost every color of the rainbow. Despite the need to dig up, clean, and store glad bulbs each fall, the plants offer marvelous, dramatic bouquets for very little effort.

Gladiola are very easy to grow. They do well in a wide range of soil types if drainage is good, and they prefer soil with a pH between 6.7 and 7. As one glad gardener said in praise of his favorite flowers, "Most garden soil that will produce a good crop of weeds will also grow good glads with little or no added fertilizer." That's almost a fact. Glads prefer full sunlight but will do reasonably well with a little high shade in early morning or late afternoon. They like good air circulation, so avoid buildings or other obstructions that might impede airflow.

Rototill or spade your ground as you would for any other garden plants. Veteran growers warn that it is best to move your glad planting from one area to another each year to help prevent disease carryover in soil. Take a soil test and apply the amount of nutrients needed from a balanced commercial fertilizer such as 5-10-10 immediately prior to planting, at a rate of 2–3 pounds per 100 square feet. Don't overfertilize.

It helps to grow a cover crop or spread compost or peat moss in fall to till under in spring. After a week or so, plant your glad corms about the time you would plant sweet corn. Avoid wet soils that can rot corms. To achieve continuous blooms for cut flowers, do subsequent plantings at 2-week intervals. Place corms 3–5 inches deep and 4–6 inches apart. For best blooms, invest in the biggest corms that will bloom from 70–100 days from planting.

As glads grow, hill along the rows to help prevent tipping in summer storms. Water well but don't overdo it, to avoid rotting corms. Your plants will tell you their needs, so pay attention to them. Glads need plenty of water but will not tolerate wet feet. Keep weeds under control by hoeing or with a mulch of straw, grass clippings, compost, or peat moss.

Even in the South, you should remove plant tops 6–8 weeks after bloom and discard elsewhere to prevent the spread of disease. It also is best to dig and divide your corms every few years and discard any damaged ones. In northern areas, corms must be dug up or they will freeze and rot in the ground. About 6–8 weeks after blooming, or in the fall, carefully loosen the soil with a spading fork or shovel and you can pull corms up with the plants. Separate the corm from the leaves, discard the old tops to avoid any disease they may carry, and clean the corms with water. Dry in shallow trays for several weeks so a corkish layer forms between the new corm and the old one and roots, and then break off and throw away the old. It pays to dust corms with a combination fungicide/insecticide dust to prevent insects or diseases. Store in mesh bags or open paper bags during winter. Any area can be used, so long as temperatures don't freeze and stay below about 60°F.

Recommended glads include two-toned Regal, a lavender Homecoming, and multicolored Mon Amor. Pepim has old-fashioned pinkish-mauve blooms, Blue Sky has a rich violet-blue color, Green Star is lime green, and Tout a Toi flowers reach 4–5 inches in shades of pink, rose, and cream. Garden centers have collections, and dozens of more exotic varieties are available by mail order. To explore gladiolus growing horizons, visit the North American Gladiolus Council website at www.gladworld.org.

IRIS

Iris can be divided into two major types: bulbous and rhizomatous. The bulbous types are described in chapter 9, the spring bulb chapter, where they rightfully belong. The rhizomatous types belong in their own category and are included here with America's favorite perennials. These iris can further be divided into three groups. Bearded iris are characterized by broad leaves, fleshy rhizomes, and a beard or pattern of hairs on the falls, which are downturned petals. Bearded iris are often called German iris, dwarf iris, border iris, or flag iris. Beardless iris are characterized by narrower leaves, thick rhizomes, and smooth falls. These include Siberian iris, Japanese iris, and many species iris. Crested iris, characterized by slender rhizomes and cockscomb-like crests on the falls, include *Iris cristata* and *Iris tectorum*.

Most rhizomatous iris prefer full sun and well-drained soil. Always plant the rhizomes horizontally. Look carefully to be sure you have the leaves up and roots down on the dried rhizomes, and never, ever plant the rhizomes more than 1 inch deep. Rhizomes must be at the surface and exposed for iris to grow properly.

Iris have a color range that rivals the rainbow in an astounding array of varieties. Iris specialists and general mail order catalogs provide selections that will treat the eye. All have their fond supporters, who adopt some special language or terms about their favorite flowers. Iris descriptions have their own specialized vocabulary. Iris can be categorized according to such characteristics as type, style of color pattern, season of bloom, height of bloom stem, and American Iris Society Awards received. To make your life simpler, here are some basics.

Bearded iris are identified by thick bushy hairs on the upper part of the falls. Within the bearded group, the American Iris Society has designated different categories based on stem height and bloom time. Tall bearded iris are the queens of the iris world, bearing magnificent 6- or 7-inch blooms on stems 25–40 inches high. Flowers are available in every color of the spectrum, growing on branched stems with up to 12 buds each. These later blooming flowers are the most popular of the bearded iris group. Arilbred iris come from crosses between tall bearded iris and aril species and grow best in warm and dry parts of the country because they are more tender.

Border bearded and table iris are small versions of the tall bearded types, with stem heights 16–28 inches and the same later summer blooming time. Intermediate iris have stems 16–28 inches but bloom just after the dwarf iris and before tall bearded. For extended early blooms, use standard dwarf bearded, which grow 9–15 inches tall with flowers 2–4 inches wide that bloom just after the miniature dwarf bearded iris in early spring. The miniature are the tiniest and earliest bearded iris, up to 10 inches in height with flowers up to 3 inches. Many gardeners like these with spring flowering bulbs for rock gardens and in borders for a blanket of color.

Beardless iris is the largest, most diverse group. They are characterized by the absence of a beard on their petals. This group contains hundreds of different species. Siberian iris, contrary to the name, are not native to Siberia but are very cold hardy, vigorous, and relatively maintenance free. Flowers are 4–5 inches wide on stems 2–4 feet tall. Louisiana iris are rooted in the southern states and are naturally a water or bog plant. Flowers reach 4–6 inches on stalks up to 4 feet high. They actually are cold hardy and disease resistant and can be at home almost everywhere in the garden as well as on the edges of ponds or streams. That gives you another plant to grace wet areas.

Most iris will thrive in any well-drained garden soils that get ample sun. If soil is heavy, add coarse sand or composted humus to improve drainage and condition. Iris experts say that gypsum is an excellent soil conditioner that can improve most clay soils. Ideal pH is 6.8, slightly acidic, but iris are fairly tolerant. Adjust the pH of your soil by adding lime to acidic soils or sulfur to alkaline soils. Soil testing gives you the best guide for soil fertility and acidity.

Iris do best in full sun, and need at least half a day of sun to bloom properly. They also need good drainage and like growing on a slope or in raised beds. In hot climates, give them some shade. Best time to plant is in July, August, or early September, because roots of newly planted iris must have time to become well established before the growing season ends.

When you select the desired site, plant the tops of iris rhizomes so they are exposed and roots spread out into the soil. Don't cover the rhizome with soil or mulch because it must be exposed to grow properly and produce desired floral results. Firm the soil around each rhizome, and water to settle the soil. Then be sure the top is exposed. A common mistake is to plant rhizomes too deeply. Space plants 12–24 inches apart. They will spread as they grow, and clumps will only need to be divided every few years. Water thoroughly after planting for several weeks, but as they mature, iris tend to do well without much water unless the weather is very dry. Excess watering can damage rhizomes.

To encourage best blooming, focus on proper fertilizing. Experts explain that a granular formulation of 6-10-10 is effective in early spring and a second light application about a month after bloom. Avoid high nitrogen fertilizers that promote vegetative growth and may encourage root rot.

Iris will spread, so they must be thinned or divided to avoid overcrowding, usually about every 3 or 4 years. Overcrowded plants won't bloom well. Easiest way to thin is to remove the old divisions at the centers of the clumps, and leave new growth in the ground. Or dig up the entire clump, remove or cut apart, and replant the large new rhizomes. Weed well so rhizome tops get plenty of sun along with the leaves. Remove spent blooms. Follow these basics and you'll be rewarded by glorious iris blooms for years to come. One of the best iris growers for several generations has been Schreiner's Iris Gardens in Salem, Oregon. Visit their website at www.schrienersgardens.com.

LILIES

Lilies are a colorful addition to gardens. True lilies include Easter lilies, Asiatic lilies, turk's-cap lilies, tiger lilies, Madonna lilies, Canada lilies, and Oriental lilies, about 100 lily species, hundreds of hybrids, and about 7,000 registered varieties! Best of all, this favorite perennial is easy to grow without much effort in even poorer garden areas. Chose early, mid, and late cultivars to enjoy lilies from June through mid-September in glorious, colorful profusion. Happily, lilies are fairly hardy and require only minimal care.

Note that other plants that have "lily" as part of their common name, such as daylily, are really not true lilies. True lilies belong to the genus *Lilium* and grow from bulbs made of fleshy, overlapping scales with no protective covering. They also have stiff stems with narrow straplike leaves. The dramatic showy flowers develop at the tip of each stem and may be trumpet, bowl, or bell shaped. Some nod downwards, while others face outwards, and all are available in luxurious colors, as you'll see when you review mail order catalogs. Some are deliciously fragrant.

The North American Lily Society can provide many details about these graceful flowers. Lilies are divided into different types and divisions. Asiatic hybrids are earliest to bloom and easiest to grow. Martagon hybrids are tall, down-facing lilies that prefer shade. Trumpet hybrids bear huge, fragrant flowers. Aurelians are midseason bloomers. Orientals are among the easiest to grow, especially in hot areas. Asiatic and Oriental are featured here as the two most popular types.

Asiatic lilies are among the easiest to grow because they are very hardy and thrive in various soils if they are well drained. A recent problem is the Asiatic beetle that has invaded the United States and feasts on these lovely plants, totally ruining flowers, leaves, and stems. There is hope with pesticides, but these beetles are a major threat.

Oriental lilies have become increasingly popular, thanks to their exotic, large, and often fragrant blooms. By improving the soil with organic materials, you can help these lilies thrive.

Lilies tend to grow tall, so keep that habit in mind when selecting sites for them. Some gardeners have success with Easter lilies outdoors, but other lilies offer far more colorful and dramatic highlights and displays.

Prepare the soil by adding organic matter and perhaps a cover crop in fall to till under before spring planting. Lilies can be planted in spring or from mid-September through mid-October. Prepotted lilies can be added all season long. Lily bulbs are more tender than spring-flowering types and must not be allowed to dry out. Be prepared to plant them when bought or received by mail. Plant Asiatic and Oriental lilies in full sunlight so they get 8 hours of direct sun daily. Martagon hybrids, a group of turk's-cap lilies, are favored because they bloom well in shadier conditions.

Plant lilies in groups of three to five identical bulbs, about 8–12 inches apart, depending on the size of the mature lilies. Dig down and plant the smaller lily bulbs 2–4 inches deep and larger bulbs 4–6 inches deep. Be sure to record which varieties are in which spot, and be aware that they'll need dividing and replanting every 3 or 4 years. Underline this key fact in your garden notes: Never plant lilies where standing water collects, such as runoff from rooftops. They require well-drained soil to prosper.

Apply 2–3 inches of mulch after the plants emerge to thwart weed competition for nutrients and water. Before winter, add 3–4 more inches of mulch to delay soil freezing and allow roots to continue growing. Mulch also helps prevent frost heaving of ground. Veteran lily growers advise leaving mulch in place in spring until danger of frost has passed. Then, remove some of the mulch as plants emerge.

Spring is the time to apply a phosphorus-rich formula such as 5-10-10. Most good gardeners know that modern, slow-release or timed-release fertilizers work well. Follow the label instructions for the type you use. Lilies have an advantage because few pests bother them. If problems occur, check with your Cooperative Extension agent for best remedies in your area.

Water early in the day and at the base of the plant rather than overhead. Soaker houses are ideal, wound through your perennial beds that include lilies. After blooms fade, deadhead flowers so no plant energy is wasted trying to set seeds. Remove old foliage in late fall after frost.

Some dramatic lilies are Strawberry Shortcake, Purple Sensation, and Lollipop, a bicolor shorter variety. Muscadet is a dwarf type for July bloom outdoors and in containers too. Check the North American Lily Society website at www.lilies.org for added knowledge.

PEONIES

Peonies are perennial favorites in the flower garden, producing exquisite, large, fragrant blossoms for cut flowers. Two types are generally grown in the home landscape: *Paeonia* hybrids, or garden peony, and *Paeonia suffruticosa*, or tree peony, but by far the favorite is the garden type. There are various flower forms, from single to anemone, Japanese, semi-double, and double, which are all well displayed in garden catalogs. Flowering usually lasts 1–2 weeks in late spring to early summer, but you can extend the blooming time by planting early, mid, and late season bloomers. Colors today are plentiful, so pick your pleasure and plant more of these perennial delights. For extra pleasure, consider trying a tree peony or two. Garden peonies grow 3–4 feet tall, but tree peonies can reach 4–6 feet. They are more temperamental than garden peonies but provide dramatic displays.

Peonies prefer sunny locations and well-drained soils but will tolerate a wide range of soil types. Best growth is in deep soil rich in organic matter with a pH between 6.5 and 7.5. To protect them in cold areas, add several inches of mulch in the fall and remove in spring. Peonies need a dormant period, so they are not well suited for southern gardens.

Prepare soil deeply before planting, adding compost and rotted manure to enrich organic content. Dig a large hole about 3 feet in diameter to accept the ample roots, add a scoop of dehydrated manure and half a cup of bonemeal, fill one-third with rich soil, and tamp down and water. Then place the peony plant in the hole with the eyes (small, red-colored buds) just 1–2 inches below the soil's surface. Fill the hole with soil, and water well. Once settled, peonies can grow undisturbed for many years. If they overgrow, use a spading fork to carefully lift out the clump and wash away the soil to expose the eyes. With a sharp knife, divide the clump into sections that have three to five eyes and a good root section. Replant in that spot or use divisions to expand your peony garden.

Follow the one-third rule for cutting peonies. Cut one-third of the blooms on one-third of their stem's length at 3–4 years old. Be sure to leave one-third of the blooms on peonies that are 5 or more years old. Cut early in the morning or late afternoon, strip off foliage below blooms, and put in a vase with room-temperature water and floral preservative for lasting display. Good growing tips are available from national peony expert Keith Swenson at P.O. Box 164, Delano, MN 55328, or e-mail info@swensongardens.com.

Peonies don't face many problems, but some diseases may occur, such as Botrytis blight and leaf blotch. Ask your garden center or Cooperative Extension agent for latest control recommendations. Ants often appear on the plants, but they are mainly attracted to the sugary liquid secreted by flower buds and don't do any real harm. At times, peonies don't bloom properly. That may be caused by overcrowding, competition from nearby plants or trees, lack of sun as trees shade peonies, and sometimes diseases. More often, peonies bloom abundantly, so consider wire hoops or stakes to support peony plants when heavy blooms appear. In late fall, after foliage is killed by frost, cut the stems back to 2 inches above ground and discard the cuttings to prevent possible disease transfer. Veterans warn not to compost peony foliage.

Peony expert Keith Swenson suggests that gardeners extend their peony blooming time by selecting peonies that will bloom early, mid, and late. By doing this, you can enjoy up to six weeks of color. He also points out that the intersectional hybrid called Bartzella actually will bloom over 2–4 weeks itself once it reaches maturity. Some recommended

varieties among singles are the rosy Bowl of Beauty and deep-red President Lincoln. Semi-double or double peonies include the brilliant red Kansas and blush-pink Nick Shavlor. You'll find more about peonies and varieties at the American Peony Society website: www.americanpeonysociety.org.

MORE POPULAR PERENNIALS

Perennials are mainstays in your landscape. Once planted they grow, mature, and return every year to reward you with their beauty. In northern areas, many perennials die back and sprout again next year. But in southern areas, they may grow continuously. Because many perennials don't flower their first season when grown from seed, veteran gardeners recommended buying started plants. As the trend toward perennials continues, many chains and garden centers now feature a wide variety of popular perennials.

Perennials have many advantages. Except for a few bulbous types, you don't need to plant them each year. Once established, they usually come back year after year, even for decades. Others fade away after a few years, so they will need replacing or dividing and renovation. Some require dividing every few years to maintain their blooming profusion. One disadvantage is that, unlike annuals, which usually bloom for a long period, perennials often have shorter blooming periods, 2–8 weeks.

However, by selecting early, mid, and late season varieties in a given plant family, you easily extend the bloom season. As you consider adding perennials, look at their foliage, which often also is appealing. A final point to consider is cost: starting perennials from seed and waiting for the second year before they begin blooming is less expensive than buying prestarted plants that offer bloom the first season in your garden.

Here are some tips to plan your perennial plantings. Select a location for perennials by learning their needs for sun, soil type, and water, and consider how they will blend with other landscape plants. You may want them in beds or borders for cutting, or just as part of the overall landscape. Plot out their place on paper, because these are long-term assets for your home grounds. A pencil on paper takes less work than digging and moving plants themselves.

Easiest way to get started with perennials is to purchase nursery-grown plants at local outlets or through mail order or online catalogs. Mail order nurseries usually ship plants at the right time for planting in your area. The right time to plant perennials varies from species to species. A rule of green thumb is that spring is a good time to plant perennials that flower in summer and fall. Late summer and fall is a good time to plant perennials that flower in spring and early summer.

Your choice of perennials is pages long, as you'll see in mail order catalogs. Many new, improved varieties are introduced each year. Focus on these key points. Select plants for flower color, bloom period, height, and light requirements and their contribution to your total landscape appearance. Bloom times may vary with weather, soil conditions, and care. Tall perennials such as delphinium, foxglove, and hollyhock often require staking, so consider dwarf varieties in windy areas. Another key to success is to group species according to their cultural requirements, such as moist or dry locations, sun or shady preferences, cold hardiness, and other special needs.

There isn't space to write about every perennial in this book, so you'll find the most popular ones here, based on surveys of gardeners nationwide. As you consider which perennials to add, check growth needs in catalogs. Although many thrive for years,

even decades, other perennials may lose their vigor after 3–4 years. That's not a major problem, because you can divide parent plants or replace old ones with improved new varieties. We're fortunate that most perennial plants may be divided to produce new plants, may be grown from seeds, or may be produced from cuttings or bought as started plants locally or by mail order.

Follow the basic cultural considerations for perennials in this chapter. You should, of course, follow specific planting and care directions that come with specific perennials you buy. Remember that when you plant a perennial, it will be in the same spot for several years, maybe much longer. Therefore, prepare the ground more thoroughly to give your plants a happy home.

BRIEF FACTS ABOUT POPULAR PERENNIALS

Here are brief tips about some of the most popular perennials.

Balloon flower (*Platycodon grandiflorus*) grows well in sun to partial shade in well-drained soils with uniform moisture. Plants grow 18–24 inches tall and produce flowers resembling balloons in mid summer. Balloon flower is slow to emerge in spring, so be careful digging near it. Two selections are Double Blue and Mariesii.

Bee balm (*Monarda didyma*) is an aromatic, ornamental perennial that attracts hummingbirds to its distinctive, attractive flowers. It grows 2–4 feet tall and can spread if underground roots aren't controlled. Bee balm prefers full sun in soils that retain moisture, and it blooms in early to mid summer. If you remove spent blooms, the plant will continue to flower for weeks. Be sure it has ample moisture, because it won't thrive in dry soil. Good cultivars include Mahogany and Blue Stocking.

Black-eyed Susan (*Rudbeckia fugida*) provides masses of yellow-petaled blooms with brown centers from summer to fall. Plants grow upright about 2–3 feet tall and prefer full sun to light shade in average garden soil. Once set, they are fairly drought tolerant. *Rudbeckia sullivantii* is the true perennial type. Prairie Sun is an All America Selection winner. Indian Summer has gigantic golden flowers and a vigorous branching habit, blooming July to frost. Goldilocks flowers are a beautiful golden orange with dark centers.

Blazing star (*Liatris spicata*) has purplish flower spikes growing 1–3 feet tall. The plants bloom in late summer to early fall and prefer sun to light shade in well-drained soil. Once established, they can tolerate some drought. Good cultivars are Kobold and August Glory.

Blanket flower (*Gaillardia* spp.) is easy to grow, tolerant of heat, humidity, and poor soil, and even handles drought well. All America Selection Gold Medal winner Arizona bears very heavily and earlier than all others and gives months of bloom. Space plants 20 inches apart. Burgundy is deep, wine-red and blooms from June to frost. Fanfare has fluted trumpets and is super hardy in all types of soils and conditions.

Bleeding heart (*Dicentra spectabilis*) blooms from late spring to early summer and prefers partial shade and adequate moisture. It matures about 2–3 feet high. Watered well, its foliage remains attractive well into fall. During dry periods, the foliage yellows and may disappear by mid-June as plants go dormant. Bleeding heart is an excellent perennial for shady sites where soil is moist but well-drained. Alba is a fine white variety.

Butterfly bush (*Buddleia*) has sweetly scented blooms on 12-inch flower spikes. Plants will bloom the first year from seed if started early, but flowers then bloom on new wood, so prune each spring.

Prune back to 12 inches. Plants grow 6–8 feet tall with white, lilac, and deep-pink blooms.

Butterfly weed (*Asclepias*) is a sun-loving perennial that handles heat and drought, is winter hardy, and tolerates damp soil. Sow in spring or fall. Cinderella has rose-purple blooms in fragrant 2-inch clusters. Space 2 feet apart. *Ascelpias tuberosa* is an orange butterfly weed worth a try to attract butterflies to your garden.

Catmint (*Nepeta nervosa*) is heat and drought tolerant and actually repels destructive insects while attracting bees. It has aromatic gray-green foliage that spreads 18–24 inches on compact plants that can be used as a border or container plant. Felix is a top variety. Blue Carpet blooms the first year from seed and gives bedding color year after year of violet-blue blooms even in poor, dry soils.

Clematis are easy to grow and prefer rich, porous, alkaline soil that allows roots to expand deeply. They need full sun but shaded roots, which a ground cover or mulch will provide. These vine plants require a year or two for setting deep roots and then reward you for many years. Avant Garde bears hundreds of 2-inch, semi-double blooms of magenta-burgundy. Niobe is a prime red clematis with 6-inch flowers. Will Goodwin is a true-blue, summer bloomer. Put these delightful flowering vines to use wherever you need to screen an unsightly area or just want to grow up more beautifully.

Columbine (*Aquilegiavulgaris* and hybrids) grow 1–3 feet tall and produce attractive blue-green foliage. In full sun to partial shade and moist soil with good drainage, these plants will provide bright flowers for weeks in spring. They can tolerate dry soil and shade, which tends to lengthen the blooming period. Prestart indoors to get blooms the first season. Columbine tends to reseed and spread, so you'll have new plants for other spots or trading with neighbors. Musi Harmony hybrids are lovely. Clementine blooms profusely and attracts butterflies. Rocky Mountain is a true-blue variety. Origami mix has blue, pink, red, rose, and yellow blooms on plants 14–18 inches tall that bloom all summer, as most other columbines will do.

Coneflower (*Echinacea* spp.) is an excellent performer, thriving in summer heat in well-drained soil in full sun. It matures 2–4 feet tall and blooms best in early summer but can continue into frost. The common purple coneflower is *Echinacea purpurea*. Magnus is a cultivar with huge 6-inch blooms for cut flowers and drying. Bravado is a purplish beauty. White Swan is snow white and fragrant. Another coneflower species is *Echinacea angustifolia*, a small variety. Paradoxa produces yellow blooms. Coneflowers have gained wide popularity for their long bloom period. Veteran growers believe slight shade improves flower color.

Coreopsis (*Coreopsis grandiflora*) is another summer garden favorite. It grows 1–2 feet tall and bears flowers from May through August if you remove the whole flower stalk after bloom, not just the flower head. It grows very well in full sun in well-drained soil but is tolerant of dry soil. In moist, fertile soil, it tends to droop. Good cultivars include Early Sunrise, an All America Selection Gold Medal winner, and Sunray. Crème Brulee has golden-yellow flowers about an inch wide on compact plants from summer to fall. Coreopsis tolerates heat, humidity, cold, poor soil, and drought, so it is a popular choice.

Daylily (*Hemerocallis* spp.) has gained amazing popularity with the introduction of many new varieties in recent years. This reliable perennial does well in sun to light shade in a variety of soils and can fill in banks or areas difficult to mow. Daylilies thrive in soils that are well drained and rich in organic matter, and they benefit from an addition of

superphosphate in the spring. Hundreds of glorious cultivars are available, and plants grow 1–4 feet tall. Newer varieties bloom from late spring to late summer. Recommended varieties include Bold Times, heavily ruffled and intense, with orange petals and 4-inch blooms in midseason. Sue Rothbauer is a fragrant rebloomer. South Seas blooms profusely during long midsummer weeks, producing tangerine-color flowers with ruffled edges. Sunday Gloves has fragrance. Stella de Oro blooms from late spring to frost, is a fine plant for ground cover, and is a winner of the Stout medal, the highest for daylilies. Plant 8–10 inches apart. Many other varieties provide colorful contrasts and dramatic blooming displays.

Delphiniums produce dramatic cut flowers. Start indoors and transplant into full sun with shelter from winds. Water freely and most will bloom the first season. When plants are established, cut back stems nearly to the ground for repeat blooms in fall. Mulch and regular watering are helpful to encourage most prolific growth. The Summer variety begins blooming weeks earlier and is heat tolerant and easy to grow. Blooms reach 1.5 inches in big, loose clusters on compact, well-branched plants. Place 6–8 inches apart. Centurian is heat tolerant and bears majestic spires with large double blooms during summer. Sky Blue is a Fleuroselect gold medal winner. Fountains is ideal for small gardens and is available in cherry, dark blue, and other hues. Aurora and Magic Fountains are two others that seed firms offer for great delphinium harvests.

Foxglove (*Digitalis* spp.) grows well in part shade in the South and sun in northern gardens. Blooms are large, trumpet shaped, and dramatic outdoors and in arrangements. Camelot hybrid is heavy flowering the first year, producing tubular florets with secondary spikes on strong stems. Cooler areas encourage higher performance. Foxy is prolific with long-blooming flowers in 5 months from seed and may reach 3 feet tall. Blends produce creamy yellow-pink and rose-red blooms in early to late summer. Grandiflora is a rare yellow foxglove.

Goldenrod (*Solidago*) hybrids are favored flowers in England. It is time we appreciated them here as a colorful, golden perennial. Forget that old tale that goldenrod causes hayfever. The pollen is too heavy. The culprit actually is ragweed. Goldenrod grows best in late summer to early fall. Plants grow 1–3 feet tall in full sun to very light shade and prefer well-drained soil of average fertility. Try Golden Baby and Peter Pan.

Lenten rose (*Helleborus*) is an overlooked but worthy perennial. It provides a long-blooming plant for shade with evergreen foliage. Plants are virtually untroubled by pests, disease, heat, or humidity and actually can bloom in winter. These plants grow 18 inches in almost any soil. You can enjoy a range of colors from purple, red, pink, and yellow to near-black blooms, and they flourish for years even in clay soil. Royal Heritage is a wonder that offers blooms in winter when we all need some color and joy. Best bet is to start them in pots and transplant outdoors, spacing 15 or more inches apart. Try a few different varieties and see how they catch your eye when all other plants are dormant.

Hibiscus (*Hibiscus moscheutos*) are available in a range of colors and produce truly dramatic blooms. Belle Hybrid has 9-inch, parasol-shaped flowers and makes a spectacular quick summer hedge. It is pest free, easy to grow, and offers nearly nonstop flowers even during drought. Southern Belle hybrid has immense displays in pink, red, and white, blooming summer to fall. Many gardeners overlook this reliable flower, but try it and see how it fits into your blooming vistas.

Hollyhocks (*Alcea rosea*) can be perennial or annual, depending on the type. These classic old-time farm flowers are making a comeback, now that hybridizers have perfected new varieties. They exude an old-fashioned warmth and are lovely in groups at the back of gardens because they are so tall. Flowers reach 3–5 inches, blooming abundantly on big plants that can be 2 feet wide and 6–8 feet tall. They self-sow and therefore are considered biennials or perennials depending on one's perspective. Old Barnyard mix is classic, with heirloom single blooms that attract hummingbirds, as most Hollyhock varieties do. These can be pink red, yellow, maroon, and pastel colors too, blooming all summer year after year as they reseed. Hollyhocks prefer moist, fertile, well-drained soil. Plant 2 feet apart and let them become a permanent blooming asset. Summer Carnival mix, an All America Selection winner, blooms 4 months from sowing, with 4-inch, semi-double flowers in red, pink, yellow, and white.

Hollyhock mallow (*Malva sylvestris*) bears distinctive 2-inch flowers of deep purple, mauve, and even true blue. They are great for landscape accents and borders. Plant 2 feet apart in sun to part shade. Plants can grow to 36 inches tall and bloom July to frost. Mystic Merlin is a fine variety.

Lily of the Valley (*Convallaria majalis*) provides one of spring's most fragrant flowers. Super easy to grow, it sets masses of small white bells that dangle from deep-green stems for weeks in shady spots. It does well in dry areas where few other flowers prosper, but it can be invasive with its underground rhizomes. It prefers organic rich soil and lots of water during blooming time, from mid to late spring. Plants reach 8–10 inches high. It makes a useful ground cover in shady areas.

Lupines (*Lupinus polyphylus*) are familiar sights in northern gardens and have won friends across

America. They provide spectacular spires of white, pink, violet, blue, red, yellow, and bicolor flowers. Very hardy and long lived with low maintenance, lupines deserve a try by those who haven't met them yet. They prefer well-drained soil in cool areas to perform well. Lupines mature 36 inches tall and bloom summer to fall. Sunrise has an incredibly fragrant, fruity scent with citrus overtones, and it blooms 9 weeks from sowing. It also is heat tolerant. Tutti Fruiti has big, beautiful blooms. Space plants 12–16 inches apart. The plants set deep tap roots, so transplanting is almost impossible, but they do self-seed.

Phlox provide one of the longer-flowering and more fragrant garden plants. Common garden phlox (*Phlox paniculata*) is the most spectacular but prone to powdery mildew. Planting in full sun with good air circulation helps solve that problem. Thin clumps to four to five shoots, and water around the base, not on foliage. Spotted phlox (*Phlox maculata*) offers earlier flowering, darker leaves, and better mildew resistance. Some good cultivars that are mildew resistant are Miss Lingard, Alpha, and Bright Eyes. Another favorite perennial, this plant is prized as a permanent part of landscapes.

Poppies (*Papaver* spp.) are favorites in borders for showy blooms on long stems borne by bushy, compact plants. Oriental poppies (*Papaver orientalis*) are bushy, spreading perennials. Iceland poppies (*Papaver croceum*) bear luscious blooms of soft pastel shades, from summer through several months of display. A different species, Blue Himalayan (*Meconopsis betonicifolia*) has rare sky-blue flowers and does best in cool areas of the northwest and northeast. Corn poppies (*Papaver rhoeas*) and California poppies (*Eschscholzia californica*) are annuals and must be seeded each year. Check mail order firms for different poppy species and varieties. Be sure to order perennial poppies from catalogs or in stores for your permanent garden displays.

Shasta daisy (*Leucanthemum* x *superbum*) provides daisylike blooms throughout summer for cutting and bright garden displays. It prefers sunny sites but tolerates part shade and produces plants 24–30 inches tall. In warmer areas it is almost evergreen. Sow outdoors in early spring. Razy Daisy is packed with petals, with fully double, stunning, buttery-eyed white blooms 2–3 inches wide. Snow Lady has super-early flowers that continue all summer on dwarf plants. White Knight has 5-inch blooms from spring to frost and is disease resistant and bushy.

Sedums (*Sedum* spp.) have bright foliage and an autumn-blooming habit. When your garden looks a bit tired in late summer, sedums can provide a fresh look. They are easy to grow even in heat and drought, offering fresh pink flowers on plants 20 inches tall. *Sedum alboroseum* is an unusual form with striking variegated leaves that sparkle in sunlight. Many other types of sedums are available and are worth exploring for their place providing early fall displays.

Verbena (*Verbena bonariensis*) is easy to grow and offers blooms the first year from spring sowing. Plants 3–4 feet tall bear masses of purplish flowers. Imagination, a moss verbena, is an All America and Fleuroselect winner with intense 2-inch clusters of violet-blue blooms. Verbena's spreading habit makes it a good ground cover, and the lacy foliage is attractive. It is very heat and drought tolerant. For those who want to try a patriotic garden, Park Seeds offers a Verbena Patriotic Collage of red, white, and blue varieties.

Yarrow (*Achillea millefolium*) is worth a try. This old-timer now is available in red, pink, yellow, and other colors. Plants blooms from seeding in 3 months. They have decorative, fernlike foliage for indoor displays. You can start indoors or seed directly in sunny locations with good soil. Check mail order firms for different types.

Naturally, there are many other perennials you can grow and enjoy. You'll find them in the colorful, free, mail order catalogs that are listed in chapter 18. As you look through catalogs, you'll find details about best varieties plus planting and cultivation tips. Some catalogs, like those from Park Seed, Johnny's, and a few others provide excellent growing ideas and advice. It pays to have a few of those useful catalogs on hand for ready reference and as guides for future perennial plantings.

PERENNIAL GROWING BASICS

Perennials are a permanent part of your home landscape, so thoughtful and careful soil or bed preparation is important to ensure years of blooming beauty. A first step is eliminating all perennial weeds even before turning the soil. Roundup, a nonselective, systemic herbicide, is useful to achieve that goal. Apply according to label directions, generally when temperatures are consistently above 50°F. Spring applications are good, but you can use in the fall before planting perennials then.

Once you have killed the weeds, turn soil under to ensure a well drained soil with ample amounts of organic matter. Add compost or peat moss too if soil is overly sandy or has excess clay. See chapter 2 on soil improvement to build that productive growing ground for perennials. Add fertilizer as needed.

Most perennials prefer well-drained soil that can retain moisture for peak plant performance. Be aware that more perennials are killed by soils that remain wet over winter than by cold temperatures. Avoid planting in low areas, and be sure to add organic matter at a rate of about 25–30 percent by volume of soil. That's about 3–4 inches of organic matter on top of the bed and worked in 10 inches deep.

It pays to check the drainage where you plan to grow perennials. Dig a hole 8–12 inches deep and fill it with water. Let it drain away and fill it again. If that water drains in less than 1 hour, your soil drainage probably will be satisfactory. Never overlook the benefits of organic matter. As a dedicated gardener, you should be making your own compost from organic materials. It's easy. All you need to know about creating compost is in chapter 2.

Organic matter truly helps improve both the physical and biological properties of soils when added in sufficient amounts and to sufficient depths. Underline this point. Don't shortcut perennial bed or planting area preparation. Organic matter improves structure and aeration of clay soil and improves moisture and nutrient retention in sandy soil. Compost works best. Rotted manure, which is now available dried in garden supply centers, is next best. Other materials to consider include peat moss and well-composted bark.

In addition to improving soil condition and organic content, it pays to add about 2 pounds of basic 5-10-5 fertilizer per 100 square feet of new garden area and till it under well. Once the preparation is done well in the beginning, you can count on having the right start for rewarding performance from perennials.

PICK PLANTING METHODS

The easiest way to begin with perennials is with started plants that will bloom the year you plant them. Seeds offer much wider varieties, but most perennials need a year to sprout, grow, and set roots for future blooming years. Whichever way you decide, here are planting and cultivation guidelines that apply to perennial gardening.

Many gardeners prefer to buy plants in containers from local garden centers. Containers can range in size from a few inches to 2 gallons. Because the plants are already growing, you get to see what they look like. Another option is mail order of bare root or packaged plants. Plants obtained through mail order usually are for spring planting only. If they arrive before you are ready to plant, keep them cool and keep their roots moist. Most can be held for several weeks this way, but read the directions that came with them to be sure.

Spring is the best planting time, but with container plants, you can get them into the ground during summer and into fall too, before frost arrives. Basically, the earlier perennials are planted, the better, so their root systems develop fully in your garden ground before the first winter. Late fall plantings can be damaged by frost heaving.

Set perennials in the ground at the same depth they were grown in the container. Planting too high can dry out plants. Perennials such as bleeding heart, iris, and peony need shallow planting to flower properly. Check instructions that come with your plants. Water container-grown plants before planting and after and about 1 inch weekly.

Soak bare-root, dormant perennials in water for an hour prior to planting to rehydrate them. Once planted, water the ground again and provide 1 inch per week so they set a proper roothold to be a permanent, beautiful, flowering part of your landscape.

Many older homes have perennial plantings that need renovation every few years. Some plants spread naturally or overgrow. Best time to transplant is in the spring as growth starts. But perennials like iris can be divided in summer. For later dividing, the Green Thumb rule is to wait until plants have flowered and then cut back by half just prior to moving. In hot summer weather, it helps to shade plants and water every few days, so they can recover and grow well.

Mulching saves you weeding work, and it benefits perennials by retaining soil moisture. When you plant new perennial beds, be sure to apply about 2 inches of mulch. Apply additional mulch in the spring as soils start to warm, because natural materials tend to decompose.

Pay attention to water for newly planted beds. Water is a vital part in helping newly planted perennial gardens get well established. Soak plants after planting, and check them regularly to prevent drying out. Mulching reduces watering frequency. The Green Thumb rule is 1 inch of water per week for established plantings. Deep watering encourages perennials to root more deeply and become better able to handle drought conditions.

Hang up the sprinkler hose. Use modern methods. The most efficient way to water perennial gardens is with soaker hoses. Many experienced gardeners weave a soaker hose through the garden and leave it there all summer. When water is needed, they turn on the faucet and water thoroughly. Today, timers are available to automatically start the water flowing. Conceal a hose by covering it with mulch.

Different plants require different amounts of fertilizer. Keep a record of what your plants need when you buy them and give them their due. Most perennials don't require large amounts of fertilizer if soil has been prepared properly. Actually, over-fertilizing produces excessive, soft growth and very few flowers, especially if the fertilizer has too much nitrogen. Follow these key points. Have soil tests made, and apply the amounts of fertilizer required by the results of those tests. Generally, perennials can benefit from 1 pound of nitrogen per 1,000 square feet. Granular fertilizers with a formulation of 12-12-12 or 10-10-10 usually are sufficient. It is smart to read and follow the directions on the package of fertilizer. To thrive and bloom beautifully, plants need to eat well. Feed perennials what they need, and they will reward you abundantly with glorious flowers and appealing landscape.

As part of your permanent landscape, perennials need periodic dividing. Different plants have different needs, so there is no set rule as to when to divide perennials. Some may need division every 3–5 years, others every 8–10 years, and some may not need any unless you think they have become overgrown. Most will give you their own signals: reduced flowering, smaller flowers, changed shape of the plant, loss of vigor, or other odd appearances. Spring is the preferred time to divide most perennials, usually when spring growth begins. But some fleshy-rooted types such as iris, peony, and poppy are best divided in mid to late summer up to very early fall.

Dividing is fairly easy. First, prepare the new sites for your divided plants, so they aren't exposed to drying air too long. Then, dig around the parent plant with a spading fork and lift the entire clump out of the ground. Use a spade or sharp knife to cut the clump into pieces about the size of a quart or gallon container plant. Keep only healthy parts; discard the dead center and any damaged roots. In the process, be sure to keep the plants moist and shaded. After planting, water well and protect these divisions from drying out.

Pay attention to water the first few weeks, so divisions take root properly. Some perennials are more difficult to divide than others because of their root systems. Take your time and you'll get the feel for doing this necessary, periodic, perennial maintenance chore. Remember your goal: to rejuvenate your perennial planting so it can continue to perform the way you intended.

To help you plan your perennial gardens for the most attractive appearance, here are lists of the best plants for different areas, environmental conditions, and landscape look.

Shorter Perennials

Goutweed (*Aegopodium podagraria*)	12 inches
Bugleweed (*Ajuga reptans*)	6 inches
Columbine (*Aquilegia* spp.)	12–36 inches
Sea Thrift (*Armeria maritima*)	6 inches
Silver Mound Artemisia (*Artemisia schmidtiana*)	12 inches
Astilbe, False Spirea (*Astilbe* spp.)	6–48 inches
Aubrieta, False Rockcress (*Aubrieta deltoidea*)	6 inches
Basket of Gold (*Aurinia saxatilis*)	6–12 inches
Heartleaf Bergenia (*Bergenia cordifolia*)	12–18 inches
Carpathian Harebell (*Campanula carpatica*)	6 inches
Snow in Summer (*Cerastium tomentosum*)	6–12 inches
Lily of the Valley (*Convallaria majalis*)	6–12 inches
Pinks (*Dianthus* spp.)	6–12 inches
Fringed Bleeding Heart (*Dicentra eximia*)	12–18 inches
Leopard's Bane (*Doronicum orientale*)	12–18 inches
Blanket Flower (*Gaillardia* x *grandiflora*)	6–24 inches
Sweet Woodruff (*Galium odoratum*)	6 inches
Cranesbill (*Geranium* spp.)	6–36 inches
Coral Bells (*Heuchera sanguinea*)	12–30 inches
Hosta (*Hosta* spp.)	12–48 inches
Candytuft (*Iberis sempervirens*)	6–12 inches
Lavender (*Lavandula angustifolia*)	12–18 inches
Catmint (*Nepeta* x *fassenii*)	12–18 inches
Creeping Phlox (*Phlox subulata*)	6 inches
Pincushion Flower (*Scabiosa caucasica*)	12–18 inches
Sedum, Stonecrop (*Sedum* spp.)	3–12 inches
Veronica (*Veronica* spp.)	6–30 inches

Taller Perennials

Yarrow (*Achillea* spp.)	3–5 feet

Monkshood (*Aconitum* spp.)	3–5 feet	Yellow Corydalis (*Corydalis lutea*)
Japanese Anemone (*Anemone* x *hybrida*)	2–4 feet	Bleeding Heart (*Dicentra* spp.)
Goatsbeard (*Aruncus dioicus*)	5 feet	Foxglove (*Digitalis purpurea*)
Butterfly Weed (*Asclepias tuberosa*)	2–3 feet	Red Barrenwort (*Epimedium* x *rubrum*)
Aster (*Aster* spp.)	3–5 feet	Ferns (various species)
False Indigo (*Baptisia australis*)	3–4 feet	Sweet Woodruff (*Galium odoratum*)
Red Valerian (*Centranthus ruber*)	2–3 feet	Cranesbill (*Geranium* spp.)
Delphinium (*Delphinium* spp.)	4–6 feet	Lenten Rose (*Helleborus orientalis*)
Bleeding Heart (*Dicentra spectabilis*)	2–3 feet	Coral Bells (*Heuchera sanguinea*)
Purple Coneflower (*Echinacea purpurea*)	3–5 feet	Hosta, Plantain Lily (*Hosta* spp.)
Globe Thistle (*Echinops ritro*)	3–4 feet	Deadnettle (*Lamium maculatum*)
False Sunflower (*Heliopsis helianthoides*)	3–4 feet	Lilyturf (*Liriope spicata*)
Daylily (*Hemerocallis* spp.)	1–4 feet	Cardinal Flower (*Lobelia cardinalis*)
Rose Mallow (*Hibiscus moscheutos*)	3–5 feet	Virginia Bluebells (*Mertensia virginica*)
Iris (*Iris* spp.)	1–4 feet	Japanese Spurge (*Pachysandra terminalis*)
Blazing Star (*Liatris* spp.)	2–4 feet	Variegated Solomon's Seal (*Polygonatum odoratum* "Variegatum")
Flax (*Linum perenne*)	2 feet	
Cardinal Flower (*Lobelia cardinalis*)	2–3 feet	Lungwort (*Pulmonaria saccharata*)
Lupine (*Lupinus* hybrids)	3–4 feet	Meadowrue (*Thalictrum* spp.)
Bee Balm (*Monarda didyma*)	2–4 feet	Foam Flower (*Tiarella cordifolia*)
Peony (*Paeonia* spp.)	2–3 feet	Globeflower (*Trollius europaeus*)
Oriental Poppy (*Papaver orientale*)	3–4 feet	
Phlox (*Phlox paniculata*)	2–4 feet	**Perennials for Moist or Wet Sites**
Orange Coneflower (*Rudbeckia fulgida* var. *sullivantii*)	2–3 feet	Goatsbeard (*Aruncus dioicus*)

Perennials for Shady Sites

Bugleweed (*Ajuga reptans*)

Snowdrop anemone (*Anemone sylvestris*)

Columbine (*Aquilegia* x *hybrida*)

Jack-in-the-Pulpit (*Arisaema* spp.)

Wild Ginger (*Asarum canadense*)

European Wild Ginger (*Asarum europaeum*)

Astilbe, False Spirea (*Astilbe* spp.)

Japanese Painted Fern (*Athyrium nipponicum* "Pictum")

Heartleaf Bergenia (*Bergenia cordifolia*)

Siberian Bugloss (*Brunnera macrophylla*)

Black Snakeroot (*Cimicifuga racemosa*)

Lily of the Valley (*Convallaria majalis*)

Perennials for Moist or Wet Sites

Goatsbeard (*Aruncus dioicus*)

Astilbe, False Spirea (*Astilbe* spp.)

Clustered Bellflower (*Campanula glomerata*)

Pink Turtlehead (*Chelone lyonii*)

Delphinium (*Delphinium elatum*)

Hibiscus (*Hibiscus moscheutos*)

Hosta (*Hosta* spp.)

Siberian Iris (*Iris sibirica*)

Japanese Iris (*Iris ensata*)

Ligularia (*Ligularia* spp.)

Cardinal Flower (*Lobelia cardinalis*)

Gooseneck Loosestrife (*Lysimachia clethroides*)

Virginia Bluebells (*Mertensia virginica*)

Bee Balm (*Monarda didyma*)

Obedient Plant (*Physostegia virginiana*)

Rock Soapwort (*Saponaria ocymoides*)

Spiderwort (*Tradescantia* x *andersoniana*)

Globeflower (*Trollius europaeus*)

Great Blue Lobelia (*Lobelia siphilitica*)

Marsh Marigold (*Caltha palustris*)

Queen-of-the-Prairie (*Fillipendula*)

Perennials for Hot and Dry Sites

Yarrow (*Achillea* spp.)

Wall Cress (*Arabis caucasica*)

Sea Thrift (*Armeria maritima*)

Silver Mound Artemisia (*Artemisia schmidtiana* "Silver Mound")

Silver King Artemisia (*Artemisia ludoviciana* "Silver King")

Butterfly Weed (*Asclepias tuberosa*)

Basket of Gold (*Aurinia saxatilis*)

False Indigo (*Baptisia australis*)

Mountain Bluet (*Centaurea montana*)

Coreopsis (*Coreopsis* spp.)

Globe Thistle (*Echinops ritro*)

Coneflower (*Echinacea purpurea*)

Sea Holly (*Eryngium amethystinum*)

Blanketflower (*Gaillardia* x *grandiflora*)

Daylily (*Hemerocallis* spp.)

Candytuft (*Iberis sempervirens*)

Red Hot Poker (*Kniphofia* hybrids)

Blazing Star (*Liatris* spp.)

Maltese Cross (*Lychnis chalcedonica*)

Primrose (*Oenothera* spp.)

Russian Sage (*Perovskia atriplicifolia*)

Orange Coneflower (*Rudbeckia fulgida* var. *sullivantii*)

Rock Soapwort (*Saponaria ocymoides*)

Sedum, Stonecrop (*Sedum* spp.)

Lamb's Ears (*Stachys byzantina*)

Veronica (*Veronica* spp.)

Perennials That Attract Hummingbirds

Bugleweed (*Ajuga reptans*)

Columbine (*Aquilegia* spp.)

Butterfly Weed (*Asclepias tuberosa*)

Bellflower (*Campanula* spp.)

Delphinium (*Delphinium elatum*)

Pinks (*Dianthus* spp.)

Bleeding Heart (*Dicentra* spp.)

Foxglove (*Digitalis* spp.)

Coral Bells (*Heuchera sanguinea*)

Daylily (*Hemerocallis* spp.)

Hibiscus (*Hibiscus moscheutos*)

Red Hot Poker (*Kniphofia* hybrids)

Lily (*Lilium* spp.)

Cardinal Flower (*Lobelia cardinalis*)

Lupine (*Lupinus* hybrids)

Bee Balm (*Monarda didyma*)

Perennials That Attract Butterflies

Aster (*Aster* spp.)

Common Yarrow (*Achillea millefolium*)

Ageratum (*Ageratum houstonianum*)

Chives (*Allium schoenoprasum*)

Butterfly Weed (*Asclepias tuberosa*)

Smooth Blue Aster (*Aster laevis*)

Blackberry Lily (*Belamcanda chinensis*)

Butterfly Bush (*Buddleia davidii*)

Purple Coneflower (*Echinacea purpurea*)

Joe-Pye Weed (*Eupatorium maculatum*)

Globe Amaranth (*Gomphrena globosa*)

Lantana (*Lantana* spp.)

Blazing Star (*Liatris spicata*)

Sweet Alyssum (*Lobularia maritima*)

Wild Bee Balm (*Monarda fistulosa*)

Flowering Tobacco (*Nicotiana alata*)

Marjoram (*Origanum majorana*)

Petunia (*Petunia* x *hybrida*)

Obedient Plant (*Physostegia virginiana*)

Mealy-cup Sage (*Salvia farinacea*)

Goldenrod (*Solidago* hybrids)

Mexican Sunflower (*Tithonia rotundifolia*)

Zinnia (*Zinnia elegans*)

GARDENING WITH GRASSES

Grasses have become decorative garden plants in recent years. Not lawn grasses, but truly decorative specialty grasses. With the popularity of ornamental grasses and their use in the landscape, it is a good idea to understand how these plants grow so you can use these plants and avoid disappointment or frustration. Look them up in garden catalogs and you'll get more details about specific varieties plus pictures.

Basically, grasses respond and start to grow based on temperature. Some start to grow in early spring when temperatures are still cool. Others wait until soil is warm and temperatures are more stable. You'll find brief details of different types here.

Cool-season grasses begin growing early in the spring and may even remain semi-evergreen over winter. They seem to do better and have better foliage quality when temperatures are cool or if they are given sufficient water during droughts. If not watered during drought, they tend to go dormant and turn brown. Cool-season grasses may require more frequent division to keep them healthy looking and vigorous or they may die out in the center. For those that remain semi-evergreen, cut off only the brown or winter-injured foliage in spring. Some of the more popular cool-season grasses are fescues, blue oat grass (*Helictotrichon*), tufted hair grass (*Deschampsia*), and autumn moor grass (*Sesleria*)

Warm-season grasses will do better during warmer times of the year, and they remain good looking even when temperatures are high and moisture is limited. They don't begin to show growth until weather becomes stable and soils warm. The previous season's growth usually browns out in the fall, requiring cutting back plants to about 4–6 inches in the spring. Warm-season grasses usually do not require as frequent division as cool-season grasses. Some popular warm-season grasses are northern sea oats (*Chasmanthium latifolium*), Japanese silver grass (*Miscanthus* spp.), hardy pampas grass (*Cortaderia*), fountain grass (*Pennisetum*), switch grass (*Panicum virgatum*), and prairie cord grass (*Spartina pectinata*).

Before planting, you should also understand the growth habit. Grasses can be either clump forming or rhizome forming. The latter is often called "running" grass. **Clump-forming grasses** will grow in very nice, neat mounds or clumps. They tend to mix well with other perennials, don't become invasive, and increase in girth slowly over time. **Rhizome-forming grasses** spread by underground stems and can become very aggressive and invasive. They have their place, but it may not be in a well-tended perennial border, since they can take over an entire area. Be sure to understand how a specific grass grows so you won't be planting a future problem. Some attractive but aggressive grasses are blue lyme grass (*Elymus arenarius*), cord grass (*Spartina*), and ribbon grass (*Phalaris*).

As with any other perennial, success depends on soil preparation before planting and good drainage. Ideally, planting areas should be prepared in the fall by deep tilling of the soil, which facilitates freezing and thawing action during the winter and improves soil tilth and workability. Spring tillage is also satisfactory. While tilling, incorporate ample organic matter. Happily, ornamental grasses do not require high amounts of fertilizer. Adding about 1 pound of a general-purpose fertilizer like 10-10-10 during soil preparation per 100 square feet of planting bed should be sufficient.

Ornamental grasses can be planted in the spring or the fall. Spring planting gives the plants adequate time to develop a good root system before winter. Fall planting is often not as reliable, so you should try to complete fall planting during August and September. Then, provide a light cover of straw or hay during the first winter for best results. Apply the mulch after several hard frosts. Maintaining uniform soil moisture around the plant hastens establishment. Plants planted too deeply tend to develop root diseases or simply rot in the ground.

Ornamental grasses require relatively low levels of fertility. Keep the level of nitrogen low so the plants don't flop over. Leaf color and vigor are good guides to nitrogen requirements. Using one-half to 1 pound of 10-10-10 fertilizer per 100 square feet of garden area, or about one-quarter cup per plant, is sufficient. Apply fertilizer when growth resumes in the spring. An application of a slow-release fertilizer such as Osmocote in the spring is enough to take care of the plants' needs throughout the summer. Fertilizer should be watered in thoroughly.

Watch watering. Plants should be well watered the first season after planting, so they can develop a good root system. Established plants do not need regular watering, but they may need supplemental watering during drought periods. The amount of water will depend on the grass species, the site, and on the quality, size, and growth rate desired.

Grasses do not need to be cut down before winter. In fact, they are attractive when left standing, and the foliage helps to insulate the crown of the plant. Cut back the foliage to about 4–6 inches in the spring before growth resumes. If you remove old growth, spring growth will begin earlier. Old foliage left on the plant can delay the crown's warming and subsequent growth by as much as 3 weeks.

You can divide most ornamental grasses rather easily. Division depends on the spacing and visual appearance of the plants as well as the overall health. Plants suffering from die-out in the center should be divided to improve appearance. Divide them in the spring before growth resumes or in the late summer or fall after the growing season. This year, try your hand at some clumps of ornamental grass. They'll give your landscape a unique new look.

9

BEST-BET BULBS

Flowering bulbs are one of the most reliable blooming beauty additions to any landscape or garden. They offer a wide variety of bloom color, flowering time, plant height, and shape. Bulbs are classified as spring flowering or summer flowering. Spring-flowering bulbs are cold hardy and can be treated as perennials in your landscape. Summer-flowering bulbs are tender. They must be planted in spring after the last frost date and must be dug in the fall and stored.

Spring-flowering bulbs such as crocus, daffodils, and tulips are planted and develop a root system in the fall, then bloom during the following spring. You can use these reliable beauties in dramatic beds and borders, along paths, naturalized in lawns and wildflower areas, and as foundation plantings.

Group bulbs together to add color wherever you wish it. They brighten evergreen shrubs in foundations. Grape hyacinths, crocus, winter aconites, snowdrops, and early maturing daffodils perform well under trees. For beautiful color contrast, match bulb blooming dates with the bloom of shrubs like forsythia and quince or in combination with flowering trees like crabapple or redbud.

Bulb plants are attractive in borders, along a path, or around a vegetable garden or later blooming flower bed. You can also enjoy bulbs as a perennial bed by themselves to add festive color that welcomes spring in March, April, and May before other perennials start to flower.

Crocus and daffodils especially are fine for naturalizing in corners of lawns and under trees. A few groupings of spring bulbs give an appealing point of focus. Naturally, bulbs do well in containers to provide portable color that you can move here and there as you wish, even as decorations for parties. Another value of bulbs is to decorate slopes that are too steep to mow. Spring-blooming bulbs can be followed by summer-blooming daylilies, for example.

As you focus on bulbs in this chapter, check out mail order firms that feature bulbs and similar perennial plants for landscapes. You'll discover a glowingly wide world of color, shapes, and sizes to beautify your home grounds. You can also find bulbs at garden centers and chain stores. Be aware that you should plant bulbs as soon as they arrive or soon after you buy them.

Here's a guide for sequence of blooming.

Early Spring

Snowdrop (*Galanthus nivalis*)

Winter Aconite (*Eranthis hyemalis*)

Crocus (*Crocus* spp.)

Glory of the Snow (*Chionodoxa luciliae*)

Siberian Squill (*Scilla siberica*)

Grecian Windflower (*Anemone blanda*)

Grape Hyacinth (*Muscari botryoides*)

Early Daffodils (*Narcissus* spp.)

Netted Iris (*Iris reticulata*)

Midspring

Species Tulips (*Tulipa* spp.)

Early Tulips (*Tulipa* spp.)

Hyacinths (*Hyacinthus orientalis*)

Medium-Cupped Daffodils (*Narcissus* spp.)

Late Spring

Dutch Hybrid Iris (*Iris* hybrids)

Midseason Tulips (*Tulipa* spp.)

Late Daffodils (*Narcissus* spp.)

Late Tulips (*Tulipa* spp.)

Some plants grow from bulbs, others from rhizomes or tubers. What they have in common is that the plants grow from an underground structure that stores their nutrient reserves to ensure the plants' survival. Bulbous plants are usually perenni-

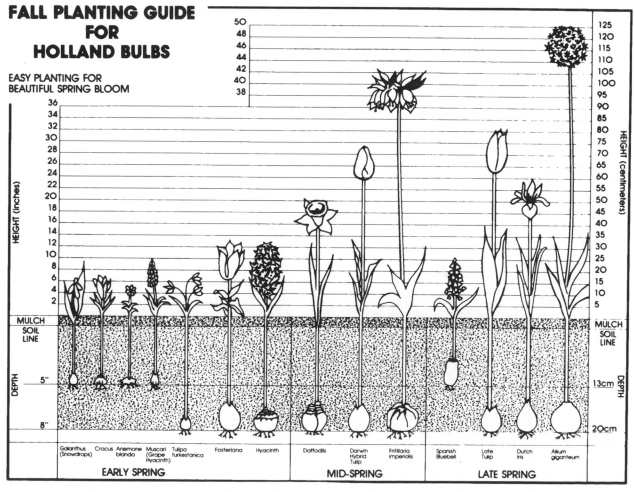

Courtesy of my friends in Holland, here's a useful fall planting guide for Dutch bulbs.

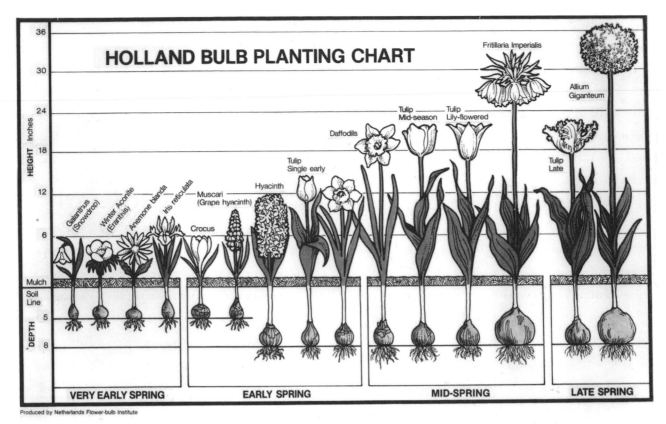

HOLLAND BULB PLANTING CHART

Produced by Netherlands Flower-bulb Institute

From Holland, a useful planting guide to be sure you plant bulbs at the proper depth.

als, having a period of growth and flowering followed by a period of dormancy when they die back to ground level. Spring bulbs flower and then end their growing season in late spring or early summer. Spring bulbs grow unseen underground in the fall and flower the following growing season.

There are six basic types of storage structures: true bulbs, corms, rhizomes, tubers, tuberous roots, and fleshy roots. Many plants such as daffodils form new bulbs, called **offsets**, around the original bulb and can produce new plants. When you see smaller flowers, it is time to dig up and divide the bulbs. Lilies can be propagated from **bulbils** that develop in the leaf axils of the plant as well as from **bulblets** that sometimes develop at the base.

A **corm** is a swollen stem base that is modified into a mass of storage tissue. Crocus and gladiolus grow from corms. When you dig gladiolus corms in the fall, save the well-developed corms and discard poor ones. You may find pea-sized **cormels** around the top of some old corms. These cormels can be saved and replanted elsewhere to mature to flowering size.

A **tuber** differs from a true bulb and corm by not having a protective tunic covering. Begonias, caladiums, dahlias, and anemones grow from tubers. **Rhizomes** grow horizontally under the surface of the soil. One example is lily of the valley.

Peonies and daylilies have **fleshy roots** and can be propagated by dividing in the fall, leaving at least three crown buds with each clump. Daylilies can be divided in fall or spring into plantlets with a single fan of leaves.

Consider the light needs of your plants before selecting their place in your home grounds. Early spring bulbs bloom before most trees leaf out, so they can be planted under trees and shrubs. You'll note that those planted near a house with a warm basement or on southern slopes bloom earlier in spring. Plan you plantings accordingly. However, be aware that many summer-blooming bulbs require full sun or partial shade. Check requirements for each as you decide the best locations for them to thrive.

PREPARE BULB AREAS WELL

Good soil drainage is essential to get the best performance from bulbs. If you have high clay content or sandy soil or otherwise need to improve it, refer to chapter 2 for details. Building better soil for more glorious gardens is easier than you think.

For both spring and summer bulbs, phosphorous is needed to encourage root development. Be aware that phosphorous moves very little once applied to the soil, and bulbs are often planted 6–8 inches deep. As you prepare for bulb planting, it helps to mix 5 tablespoons of 10-10-10 soluble fertilizer or equivalent bulb fertilizer plus two cups of bonemeal per 10 square foot area. When shoots break through the ground in the spring, repeat that soluble fertilizer application.

For summer-flowering bulbs, to encourage superior flowering, plan to apply 7 tablespoons of 10-10-10 soluble fertilizer or equivalent bulb fertilizer over a 10 square foot area, two times. Soil tests can guide you best. Note that optimum pH range for bulbs is betweeen 6 and 7.

The best Green Thumb rule for planting spring bulbs is to plant 2–3 times as deep as the bulb is tall. Most large bulbs like tulips or daffodils will be planted about 8 inches deep. Smaller bulbs will be planted 3–4 inches deep. A planting depth chart is included in this chapter for guidance. Measure planting depth from the bottom of the bulb. However, this depth rule does not apply to summer bulbs. They have varied planting requirements, so check the instructions supplied with the bulbs.

Point bulb noses up for daffodils, hyacinths, and tulips. For beds and larger areas, till or dig the entire bed to the proper depth, press all bulbs into the soil, and cover with soil. Well-dug soil has the good drainage that plants prefer. For smaller plantings, tools called bulb planters are useful, especially for naturalizing numerous bulbs in lawn or wildflower areas.

Mulch works wonders to retain moisture and thwart competitive weeds. Apply 2–3 inches of peat moss or similar organic mulch that is attractive as a ground cover until bulbs sprout. In future years, add an inch or so for appearance and weed control.

Once spring bulbs have bloomed, their foliage is needed to replace growing energy in the bulbs for next year. As foliage yellows, tie it together, and finally remove it when it has served its purpose. If your daffodils, tulips, or crocus seem crowded with smaller flowers, consider digging them up and replanting, about every 5 years for daffs and crocus.

TIPS FOR SUMMER BULBS

In contrast to spring-flowering bulbs like crocus and tulips, most summer-flowering bulbs should be dug up and stored when the plant leaves turn yellow. Use a spading fork to gently lift bulbs from the garden. For most bulbs, just wash away the soil and store them in a cool, dark place, about 60–65°F, for planting next spring. However, leave the soil on begonia, canna, caladium, and dahlia bulbs and store them in clumps on a slightly moistened layer of peat moss or sawdust in a cool place. Then, just before planting, wash and separate them. Be sure to label all bulbs and varieties, so you know what they are and where they should be added to your garden

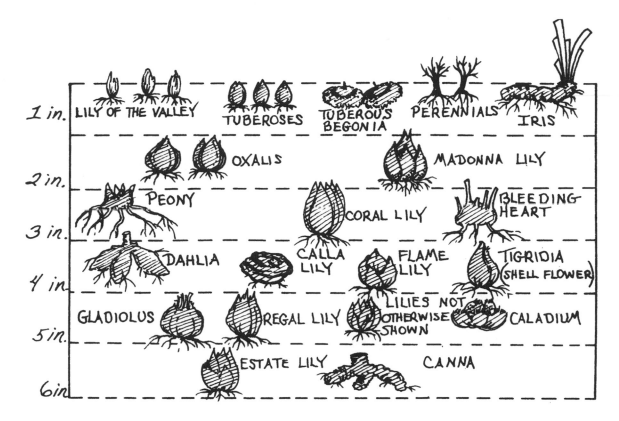

For summer-blooming plants, here's a handy guide to depths for planting bulbs from one of our nationally syndicated garden columns.

next year. It helps to store bulbs on screen trays for good air circulation. Never store bulbs more than two to three layers deep, because deep piles of bulbs generate heat and may decay.

masses and is fine for naturalizing, since it will self-sow. Soak tubers overnight before planting, and place the tubers 3 inches deep and 4–6 inches apart in early fall.

ACONITE

Winter aconite is a member of the buttercup family and one of the earliest flowers to bloom after winter. It has an upright growth of 3–8 inches and basal, deeply divided, leafy bracts under the flowers. Plants die down in summer. The flower is solitary, measures about 1 inch across the yellow petal–like sepals, and appears very early, hence the name winter aconite.

This plant prefers partial shade to full sun in well-drained, moist soil. It looks best planted in

ANEMONES

Anemones have an underground rootstock and usually deeply cut leaves. Flowers can be one or several, and the colors are white, red, blue, or rarely yellow. Seeds can be spread by the wind, which gives them their popular name of windflower. Anemones grow best in a loamy soil, enriched with compost or well-rotted manure. Plan to plant in October for flowering in May and June. You also can grow them from seed. Two fine varieties are *Anemone blanda*, or Greek windflower, which grows

4–6 inches tall, and *Anemone coronaria*, the poppy anemone, which bears large poppylike blossoms and is 12–18 inches tall.

Plant the tuberous root 2–3 inches deep and 3–4 inches apart in humus-rich, loamy soil. Anemones can tolerate a high pH and partial shade. Protection from wind prolongs flowering.

CROCUS

Crocus, a favorite harbinger of spring, should be planted in fall for spring blooms. The Dutch crocus is the most popular and has larger flowers than other types. The fall-blooming saffron crocus adds color in autumn but is planted in spring. Crocus prefer well-drained soil with full sun or partial shade. They may be naturalized in lawns for early spring beauty, but the foliage should be allowed to mature properly before mowing.

Plant the corms 3 inches deep and 4 inches apart in fall. Crocus have an upright growth habit with grasslike leaves. Flowers are 1.5–6 inches long and usually single. Common colors are white, yellow, purple, and striped. The flowers close at night and on cloudy days. Plant fall-blooming crocus in spring. Crocus are especially beautiful when they are planted for a massed effect, 100–150 corms for truly glorious display. Landscape designers say a good proportion to use for a mix of large-flowering crocus varieties is 50 percent blue and purple, 25 percent yellow, 15 percent white, and 10 percent striped.

Because of their early flowering, crocus are suitable for planting on top of other bulbous plants. After the crocus pass their peak bloom, other plants such as daffodils, hyacinths, and tulips can take over. To achieve such a succession, first plant the larger bulbs and cover them with soil up to the level of their noses. Then plant an ample amount of crocus on top. This gives continuing bloom from crocus to other later flowering plants.

Crocus experts suggest these varieties: Flower Record, a shiny violet-mauve; Grand Maitre, a lavender-violet; King of the Striped, violet with lighter stripes; Purpureus Grandiflorus, a violet-purple; Queen of the Blues, deep blue with lighter margins; and Striped Beauty, violet stripes on a white background.

DAFFODILS

Their botanical name is *Narcissus*, but gardeners call these appealing plants with their trumpet-shaped spring flowers either daffodils, narcissus, or jonquils, depending on their characteristics. The plants have an upright growth habit, and heights range from 6 to 24 inches, depending on the variety. There are many types of daffodils, producing one or even several flowers to a stalk, with the six lower segments usually white or yellow. The trumpet may be long and tubular or short and cuplike, in various shades from white, pink, yellow, orange, to orange-red. The flowers may be single or double blooms. The shiny green leaves can grow up to 15 inches long.

Daffodils prefer a well-drained soil enriched with organic matter. They thrive in sun but tolerate partial shade. Plant bulbs 6 inches deep and 6–12 inches apart for most, but somewhat less for smaller species bulbs. Remove faded flowers so they don't set seeds. Divide clumps every 3 or 4 years, usually after the leaves have died. Daffodils may form bulblets that can be used to establish new plants that will mature and bloom in future years.

GLORY OF THE SNOW

The small, lily-like flowers of the *Chionodoxa* have been a delight in many gardens, gracing them with tiny blooms while snow still lingers on the ground. Glory of the snow are perfect planted in masses for naturalizing. Plants are 3–6 inches tall, and they blossom especially early in the spring. Plant bulbs as you would crocus. *Chionodoxa luciliae* and *C. sardensis* are the two species most generally grown and recommended. You may find others in mail order catalogs.

HYACINTHS

Hyacinths have an upright growth, a height of about 12 inches, and often very fragrant blooms, 5–8 inches tall, in yellow, rose, pink, blue, salmon, or white. Hyacinths bloom typically in midspring. Foliage is four to six basal leaves about 12 inches long.

Hyacinths like full sun, good drainage, and fertile sandy loam soil improved with organic matter. You should remove spent flower stalks. Floral display gradually decreases each year, so you will eventually dig up and discard old bulbs and plant new varieties. Plant 7 inches deep and 6–9 inches apart in fall.

GRAPE HYACINTHS

Grape hyacinths are an early spring flower. The flower stems grow 6–10 inches tall with 12–20 tiny blooms in a terminal cluster. The urn-shaped flowers are usually blue or white. Foliage is six to eight dark-green basal leaves up to 12 inches long and one-third of an inch wide. The plants prefer fertile, sandy soil in full sun or partial shade. For best display, plant in masses, setting bulbs 3 inches deep and 4 inches apart in early fall.

IRIS

There are well over 200 different species of iris. The familiar Dutch iris, which blooms in June or July and grows from a rhizome, is covered in chapter 8, the chapter on perennials. Here we focus on spring-blooming iris, which are much shorter than the Dutch iris and usually referred to as dwarf iris. These iris have bulbs instead of rhizomes, and they bloom about the same time as crocus. Two popular spring-blooming types are reticulata iris (*Iris reticulata*) and Danford iris (*Iris danfordiae*).

The wild *Iris reticulata* has been extensively cultivated to produce more than a dozen different named varieties in beautiful shades of blue and purple and is the species of dwarf iris most often sold commercially. Also called netted iris, it gets its name from the netlike skin that covers the bulbs. It blooms very early in spring. The flower is quite large in relationship to the plant and has a wonderful fragrance. These are very easy to grow, come back year after year, and even multiply. Harmony and J. S. Dijt are popular varieties. Plants grow 4–6 inches tall, with small purple and gold ridged flowers that open in late winter or early spring. Leaves are narrow and short at flowering time but elongate to 12–18 inches afterward. Plant 3 inches deep and 6 inches apart in full sun.

Danford iris is a neat little plant, 4–6 inches high. It bears lemon-yellow blooms with green markings and bright yellowish-green to orange markings on the haft of the falls. Although hardy, flowering in January or February, it needs protection in cold and wet areas to prevent flower damage. They are easily grown in average, medium wet, well-drained soil with full sun to part shade. It helps for soil to be relatively dry during summer for the bulbs to set buds for the following year. Plant bulbs 3–4 inches deep and 3–4 inches apart in fall. The bulbs tend to separate into bulblets after bloom. Bulbs can be dug and divided and offsets removed after bloom. However, this is suggested only if flowering has significantly declined.

SNOWDROPS

Snowdrops (*Galanthus* spp.) often compete with glory of the snow and winter aconite for the earliest bloom. Two or three dark-green, straplike leaves grow from each bulb. White flowers are usually borne singly, sometimes in mid to late winter, which often makes them the earliest flowering bulb. Snowdrops will thrive in sun or shade and are great for rock gardens or as edging plants. Plant bulbs 3–4 inches deep in early autumn in fertile soil. Left undisturbed, they will reward you for many winters. To transplant some, dig up carefully just as their flowers fade.

SIBERIAN SQUILL

These lovely greeters of spring usually have blue blooms, but white and pink species also exist. They look best when planted in masses, and they will grow in almost any kind of soil so long as it is moist in spring. Despite the name, it is not from Siberia, but it is a very hardy plant that can grow in zones 2–8.

Quality bulbs will often produce more than one 8-inch flowering stem bearing up to six brilliant blue flowers on each. Leaves are bright green, 8 inches in length. Spring Beauty is a popular variety.

Set the bulbs 3–4 inches deep and 6–8 inches apart. They need not be lifted or divided unless you intend to propagate. Fortunately, unlike many spring-flowering bulbs, squill is not bothered by voles, chipmunks, rabbits, or deer. Flowers tolerate late cold snaps and aren't injured by snow or freezing temperatures. Squill need sun to thrive but are nice naturalized under deciduous trees and shrubs because leafless branches allow the sun through when the bulbs are actively growing. Some experts recommend never planting fewer than 100 bulbs. They mix well with other early bloomers, such as giant crocus, yellow winter aconite, snowdrops, glory of the snow, and very early daffodils. They can accent beds and borders or grace herb or rock gardens.

TULIPS

Many hundreds of tulip varieties are available. You can find them at garden centers each fall and in mail order catalogs too. Tulips have an upright growth, maturing to heights of 6–30 inches, depending on type. Tulip flowers are usually solitary, erect, saucer-shaped blooms with 6 petals and sepals. They come in a multitude of colors and flower forms, and more than 400 named cultivars. Common classes are Mendel, Fosteriana hybrids, Kaufmanniana hybrids, Greigii hybrids, Triumph, Darwin hybrid, Lily-flowered, Cottage, Rembrandt, Parrot, Double-flowered, and Species tulips. They provide delights from early through late spring. And *Greigii* hybrids often have burgundy- or purple-mottled leaves.

Tulips prefer well-drained, sandy, humus-rich soil in full sun or partial shade. There are many types and styles, so select those that please you and give you early, mid, and late season blooms. It is best to plant tulips in masses. Because most tulips don't multiply or last as long as other bulbs, some gardeners plant new bulbs each year. Plant bulbs 4–8 inches deep and 4–8 inches apart in fall. Species tulips usually require shallower planting.

10

ROSES ARE THE RAGE

Roses are not only beautiful but also one of the oldest known flowers. Fossil records of the rose date back 35 million years. Sappho, in her 600 BCE "Ode to the Rose," referred to this beauty as the queen of flowers. In fashionable France in 1798, Empress Josephine created the most remarkable rose garden ever planted, which included every variety known at the time, about 250 then. Modern rose hybrids date back to 1867. By 1920, hybrid teas dominated the market and remain the most popular type today. One of the most popular roses of all time, the Peace rose, was smuggled to the United States from occupied France in 1945.

The rose family contains about 107 genera and 3,100 species. Curiously, the family contains many of the most important fruit trees grown in temperate areas: apple, pear, peach, plum, cherry, apricot, and nectarine, plus the raspberry, blackberry, and strawberry. The rose has been grown and appreciated for its fragrance and beauty since ancient times and today remains the world's most popular and widely cultivated garden flower. Fact is, there are more than 20,000 cultivars, and several hundred new cultivars are introduced each year. In the United States, about 20 million rose plants are grown annually for cut flowers, and about 40 million are produced for home landscape and orna-

mental purposes. Despite major efforts by David Burpee in support of the marigold, the rose won out to become our nation's flower.

The American Rose Society (ARS) (www.ars .org) in cooperation with the World Federation of Rose Societies adopted a classification system that reflects both the botanical and evolutionary progress of the rose. This is not the only classification system in use, but the majority of the established rose societies in the world use this method for classifying roses for competitions and identification. The system recognizes three main groupings of roses: **species**, like the wild roses; **old garden**, classes of roses in existence before 1867; and **modern**, classes of roses not in existence before 1867.

Roses are available in many colors. Red remains most popular, but other colors have their supporters. For fun, here's an old rosarian chart (a rose expert is called a rosarian) that matches some of the most popular rose colors with the sentiments they are said to express.

Color	Symbolism
Red	Love, respect
Deep pink	Gratitude, appreciation
Light pink	Admiration, sympathy
Yellow	Joy, gladness

Orange	Enthusiasm, desire
Red and yellow	Gaiety, joviality
Yellow	Sociability, friendship

SWEET SMELL OF ROSES

Fragrance is probably the most common attribute gardeners love about roses. From spicy to fruity to musky, a rose's scent is hard to resist. When was the last time you didn't stop to smell the roses? (But one caution before you buy a rose bush: not all rose varieties have a scent. Some are bred for the appearance of their blooms.)

Best time to smell roses is midmorning, just as the sun has reached the garden. Rose experts say that fragrance will be most intense when the bloom is one-quarter to two-thirds open. According to the All America Rose Selections (AARS), a group formed in 1938 that tests new rose varieties to determine which to recommend to the public, here are some of the most fragrant: Amber Queen, America, Arizona, Bonica, Broadway, Chrysler Imperial, Double Delight, Mister Lincoln, Perfume Delight, Sheer Bliss, Sun Flare, Sutter's Gold, Sweet Surrender, Tiffany, Tropicana, Voo Doo, and White Lightnin.

Old-fashioned roses are famed for their aroma. With the increasing interest in old garden roses, a survey was taken among rose growers to determine their favorites, according to rosarian Steve Jones. There were two groups in this survey: well-known and respected old garden rose people in the American Rose Society, and others who responded to a query in *Rose Magazine*. The top ten fragrant old garden roses were Baronne Prévost, Mme. Isaac Pereire, Celsiana tied with Marchesa Boccella, Louise Odier, Autumn Damask tied with Sombreuil, Rose de Rescht, Charles de Mills tied with Königin von Dänemark.

Another national poll among rose growers provided more favorite fragrance roses. Note that most are hybrid tea roses, indicated by HT. The abbreviation ER indicates an English rose, and HP means hybrid perpetual.

HT: Double Delight, red-white bicolor
HT: Fragrant Cloud, reddish-orange
HT: Mr. Lincoln, dark red
HT: Crimson Glory, red
HT: Chrysler Imperial, red
HT: Papa Meilland, dark red
HT: Perfume Delight, pink
HT: Secret
ER: Gertrude Jekyll, pink
ER: Othello, dark red
Alba: Félicité Parmentier, once-blooming
Damask: Mme. Hardy, white, once-blooming
Tea: Sombreuil, cream-white
Bourbon: Souvenir de la Malmaison
HP: Souvenir du Dr Jamain

Although roses are famed for their appealing aromas, some beautiful roses don't have much scent at all. When hybridizers were competing to produce bigger and more dramatic rose blooms, they neglected the fragrance. Rose lovers objected, however, and today rose breeders are again focusing on imparting sweet smells to new roses they introduce. You can find more details about rose history, heritage, culture, and varieties at the ARS website: www.ars.org.

PICK THE BEST ROSES FOR YOUR GARDEN DESIGN

Different types of roses are available to serve various landscape and garden design purposes as well as provide appealing fragrance.

Climbing roses need support but will climb fences, arbors, trellises to add delightful color in profusion. A national favorite is bright-red Blaze.

Floribunda roses are bushy shrubs that produce flower clusters of 3–15 blooms. Most rose growers say these are the most colorful of rose types.

Hybrid tea probably is the most popular rose type, producing large blooms on upright bushes, generally one flower per stem but several stems per bush. Great for cut flowers, and many have appealing rose fragrance.

Grandiflora roses are crosses between a floribunda and a hybrid tea which grow up to 6 feet tall bearing clusters of classic hybrid tea flowers. That's a neat combination.

Shrub and landscape roses in various shapes and sizes have a spreading habit, growing close to the ground. They are useful as ground covers and on banks you can't mow.

Miniature roses grow on plants only 6–24 inches tall. Being hardy and blooming continuously, they are excellent for container gardening.

Tree roses are truly distinctive and dramatic but require extra care because of their creation through grafts.

ROSES FOR YOUR LANDSCAPE

Roses offer an amazing variety of growth habits, shapes, and sizes as well as many flower colors and forms. They bloom the first year planted, and with proper care they reward you with glorious blooms for many years. With their special blooming beauty value, roses deserve a place in home landscapes. It's up to you to decide which type works best and where you want to see them blooming week after delightful week.

Consider a classic bed of roses in whatever size or shape you wish. As you look for the best spot, remember that roses like 6 hours of sun per day, as well as loamy, well-drained soil and good air ventilation. Masses of roses are especially magical and magnificent. Hybrid teas, floribundas, grandifloras, miniatures, and landscape roses do best in beds.

How about rose hedges? They are marvelous as property borders, along drives and walks, and to screen unsightly areas too. Floribundas or landscape shrub roses do well as hedge plantings. Set plants in a single row 24 inches apart, or for a thicker display, plant a staggered double row with 24–36 inches between each plant and 18–24 inches between each row.

Try rose borders too, either straight or winding. Think fragrance and plant especially fragrant roses to welcome guests to your home and garden. Consider mix and match designs of different types—hybrid teas, floribundas, grandifloras, shrub, and even tree roses interspersed with other landscape plants. That will provide eye appeal and guarantee longer seasons of bloom from spring through fall.

Patios and balconies benefit from roses too. Most types of roses do well so long as they get 6 hours of sun and you tend them properly with water and fertilizer in their containers. You can roll out a red carpet of roses, or any other colors you prefer, for visitors with dramatic tree or tiny miniature roses in containers. In cities, roses in containers will grace sunny balconies, decks, terraces, and even rooftops. You can use them too on exterior stairways, indoor window ledges, or hanging baskets.

Considering the thousands of roses available, it helps to have a reliable system to help you make the best choice for your garden. The ARS has a rating system, from 1 for the worst to 10 for best, as a useful guide to new roses. The ARS ratings are printed yearly in the Handbook for Selecting Roses and can be obtained from the American Rose Society, P.O. Box 30,000, Shreveport, LA 71130-0030. Or visit their website at www.ars.org for more great rose growing ideas and advice than can fit in this chapter.

WHAT IS A WINNING ROSE?

The AARS, a nonprofit association, has encouraged the rose industry to improve the quality, strength, and beauty of roses. Their test gardens program nationwide provides a proving ground to evaluate new roses, and AARS winners embody all of the characteristics that home gardeners desire in a garden plant. Every AARS winner must come through an extensive two-year trial program. This sophisticated evaluation process guarantees that only the best of the crop make it into your garden. You can visit the AARS website at www.rose.org to find many winners. They also are listed by mail order firms that offer roses, as well as leading rose breeders.

To be awarded national honors, roses must be judged in competition with many new varieties being evaluated on 15 key gardening characteristics, including disease resistance, hardiness, color, form, flowering effect, fragrance, vigor, and novelty.

The AARS is dedicated to the introduction and promotion of exceptional roses. Their program is one of the most successful and highly regarded of its kind, having brought to the forefront such roses as Peace, Mister Lincoln, Knock Out, and Bonica.

Roses are evaluated in 20 test gardens in varying climates across the country, from Iowa to Georgia to California and Oregon. These gardens provide similar conditions and challenges inherent in most American gardens in order to provide a comprehensive test environment. "Only the very best can meet the standards of the All America Rose Selections," said AARS President Charlie Anderson. "We are truly awed by the creativity of the introducers who breed such exciting and inspiring varieties."

Some recent winners are listed below, along with their AARS descriptions. These remarkable winning roses will brighten up any garden and capture the hearts and minds of rose lovers everywhere.

2006 AARS Winners

Julia Child is a floribunda destined to be as famous as her namesake. Personally chosen by the award-winning chef herself, this rose combines old-fashioned style with delicious fragrance rarely found in a free-flowering plant. This rose has a rounded habit and excellent disease resistance, raising the bar for any English-style rose. Julia Child also features a sweet licorice perfume that exudes from each fully petaled flower, as well as a butter-gold color that's perfectly suited to any landscape. Julia Child was hybridized by Tom Carruth and introduced by Weeks Roses of Upland, California.

Rainbow Sorbet is as cool and delicious as it sounds. This multicolor floribunda harkens back to the popular variety Playboy from which it is a descendant. More rugged and winter hardy, Rainbow Sorbet shows a resistance to black spot similar to many shrub roses on the market. With a symphony of bright color uninterrupted throughout the season, Rainbow Sorbet can be used either as a powerful accent or as a bold border for those who like to make a statement in their garden. Rainbow Sorbet was developed by Ping Lim of Bailey Nurseries and introduced by the Conard Pyle Company of West Grove, Pennsylvania.

Tahitian Sunset offers a little slice of paradise. This brightly hued hybrid tea features splendid blossoms starting from high-centered orange-yellow buds that open fully to a peachy apricot-pink with yellow highlights. The vigorous plant produces 14–16 inch stems, and flowers with about 30 petals to create blooms up to 5 inches in diameter. With its complex color, delightful licorice fragrance, and semi-glossy foliage, this perfectly formed rose makes a strong focal point in any garden. Tahitian Sunset was hybridized by Keith W. Zary and introduced by Jackson & Perkins of Medford, Oregon.

Wild Blue Yonder offers a journey into uncharted territory. This lavender blend is the first rose in this color range to garner the AARS designation since 1984. Every large wavy petal is a velvety warm wine-purple layered onto rich lavender, making Wild Blue Yonder a unique rose to behold. Each lovely blossom exudes the perfume of sweet citrus and rose. A vigorous "shrubby" bush, its abundant, deep-green leaves provide the perfect accent to the extraordinarily novel color. Hybridized by Tom Carruth, Wild Blue Yonder is introduced by Weeks Roses of Upland, California.

2005 AARS Winners

DayDream may seem like a fantasy. It is a low-growing compact landscape shrub rose reaching just 2 feet in height. It has a unique color in the shrub category, massive clusters of lightly scented, fuchsia-pink blooms that flower all summer long. Foliage is glossy, deep green and highly disease resistant. DayDream's moderate size and neat round habit make it an appropriate choice for a variety of garden situations. It is

crown hardy to zone 4. DayDream was hybridized by Ping Lim and introduced by Bailey Nurseries of St. Paul, Minnesota.

Elle is chic as a Parisian fashion house and sleek as the world-renowned supermodel. Elle combines a strong spicy, citrusy fragrance with a high-centered classic rose bud. It is a hybrid tea that produces shell-pink flowers with deep yellow undertones. The dark glossy foliage provides a nice contrast to the soft, nonfading flower and offers above average disease tolerance to mildew and black spot. Elle's flowers bloom on 10–14 inch stems and are 4–5 inches wide with a petal count of 50–55. Elle was developed by Meilland International and was introduced by the Conard Pyle Company/Star Roses of West Grove, Pennsylvania.

Lady Elsie May is a rose unlike any other. An upright, spreading shrub rose, Lady Elsie May offers a vigorous, uniform growth habit and excellent disease resistance. An abundance of flowers bloom in clusters on strong 12–20 inch cutting stems. Each flower is approximately 3.5–4 inches wide and has 12–14 petals. The fragrance is slight. Foliage is dark green and rugged. It was hybridized by Reinhard Noack and introduced by Angelica Nurseries of Kennedyville, Maryland.

About Face is a grandiflora with a novel "backwards" bicolor whose color of deep golden yellow is carried on the inside of the petals with a darker bronzy orange-red on the backside. This super-vigorous plant yields long stems with full old-fashioned blossoms that catch attention throughout the life of the bloom. The flowers are up to 5 inches in diameter and offer a mild fresh apple fragrance. They are beautifully complemented by lush, clean green leaves. Hybridized by Tom Carruth, About Face was introduced by Weeks Roses of Upland, California.

2004 AARS Winners

Day Breaker is an upright, bushy floribunda with bright, multishade blooms in yellow, blending to pink and apricot. From pointed and shapely buds, its spiraled blooms grow to 4–4.5 inches in diameter, with 30–35 petals per flower, each nestled among dark, glossy green foliage on a plant that reaches a medium height. According to judges, "Day Breaker is an awakening of the senses, not only for its exquisite beauty, but also for its sharp moderate tea fragrance. Day Breaker truly earns its floribunda classification with its brilliantly colorful, long-lasting clusters of flowers in a hardy, continuous bloom. Hybridized by Gareth Fryer, Day Breaker was introduced by Edmunds' Roses of Wilsonville, Oregon.

Honey Perfume is a knockout performer. Its bright apricot yellow blooms grow in large, open clusters with fast repeat on an upright, well-branched plant. Flowers are 4 inches in diameter with 25–30 petals each on 12–14 inch long stems. Honey Perfume grows to about 3.5 feet high and 2.5 feet wide and features dark green and glossy foliage. Honey of a winner is appropriate to this rose. This classic floribunda has a great spicy scent and exhibits very good resistance to disease, including rust and powdery mildew. Honey Perfume was hybridized by Keith Zary and was introduced by Jackson & Perkins of Medford, Oregon.

Memorial Day, like its namesake holiday, is truly worth celebrating. This medium-tall, hybrid tea rose is upright and bushy with very large, full, spiraled blooms having more than 50 petals per flower. Evolving from pointed and ovoid buds, Memorial Day's clear pink flowers are accented with a lavender wash and grow to up to 5 inches in diameter. Its long cutting stems are beautifully clothed with rich green foliage to accent the large blossoms. With its classic, strong damask rose fragrance, a single Memorial Day rose can fill an entire room with sweet rose perfume. A productive performer, Memorial Day is highly disease resistant and especially loves hot weather so it makes a great, easy-to-grow addition to any garden. Memorial Day was hybridized by Tom Carruth and was introduced by Weeks Roses of Upland, California.

AARS award winners are available by mail order through selected catalogs and at retail garden stores nationwide. Additional information about AARS winners, along with photos, is available at the AARS Rose Resource website: www.rose.org.

One of the best ways to learn more about the best roses available for home gardeners is to stop and smell the roses at one of the more than 130 AARS-accredited public rose gardens. Each blooms with hundreds, and sometimes thousands, of roses. These gardens showcase AARS award-winning roses. Garden visitors can enjoy the winners as they grow and bloom, and they can check metal markers to identify the rose by name and award year.

For now, thumb through those colorful rose catalogs and begin planning your new rose growing horizons.

PICK THE BEST PLANTING SITE

Roses are more easily grown than most gardeners may realize. To have them perform to perfection, give them what they need. Note these key points. To bloom best, roses need 5–6 hours of direct sun each day, preferably morning sun as buds open and bloom. Be sure the site has good air movement to dry overnight rain and morning dew and to prevent fungus and mildew problems. Protect roses from strong winds with a building or board fence.

Select loamy, well-drained soil, because roses can't abide soggy roots. Also, don't grow roses near large trees or shrubs that compete for light, water, and nutrients. You can improve the soil with tips from chapter 2 in this book to give roses what they need. To have most glorious displays, plant groups of roses for massed blooms.

Once you have found the right site that meets rose needs, and perhaps improved soil with addition of compost, peat moss, or other organic materials to provide a loamy condition, you're ready for the next step: planting your roses.

TAKE THE TIME TO PLANT RIGHT

Veteran gardeners realize that roses return more for your time and effort than almost any other flower. After you pick the right spot, take that little bit of extra time to plant them right. Rose experts explain that spring is the ideal time to plant. However, you can have success at other times, especially in southern areas.

Gardeners buy many millions of roses from mail order firms so they can obtain very special varieties not often available locally. One of America's oldest and foremost rose producers, Jackson & Perkins, has kindly provided tips for proper care and planting of roses. I've followed their advice for years and can attest that their advice works wonders.

When your roses arrive, open the box immediately and soak roots in lukewarm water for 12–24 hours. If you can't plant them right away, you may leave them in their boxes for up to a week in a cool, dark place. Sprinkle roots with water every few days.

When ready to plant, dig a hole about 18 inches deep and 24 inches wide. That may seem large, but you are planting a valuable perennial that you want to reward you for many years. Make sure that the hole is large enough to give the roots plenty of room to develop after planting. Loosen the soil at the bottom and sides.

Next, build a mound in the center of the hole and set the rose plant on top. Fill the hole with two-thirds of the remaining soil. Add water, let it soak in, then finish filling the hole. Tamp down lightly to remove air pockets, and water well. Spread mulch around the plant to suppress weeds and retain moisture. Water three or four times a week until leaves begin to grow and weekly thereafter.

Roses may be the flowers of love, but there's nothing romantic about a bush that doesn't produce beautiful blooms. Pay attention to rose needs and you'll have glorious gardens and beautiful rose beds. Roses need to be fed, just as you do, so plan to fertilize them regularly.

First feeding should be done when the bush first leafs out. For the remainder of the growing season, fertilize after each flush of blooms. Stop fertilizing about 2 months before the first frost. Otherwise you may promote tender growth that is susceptible to winter kill. Use a commercial rose food or general-purpose fertilizer applied according to package instructions. Scratch dry fertilizers into the soil beneath the leaves but keep away from the canes or bud union. Then water well.

Roses thrive when mulched. Not only does mulching set them off attractively, but mulch helps minimize weeds, it keeps soil moist and loose, and it adds minor nutrients. Organic mulch is best, such as wood chips and shavings, shredded bark, or peat nuggets. Remember that when you use a cellulose mulch such as wood chips, you must add extra fertilizer periodically, since the decay process uses

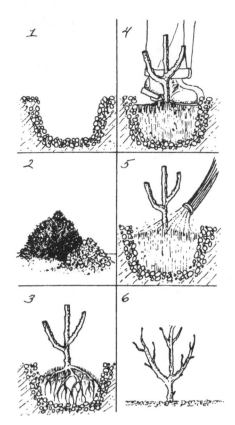

How to Plant a Rose

(1) *Dig a hole large enough to let roots spread naturally.*

(2) *Enrich soil by mixing compost or rotted manure with soil from the hole.*

(3) *Place rosebush in hole so that roots will spread naturally.*

(4) *Fill with enriched soil mixture and firm down to eliminate air pockets in the soil.*

(5) *Water well and daily until plant begins sprouting new shoots.*

(6) *Prune as necessary to obtain bushy, desirable shape.*

Here's a handy guide to planting roses that was popular with my syndicated garden columns and in my periodic gardener's almanacs.

nitrogen. Apply mulch in the spring when soil warms and before weeds start to grow. Actually, mulch can be applied anytime during the growing season, provided you remove weeds first and lightly cultivate the soil surface. About 2–4 inches thick is a good application.

For extra reference, AARS rose experts have provided some easy rose-planting steps, which you'll find here.

Step 1: Dig a hole 18 inches wide and 18 inches deep. Add a quart of peat moss or compost and mix well with the soil. Form a mound of the mixture at the bottom of the hole.

Step 2: Position the rose on the soil mound. In warmer climates, position the rose so that the bud union is at or just above ground level. In colder climates, position the bud union 1–2 inches below ground level and mulch over. Carefully arrange the roots of the plant around the soil mound.

Step 3: Work the soil mixture around the roots to eliminate any air pockets. Firm the soil around the roots and add more soil until the hole is three-quarters full.

Step 4: Fill the hole with water and let it soak in, then refill. Trim canes back to 8 inches, making 45-degree angle cuts one-quarter inch above outward facing buds.

Step 5: Create a 6-inch soil mound over the plant to protect canes from drying out. When buds sprout—about 2 weeks—remove the mound.

Not all garden roses come in bare-root form. If you have purchased a container rose, which should already have plenty of leaves and maybe some blooms, follow these simple instructions:

Step 1: The planting hole for your rose bush should be the same depth as the container and about 18 inches wide.

Step 2: Loosen the soil around the root ball to expose the roots. If the ball is rootbound, score it by making vertical cuts with a sharp knife. Open the scores about an inch to allow roots to form.

Step 3: Center the rose bush in the hole and fill in with soil that's been amended with peat moss or compost.

Step 4: Work the soil mixture around the roots to eliminate any air pockets. Firm the soil around the rose bush with your hands.

Step 5: Water thoroughly to establish good soil contact, then apply an organic mulch like wood chips, shredded bark, pine needles, or peat nuggets.

OTHER KINDLY ROSE CARE

Roses perform best with adequate water throughout their blooming season. They actually need more than most other flowering plants if you want them to bloom most profusely over a longer time. Don't rely on rainfall. Water a few mornings a week. Watering frequency depends on your soil and climate as well as the age of the plants. Add water slowly until the soil is thoroughly soaked 10–15 inches deep. Soaker hoses or a hose with a bubbler attachment will help keep water from splashing onto foliage and possibly spreading diseases. Soil-level and drip-irrigation systems are also effective, and combined with a timer work well.

Emphasis is needed about watering, because rose experts explain that nothing is more impor-tant for a rose bush's survival and performance than water. Roses absolutely love water. The key is to adopt correct watering practices for your particular rose situation, soil, and climate. In general, roses should be watered deeply, but infrequently.

Roses in containers are in a very controlled environment, so keep close watch on the soil's moisture condition. Initially, water the plant well to get it firmly established. During growth, stick a finger in the soil to check for moisture. If your finger comes out dry, add water. Muddy soil means the plant is getting too much water, which can kill plants by drowning their roots. Moist soil is an indicator that the water amount is just about right. Remember that roses need 6 hours of sun per day, so be sure you have positioned your containers to give roses that amount.

WINTER CARE POINTERS

When winter winds wail, gardeners who live where temperatures drop below 5°F should protect their roses to lessen the effects of freezing and thawing. It also is important to keep branches from whipping about, which can damage roots. Some rose lovers believe that winter protection is overly debated. It is useful to share the tips from AARS, since they are qualified authorities. Here is the system that has proven effective in AARS public and trial gardens across the United States:

The AARS rose experts provide these tips for winter rose care. Sometime after the first hard frost, cut back rose plants to about 24 inches. This makes the plants easier to work with and prevents them from becoming battered by wind and ice. Next, tie the canes together with twine to protect from winds. For each rose plant, form an 8–12 inch mound of fresh, loose soil or compost around the base. An additional layer of hay or straw may be added over the mound, if desired. Then, come spring, simply remove the mounds.

ROSE-PICKING TIPS

Rose lovers have compiled the following handy tips to get the most out of rose blooms. Avoid picking flowers the first year, and never take more than one-third of the flower stem so you keep the bush productive and shapely. Use a sharp blade and cut to an outward facing bud. If the bush is not growing vigorously, remove flowers without taking any leaves. Cut roses early in the morning, when moisture and sugar levels are high.

To achieve the largest, prize-winning blooms for your cut flower displays, consider "disbudding" roses. This simply means removing all side buds while they are still small. This lets the plant concentrate all its energy on making the top bud bloom larger. You'll have fewer but larger blossoms.

SPACE NOTES FOR ROSES

Beginners often are puzzled about planting space for roses. Ramblers require about 10 feet between them, climbers 7 feet, large shrub roses 5 feet, tree roses 4 feet, tall hybrid teas 3 feet, floribundas 2 feet, and miniature roses 1 foot. Landscape or ground cover roses tend to grow wide sideways. They can be spaced by personal preference.

For rose beds, remember roses need at least 6 hours of full sun daily. Dig or rototill to a depth of 1 foot. Incorporate some well-rotted manure, compost, or peat moss. Arrange tallest roses in the center or at the back of a bed. Add medium ones next and smaller ones in the foreground. Tree roses can be used in the center instead of tall rose bushes.

For hedges, choose roses that are hardy, disease resistant, repeat flowering, and have lots of foliage. Tall 5-foot bushes should be planted 3 feet apart. Medium bushes, about 3.5 feet tall, should be planted 1.5 feet apart. If you have banks or areas where you want a colorful, long-lasting ground cover, roses may fit well. New types of landscape roses have been introduced in recent years and are superb. These landscape roses produce 5-foot canes that grow in all directions and really cover the ground, even crowding out most weeds.

Climbing roses are vigorous and easy to grow, provide a plentiful amount of blooms and fragrance, and make a dramatic addition to a landscape. Their size and climbing habit allows them to be used as an architectural feature. Climbers can be trained on a fence or trellis to provide screening. They can create a dazzling entry or doorway to other parts of the garden and be used as a focal point on a pillar frame.

Be aware that climbing roses do not twine or have tendrils to attach themselves to a structure. They need something sturdy that they can be loosely secured to or woven through. One trick to make climbing roses produce more bloom is to train them more laterally than vertically, so they will produce short spurs along their main stems or canes that will produce blooms.

It takes a lot of energy to produce all those large, magnificent blooms on climbers! Fertilize regularly with a balanced fertilizer. Climbers need little or no pruning the first two years. Many of the older climbing varieties tend to bloom on second-year canes, so prune climbing roses every 3 or 4 years. Remove small twiggy canes and old woody canes at the base of the plant in favor of young vigorous canes that are long and flexible. These can then be trained onto or through the structure provided.

ROSE PRUNING POINTERS

All roses benefit from judicious pruning. The main aim of pruning is to remove old wood that will no longer flower and encourage development of young, vigorous, and healthy stems. Pruning also trains roses to a desired shape and manageable size. The best time is when the plants are dormant. There are three ways to prune, as rosarians have learned and share.

First is **hard pruning**, which is cutting stems back to only three or four buds. Hard pruning is recommended for newly planted roses or to rejuvenate neglected roses. It results in larger but fewer blooms. In **moderate pruning**, you cut stems back to half their length. This is recommended for all established roses. **Light pruning** is cutting stems back to two-thirds their length, so that the main stems are merely tipped. This method is used with very vigorous varieties. Light pruning generally results in a profusion of flowers.

Follow these five key points.

- Remove all dead, old, or diseased stems and remove any old branches that look dull and gray compared to new growth which is green and shiny.
- Cut the stem off at the bud union.
- Remove very thin stems and branches that cross each other or are crowding the center of the plant.
- Prune away any suckers growing from below the bud union. This process should leave only healthy branches. Prune these to the length required, depending on whether you are pruning hard or light.
- When making your cuts, cut on a 45-degree angle just above an outward facing bud.

PROBLEM-SOLVING TIPS

Despite your best efforts, sometimes you may have problems with roses. Biggest question is "Why don't my roses bloom?" Perhaps the plant is not getting sufficient sun. Roses need at least 6 hours of direct sun a day to perform well. Consider transplanting to a sunnier site. Maybe the plant needs more water. Roses need at least 1 inch of water per week during the growing season. Set your schedule to give them what they need. Try drip irrigation.

Think about plant nutrition. Has the rose been given too much fertilizer, especially nitrogen? Too much fertilizer can damage the plant or cause it to grow extra leaves and stems at the expense of blooms. That's true with many plants, so watch the fertilizer mixture you use.

Another problem may be that your rose is a "once blooming" variety, which means it will bloom only once a year in the late spring or early summer. Perhaps your soil pH is too low or too high. If the pH is not in the range of 6.0–6.8, and ideally 6.5, needed nutrient uptake will be reduced. Essentially the plant won't be getting the food it needs to produce flowers.

Finally, your plant may not have enough foliage. If the bush doesn't have adequate foliage, it can't produce the food it needs to make new flowers. Inadequate foliage may result from disease or too little fertilizer. Many brands of rose fertilizers are available in stores. Or you may wish to try one of the special rose fertilizers available from a major mail order rose firm.

CELEBRATED ROSES

Roses have been named for various celebrities over the years, such as the Julia Child and Elle roses described earlier in this chapter. For 2004, Jackson & Perkins hybridizers introduced a pair of roses, the Ronald Reagan and the Nancy Reagan, to recognize an extraordinary couple who inspired many. Fact is, in 1986 President Reagan signed a resolution making the rose our national flower. The Ronald Reagan rose has light red petals with a crisp, white reverse, and the red deepens in color after the petals open. The Nancy Reagan is a rich coppery apricot that opens to a light peachy apricot.

Some roses are honored internationally. The World Federation of Rose Societies (WFRS), an organization formed to encourage the exchange of information about roses, promote uniform standards for judging, and grant awards for the best roses worldwide, has established a Hall of Fame for roses, along with an Old Rose Hall of Fame. The Old Rose Hall of Fame recognizes roses of historical or genealogical importance and those roses which have enjoyed continued popularity over a great many years. The following roses have been so recognized:

Cecile Brunner: Synonyms: Mme. Cecile Brunner, Mlle. Cecile Brunner, Mignon, Sweetheart Rose. Polyantha, light pink. Introduced in 1881. Hybridized by Ducher of France.

Gloire de Dijon: Climbing Tea (Old Garden Rose), orange pink. Introduced in 1853. Hybridized by Jacotot of France.

Gruss an Teplitz: Synonyms: Virginia R. Coxe, Salut a Teplitz. Bourbon (Old Garden Rose), medium red. Introduced in 1897. Hybridized by Geschwind of Slovakia.

Old Blush: Synonyms: Common Monthly, China Monthly, Common Blush China, Old Pink Daily, Old Pink Monthly, Parson's Pink China. China (Old Garden Rose), medium pink. Introduced in Sweden in 1752 and into England before 1759.

Souvenir de la Malmaison: Synonyms: Queen of Beauty and Fragrance. Bourbon (Old Garden Rose), light pink. Introduced in 1843. Hybridized by Béluze of France.

For more information about these and other internationally celebrated roses, visit the WFRS website at www.worldrose.org.

This year, get into a fragrant mood and mode. You'll find that roses provide some of the most delightful scenes, blooms, and scents you can add to your more glorious garden.

II

ALL ABOUT ANNUALS

Spring sprouts every year. We gardeners count the days until it does. In this chapter, you'll find a path to success annually, with annuals. In recent years there has been a shift to planting perennials. That's true. Serious gardeners use perennials for beauty that returns from one year to the next, but they also indulge in annuals to bring season-long color to the garden. Although annuals only live for one season, they offer many advantages. Annuals fill in bare spaces between newly planted perennials and provide continuous color to augment the shorter bloom times of most perennials. Annual flowers provide dramatic color to accent and enliven a home's landscape. Flowering trees and shrubs do provide short bursts of color and perennials have

their value. However, annuals give big early rewards, blooming within a month of planting, and many continue flowering until frost.

The wide range of colors, sizes, and species adapted to either sun or shade makes it possible to plant annual flowers almost anywhere. Annuals are perfect for beds, borders, rock gardens, windowboxes, hanging baskets, or as temporary ground covers and fillers. By definition, annuals are nonwoody plants that complete their life cycle in one season, ending with seed production, and then they die. Confusion may arise when an annual reseeds itself and appears to have a perennial habit. Many of these are properly known as biennials, growing the first year and flowering and setting seed their second year.

Flowers are fun and appealing, and children can enjoy selling the ones they grow at their own little roadside stand.

Children enjoy exhibiting their flowers at local shows to win prizes.

ANNUALS DESERVE LANDSCAPE SPACE

Annuals deserve not only applause but garden space. These worthwhile flowers can play an important role in a well-designed landscape. Compared to most perennials, annuals require higher levels of maintenance and water. It is helpful to plant annual beds near water sources and pair annuals in beds with other annuals having similar growth, care, and water requirements.

Annuals offer several assets. They provide a variety of interesting textures and forms to the landscape but are most praiseworthy for the color they provide. You can color coordinate your gardens with annuals. Try related colors, such as red, orange, and yellow, the so-called warm colors. Or try green, blue, and purple, known as cool colors. Warm-colored flowers bring excitement into the landscape and appear close to the viewer. That makes their space seem smaller. Cool-colored flowers appear more distant, which imparts a greater sense of garden space. Cool colors also tend to relax and soothe viewers, according to horticultural authorities.

Landscaping experts explain that annuals are an excellent way to draw attention to building and home entrances, walkways, and outdoor living spaces. Plant height is an important design consideration. A flower border usually has the tallest plants in the back, medium high ones in the middle, and short plants in the front. An island planting places the tallest plants in the middle of the bed, surrounded by plants of decreasing heights. As you create an annual plant bed, be sure it fits with the overall style of your landscape's formal or informal design. Formal designs are made up of geometric lines and symmetry, with strong focal points to attract the eye. Informal designs are more relaxed and natural, using curved, flowing lines that seem to follow natural terrain features.

Wherever you decide to plant annual flowers, learn what these plants need to thrive and prosper. Consider soil type, fertility, drainage, and exposure to sun and wind. Compare site characteristics with specific plant requirements. When plants are matched well with the growing site, they naturally grow more vigorously and reward you more beautifully. Be mindful that some annuals are intolerant of heat and sun and love shade. Some like to climb while others are best for low borders. Get to know your annual flower friends and meet their needs. They'll repay you gloriously.

Annual flowers can be landscape mainstays. We love them for several reasons. They deliver joyous color in all shades and hues, including colorful foliage. Annuals provide constant blooming and a steady supply of cut flowers. They offer diversity in dozens of shapes and sizes. They provide versatility to edge beds, punctuate borders, climb arbors, carpet the ground, hang from the porch roof, and overflow all types of containers. Finally, annuals are reliable, performing to our high expectations, especially the award-winning new varieties that are All America Selections.

Comparing annual and perennial flowers is like comparing apples and oranges. Each type has its own advantages. Annual flowers complete their life cycle in just one growing season. You plant a seed or transplant, it grows foliage, flowers, sets seeds, and then the plant dies all in the same year. Many popular annual flowers tend to bloom from spring until autumn frost. Yes, they must be replanted each year, but annuals are hard to beat in terms of showy, season-long color. The most popular, best-known annual flowers include petunias, marigolds, zinnias, and impatiens. If you can't decide whether to plant annuals or perennials, do both. You'll find perennials covered in chapter 8 in this book, so you can combine annuals and perennials to reap the best of both!

TYPES OF ANNUALS

Annual flowers differ in their tolerance to cold weather and frost. **Hardy annuals** are the most cold tolerant. These can take light frost without being killed. Hardy annuals include calendula, cornflower, foxglove, larkspur, pansy, sweet alyssum, stocks, viola, and many dianthus cultivars.

The drawback is that most hardy annuals are not heat tolerant, and you may find that they decline or die during hot summer temperatures.

Half-hardy annuals will tolerate periods of cold, damp weather but are damaged by frost. Most half-hardy annuals can be seeded directly outdoors in early spring because they don't need warm soil temperatures to germinate. Examples of half-hardy annuals are baby's breath, candytuft, cleome, forget-me-not, love-in-a-mist, and strawflower. They tend to decline in the midsummer heat.

Tender annuals are sensitive to cold soil temperatures and easily damaged by frost. You can start them indoors to get a jump on spring or wait 2–3 weeks after the last spring frost to sow seeds for transplant outdoors. Tender annuals include ageratum, balsam, begonia, celosia, coleus, impatiens, marigold, morning glory, nasturtium, nicotiana, petunia, verbena, vinca, and zinnia.

TIPS FOR USING ANNUALS

Annual vines are often useful to cover a fence, hide unsightly areas or just provide blooming beauty growing higher than usual ground-bound annuals. Consider black-eyed Susan vine, cardinal climber, canary creeper, firecracker vine, morning glory, scarlet runner bean and sweet peas. Look them up to see where and how they may fit into your garden.

Birds love flowers as much as gardeners do. If you also love birds, consider balsam, cleome, four o'clocks, forget-me-not, impatiens, larkspur, nicotiana, marigold, nasturtium, petunia, poppy, snapdragon, sweet William, verbena, and zinnia.

If you like to watch butterflies flitting around your home grounds, welcome them with annuals such as cleome, gloriosa daisy, nasturtium, pansy, snapdragon, sunflower, sweet alyssum, toadflax, and wallflower.

Some annuals thrive colorfully all season despite heat. Nicotiana, or flowering tobacco, comes in a variety of heights and colors, including red, white, and pink. It is appealing to hummingbirds. Dwarf butterfly pentas bear rounded pink, lavender, or red flowers and have good heat tolerance. Verbena provides classic trailing plants for window-boxes and containers in dark purple to hot pink, with good heat tolerance.

Cosmos, with their fernlike foliage and appealing flowers, belong in every garden. Plants grow from 12–48 inches tall, depending on the variety. Sow seeds in full sun in groups or scattered among tall perennials. Stake tallest types. Fertilize all cosmos once or twice during the season if you cut flowers often for arrangements. Cosmos are fairly drought tolerant.

Marigold are hardy and perform well when directly seeded. David Burpee did a lot to popularize marigolds in the United States, and his famous mail order firm perfected hundreds of types. (Although he worked for years to have marigolds named America's national flower, roses won out.)

The French marigold (*Tagetes patula*) is small-flowered and shorter than the African or American marigolds (*Tagetes erecta*). French marigolds bear single or double blooms in bright yellow, orange, red, and combinations. Sow seeds thinly, and space seedlings 6–8 inches apart in any good garden soil in full sun. Pinch growing tips of young plants to encourage bushy, compact growth. Fertilize midway through the season. Marigolds are fairly drought tolerant but need supplemental water in dry spells. Use low-growing types to edge beds and borders. Taller varieties can provide colorful backgrounds. Marigolds do especially well in container planting. Use them to advantage in vegetable gardens too, because they help repel root nematodes.

Morning glories can climb high to decorate an arbor or fence with masses of heart-shaped leaves and dramatic flowers. You have a wide choice of colors, from traditional blue to red to pink and those with contrasting markings. Related moonflowers are larger, fragrant, and open at dusk. Soak both types of seeds overnight in damp paper toweling before planting in full sun. Give them a sturdy support, and after a somewhat slow start they quickly climb skyward to a height of 10 feet or more. Grow both glories and moonflowers for morning to evening color.

Sunflowers are an American native, now perfected in yellow, gold, orange, bronze, and multicolored blooms. We've had dozens of cutting beds for years because neighbors love the sight and birds enjoy the seeds on fall migration. Seeds are easy for kids to handle, and they can grow shorter new varieties or the giant Russian that matures 10–15 feet tall with huge blooms. Sunflowers are drought tolerant, and as their name implies, they enjoy full sun.

Another old-time favorite, zinnias produce flowers nonstop all season. Sow seeds thinly, because germination rates are high and plants grow better when not crowded. Fertilize at least once a month and water frequently for best displays. Luckily zinnias aren't fussy about soil as long as it drains well, so they fit in problem areas. You have a wide color range, from cherry and orange to yellow and white. Zinnias are one of the best cutting flowers for bouquets.

If you look forward to early blooming, there are other easily sown annual flowers that can provide compelling displays outdoors, as cut flowers, and as sources for dried arrangements too. Try bachelor's buttons, nasturtiums, poppies, and strawflowers.

USE ANNUALS FOR COLOR

One question about annuals is what are the best colors. Pick what you prefer is the best answer.

However, suggestions from landscape designers might be helpful.

Bright colors stand out, while dark colors retreat into the background. A bed of red flowers can easily be seen from a distance, but blue and purple flowers can only be enjoyed up close. Bright colors draw attention to an area and also appear closer, while dark colors make the area appear farther away. White is the last color to fade from sight as darkness falls and is good for areas used at night.

Colors influence how people feel. Red and yellow are considered warm colors. Green, blue, and violet are considered cool colors. Planting warm-colored flowers around a deck or patio will make it seem warmer. Red tends to excite people. Yellow is associated with liveliness and exuberance. White gives the feeling of cleanliness. Blue is perceived as cool and calming.

GROW THE BEST IN AMERICA

How do you grow the best annuals? The secret begins in the seeds. Take advantage of millions of dollars that plant breeders put into developing and testing new, high-performance hybrid flowers. It is being done to provide you with assurance of growing success. There are 235 test and display gardens in America, coast to coast, in all soils and climates, where new varieties are being evaluated every year. It's part of the All America Selections (AAS) program. Trial rows of entries are grown in side-by-side comparison with the most similar variety already available. Thus, when you see the AAS award insignia on a new variety, you can be sure it is not only the best in its class but also is adapted to a wide range of soils, climates, and gardening practices.

In the 1920s and 1930s, magazines were hungry for garden news, but little reliable information was available. In 1932, W. Ray Hastings, then president of the Southern Seedsmen's Association, proposed the idea of All America Selections so that home gardeners could learn which new varieties are truly improved. He encouraged all seed companies to set up trial grounds, cooperatively test new varieties, and agree to develop marketing efforts for new vegetables and flowers. He wisely recommended a national network of trial grounds throughout North American climates where flower and vegetable varieties would be grown and assessed by skilled, impartial judges.

AAS winners have been introduced each year since 1933. There is an AAS Gold Medal award reserved for a breeding breakthrough. Gold Medal awards have been rare, only given once or twice a decade. The other AAS awards recognize a flower or vegetable for significant achievements, proven to be superior to all others on the market. AAS is the oldest, most established international testing organization in North America.

A trial ground is a test site that conducts comparison trials and is supervised by a judge who is responsible for the growing and evaluation of the flowers, fruits, or vegetables. AAS display gardens provide the public an opportunity to view the new AAS winners in an attractive setting. They also offer educational programs during open house or field days during the peak season for garden flowers and vegetables. Nearly 200 botanical gardens, arboretums, colleges, universities, Cooperative Extension agencies, garden centers, seed companies, city civic centers, and public parks create AAS display gardens. In an average year, a display garden will be sent 45–55 AAS flower and vegetable winners. Approximately one-third of the winners are vegetables, two-thirds are flowers.

Some Recent AAS Winners
Vinca, First Kiss Blueberry: The large 2-inch single blooms have a darker eye which accentuates

the violet blue color. For decades breeders have been diligently working towards a blue Vinca. First Kiss Blueberry fills the color void. This is heat and drought tolerant, mature plants about 11 inches tall and spread 16 inches in adequate growing conditions.

Zinnia F1, Magellan Coral: Fully double, dahlia flowered, 5–6 inch blooms with brilliant coral petals. Flower quality and color are superior to other *Zinnia elegans*. Consistent flower production and earliness are improved qualities. Mature zinnia plants reach about 15–17 inches tall and spread 15–19 inches. Like all zinnias, this one performs best in full sun.

Celosia plumosa, Fresh Look Red: A Gold Medal award winner. It performs like a fresh floral arrangement all summer, thriving in the summer heat and humidity with drought or rainy condition. It won the coveted Gold Medal for its consistent performance with minimal maintenance and pest-free growth. Plants mature at 12–18 inches tall and spread 12–20 inches.

Celosia plumosa, Fresh Look Yellow: A flower winner that offers season-long garden color with minimal care. The golden-yellow plumes are produced in abundance, at times covering the plant. The plant attains a height of about 12–17 inches and spreads 12–15 inches.

Petunia, Limbo Violet: Differs from all other single grandiflora petunias as a unique combination of large flowers on a compact plant. Ultimate plant size is only 6–7 inches tall, spreading 10–12 inches, designed for small-space gardens such as urban residences or formal gardens requiring neat, tidy plants.

MORE KEY ANNUAL PLANT LISTS

Gardeners want plants that endure. Reliable annuals that do are balsam, calliopsis, cockscomb, godetia, lobelia, monkeyflower, periwinkle, and stock.

For annuals that thrive in very poor soil, your choice is California poppy, calliopsis, corn poppy, four o'clock, gaillardia, balsam, godetia, love-lies-bleeding, nasturtium, petunia, rose moss or portulaca grandiflora, and sweet alyssum.

Looking for fragrant annuals? Try sweet alyssum, calendula or pot marigold, centaurea or sweet sultan, heliotrope, candytuft, yellow lupine, and others you can find that are flagged as fragrant plants in flower catalogs.

Cool and shady areas require special attention. Here are some good annuals to try: Canterbury bells, evening primrose, impatiens, balsam, and nicotiana.

Annual vines are fine for growing up, up and away as you wish. There's something irresistibly romantic about a split-rail fence covered with sweet peas. Flowering vines of all types add their artful growing patterns to outdoor living areas. Think about a living curtain of morning glories outside your kitchen window or bright black-eyed Susan vines hiding an ugly wall or area you don't want to see.

Many annual vines grow fast enough to cover a trellis in a few weeks. Your vine options are endless. One wonderful way, especially with limited room, is to construct a trellis in a planter box on a deck or balcony. Annual vines growing on the trellis will add beauty without sacrificing room. Most annual vines attach themselves to a supporting structure with twining stems or tendrils. It may take some training to start them on a trellis, but once they've taken hold, just step back and enjoy the beauty.

Sweet peas are old-fashioned vining favorites and available in all sizes, from 2 feet and bushy to 8-foot climbers. Blossoms range from scarlet to soft pink to white to purple with combinations of bicolors. Best part is their fragrance. Sweet peas bloom best in full sun in the cooler weather of spring and summer. They need rich soil that retains moisture.

Morning glories are now available in many colors, so take your pick of blue, pink, scarlet or magenta, or bicolors. Once started, they grow fast, and their whorled buds unfurl gracefully each morning and fade by early evening. New buds replace them the next morning. Because morning glory seed has a hard coat, soak seeds overnight or nick the coat with a file before sowing.

Try an evening treat of moonflower or moon vine. Crystal white flowers resemble morning glory blooms but instead open as dusk approaches and remain open through the night, with what some call a sensual perfume through the evening.

Balloon vine, love-in-a-puff, or cup-and-saucer vine will cover a trellis or pergola quickly to give you shade or a solid screen. Balloon vines grow to 10 feet with tiny, white, orchidlike flowers followed by greenish balloon fruits. Plant in full sun and average garden soil after danger of frost. Cup-and-saucer vines have reddish-purple, cup-shaped flowers nestled in light-green saucers. Start seeds indoors 6–8 weeks before the last frost or seed directly into the garden after frost has passed. These prolific vines can reach 20 feet in one season.

Nasturtiums, another old-fashioned flower, may grow only 6 feet, but they are a beautiful companion to taller vines. The bright yellow, orange, red, or white spurred flowers appear like jewels amid the dusty green leaves. Blooms have an extraordinarily sweet scent that can fill a room when cut and brought indoors. A related plant, canary bird vine, will envelop a trellis with tiny yellow flowers and delicate palmate leaves. Fortunately, nasturtiums grow and bloom best in poor soil. Rich soil will produce abundant foliage but very few flowers. Seed nasturtiums and canary bird vine directly into the garden after the soil has warmed.

Black-eyed Susan vine can be trained onto a trellis or grown in a hanging basket to cascade down. Blue-green foliage is offset with bright orange, gold, yellow, or white flowers with dark-brown eyes. Older flowers turn varying shades of cream to yellow to give the plant many variations of color at one time. Start indoors 6 weeks before the last frost and transplant to well-drained soil in full sun.

Hyacinth bean produces attractive blue-green leaves that complement its striking dark-purple, pealike flowers and eventual purple bean pods. These can grow 15 feet or more in a summer in average garden soil with ample water. Sow seeds directly in the garden after frost has passed.

Don't overlook the value of combinations of vines to stretch the blooming seasons and complement each other with contrasting blooms and foliage.

ANNUAL SEEDING REVIEW

Your choice of annuals may include the most popular or some of the more exotic flowers. Whichever you prefer, focus on proper seeding to get annuals off to a well-rooted start. Here are key notes to highlight in this book and your mind. These tips apply to all annuals.

For direct seeding outdoors, cover seeds with enough soil to protect them from wind and birds, about one-quarter to one-half inch, or 2–3 times their thickness as the packages direct. Then, water the seedbed to keep it evenly moist until seeds germinate.

When seedlings have grown several inches tall, thin them to the spacing that their seed packets direct. Mulch plants when they are a few inches tall to prevent weeds and conserve soil moisture. Use about 2–3 inches of mulch.

Fertilize most annuals at least about midway through the growing season to give them the nutritional boost they need to perform beautifully until frost.

STARTING SEEDS INDOORS

To get a jump on spring, see chapter 14, which is filled with tips to let you achieve your goals from the time you start seeds until you transplant seedlings outdoors. To reinforce those guidelines, key points are included here. Some annuals have small seeds or are frost sensitive. To extend the blooming season, start those seeds indoors to have transplants to set outdoors when all danger of frost is past. Another advantage is that starting seeds lets your entire family experience the magic of watching seeds sprout and grow as you all anticipate another gardening season together. Follow these guidelines.

First, obtain suitable containers of any type that hold soil, such as flats with or without individual cells, peat or paper pots, egg carton bottoms, or halved milk cartons. For transplanting seedlings, plastic, clay, or peat pots about 2–4 inches in diameter are helpful. Chain stores provide a myriad of planting pots and kits every spring. So do many mail order firms. Look around to see what may work best for you, and try some different seed-starting systems. To ensure even moisture for seeds and save yourself time, consider self-watering seed-starting kits.

You'll also need a germinating mix. Some come with minute amounts of fertilizer to give seedlings a useful growth boost. A mister or spray bottle is helpful to insure seedlings have a moist growing environment in the dry environment of most homes, especially those with forced air heat.

Wet the germinating mix thoroughly so it is moist but not soggy. Then, fill flats or individual pots with the mix to within about an inch of the top. We have always preferred peat pots, because once seedlings set good roots, you can plant the pot into the ground easily and roots grow right though the peat walls. This avoids transplanting setbacks that could occur if roots are damaged in moving from trays.

However, starting in flats or other containers works well for many gardeners, especially when growing large quantities of seedlings. If you prefer trays, make shallow row indentations with your finger in the flats. It's easier to separate seedlings at transplanting time if you sow in rows. Sow thinly to space seeds. If using pots, make shallow holes in the germinating mix and sow three to four seeds in each pot.

Some seeds need light to germinate properly, so check your seed packet and don't cover those types. Most seeds need darkness, so cover the seeds with one-quarter to one-half inch of mix and tamp it down. Then mist the surface with water to settle the seeds.

Veteran gardeners know it helps to cover flats with a sheet of plastic wrap or set them in plastic bags, like a mini-greenhouse to keep the mix from drying out while seeds germinate. Check periodically, and moisten if necessary by light misting with water. Place flats in a warm location and double check the seed packet for specific soil temperatures for germination. Generally, seeds germinate with soil temperatures of 70-75°F. You may find special plant heating pads in kits will give you better success.

When the seedlings emerge, usually in 7–14 days as the packet advises, remove the plastic covering. Keep the mix evenly moist and try to water from the bottom by setting flats and pots in a sink filled with a couple of inches of water. Remove them when moisture reaches the surface.

Next simple step is transplanting. Botanists explain that the first leaves on a seedling are cotyledons, not true leaves. Their shapes usually do not look like the plant's familiar leaves. When seedlings in flats grow at least two sets of true leaves, it is time to move them to pots or containers of transplanting mix. Frankly, a good potting soil will do, but a mix specifically formulated for young seedlings is better. That usually contains a coarser grade of sphagnum peat moss than a germinating mix and often includes fertilizer. Don't overlook fertilizer as you bring along your young plants. Fertilizer labels always list the main nutrients plants need, which include nitrogen, phosphorus, and potassium, in that order, with numbers to indicate percentages, such as 5-10-5, 10-10-10.

Moisten the mix, then fill the 2–4 inch pots about three-quarters full. With your fingers, carefully pick each seedling out of the original flat by holding each by the leaves, not the stem, because plants readily grow new leaves but not broken stems. Then set the transplant in the pot and fill in around the roots with more mix and lightly tamp it down. That's it. Place pots in a tray to hold water and place on a sunny windowsill.

While awaiting outdoor planting time, water transplants regularly from the bottom until they grow 3–4 inches tall. Then you can water from the top. Feed your plants with a water-soluble fertilizer according to package directions. It helps to encourage compact, bushy plants by pinching off the growing tips of most flowering plants.

To give young plants their proper share of sun, turn them a quarter-turn every week, which helps them grow straight instead of bending toward the light. Because it is difficult to tell what tiny plants are, always label seed containers when you plant them. It is best to plant only one variety in each container to avoid confusion. A last and vital tip: go easy on water. Too much water can rot roots. Keep soil moist, never wet.

Because it can be difficult to produce quality transplants at home or you don't have the time or space, you may be better off purchasing young bedding plants from a garden center to transplant in your garden. Look for stocky plants with dense foliage and rich colors. Avoid seedlings that are leggy, yellowish, or dry looking. If possible, check the root system. Most healthy plant roots are white. While it is tempting to choose blooming plants, it is better to select those that are not.

Just prior to planting, water bedding plants well to thoroughly moisten the soil. Ideally, the garden bed should also be slightly moist prior to planting. Lift plants from the cell packs or pots by gently squeezing or pushing up the bottom, or turn it upside down, tap it lightly, and the plant will fall into your hand. If roots are compacted, loosen roots by either breaking the soil ball apart slightly or cutting the sides of the root ball with a knife, which helps to encourage better rooting in the garden. If flats don't have individual cells, separate plants gently by hand or use a knife to cut them apart.

ANNUAL GARDEN SEEDING POINTERS

Happily, most annuals are easy to grow from seed right in the garden. Fact is, direct seeding outdoors is the preferred method for certain annuals that do not transplant well. Also, young seedlings grown from seed sown outdoors directly into the soil are immediately acclimated and don't face transplanting setback.

Seeds will grow in all kinds of unconventional situations, even when stressed. However a well-prepared seedbed gives them growing advantages. When the soil has warmed and dried out in spring, dig down or rototill 8–10 inches to loosen the soil.

In the process, mix in some organic matter such as compost or peat moss to help hold moisture. To ensure even better success, mix in some granular, slow-acting, general-purpose fertilizer to provide consistent nutrition over many weeks. Pelleted, slow-release fertilizer works especially well to help annuals sustain their fullest flowering. Rake the soil level and smooth.

For a natural look in your garden, you can sow seeds in a free-handed, broadcast way in a bed or border. If you are planting tiny seeds, such as portulaca or petunia, mix them with a bit of coarse sand or vermiculite to spread more evenly. Toss larger seeds freestyle and then rake them gently into the soil where they fall. If the package label says seeds must be covered with soil, sprinkle some garden soil or packaged potting medium over them and moisten the seedbed.

If you prefer more formal gardens, sow annual seeds in rows. Just make lines in the soil and space seeds as the packet suggests. Most should be set one-quarter to one-half inch deep and covered with soil or soil mix and then moistened. Water periodically.

An advantage of the hardy annuals is that they tend to be self-sowing. Seeds they released as they died the previous fall can withstand winter weather and often will germinate on their own the following spring. To encourage this, don't deadhead faded flowers as fall approaches. Let them develop seedheads. Let these mature seeds fall where the plants are growing. You can even pick dried seed heads and shake the seeds loose over an area where you would like to have the flowers next season. Try it and test your skills with these special annuals.

For your annual flower planning, some of the best that are easiest to grow from seeds are alyssum, balsam, calendula, California poppy, coreopsis, celosia, cosmos, marigold, nasturtium, portulaca, rudbeckia, sunflower, sweet pea, viola, and zinnia.

ANNUAL CULTURE KNOW-HOW

Gardeners sometimes overlook the basics in their rush to plant, landscape, or expand their growing horizons. We neglect basics at our peril. Fertilizer is a basic. Nitrogen is the nutrient that most frequently limits plant growth. Unfortunately, nitrogen is the most difficult nutrient to manage. Nitrogen is easily leached from the soil. The challenge is to maintain adequate nitrogen levels to meet the plant requirements without damaging the plants or the environment. Because nitrogen promotes foliage, other fertilizer elements are needed to produce desired plant growth and desired profuse flowering.

Growth rate and foliage color are the primary guides for determining the need for additional fertilizer applications during the growing season. However, some general guidelines can be used. Nitrogen can be applied in a quick-release, water-soluble form using a liquid or granular fertilizer or in a slow-release, granular form. Make applications of a quick-release fertilizer, such as 10-10-10, every 4–8 weeks throughout the season at the rate of 1 pound per 100 square feet. Experts note that liquid, water-soluble fertilizers should be applied about every 2 weeks. With slow-release fertilizers, make only two applications: the first incorporated into the bed just before planting, and the second broadcast over the bed midway through the growing season. Plant nutrition experts also advise that the total seasonal application of slow-release fertilizer should not exceed 4–6 pounds of nitrogen per 1,000 square feet.

Water is another key element that we can overdo. Novices tend to overfertilize and overwater their gardens. Be wise and don't overdo fertilizer or water. Naturally, different plants have different needs, so try to learn all you can about your favorite plants. When you give them the optimum conditions they need, they will perform abundantly. Although some flowers will tolerate moderate periods of dry weather, others must have a continuous supply of water. Flowering of most annuals will slow or stop during extended hot, dry summer weather. To minimize the need for watering, select drought-tolerant annuals such as globe amaranth, blue blaze, gazania, gomphrena, portulaca, and creeping zinnia.

Supplemental watering will probably be required at some point during the growing season. Soil type as well as plant growth, the use of mulches, and temperature changes influence watering frequency. Plants growing in a clay soil may need to be watered only once a week. Plants in a sandy soil may have to be watered several times a week. This will vary with the time of year, amount of sunlight or shade, plant growth, and other conditions. Most plants need I inch of water per week but may require more when flowering profusely. Additional water may be needed when plants are exposed to high temperatures or windy conditions. A Green Thumb rule says moisten the entire bed thoroughly but do not water so heavily that the soil becomes soggy. After watering, allow soil to dry moderately before watering again.

Modern gardening conveniences are welcome. A soaker hose is excellent for watering flowerbeds. Water seeps directly into the soil without waste and without wetting leaves and flowers that might encourage mildew. The slow-moving water does not disturb the soil or reduce its capacity to absorb water. Sprinklers tend to wet flowers and foliage and make them more susceptible to diseases.

As you may have guessed, the least effective method for watering is with a handheld hose, which has all the disadvantages of watering with a sprinkler. Most gardeners seldom are patient enough to do a thorough job of watering with a hose and don't apply enough water or distribute it evenly over the bed. Invest in soaker hoses or a drip irrigation system and you'll discover that they, with a timer, are one of the better garden investments that contribute to more productive, beautiful gardens.

Another key factor to help annuals to produce more flowers is a simple process called deadheading. That is simply the removal of dead or faded flowers and seed pods. When annuals expend energy to produce seed, they don't continue to produce flowers as abundantly. It pays to remove spent flowers and seed pods especially on such flowers as ageratum, calendula, celosia, coleus, cosmos, geranium, marigold, scabiosa, salvia, rudbeckia, and zinnia. Many modern cultivars are self-cleaning, which means that their spent flowers disappear quickly. Other cultivars are sterile and do not produce seeds. If you see spent flower heads begin to form seeds, deadhead and give the plants encouragement to set more blooms.

ENJOY A BUTTERFLY GARDEN

Butterflies delight us all. On a warm sunny day, these playful visitors provide their own flying colors that add to the pleasure of gardening. To attract them, think in terms of massed splashes of color. Butterfly-attracting plants should be good nectar producers. Perennials can be your base, with annuals added for accents each year. It is best to have butterfly gardens in full sunlight to achieve most blooms. They also need shallow pools of water, and the garden should be screened from winds.

Adult butterflies are attracted to bee balm, butterfly bush, candytuft, cardinal flower, gaillardia, heliotrope, lobelia, lantana, lavender, liatris, lupine, monarda, ox-eye daisy, phlox, Joe-Pye weed, purple coneflower, black-eyed Susan or rudbeckia species, scarlet sage, sedum, tickseed coreopsis, verbena, yarrow, and zinnia. Mature butterflies need nectar to thrive. As you plan butterfly-luring flowers, focus on clusters of small florets that provide many sips plus a place to rest; are brightly colored in lavender, purple, red, orange, and yellow and are single-flowered types where the nectar is more accessible. Flowers with fragrance, planted in clusters, are especially effective.

Butterflies will visit and often lay eggs wherever there is a variety of plants for food and shelter, some moisture, and no pesticides. Your challenge is to provide diversity of plants to support both larvae and adults. Variety is the key. Incorporate herbs, annuals, and perennials. Use flowers as vines, ground covers, and in beds. Wildflower meadows featuring native plants are ideal. Allow an area to remain weedy and undeveloped to lure female butterflies to lay eggs. Plants that attract butterfly larvae include asters, clover, lupine, mallow, marigold, parsley, snapdragon, and violets, as well as plantain and sorrel.

GROW A LIVING AMERICAN FLAG

You can let the breeze wave your living American flag as it grows in your garden. Here's a patriotic challenge. Try planting an Old Glory with glorious red, white, and blue blooms in your own yard. Pick a sunny spot with good soil and dig in. Apply a general all-purpose fertilizer to the soil before you till the ground, spreading about 2–3 pounds of fertilizer per 100 square feet. Leave a wide margin around the edge of your living flag so you can weed, remove old blooms, and water your garden.

Next step is to mark out straight or waving lines for your flag's stripes. Stake the rows with cord so you can plant seed or seedlings evenly. For a 13-star Colonial Old Glory, place 13 wood stakes in a circle

where you'll plant the white flowers for the stars representing the original 13 states. Plant your red and white flower seeds in rows as directions on the seed package advise. Cover lightly with soil. Next plant seeds of blue flowers to be your field of blue, and then the white flower seeds where you made the ring of stakes.

To ensure good germination, water your flag garden every day until seeds sprout. Leave cords in place so you'll know where your flowers will sprout. Remove competing weeds every few days. To have faster results, you can prestart plants in peat pots and bring them along until they begin to bloom. Or buy red, white, and blue flower plants at a garden center. It's more costly, but you get to see results faster with started plants and avoid weeding chores. Once plants are well established, mulch with peat moss or bark mulch to smother weeds and hold in soil moisture that benefits your flag garden plants.

For cooler weather flowers, here are some to try. Reds: aster, begonia, petunia, snapdragon, stock. Whites: aster, alyssum, baby's breath, stock. Blues, aster, ageratum, lobelia, larkspur.

If you need heat-resistant flowers for hot weather areas, try the following. Red: celosia, geranium, impatiens, pinks, salvia, zinnia. White: cleome, geranium, petunia, daisy, impatiens. Blue: blue lace flower, petunia, verbena, blue salvia.

As your flag bursts into bloom, you'll have earned, as the song says, "a hurray for the red, white and blue."

SAVE AND RECYCLE POTS

Reusing plastic pots is a good idea. Here's how to make sure you avoid problems when you recycle pots that held last year's plants. Be aware that disease-causing bacteria and fungi that attack

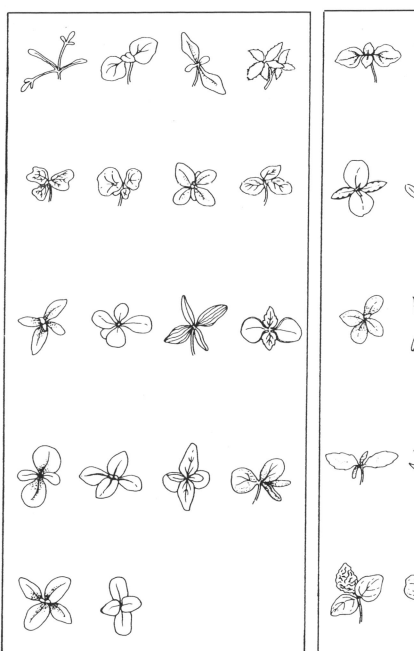
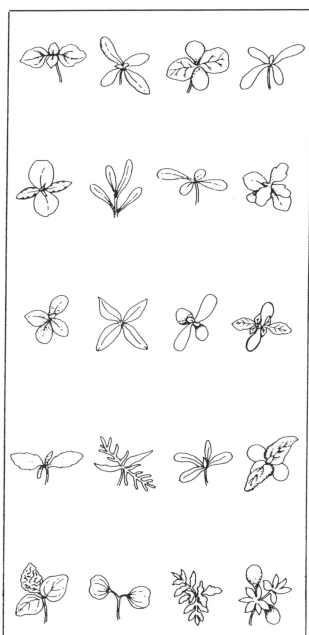

Weeds can get a head start when unconfident gardeners aren't sure which is a flower and which is a weed. Here is a visual guide depicting the most common flower seedlings. Left column: row 1: kochia, linaria, lobelia, lupine; row 2: morning glory, nasturtium, nicotiana, pansy; row 3: petunia, phlox, portulaca, salvia; row 4: Shasta daisy, snapdragon, sunflower, sweet pea; row 5: verbena, zinnia. Right column: row 1: ageratum, alyssum, aster, bachelor's button; row 2: balsam, calliopsis, calendula, candytuft; row 3: carnation, celosia, chrysanthemum, cleome; row 4: coleus, cosmos, dianthus, four o'clock; row 5: hollyhock, impatiens, marigold, larkspur.

seedlings are common inhabitants of soil and can be spread with soil particles. Old soil clinging to pots can carry these troublesome microbes, which can cause poor seed germination or damping-off of seedlings. Plant debris, including parts of old roots or leaves, also can transmit these pathogens.

Wash pots and flats with soap and water, using a stiff scrub brush if necessary to remove debris. Microbes can survive on particles too small to see. To disinfect your planters, prepare a solution of 1 part bleach and 9 parts water, and soak pots and flats in it for 30 minutes. Pots and flats must be completely free of soil and totally immersed in this liquid to achieve desired results. Rinse the containers thoroughly to remove bleach residues, then dry and store until you need them.

CELEBRATE CUT FLOWERS

A bouquet of flowers is a treat to receive, and also to give to family and friends for special occasions or just to celebrate the joys of gardening beauty. Think how marvelous it is to be surrounded indoors by bouquets and arrangements of fragrant, colorful blossoms. You can treat yourself and friends more easily than you imagine. Plan a cutting garden. Annuals are ideal because they bloom so profusely. In addition, plan ahead to have not only home-grown blossoms, but decorative foliage and even seedheads for fresh or dried floral decorating. One problem is that by picking flowers from the garden, you reduce the blossom show. A simple solution is to have a separate cultivated area as a cutting garden to have your flowers and pick them too!

Since you'll be cutting regularly, use an area perhaps near your veggie patch or herb bed. Plant the flowers you love best as cut flowers, especially the most fragrant ones. Don't worry about design, since you'll be cutting it down regularly. Pick a site

that receives generous sun. Prepare the soil so that it drains well. Add humus, compost, peat moss, or chopped leaves to improve clay or sandy soil. Create one or more beds of whatever size and shape you wish, perhaps tucked into sunny spots along the back boundary, in a neglected corner, or behind the garage. Space rows widely enough apart so they are easy to tend while fertilizing, deadheading, and harvesting.

Although perennials, once beds are established, produce cutting flowers every year, most annuals are favored for their profuse blooming habit. To enjoy maximum production, plant annuals in succession to have early, mid, and late bloomers together. Cluster plants with similar requirements for sun, water, and drainage for easier maintenance. Plant tall types together and lower ones together so tall plants won't shade lower growers. Mulch with a 2–3 inch layer to minimize watering and weeding.

To encourage flower production of annuals, pick blossoms regularly and deadhead as needed. Be alert for aphids on tender young growth. Simply pinch off infested tips or spray with insecticidal soap to eliminate stubborn infestations. When blossoms from one group of annuals have been cut, be bold. Pull them up or till under and plant new seedlings to provide cut flowers for the weeks that remain. Pansies, for example, are early and cool weather bloomers. When heat slows them, interplant marigolds, but leave some pansies to rebloom in cool fall weather.

You probably have your own cutting-flower favorites. Grow what you wish. To help your planning, here are thoughts about flowers that provide dependable cut-flower success. Long-stemmed types are most useful. All varieties of daisies are popular and combine well with many other flowers. Here's a brief list of recommended annuals from some veteran gardeners, which is just a beginning:

ageratum, amaranthus or love-lies-bleeding, anemone, bells of Ireland, calendula, China aster, celosia or cockscomb, baby's breath, bachelor's buttons, cleome, cosmos, everlasting, marigold, stock, pansy, petunia, phlox, snapdragon, strawflower, sunflower, sweet pea, and verbena. Note that celosia and baby's breath are excellent for dried flower arranging.

The fresher cut flowers look, the more appealing your displays will be. Follow these tips to prolong the vase life of your cut flowers. Cut flowers early in the morning or early evening. Be sure your vases are filled with a cut-flower preservative solution. If you arrange flowers in one of the foamlike materials that florists use, be sure that water in the vase covers the top of the foam to ensure all the plants have an ample supply of water. To keep blooms nicer, recut all loose bunched flowers to open stems so they can drink up water better. Avoid damage to stems. Remove any foliage that will be under water in the arrangement. Select a location in your home or office where the flowers can be prominently displayed but have cool temperatures and high relative humidity. Display them away from drafts, heat, and air-conditioning ducts or appliances that give off heat. Attention to these tips will ensure longer-blooming beauty from your cut flowers.

12

GARDEN FOR
SCENIC BEAUTY

Colorful gardens brighten our lives. One of your objectives should be to paint colorful pictures with your home plantscaping. You'll find landscaping details in chapter 7. In this chapter, you'll find related ideas but more focused on projects that will provide you with ways to give your home special surroundings.

One way is with color. For generations, gardeners have focused on ways to have colorful greetings from flowers as soon as snow melts in spring right through to the last glow of fall foliage. Some of the secrets are with bulbs, from earliest crocuses that burst forth in early spring to daffodils, hyacinths, tulips, lilies, and other bulbous plants that provide colorful horizons into summer. You'll find details about making them bloom bountifully in chapter 9. Here you can savor the ideas harvested from around our country to give your land even more glorious vistas as well as create colorful nooks and crannies.

For the past several years, the National Garden Bureau (NGB) has addressed color in the garden. With thanks to those respected experts, here is a collection of tips from them for using color, and focused thoughts from a color expert which you can put to use where you live.

First, when planning a garden, think of it as a three-dimensional painting. Envision colorful annuals for beds and containers as colors on an artist's palette. Some colors will dominate and be spread with broad brush strokes. Other colors can give depth and dimension with small dabs here and there. Try to envision the entire panorama of your garden as you want it to look when it is at its best, and plan accordingly.

To brighten shady areas, the NGB experts suggest using light-colored annuals such as white, light pink, or palest blues, because dark colors tend to get lost in shady areas. Also think about foliage plants such as coleus that have bright, multicolored leaves and thrive in shady areas. Yes, you can use deep colors in a shady area, but be certain to use lighter colors around or behind them to provide contrast so that they stand out. For example, burgundy impatiens surrounded by pale green coleus or coral impatiens will stand out because of the contrast.

To achieve maximum impact, think how the colors of plants will blend or contrast with their surroundings and each other. For example, deep-red geraniums or red salvia planted against a red brick wall or redwood fence will become lost and not stand out as well as white or pink geraniums. Same problems with white flowers against a white fence or siding. Think of using a more dramatic color scheme such as purple or magenta against a white or light-color background, and something lighter, such as peach or pink, against darker surfaces.

National Garden Bureau design experts also note that you can learn from home interior decorators. Just as they use three or four colors as a theme throughout a home, you as an exterior garden decorator can do the same. Theme colors used repeatedly will unify different garden areas, just as colors unify rooms of a house. For example, bordering all your garden plots with rows of yellow marigolds or creamy petunias can tie different garden areas together for a unified look. Repeating the same colors but in different plant types can produce the same effect. If white and blue are your colors, for example, plant different types of flowers such as lavender, blue petunias, and blue salvia and for white use white geraniums, impatiens, or petunias to carry the theme but vary the look. Take advantage of different flower forms, sizes, and shapes as well as the plants themselves with their foliage.

Interior decorators point out that each room should have a focal point. Same with each area of your garden. If you don't have a natural focal point such as a pool of water or garden statuary, color can create one. Avoid long, uninterrupted rows of flowers. Instead, create a focal point by planting a mass of one color in the center of a bed. Then surround it with flowers or plants that contrast in color, texture, or height. Use color to draw the eye away from an unsightly area, such as a compost pile, storage area, or telephone pole. Plant a colorful focal point away from the object to draw attention to a more pleasing group of colorful plants.

Psychologists point out that colors affect our emotions. Bright colors such as red and yellow ex-cite us and can make us feel warm. Advertising agencies know that fact from studies and often call those "hot" or "warm" colors. Notice which packages catch your eye in stores, those with hot reds and yellows.

In contrast, colors such as blue, lavender, green, pink, and peach are considered cooler and calmer. Consider how to draw favorable attention to the entrance of your home. Give it a feeling of warmth and excitement with more exciting colors such as yellow marigolds and scarlet dianthus. For a quiet meditation garden area, you may want to create a more relaxing and serene mood by choosing cooler or softer colors such as pansy rose shades with blue violas.

One final key point about colors to consider. Dramatic color combinations can give your garden beds a distinctive look. Instead of something as ordinary as red and white, consider orange and blue, which actually are direct complements on the color wheel, or light pink and green. Plant breeders have been producing a much wider range of colors in many different flower varieties. Take advantage of those opportunities to redecorate your garden with colors.

Many of today's annuals are available in more colors, tones, and shades than ever before. Impatiens, for instance, now come in 24 separate designer colors or blends. Creating a colorful fresh new look is easier than ever.

As times change, so do home and garden decorating ideas. Perhaps a look at "fashionable" color trends might be helpful. National Garden Bureau color expert Ken Charbonnau, director of color marketing for the Benjamin Moore Paint Company in Montvale, New Jersey, offers some worthwhile considerations.

"The biggest thing affecting color over the last five years has been the economy," says Charbonnau.

"People want more value for their money, so we are seeing a return to more classic colors and color combinations. Colors will be less trendy and more long-lasting."

According to Charbonnau, purple and violet are big news in color, but as he says, "in small doses. Purple and blue-violet bring out the rest of the palette." An avid gardener himself, he notes that purples and blues tend to fade away in the garden. They need lots of sun to highlight them, be massed to be seen, or combined with white or yellow to really show off. You can bring little doses of purple to your gardens with plants like petunias and a wide choice of other annuals.

Charbonnau also notes that coral has gained attention. In his yard, he has masses of coral- and peach-colored flowers against a weathered gray fence. "People are just amazed when they see it. We are also seeing color being used to link new things with things from the past," he says, calling them bridging colors. "For example, people tend to think of salvia splendens only in red, but today it comes in twelve decorator colors."

Salvia, a longtime favorite, is now fresh and new with its new colors. The past is linked to the new. Charbonnau also gives an example from the windowboxes at the front of his brownstone home in New York. "I combined purple salvia, blue ageratum, and magenta geraniums. People would stop and take pictures!" Those colors are the same colors in the slipcovers in one of his rooms. "I took our interior colors to the outside," he says.

Magenta is another important color, Charbonnau believes. "What was pink is now moving into magenta. Mauve is rapidly declining because it was so trendy and so everywhere that people became tired of it," he notes. But, yellow is returning to the color palette after a long absence, he believes. He extols combinations such as yellow and white and periwinkle, or yellow and white and purple, pointing out the value of purple in small doses to bring out the other colors.

"Reds are still doing well, but in the classic shades such as wine and burgundy. Bright but not too orange." Generally speaking of color trends, he thinks that colors will tend to be brighter and stronger than pastels, but still softer and what he calls relaxed. He thinks that this relaxed feeling will extend to our gardens, and we will see garden designs and floral arrangements that are less formal or structured. "People will experiment more with color combinations and not worry so much about what goes together perfectly," Charbonnau says. My thanks to the National Garden Bureau for sharing these timely observations from a noted color design authority.

New, bright, and also muted colors give us all an opportunity to paint our outdoor living areas with the colors and types of flowers we like best. Actually, adding color to our lives is often why we garden in the first place. Color can excite and stimulate. They can soothe and refresh. Perhaps most importantly, the colors of our garden are a reflection of who we are. Besides, who isn't happy while sitting on a bench in the midst of a mass of colorful blooming beauty whichever way you wish to look across your landscape.

As you plan to redecorate with garden colors, keep in mind that white is the most versatile color of all. It blends other colors and lightens the garden. Garden Bureau specialists point out that whites tie together garden areas, soften strong colors, and lead the gaze from one area to another. Pale colors such as pastel pinks and yellows brighten and accent dark corners of the garden or shady retreats. Dark colors such as maroons and plums make their strongest impact when used in full sun, although they will add beautiful emphasis to darker areas when set off with white or silver.

Next, think in terms of monochromatic gardens. These emphasize a single color with flowers and foliage of various tints and shades of that color. Although the emphasis is on one color, not everything is the same shade or tone. Instead, there will be different shades that reflect the original color. In fact, even an all-white garden is best emphasized with shades of silver, cream, and pale yellow to set off the whites.

Another worthwhile observation from the National Garden Bureau is that complementary themes such as mauve, pink, and blue or yellow, orange, and brown are soothing. But it pays to add something of contrast for interest and tie the colors together with white and gray. Major contrasts such as yellow and purple or red and blue can be dramatic and exciting. Experts explain that the ultimate polychromatic garden includes all colors. A riot of colors is exuberant, as we noted during our visits to the famed Keukenhof Gardens in Holland. There garden designers used massed colors and mixed colors to showcase new tulips. The results were truly dramatic.

Walking among those 7 million blooms of tulips, daffs, and hyacinths, you can see the value of color dramatically displayed. Frankly, color is a superb way to complement other elements in the garden, such as the house, a fence, a statue, or a planter. Here are some other suggestions, courtesy of the National Garden Bureau. A gray weathered fence is a spectacular backdrop for peach and salmon foxgloves and delphiniums. A red brick patio is dramatic when adorned with silver and white mealycup sage and fragrant flowering tobacco. A white windowpane trellis or white picket fence is exquisite when draped with creamy peach sweet peas and periwinkle-blue morning glories.

As you plan for your own all-season display, the colors that naturally fall into place in spring are the bright new greens of emerging leaves, bright yellows and pinks of tulips and daffodils, and soft pastel pinks and purples of pansies, anemones, and peonies. Summer, with the brightest sun and clearest days, brings the exuberant colors of bright yellows, oranges, and reds of sunflowers, lilies, and zinnias. Fall delivers muted crimson and gold mums and blazing purple asters set against a backdrop of golden birch, red maple, and bronze magnolias. Winter is the time to enjoy muted greens and grays set against crisp sparkling snow and striking bark colors of red, gold, velvety gray, and hushed black.

You can page though colorful mail order garden catalogs to find hundreds of new varieties in a wide range of colors. Whether you prefer perennials for their lower upkeep, want annuals for their dramatic displays, or enjoy mixing and matching flowers and plants, you can paint your home grounds as gloriously colorful as you wish.

TRY GROWING WILD

There is another way to enjoy colorful beauty that may prove even easier in the years ahead. Try growing wild. It can be a wonderful new horizon for your gardening pleasure. Lawns may look nice, but you can save time and money while enjoying natural beauty when you grow wild.

You'll be amazed at how many delightful, different flowers will grace a natural meadow. Many sprout from roots or dormant seeds. Others grow from seeds brought by wind or birds. One senior gardener, my neighbor Bligh Parker when I lived in Basking Ridge, New Jersey, let a plot of lawn "go natural," as he described it. He didn't mow about a quarter-acre of lawn. I could see it when I mowed my lawn adjacent to his property. His effort to grow wild impressed me and I wrote about growing wild in a 12-part series of my nationally syndicated Gardener's Notebook columns.

In early spring, tiny bluets in a moist area near maple trees bloomed. Hundreds of them blossomed all around the tree without a power mower to lop off their bluish-white flowers. Violets appeared next. The second year, enough had naturalized from parent plant seed to give the lawn area a purplish haze for several spring weeks. Then hawkweed sprouted. What seemed to be dandelions at first glance thrust 10 inch-tall stalks that burst with yellow and golden looms. They flourished, unthreatened by herbicides or mower blades. Naturally, dandelions joined in with their golden display.

Next, he reported that daisies bloomed. Their fernlike foliage matured, supporting bright white ox-eye blooms with golden-yellow centers. Red and white clover reappeared, beckoning bees to a harvest of pollen. Even rabbit's foot and tall yellow clover graced the property border. As the season progressed, scattered black-eyed Susans burst into bloom. Their radiant yellow petals surrounding dark centers brightened the unmowed, waving green grass. Finally, asters sprouted, cascading white and even purple-hued blooms through the fall.

Perhaps the richest reward was the time saved. He used it to enjoy this natural wildflower world, a colorful bouquet in his own backyard. As far as I know, it grows on to this day, glorious and untended, naturally in New Jersey. Perhaps you may wish to transplant that idea to part of your own home grounds. You can let an area grow wild without mowing, or buy or collect wildflowers. Here are some tips to help you. These tips are from my garden columns that appeared in newspapers nationwide.

Wildflowers have advantages over cultivated ones. They are naturally hardy, usually self-propagating, and almost as indestructible as weeds.

Better yet, they provide wild beauty to those difficult spots where soil or growing conditions are inhospitable to cultivated plants. Select healthy material, whether you purchase it or collect plants from the wild—with permission of the landowner, of course. Always plant immediately after you bring plants home. Give plants the same kind of soil in which they grew in their native habitat. It pays to gather extra soil with the plants you dig so they will be comfortable in their new setting. Set them at the same depth at which they grew naturally. Clear space around the new planting to avoid competition from weeds.

Water newly planted wildflowers the first few days and then weekly until they are clearly well established. Collect woodland or field litter, the decaying humus around the plants where they grew. Spread it around them both as a mulch and to let the natural soil organisms work their wonders as they did where the plants grew. Start simply, a few clumps of plants at a time.

Check with your local garden club or state conservation officials before you embark on wildflower collection. Some plants are on rare and restricted lists and should be left alone in their native habit. Several wildflower specialist nurseries provide individual plants, seeds, and collections of mixed varieties that are native to certain parts of America. Those specialty firms also provide you with helpful ideas and advice to launch your wildflower gardens and get them growing to perfection.

Wildflowers are flowering plants that grow in their natural state with little interference from humans. They are not bred or crossbred the way hybrids and other cultivated annuals and perennials may be, and generally may be considered "natural" because they grow in open fields without someone planning where they should be planted. One of the many appeals of wildflowers is their low-maintenance need. Designed by nature to tolerate natural growing conditions, wildflowers usually require less attention than cultivated flowers. Deciding which wildflowers to grow in your garden depends on where you live and where in your garden you want to grow the wildflowers.

Today, wildflowers can be purchased as seeds or plants, as a single species or in mixes. If you want only a few specific wildflowers, purchasing growing plants or buying seed packets may be your best choice. Started plants offer you the advantage of avoiding the germination stage and may give you a better idea of what a plant really looks like.

To make life even easier, it is best to purchase wildflower mixes for your area. These are a popular way of purchasing wildflowers. Mixes offer the advantage of combining a wide range of species that offer a full season of color and growth. They also offer the free-form look of varying heights, sizes, and colors, one of the natural appeals of wildflowers.

Major mail order firms also offer packages. Mixes are available that will do best in sunny locations or shady locations. There are also regional mixes, such as for the Midwest, South, Northeast, and New England, specially blended with annuals and perennials suited to the particular growing area. That takes some of the guesswork out of what will grow where.

You also can buy prestarted wildflower plants and seeded mats. The advantage of mats is that they are easy to handle and can be cut to fit circular and irregularly shaped beds. Usually these mats just need to be put in place and watered. They are often made of a wood fiber material that is biodegradable. They also serve as a mulch to help keep down weeds and will eventually disappear into the soil. Wildflower sod is also becoming available but is rather expensive.

You'll find sources for wildflowers in chapter 18. More information about wildflower seed suppliers and tips are available from the National Garden Bureau, Suite 310, 1311 Butterfield Road, Downers Grove, IL 60515.

TRY SOME WILDFLOWERS

Here are growing tips for some of the most popular wildflowers. Give some a try.

You'll enjoy more than a daisy a day when you grow **ox-eye daisies**. Originally from Europe, these well-established flowers are truly naturalized Americans that grow well all across the United States. Fernlike leaves give the plants a graceful look. The sparkling white petals surround bright yellow-gold centers. Blooms stand 15–24 inches tall on sturdy stems. Flowers are 1–1.5 inches across, ideal for cutting and long-lasting in water for indoor decorations.

Daisies love sun. Since they thrive on a wide range of soils, daisies are easily grown in most garden areas. Best planting time is spring or fall. From wild plants, select and divide large clumps. Keep roots wrapped in moist moss covered with plastic until you plant them. Or collect seeds in late summer from mature plants and sow them in the fall, as nature would.

Black-eyed Susans will never give your garden a black eye. You'll delight in their nodding blooms of bright golden petals around dark-brown centers. Their dark-brown "eyes" give them their popular name. They also are called coneflowers and are hardy, native American flowers that grow gloriously in sunny fields and meadows across our continent.

This beautiful flower prefers well-drained, even fairly dry soils. Their ability to grow well even in poorer, sandy soils makes them a perfect match for daisies and clover in a natural meadow habitat.

Foliage and leaves are rough and bristly. Flowers burst into bloom on stems 2–3 feet tall with golden-yellow petals and purple-brown centers 1.5–2.5 inches across. Mature plants can be moved easily in the fall. Young plants can be set in early spring. Seeds are widely available or you can collect from wild plants. Sow seeds in summer to germinate and winter over as young plants to bloom the following year.

Sundews are sticky and surprising because they lure, catch, and eat live insects. Enzymes secreted by the plants digest the protein of the insects, which becomes the plants' nourishment. These plant oddities are native to boggy areas across America, in swamps, roadside ditches, lake sides, and wetlands. Bugs are lured by the dozens of glistening, reddish tentacles on each inch-long leaf. When insects land, the glue-like secretions stick the prey tight until other tentacles wrap around to digest it. Typical plants have 6–15 leaves radiating from the center. Depending on the variety, sundews bear violet to purple flowers, each with five petals.

Sundews thrive in wet spots with full sun and must never be allowed to dry out. Transplant young plants in spring with enough acid soil and sphagnum moss to provide a suitable new habitat. Specialized plant firms sell them too. Since sundews are a bog plant, it is best to grow them with other moisture-loving wildlings. Purple pitcher plant, another meat-eater, makes a good companion.

You have a wide choice among the wild **violet** family. Some like sun, and others thrive in shade. Some tolerate poor soil, while others prefer richer conditions. All grow low, so they fit well in beds and borders, around trees and shrubs, and in rock gardens too. With time, most will form dense clumps. Try fragrant white violets, which are adaptable to acid or alkaline conditions in dry or moist

Common blue-violet wildflowers.

Common ox-eye daisy wildflowers.

Black-eyed Susan wildflowers.

ground, light or heavy soil. Common violets are uncommonly easy to grow. Found from Maine to Georgia in moist meadows and stream sides, these prefer loamy soil and sun. They grow 3–7 inches tall with half-inch rich purple flowers. Downy yellow violets are native to dry, rich woodland soil. The flowers bloom in early spring on plants that can reach 15 inches in height. No matter where you live, there are wild native violets for rock gardens, beds, borders, or just growing wild in your uncut lawn areas. Transplant by dividing clumps in spring or fall. Most root readily and spread themselves by seeds through the years.

Iris blooms have been admired throughout history. The fleur-de-lis pattern has been captured in tapestries, carvings, and ceremonial banners from ancient times through the present. Wild flag iris have a long, hardy tradition that you can add to your home gardens. The large blue flag iris shoots

its lance-shaped leaves from wet meadows and pastures in early spring. Its neatly furled buds burst into violet blossom on 16–30 inch stems. Although this iris prefers marshes, wet pastures, and banks of streams, it will flourish in moist garden soils or boggy areas if provided regularly with ample moisture. Blue flags will reward you profusely each year with violet-blue, purplish, and slate-blue blooms.

Yellow flag or sword flag iris produces 3–4 foot stems, flanked by 12–18 inch leaves. This is also a marsh plant, favoring borders of swamps, ditches, and streams. It must be well watered to thrive. All wild iris, like their domesticated relatives, can easily be transplanted by moving entire clumps. Or you can divide the rhizomes with a sharp knife. Then replant the rhizomes at the soil surface, just tucked in enough to stay in place.

Wild **asters** give us sparkle and color in the fall after most other flowers have passed their prime and gone to seed. And they are especially prolific, providing dozens of dainty blooms in shades of silver to rich purple. They also are hardy and grow well even in poorer soils. Asters deserve a place wherever you wish to grow wild. Low-growing types cling to the ground and are ideal for rock gardens, slopes, low beds, and borders. Taller types 2–5 feet tall bear profusions of blooms as a backdrop for lower plants or screens along property lines. Asters are common in sunny meadows, along roadsides, and at the seashore. Other types prefer shade and thrive in wooded settings.

Canada lilies are brilliant, eye-catching wildflowers that deserve a place even in cultivated plant gardens. They're sturdy and lend a touch of wild elegance as they bloom. The Canada lily, one of the most beautiful of all wild lilies, is native to sunny meadows in the eastern United States. Its buff-yellow blooms are spotted with purple brown. A southern relative is shorter and has redder flowers.

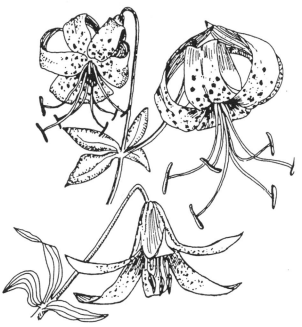

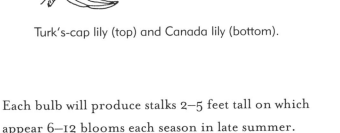

Turk's-cap lily (top) and Canada lily (bottom).

Common wild sunflower.

Each bulb will produce stalks 2–5 feet tall on which appear 6–12 blooms each season in late summer.

Turk's-cap lilies are even more elegant beauties, found in sunny, moist meadows, partially shaded roadsides, and bog borders. Their brilliantly colored mass blooms make a striking picture. Turk's-cap lilies may have 6–18 flowers appearing in a pyramid of bloom atop 3–6 foot stems. Blossoms resemble a sultan's headdress of buff-orange to vermilion, spotted with brown. The petals seem to curl upward. This plant is a favorite of monarch butterflies and blooms from July through August. Propagation is relatively easy. Transplant bulbs or bulblets formed on parent-plant bulbs. Dig 6–8 inches deep and mix leaf mold or compost in the hole. Plant bulbs and cover. Mulch and they'll take root to give years of brilliant color. Plant the tiny bulblets 4–6 inches deep.

Marvelous **sunflowers** turn their beautiful blooming heads to follow the sun in its daily journey east to west across the sky. These radiant flowers, the official state flower of Kansas, are hardy natives. Their golden-yellow blooms are common in fields and meadows in sunny areas. They will thrive even in poor, sandy, gravelly soils, but are most productive in sandy loam. The common sunflower is an annual with yellow petals radiating from a darker yellow center. The stems are 3–10 feet tall, while blooms are 3–6 inches across. Sunflowers will grow in all states but do best outside the deep South.

GROW YOUR OWN STATE FLOWER

Native American wildflowers are delightful additions to any home garden. Being native, they are hardy and adaptable. Best of all, they are beautiful. Some states have selected native wildflowers as their official state flowers. Other states have selected flowers that may be cultivated plants but truly represent the state well.

Every state has its official flower, selected as representative of that state. Sometimes more than one state has chosen the same flower.

By growing these flowers, you can cultivate the plant of the state where you were born or salute the state where you have been transplanted. Here's a list of all of America's state flowers.

Alabama: Camellia; **Alaska**: Forget-me-not; **Arizona**: Saguaro cactus; **Arkansas**: Apple blossom; **California**: Golden poppy; **Colorado**: Columbine; **Connecticut**: Mountain laurel; **Delaware**: Peach blossom; **District of Columbia**: American Beauty rose; **Florida**: Orange blossom; **Georgia**: Cherokee rose; **Hawaii**: Hibiscus; **Idaho**: Syringa; **Illinois**: Violet; **Indiana**: Peony; **Iowa**: Wild rose; **Kansas**: Wild sunflower; **Kentucky**: Goldenrod; **Louisiana**: Magnolia; **Maine**: Pine cone and tassel; **Maryland**: Black-eyed Susan; **Massachusetts**: Mayflower; **Michigan**: Apple blossom; **Minnesota**: Lady's slipper; **Mississippi**: Magnolia; **Missouri**: Hawthorne; **Montana**: Bitterroot; **Nebraska**: Goldenrod; **Nevada**: Sagebrush; **New Hampshire**: Purple lilac; **New Jersey**: Violet; **New Mexico**: Yucca flower; **New York**: Rose; **North Carolina**: Dogwood; **North Dakota**: Wild rose; **Ohio**: Scarlet carnation; **Oklahoma**: Mistletoe; **Oregon**: Oregon grape; **Pennsylvania**: Mountain laurel; **Rhode Island**: Violet; **South Carolina**: Yellow jasmine; **South Dakota**: American pasqueflower; **Tennessee**: Iris; **Texas**: Bluebonnet; **Utah**: Sego lily; **Vermont**: Red clover; **Virginia**: Dogwood; **Washington**: Rhododendron; **West Virginia**: Rhododendron; **Wisconsin**: Violet; **Wyoming**: Indian paintbrush.

GROW FLOWERS
OF SHAKESPEARE

William Shakespeare must have been a gardener. His plays come alive with marvelous words and im-

agery relating to flowers, herbs, and other plants. No doubt the Bard also loved the flowers of those elegant English gardens of his era. Fortunately, many of those flowers remained popular and have come down to us for landscaping and gardening delights over the years. So have the herbs and other plants mentioned in his plays. Actually, more than 150 plants appear in Shakespeare's works. Through his colorful descriptions, we can picture the customs of the day, the clothes people wore, the food they ate, and the beautiful flowers, refreshing herbs, and handsome other plants.

Elizabethan gardens were renowned for their beauty and dramatic designs. Even smaller homes copied the style of the wealthy mansion gardens. In Shakespeare's plays, nearly 30 scenes, from comic and romantic to tragic and historic, unfold against a garden backdrop. You can read about these plants and grow some of them in your own gardens. Here's a checklist of Shakespearean flowers, herbs, and other enchanting plants. You'll find the delightful, poetic passages included and the names of the plays in which they are found. Look them over, muse about their significance in historic literature, and plant as you wish.

Flowers of Shakespeare

Bluebell—harebell—*Endymion nonscriptus*: "thou shall not lack the flower that's like thy face, pale primrose, nor the azured harebell like thy veins" (*Cymbeline*).

Buttercup—cuckoo-buds—*Ranuculus acris*: "And cuckoo-buds of yellow hue, do paint the meadows with delight" (*Love's Labor's Lost*).

Camomile—*Chamaemelum nobile*: "for though the camomile, the more it is trodden on, the faster it grows, yet as youth, the more it is wasted, the sooner it wears" (*Henry IV*).

Carnation—Pink—*Dianthus caryopyllus*: "Of trembling winter, the fairest flower o' the season are our carnations, and streak'd gillyvors" (*The Winter's Tale*).

Clover—*Trifolium pratense*: "and green clover, wanting the scythe, all uncorrected, rank" (*Henry V*).

Columbine—*Aquilegia vulgaris*: "I am that flower, that columbine" (*Love's Labor's Lost*).

Cowslip—*Primula veris*: "The cowslips tall her pensioners be; in their gold coats spot you see" (*A Midsummer Night's Dream*).

Crabapple—*Malus sylvertris*: "And sometimes lurk I in a gossip's bowl. In very likeness of a roasted crab" (*A Midsummer Night's Dream*).

Crow-flower—*Lychnis flosuculi*: "There with fantastic garlands did she come. Of crow-flowers, nettles, daisies" (*Hamlet*).

Crown imperial—*Fritallaria imperialis*: "Bold oxslips and the crown imperial" (*The Winter's Tale*).

Daffodil—*Narcissus pseudonarcissus*: "When daffodils begin to appear, . . . why, then comes in the sweet o' the year" (*The Winter's Tale*).

Daisy—*Bellis perennis*: "When daisies pied and violets blue, do paint the meadows with delight" (*Love's Labor's Lost*).

Eglantine—*Rosa rubiginosa*: "With sweet musk-roses and with eglantine" (*A Midsummer Night's Dream*).

Flower-de-luce—*Iris pseudacorus*: "Cropp'd are the flower-de-luces in your arms" (*Henry VI*).

Honeysuckle—*Lonicera periclymenum*: "So doth the woodbine the sweet honeysuckle gently entwist" (*A Midsummer Night's Dream*).

Lady-smock—*Gardamine pratensis*: "And lady-smocks all silver white" (*Love's Labor's Lost*).

Lancaster rose—*Rosa gallia*/York Rose—*Rosa alba*: "Shall send between the red rose and the white a thousand souls to death and deadly night" (*Henry VI*).

Lavender—*Lavandula spica*: "Here's flowers for you; hot lavender, mints, savory, marjoram" (*The Winter's Tale*).

Lily—*Lilium candidum*: "To guild refined gold, to paint the lily" (*King John*).

Marigold—*Calendula officinalis*: "The marigold, that goes to bed wi' the sun, and with him rises weeping" (*The Winter's Tale*).

Musk rose—*Rosa arvensis*: "And stick musk-roses in they sleek smother head" (*A Midsummer Night's Dream*).

Oxslip—*Primula elatior*: "I know a bank whereon the wild thyme blows, where oxlips and the nodding violet grows" (*A Midsummer Night's Dream*).

Pansy—Heartsease—*Viola tricolor*: "and there is pansies, that's for thoughts" (*Hamlet*)

Poppy—*Papaver rhoeas*: "Not poppy, nor mandragora, nor all the drowsy syrups of the world, shall ever medicine thee to that sweet sleep" (*Othello*).

Primrose—*Primula vulgaris*: "Primrose, first-born child of Ver, merry spring-time's harbinger" (*Two Noble Kinsman*)

Rose—*Rosa*: "What's in a name? That which we call a rose by any other name would smell as sweet" (*Romeo and Juliet*).

Thistle—*Cirsium vulgare*: "There thou prick'st her with a thistle" (*Much Ado about Nothing*).

Vetch—*Viscia sativa*: "Ceres most bounteous lady, thy rich leas, of wheat, rye, barley, vetches, oats and pease" (*The Tempest*).

Violet—*Viola ordorata*: "as gentle as zephyrs, blowing below the violet, not wagging his sweet head" (*Cymbeline*).

Herbs of Shakespeare

Belladonna—*Atropa belladonna*: "Within the infant rind of this weak flower, poison hath residence, and medicine power" (*Romeo and Juliet*).

Fennel—*Foeniculum vulgare*: "There's fennel for you and columbines" (*Hamlet*).

Hemlock—*Conium maculatum*: "Root of hemlock digg'd in the dark" (*Macbeth*).

Hyssop—*Hyssopus officinalis*: "so that if we will plant nettles, or so lettuce; set hyssop" (*Othello*).

Marjoram—*Majorana hortensis*: "She was the sweet marjoram of the salad" (*All's Well That End's Well*).

Mint—*Mentha spicata*: "Here's flowers for you, hot lavender, mints, savory, marjoram" (*The Winter's Tale*).

Monkshood—*Aconitum napelum*: "Though it do work as strong as aconitum" (*Henry IV*).

Nettle—*Urtica dioica*: "Yield stinging nettles to mine enemies" (*Richard II*).

Rosemary—*Rosmarinus officianalis*: "There's rosemary, that's for remembrance; pray you, love, remember" (*Hamlet*).

Rue—*Ruta gravelens*: "Here did she fall a tear; here, in this place, I'll set a bank of rue, sour herb of grace" (*Richard II*)

Thyme—*Thymus serpyllum*: "I know a bank whereon the wild thyme blows" (*A Midsummer Night's Dream*).

Wormwood—*Artemisia absinthium*: "Dian's bud o'er Cupid's flower hath such force and blessed power" (*A Midsummer Night's Dream*).

Other Plants of Shakespeare

Blackberry—*Rubus tuberculatus*: "and elegies on brambles" (*As You Like It*).

Broom—*Cytisus scoparius*: "and they broom-groves whose shadow the dismissed bachelor loves" (*The Tempest*).

Burdock—*Arctium lappa*: "Crown'd with burdocks, hemlock, nettles, cuckoo-flowers" (*King Lear*).

Cherry—*Prunus avium*: "So we grew together, like to a double cherry" (*A Midsummer Night's Dream*).

Oak—*Quercus robur*: "that all their elves, for fear, creep into acorn-cups, and hide them there" (*A Midsummer Night's Dream*).

Pomegranate—*Punica granatum*: "Nightly she sings on yon pomegranate tree" (*Romeo and Juliet*).

Rushes—*Butomus umbellatus*: "She bids you upon the wanton rushes lay you down, and rest your gentle head upon her lap" (*Henry IV*).

Strawberry—*Fragaria vesca*: "The strawberry grows underneath the nettle" (*Henry V*).

Vines—*Vitis vinifera*: "Vines, with clustering bunches growing" (*The Tempest*).

Often the best way to transplant garden ideas is to see them growing in display gardens. If possible you might visit one of these gardens that feature plants mentioned by the Bard. Or try a visit on the Internet. Use Google to look up Shakespeare gardens in Boulder, Colorado; Golden Gate Park in California; the Brooklyn Botanic Gardens; Plainfield, New Jersey; Cleveland, Ohio; Cedar Rapids, Iowa; San Marino, California; Sewanee and Chattanooga Tennessee; Evanston, Illinois; Wichita, Kansas; and Montgomery, Alabama. Other Shakespearean gardens worldwide may be available via Internet search.

PLANTS OF THE SCRIPTURES

The Holy Land, Asia Minor, and the countries bordering the Mediterranean Sea are the sources of the classic bulbous flowering plants so popular in America today. From these regions have come crocus and cyclamens, hyacinths and iris, lilies and tulips. These flowers developed there under the hot dry season that forced them into dormancy and then the brief moist period that forced them into bloom.

Biblical gardens are gaining popularity across America. I've written several books about such gardens, including *Plants of the Bible and How to Grow Them*, *Flowers of the Bible and How to Grow Them*, and *Herbs of the Bible and How to Grow Them*. It seems appropriate to include some details here about biblical plants so that all who wish to pursue this type of colorful growing experience can do so.

Perhaps it is best to focus on passages about flowers of the Holy Land to learn more about their rich history. As the Bible describes, God created the earth and the waters, and then the plants on the third day. As we read in Genesis 1:11–12: "Let the earth bring forth grass, the herb yielding seed, and the fruit tree yielding fruit after his kind, whose seed is in itself, upon the earth: and it was so. And the earth brought forth grass, and the herb yielding seed after his kind, and the tree yielding fruit, whose seed was in itself, after his kind: and God saw that it was good" (King James Version).

As we read further, we discover that God's primary purpose for creating people was to be gardeners of the good earth. Many gardens are mentioned, from Eden to Gethsemane. King Solomon's garden contained many flowering and aromatic plants, including lilies and crocus. In biblical times, the average person could not afford such a luxurious garden as Solomon's, but they lived in a land where the hillsides and valleys were profuse with wild anemone, narcissus, hyacinth, tulip, and many other flowering delights.

In my years of biblical plant research, I focused on the flowers that most biblical and botanical scholars have identified as being mentioned in the scriptures. My goal is to help millions of home gardeners enjoy the beauty that plants of the Bible can provide for their landscapes.

The following plant list is based on five key considerations: (1) Biblical and botanical scholars generally agree that the plants are mentioned in the scriptures. (2) The plants grow in the Holy Land but may not be specifically identified in scriptural passages. (3) The flowers must have eye appeal and be beautiful. (4) The plants must be reasonably available, either the actual species or closely related family members that can be purchased locally or from reputable mail order firms. (5) The plants must be those which can be grown in most parts of the United States.

When earliest translations of the Bible were made, there were honest differences of opinion about what specific words meant. Ancient Hebrew and Greek words could be interpreted to mean several different things. Problems arose whenever people translated a biblical text from one language to another. Also, there was no botanical nomenclature when the scriptures were first translated. Therefore, the following lists include the flowers that most authorities agree are the likely flowers referred to in the scriptures. Each entry includes the name of a plant followed by the scriptural source and the botanical name.

Anemone—Matthew 6:28—*Anemone coronaria*

Saffron crocus—Isaiah 35:1, Song of Solomon 4:13—*Crocus sativum*

Cyclamen—Song of Solomon—*Cyclamen persicum*

Daffodil, trumpet narcissus—Matthew 6:29, Isaiah 35:1—*Narcissus* spp. *or N. tazetta*

Hyacinth—Song of Solomon 6:2–3—*Hyacinthus orientalis*

Iris, blue flag—Hosea 14:5, Song of Solomon—*Iris versicolor*

Iris, yellow flag—Hosea 14:5—*Iris pseudacorus*

Lily, madonna—Song of Songs 2:1–2—*Lilium candidum*

Narcissis, daffodil—Matthew 6:30, Song of Solomon—*Narcissus tazetta*

Star of Bethlehem—II Kings 6:25—*Ornithogalum umbellatum*

Tulip, red, Sharon—Song of Solomon 2:12—*Tulipa* spp.

Blue flag (left) and yellow flag (right) iris wildflowers.

There are many other flowers that could be identified as having been mentioned in the scriptures, but in more generic terms. They do indeed grow in the Holy Land and their roots have been there for centuries. For this reason, many who have planted biblical gardens have included these other flowers in their plantings. To present the widest diversity of biblical flowers so you can have a broad choice for your own home Holy Land gardens, here are some of those other flowers.

Buttercup—Psalms 4:5—*Ranunculus*
Daisy, shasta—1 Kings 6:29, Psalm 45—*Chrysanthemum* spp.
Dandelion—Exodus 12:8—*Taraxacum officianale*
Flax, blue—John 19:40, Proverbs 31:13—*Linum perenne*

Hibiscus—James 1:9–10, Job 30:4—*Hisbiscus syriacus*
Hollyhock—Job 6: 6–7—*Alcea setosa*
Hyacinth, Grape—Song of Solomon 6:3—*Muscari sp.*
Iris, purple—Hosea 14:5—*Iris astropupurea*
Larkspur, delphinium—Luke 12:27, Song of Solomon 6:24—*Delphinium ajacis*
Lavender—Song of Solomun 6:24—*Lavendula stoechas*
Lenton rose—Song of Solomon 6:24—*Helleborus*
Lily, water—1 Kings 7:19, 1 Kings 7:22—*Nymphaea lotus, N. caerulea*
Lupine—James 1:9–10—*Lupinus augustifolius*
Loosestrife—Song of Solomon 1:14—*Lythrum salicaria*
Mallow—Job 6:6—*Malva moschata*
Mum, hardy—James 1:9–10—*Chrysanthemum* spp.
Poppy, common—Isaiah 40:6, Jeremiah 8:14—*Papaver rhoeas*
Poppy, Icelandic—Isaiah 40:8—*Papaver alpinum*
Poppy, oriental—Isaiah 40:6—*Papaver orientale*
Red buttercup—1 Peter 1:24—*Ranunculus asiaticus*
Rockrose—Isaiah 35:1—*Cistus* spp., *C. creticus*
Rose, rugosa—Isaiah 35:1, Wisdom 24:14—*Rosa rugosa*
Phoenicia rose—Eccesiasticus 24:14—*Rosa phoenicia*
Salvia, sage—Exodus 25:31–33—*Salvia officinalis*
Globe thistle—Judges 8:16—*Echinops viscosus*
Violet—James 1:10, Song of Songs—*Viola odorata*

You'll find details about growing the perennial plants in chapter 8, bulbs in chapter 9, roses in chapter 10, and annuals in chapter 11. In those and other chapters, you'll find ideas for distinctive types of gardening, such as tuneful plantings that encourage birds, butterfly garden, and even tasteful international flavor gardening. The potential for expanding growing horizons often seems endless. Dig in and try new growing experiences each year. The rewards are endless too.

13

ENJOY A TUNEFUL GARDEN

Birds are a tuneful boon to gardeners. They'll reward you with their singing, colorful, amusing antics, and most importantly, they will help you win the battle with the bugs. Some species eat many times their weight in insects every year. Get to know some of the bug catchers: tree and cliff swallows, swifts, wrens, and flycatchers. Swallows earn their name, swallowing a thousand insect pests each day. Wrens devour hundreds of spiders and caterpillars daily. Add other feathered friends to your bird cultivation list: juncos, kinglets, song sparrows, tanagers, vireos, warblers. There are more from bluebirds, flycatchers, phoebes, and meadowlarks to mockingbirds, thrashers, and woodpeckers that hunt out hidden pests beneath bark or lurking in secluded crevices. Your feathered insect-eating al-

lies willingly work long hours to feed their families. They'll help keep your home grounds virtually pest free.

We've erected tree swallow, bluebird, and wren houses every year. Bird families seem to remember our hospitality, returning each spring to take up housekeeping and insect-catching chores. It pays to provide the proper birdhouses, baths, nesting boxes, and shelves that different bird species need. It also is important to plant shrubs, flowers, trees, vines, and windbreaks, because birds need food, safeguards, and shelter, just as we need our food, clothing, and shelter.

The tips in this chapter will help you cultivate birds to help around your garden. Choose flowering shrubs and plants that provide seeds, berries,

Birds and butterflies bring joy to any garden.

and nuts. These will add color to your grounds and benefit birds too. Birds have different habits. Some like to nest high. Others prefer low, bushy sites. Hedges are a good starting point. Consider them for borders or property lines and as screens to hide compost piles, vegetable gardens, and storage areas.

You've already learned in chapter 7 on landscaping about the value of multipurpose trees and shrubs for blooming beauty in spring and berries plus fall foliage in autumn. You can invite an abundance of birds to your garden by choosing plantings that provide shelter, food, and nesting sites for them.

For years, the Audubon Society has provided worthwhile tips and advice to bird watchers. According to the society and other bird experts, landscaping for birds involves nine basic principles. With thanks to the Audubon Society, here's a useful checklist as you plan bird and wildlife plantings.

Food: Every bird species has its own unique food requirements, and these may change as the birds mature and seasons change. Learn the food habits of the birds you wish to attract. Then plant the appropriate trees, shrubs, or flowers that will provide fruits, berries, grains, seeds, acorns, nuts, or nectar.

Water: Experts say you can double the number of bird species in your yard by providing a source of water. A birdbath or water garden will get lots of use, especially if the water is dripping, splashing, or moving in some way. A circulator pump helps.

Shelter: Birds need places where they can hide from predators and escape from severe weather. Trees, shrubs, tall grass, and birdhouses provide such shelter.

Diversity: The best landscaping plan is one that includes a wide variety of plants to attract a greater

Attract birds by providing what they need: shelter, water, and food.

number of bird species; the more the merrier and more songful.

Four-Seasons Care: It is important to provide birds with food and shelter during all four seasons of the year. Plant trees, shrubs, and flowers that will provide year-round food and shelter. Different plants provide foods in different seasons.

Arrangement of Shelter: Consider the effects of prevailing winds and blowing or drifting snow so your yard will be protected from harsh winter weather. Think about use of plant windbreaks or hedges and fences too.

Protection: When placing bird feeders and nest boxes, consider protection from predators. Also, be cautious about the kinds of pesticides you use; apply only when necessary and strictly according to label instructions.

Hardiness Zones: Consult a plant hardiness zone map to be sure the plants you want are rated for the winter hardiness zone classification of your area.

Soils and Topography: Consult with your local garden center or county Cooperative Extension office to have a soil test done for your yard. By knowing what type of soil you have, you can select the types of plants that will grow best in your yard for you and your feathered friends.

As you use these key points to plan your bird landscape habitats, note that there are several types of plants important for birds.

Conifers—evergreen trees and shrubs that include pines, spruces, firs, arborvitae, junipers, cedars, and yews—are important as escape cover, winter shelter, and summer nesting sites. Some also provide buds and seeds.

Grasses and legumes can provide cover for ground nesting birds, especially if the area is not mowed during the nesting season. Some grasses and legumes provide seeds as well.

Nectar-producing plants attract hummingbirds and orioles. Flowers with tubular red corollas are especially attractive to hummingbirds.

Summer-fruiting plants produce fruits or berries from May through August. These include various species of cherry, chokecherry, honeysuckle, raspberry, serviceberry, blackberry, blueberry, grape, mulberry, plum, and elderberry. These attract thrashers, catbirds, robins, thrushes, waxwings, woodpeckers, orioles, cardinals, towhees, and grosbeaks.

Fall-fruiting plants are important for migratory birds, which need to build up fat reserves prior to migration. They also provide food for non-migratory species that need to enter the winter season in good physical condition. Fall-fruiting plants include dogwoods, mountain ash, winterberries, and cotoneasters.

Winter-fruiting plants offer fruits that are attached to the plants long after they first ripen in the fall. Examples are glossy black chokecherry, Siberian crabapple, snowberry, bittersweet, sumacs, American highbush cranberry, and Virginia creeper.

Nuts and acorns from oak, hickory, buckeye, butternut, walnut, and hazel trees are also of value.

TREES AND SHRUBS THAT ATTRACT BIRDS

Consider some of these trees and shrubs that attract birds. Remember that when birds feed on the seeds or berries of plants, they spread them later in their droppings. This seed dispersal often leads to the propagation of new plants. Therefore, it is a good idea to use native plants instead of introduced ones to attract birds. Natives are well adapted to local soil types and climates and don't require special winter protection or soil amendments to thrive. Here are tips from my popular syndicated newspaper columns about tuneful gardening.

Trees That Attract Birds

Birch (*Betula*) offers several native species that feed siskins and redpolls, and the shed bark is used for nesting material. Trees yield conelike fruit in fall.

Evergreens such as cedar (*Cedrus*), juniper (*Juniperus*), spruce (*Picea*), pine (*Pinus*), hemlock (*Tsuga*) all have thick branches that provide birds with necessary winter shelter from the elements and year-round protection from predators. Game birds and waxwings eat the berries of cedars and junipers. Chickadees, crossbills, goldfinches, nuthatches, siskins, and woodpeckers pick the winged seeds from pine and spruce cones.

Common hackberry (*Celtis occidentalis*) is native to the eastern states and attracts game birds, finches, thrushes, and woodpeckers. Western hackberry (*C. reticulata*) has tiny red or brown berries.

Flowering dogwood (*Cornus florida*) grows in shade or sun and produces red berries that attract many songbirds.

American beech (*Fagus grandifolia*) has nuts as food for blackbirds, chickadees, jays, and tufted titmice.

American holly (*Ilex opaca*) has a bounty of vibrant red berries against pointed dark green leaves for cedar waxwings, finches, mockingbirds, thrushes, and woodpeckers. Holly plants are male or female, and both are required for the female to bear fruit.

Crabapple (*Malus*) is popular with landscapers for its beautiful flowers, and cedar waxwings, finches, and mockingbirds enjoy the fruits into winter.

Cherry species such as pin cherry (*P. pensylvanica*), black cherry (*P. serotina*), and chokecherry (*P. virginiana*) are among the best trees for attracting birds. Cedar waxwings, finches, flycatchers, grosbeaks, jays, mockingbirds, thrushes, vireos, and woodpeckers feed on the fruits.

American mountain ash (*Sorbus americana*) provides clusters of scarlet berries for thrushes, waxwings, and woodpeckers to eat in the fall.

Shrubs

Holly (*Ilex*) may be evergreen, such as inkberry (*I. glabra*), or deciduous such as winterberry (*I. verticillata*). Female plants produce berries that sustain cedar waxwings, finches, mockingbirds, thrushes, and woodpeckers.

Bayberry (*Myrica pensylvanica*) is a hardy native shrub commonly found in sandy soil along coastal areas. Female plants produce an abundance of hard, waxy berries that attract bluebirds, crows, game birds, meadowlarks, myrtle warblers, tree swallows, and woodpeckers.

Roses (*Rosa*) produce rose hips, a winter food source for game birds and songbirds.

Yew (*Taxus canadensis*) offers dense evergreen growth as security for mockingbirds, robins, and sparrows, which also enjoy the juicy red fruits.

Viburnum (*Viburnum*) are deciduous or evergreen shrubs with appealing form and blooms that also produce red, blue, or black berries favored by finches, game birds, mockingbirds, thrushes, waxwings, and woodpeckers.

Other plants that provide food for birds are aromatic sumac, firethorn, bittersweet, and barberry. Some birds will eat your garden berries but usually prefer acid, bitter, or sour fruits. As you plan bird plantings, consider groupings of autumn olive, ornamental crabapples, and flowering dogwoods. Hedges of honeysuckle, roses, and mulberries are multipurpose too, providing privacy, nesting areas, and food.

Birds like variety just as you do, so blend a few dogwoods against a darker cedar or hemlock. Use low-growing trees and shrubs where they will be set off against a background of taller evergreen trees. Aim for a longer season of beauty by selecting plants that give you flowering pleasure in spring and summer plus the bonus of fruit, berries, and colorful foliage each fall.

Birds sing for their suppers, so provide some cover near your home, especially the kitchen, dining room, and bedroom windows. Consider training vines up around windows. Use arbors or trellises to provide a quiet, secluded cover near the house. Perhaps these extra notes about some plants will prove helpful too.

Autumn olive attracts 25 different species of birds and is a valuable addition to your landscaping. Maturing to 20 feet tall, it is a large, spreading shrub with gray-green foliage. The fragrant, small, yellowish blooms appear in May to July. Abundant speckled, red fruits ripen in September and may last to February. The cardinal variety is winter hardy in most areas and likes deep, moist soil in sun or light shade.

Bittersweet is a twining vine that bears bright red berries in yellow husks in September through December. It attracts about 10 types of birds and grows best in well-drained to dry soil in sun or light shade. A plus are the colorful berries on stems for dried indoor decorations.

Crabapples are one of the best bird-attracting landscape plants. You have your choice of many shapes, colors, and sizes ranging from 15 to 25 feet tall. They provide a marvelous display each spring of white, pink, or red blossoms, de-

pending on the variety. In fall, reddish, orange, or yellow fruits feed the birds. Most crabapples prefer a dry soil in good sun.

Dogwoods, both pink and white, provide profusions of color during spring and fall. These range in size from shrubs such as red osier to trees growing up to 30 feet. Dogwoods bear white to reddish blooms from April to June. They thrive in well-drained to dry soil with moderate sun or shade. Bunched fruits appears in fall, when leaves are a bronze color.

Holly is useful for birds and your holiday decorating too. About 20 species of birds enjoy holly berries. You have a choice of shrub and tree forms, deciduous or evergreen. Tiny white blooms appear in spring and bright red fruits by fall.

Birds also like to bathe, so be sure to provide fresh, cool water to drink and wash. Place a birdbath off the ground with some protection from cats and other predators. When baby birds hatch, the parents need a readily available water supply. Fact is, the closer their food and water supply, the more inclined birds will be to nest and live on your property. Keep water available in all seasons. A heater in winter encourages more birds to stay in your neighborhood. Bird feeders are needed too, of course.

Most birds prefer to build their own nests in bushes or trees where they can raise their young. Other birds prefer and will use houses you provide. Those you make from kits are a fun project for children. Bluebirds, chickadees, flycatchers, flickers, nuthatches, titmice, and wrens enjoy birdhouses.

Tree swallows also like birdhouses, and several families will make their homes as a colony in your backyard if you provide sufficient houses for them.

We've learned that tree swallows are one of the best birds to keep our home grounds pest free, eating most gnats, mosquitoes, and black flies as they raise their young.

You don't need to be an avid birdwatcher to appreciate the value birds add to your garden. They please you with music and song, the antics of youngsters, and flashes of color, but most important, birds eat bugs by the bushel. Attract them with homes, cultivate their friendship with natural habitats, and they'll remain your first line of defense against insect invasions.

14

GET A JUMP ON SPRING

Starting your garden from seeds is a good idea, for several reasons. You have a much wider choice of varieties available from seeds, as you'll discover when you scan a few mail order gardening catalogs. Seeds are much less expensive than started plants. They also provide you with an abundance of seedlings to trade with other gardeners to expand your growing horizons. You can choose annuals or perennials and even opt for growing rare, antique heirloom varieties that are being rediscovered and offered by specialty firms.

However, seeds can present some challenges because of their tiny size, the slowness of some varieties to germinate, and the time and patience seed starting requires. In this chapter, you'll find ways to get growing better and truly get a big jump on spring and better gardening with seeds. Veteran gardeners vow that starting plants yourself from seeds doubles the pleasure of gardening. When you grow varieties that few others ever do or see, seeds do offer appealing opportunities for flowers and more delicious veggies than most garden centers ever offer as preplants.

You may believe that growing from seed is difficult and takes too much time and equipment. Take heart. The steps and tips here will dispel any appre-

hensions. Basically all you need to know about specific seeds is whether or not they require light to germinate and the number of days germination takes. With a very sunny window, a few containers, and a good germinating mix, you'll be on your way to success.

Frankly, the growing season is too short in much of America to allow many annual plants that need warm soil and hot weather to mature and bear flowers or fruit if you sow them directly in the ground. That includes popular plants such as tomatoes, peppers, petunias, and salvias. Some plants have very tiny seeds that are easier to sow and tend indoors, such as begonia seeds that are so fine they look almost like powder. Veteran gardeners still enjoy the magic of planting seeds and watching a seedling push up and become a young plant, offering a special bond between you and nature.

First, focus on materials. There are many types of containers, from trays with heating pads to those that are marvelous miniature greenhouses. Catalogs offer a range of useful seed starting tools, trays, pots, and materials. So do many garden centers and chain stores. Containers can be any shallow receptacle that holds soil, such as flats with or without individual cells, peat or paper pots, egg carton bottoms, or halved milk cartons. For transplanting seedlings once they get started, you'll need 2—4 inch plastic, clay, or peat pots. To ensure even moisture for seeds and save time, look for self-watering seed starting kits.

Next requirement is germinating mix, either commercial or homemade. You can mix your own with a 50-50 combination of fine sphagnum peat moss and vermiculite. Seed starting mixes are readily available and are a good bet for ease and without risk of contaminants.

Naturally, you'll need to order your seeds, the special varieties you want of annuals, perennials, vegetables, herbs. Talk to fellow gardeners and arrange to grow some new varieties you can share,

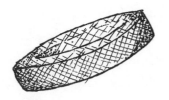

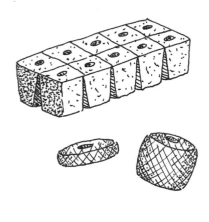

Jiffy 7 peat pellets (top) enlarge with water for starting seeds. The seedling roots can grow right through the peat pots when planted in the garden.

Use peat blocks or peat pots to start seedlings indoors.

compare, and swap. Remember that All America Selection winners have been proved successful in climates, soils, and growing conditions nationwide and are sure to perform well. Various seed firms offer winners from the present year as well as best from previous years.

Other materials include plastic bags or plastic wrap, a mister, and a transplanting mix. This is different from a seed starting mix. You need it to grow the tiny transplants into the size they should be for planting in your outdoor garden areas. A good potting soil will do, but a mix specifically formulated for young seedlings is better because it usually contains a coarser grade of sphagnum peat moss than a germinating mix and often includes fertilizer.

To encourage your plants, you'll need a balanced all purpose fertilizer. Labels always list the main nutrients plants need, including nitrogen, phosphorus, and potassium, with numbers to indicate percentages, such as 5-10-5, 10-10-10. If you prefer to grow with organic rather than chemical fertilizers, you can use fish emulsion, which is smelly, or other types usually available in garden centers.

Finally, be sure to have plant labels to identify what seeds are in which container, date planted, and days to germinate. Always save seed packets for reference. There is valuable information on those small packets you should not overlook.

GET STARTED EARLY

One main reason for starting many types of plants indoors is to get a jump on spring. The plants are too tender to plant until the soil is warm enough and no frost threatens in spring. You really need more weeks of growing time so vegetables especially will have sufficient time to set abundant crops and bear more produce than if you waited to plant directly outdoors. For example, a few extra weeks for melons can yield dozens more ripe ones before fall frost kills the plants.

Most longtime gardeners like to use small peat pots to start seeds, rather than trays or flats. A main reason is that seedlings can grow well in these pots with planting mix, and they can be placed directly into the outdoor garden soil when ready. Roots will grow right through the pot, which will decompose in the garden ground. This method avoids transplanting shock.

Fill flats or individual pots with the mix to within about 1 inch of the top. Wet the germinating mix thoroughly. It should be moist but never soggy. If using pots, make shallow holes and sow three to four seeds in each pot. In flats, make shallow row indentations with a ruler or your finger. Note, it is easier to separate seedlings when transplanting time comes if you sow in rows. Sow thinly so you do not waste seed.

Before you plant, read seed packet to see if the seeds need light to germinate. If they do, press them just lightly into the surface. If they require darkness, cover with one-quarter to one-half inch of mix and tamp it down. Then, lightly mist the surface with water to settle the seeds.

Veteran gardeners suggest covering flats with a sheet of plastic wrap or set them in plastic bags. You can place pots in plastic bags and close with twist ties. This procedure keeps the mix from drying out while the seeds germinate. However, check the mix occasionally and moisten if necessary by misting with water. A clothes mister works well. Don't pour water on pots or flats, which can disturb tiny seeds when they are trying to set roots. Mist them instead.

Place the pots or flats in a warm location. Be sure to review the seed packet for specific soil temperatures for germination. Generally, seeds germinate with soil temperatures of 70–75°F. Some plants may benefit from use of a heating mat under the pots. You may find starter kits with a heat mat, and some starter kits have self-watering systems. Depending on your budget, they may be worth a try.

Keep watch, which every gardener tends to do, like waiting for a pot to boil on the stove. Eventually, seeds will sprout if you have followed these basic instructions. When seedlings emerge, remove the plastic covering so you don't overheat them. Seed packets give you an idea of germination time, usually 7–10 days, but some take as long as 2 or 3 weeks.

During this period, keep the mix evenly moist, not soggy. It is best to water from the bottom by setting flats and pots in a larger tray or sink filled with a couple of inches of water. Simply remove them when you see moisture on the surface of the mix.

The first leaves on a seedling are called cotyledons, not true leaves. Their shapes usually do not look like the plant's familiar leaves. When seedlings in flats grow at least two sets of true leaves, transplant them into pots. Moisten the transplanting mix and let it drain. If you plan to use a commercial all-purpose potting soil, veteran gardeners say it helps to add a handful of vermiculite or shredded sphagnum moss for each quart of mix to lighten the texture. Fill 2–4 inch pots about three-quarters full. With your fingers or long tweezers, carefully pick each seedling out of the flat, holding each by the leaves, not the stem, because plants easily grow new leaves but not stems. Set the transplant into the pot and fill around the roots with more mix and firm the mix down. When finished transplanting, place pots on a sunny window, preferably south facing, or use a Gro-Light to bring them along. Give pots on windowsills a quarter-turn every week so plants grow straight instead of bending toward the light.

During this seedling cultivation period, water transplants regularly from the bottom until they grow 3–4 inches tall. Then you can begin to water from the top, since they will have grown proper rootholds. At this time, you also should begin feeding them by diluting a water-soluble fertilizer to half the strength that is suggested by the label. That should give you well-developed seedlings that are large enough to plant outdoors when danger of frost has passed.

Some vegetables, especially tomatoes, produce extensive root systems and grow quickly into lush plants. They may need transplanting into somewhat larger pots before the weather warms up enough to plant them in the garden.

Strange as it may seem, many seeds germinate more quickly and well if you don't cover them with a starting mixture when you sow them. These include ageratum, begonia, coleus, columbine, dill, feverfew, gaillardia, impatiens, lettuce, nicotiana, petunia, parsley, oriental poppy, salvia, savory, and yarrow.

A few more pointers might be useful too. Label your seed containers as you sow, so you'll know what you planted when and where. Let me repeat that point! Label seed trays or pots, so you can identify your plants and move them to their spot in your garden. Get to know the date of the average last spring frost in your area, because you'll need to start most plants indoors a certain number of weeks before that date. Seed packets include that information.

If this is your first try at starting seeds indoors, focus on the easiest plants to get the feel of it. These include basil, coreopsis, dianthus, gaillardia, gloriosa daisy, marigold, oregano, yarrow, and zinnia. Keep seed packets for reference, especially for new hybrid varieties and old heirloom types. They may have special starting and growing tips you need to follow. Sealing the used packet in a plastic bag and stapling or taping it to a row marker is one good way to have the information handy.

Perhaps a few classic "Don'ts" should be included and emphasized to save you worry and avoid problems. Make a mental note of these key points:

Don't combine different varieties of seeds in one flat unless they germinate in the same number of days.

Don't forget to identify with labels or in some other way what varieties are planted in which flats or pots.

Don't let seedlings in flats grow too large before you transplant them or their roots will become entwined, which makes them difficult to separate without damage.

Don't overwater seedlings; soggy soil encourages fungus and root rot.

Another point to consider when starting seeds is that some plants resent being transplanted. These include annual phlox, chervil, cucumber, dill, fennel, lupine, nasturtium, and poppies. The way around that problem is to start them indoors in individual peat or paper pots that are biodegradable. You simply plant the whole pot in the garden and let the roots grow through the sides. Water well the first week or so to encourage that action and decay of the peat pot.

IMPORTANT PLANT FACTS

Some people believe that all new varieties are hybrids, which isn't true. There are new flowers and vegetables introduced each year that are open-pollinated varieties. To understand the difference between a hybrid and an open-pollinated variety, think of plant parents. An open-pollinated plant has one parent; a hybrid has two parents. Basically, hybrid seed can be defined as the seed that results from the cross-pollination of two inbred parent plants. Open-pollinated varieties have only one parent line. Many seeds being offered for sale in packets from mail order firms and at nurseries are indeed F1 hybrids. (That means they are the first filial generation resulting from crossing two distinctly different parent plants. Be aware that seeds from your hybrid won't produce a plant that is the same as the parent plant, so don't save the seeds.) But there are classes of plants where this method of hybridization does not work.

Open-pollinated flowers or vegetables are often easier and faster to breed and produce. Breeders create new varieties by selecting "parent" plants by repeatedly self-pollinating a particular plant and resulting progeny over several generations. To make sure that the variety is true to type, the best individual plants are chosen, these are self-pollinated, and the whole process is repeated anywhere from three to eight or more times. When a promising line has been developed, it is then tested under various climatic conditions. Outstanding varieties may be considered for entry in the All America Selection or Fleuroselect (European) trials. You'll find facts about the type of variety in seed catalogs, so try your luck with those that appeal.

Another question arises about seeds. What are organic seeds? Simply, they are seeds harvested from plants that have been grown without the use of synthetic chemical fertilizers or pesticides. Also, organic seeds are not treated with any fungicide or other synthetic chemical after harvesting prior to sale. Organic seeds are sold through retail outlets and mail order firms. Typically they are more expensive.

RECYCLE FOR HANDY GARDEN AIDS

That good old saying "Waste Not, Want Not" had a purpose, and today we can apply it to our gardening projects. Now we call it recycling. In your home, you probably can find many free gardening aids among everyday food containers such as milk cartons and jugs, ice cream and yogurt cups, egg cartons, plastic glasses, ice cream cups, and sticks from popsicles. Save some, wash them out, add seed starting mix, and use to sow seeds. Just mark the variety and date planted with crayon or felt-tip pen on the container, or write the information on popsicle sticks. They also make handy row stakes with empty seed packets stapled to them inside a clear plastic bag. That way you'll have useful seed packet tips for thinning and transplanting and harvest time too.

Wire coat hangers are handy, as are plastic bags from dry cleaners. Cut coat hangars with pliers and form into hoops. Set them in the ground and cut plastic bags to cover them, making a row cover to ward off late frosts. Remove the plastic on warm days to avoid overheating young plants.

Recycle milk cartons as seed starting containers by cutting one side from quart or half-gallon cartons. Fill with seed starting mix and use pieces of the side you removed to make dividers within the milk carton. When seedlings are ready to transplant outdoors, cut the sides of those cartons and slide out the root cube gently to avoid disturbing tender roots.

Plastic milk containers have other uses. Cut off the bottoms and use them as plant saucers to keep

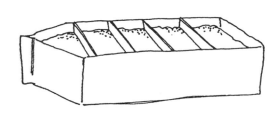

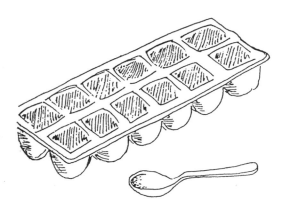

Recycle household containers for your garden. Cut a milk carton in half and fill with starting mix (left). Use an egg carton with starting mix (right). A butter or ice cream container can be a seed starting unit (lower left).

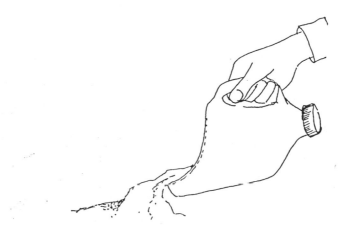

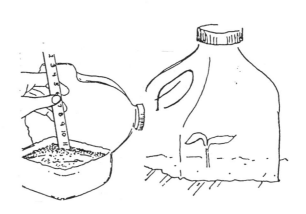

Gallon milk jugs are handy as protection for seedlings against frost,
as scoops to spread fertilizer, and in other ways too.

water from staining windowsills or table tops. You also can use these as seed starter dishes. Tops can be used over tender seedlings to keep frost from damaging them. Simply press the bottomless jugs into the ground. Remove them in the morning and replace at night until all danger of late frost is over. These also can be used as scoops to scatter fertilizer along rows and around plants. Quart containers are handy as funnels.

Thwart cutworms that attack cabbages, broccoli, and tender, tempting seedlings. Cut milk containers into 3-inch sections and press them into the ground as collars around seedlings to stop cutworms. Save the plastic containers from margerine and use them for seed starting containers or for transplants. Save a few egg cartons too. Remove the top and fill the egg areas with seed starting mix, then sow your seeds. When ready to transplant, moisten the tray and gently scoop out the seedlings to plant outdoors.

Clear plastic drinking cups, ice cream cups, or similar food containers hold humidity as you start seeds that are slow to germinate, and they give cuttings a better habitat for setting roots. Clear plastic

Wire coat hangers can be cut and used to hold clear plastic to protect young seedlings from late frost outdoors. Cut milk cartons act as shields to thwart cutworms in the garden (above right).

and glass jars also provide a greenhouse effect over tubs and pots when you start seedlings or grow cuttings of favorite plants. Don't put these in hot, direct sun: north and west windows are better to avoid overheating tiny plants.

While enjoying breakfast, look around your kitchen and recycle some food containers as handy gardening aids.

COLD FRAME POINTERS

Cold frames have proved their value to millions of veteran gardeners for decades. They offer protection from unpredictable weather in spring and even can be used to give late planted crops a place to mature right up toward winter time. On a small scale, cloches and similar plant protectors are often the

answer. But a cold frame or a small portable greenhouse may be just what you are looking for. The catalog for Charley's Greenhouses will show you a number of options.

Cold frames and portable greenhouses create an area of controlled conditions that give gardeners the ability to stretch the season and grow plants that are used to warmer climates. Cold frames that have an electric heating cable or use heat from rotting manure or compost are often called hotbeds. According to the specialists at Charley's, keep the following points in mind as you shop for a cold frame or consider making one.

In early spring, use a cold frame to start seedlings or harden them off before planting outside. It lets you expose seedlings gradually to full sun by keeping the vent open for longer periods

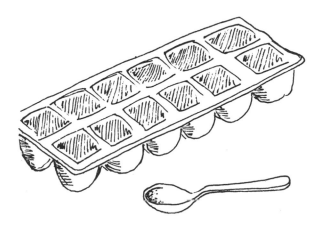

Recycle an egg carton as a seed planter with soil mix in each part.

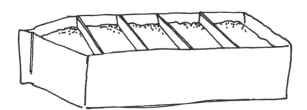

A gallon milk jug protects a young seedling from frost (top). Quart milk containers are handy for starting seeds (below)—place one on your windowsill. Use the cut side to make dividers.

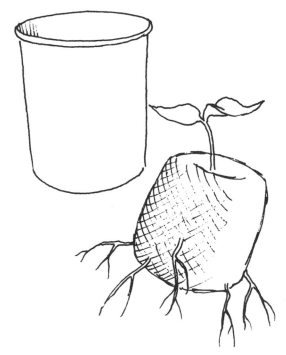

Put peat pots into old plastic cups, and when roots begin growing through, transplant into the outdoor garden.

each day. In the summer, cold frames are handy for rooting herbaceous and woody cuttings with adequate shading. If you provide shade and adequate moisture, you can also start fall crops of carrots and beets for picking well into winter.

Lettuce, spinach, and other late-fall leaf crops thrive inside a cold frame, well after frosts that normally would have killed them. A cold frame is also an excellent place to store plants that are not quite hardy enough to be in the garden all winter.

Before forcing spring bulbs as fun projects in pots or tubs, give them their cold treatment in the cold frame. Experts note that seeds of some trees, shrubs, wildflowers, and perennials need a cold treatment before germination in the spring.

The garden advisors at Charley's recommend choosing a site for your cold frame that will face south to get maximum benefit from the low winter sun. A level and well-drained area of the garden protected from winds is ideal. Place the cold frame near a water source and in an area you will be able to check on periodically. Even in winter, temperatures can heat up dramatically, so venting on warm days is essential.

A cold frame or even a small greenhouse lets you stretch the growing season into the fall.

Portable greenhouses and patio-wall gardens are a cost-effective way of getting your seedlings out of the house and into a greenhouse, even if space is limited. You can use one just as you would a cold frame. There are insulated patio garden models with glass panes and poly-covered models that assemble in less than an hour. We have used old storm windows to make a growing area that can keep tomatoes ripening right up to September. Today, modern, affordable, and easy to assemble portable and miniature greenhouses make sense to avid gardeners. Some types attach to a wall as a lean-to. You can find plans to build some of these useful devises at websites included in chapter 18.

GREAT GARDENERS USE SEED

The National Garden Bureau has a campaign called "Great Gardeners Use Seed," which is a commitment to reach teachers, youth, and adults, teaching the benefits of gardening with plants from seed. The National Garden Bureau was founded in 1920 to disseminate basic instructions for backyard gardening, and its experts have been of great value to gardeners of all ages and stages of experience for many years. The organization publishes Today's Garden and the "Year of" fact sheets and offers valuable gardening advice on its website: www.ngb.org.

The organization also sponsors programs that teach youth science with the use of garden-based activities. The National Garden Bureau acknowledges that previous generations were taught to garden by their parents, grandparents, or other family members. Today, in our fast-paced world with many activities competing for time, millions of children have not had the opportunity to sow a seed and nurture the plant grown from seed.

Therefore, the National Garden Bureau has supported an innovative project, the GrowLab Program. Over 50 GrowLabs have been donated to teachers for classroom use. A GrowLab is a tabletop structure that serves as a germination chamber and growing laboratory for children to sow seed, nurture growing plants, learn botany, and become familiar with plant needs. Teachers are given guidelines, seed, soil, and the tools to lead youth through the growing process. Teachers applaud this program.

To ensure that this innovative and worthwhile program meets its goals, the National Garden Bureau partners with the National Gardening Association to distribute educational kits to teachers. Each year more than 500 educational kits are sent to teachers upon request, and 37,000 teachers have received seed packets donated primarily by the National Garden Bureau members.

TYPES OF GARDENS FOR YOUR SEEDLINGS

As you start seeds and watch them sprout and prepare to be part of your home garden vistas and plantscapes, take a moment to envision the types of gardens that you may wish to create. Naturally, gardeners have classified different types of gardens, so perhaps a quick review might be helpful here.

Is your garden a certain style? Or is it eclectic: a little of this, a little of that? If you find it hard to resist a new plant, your garden is probably eclectic. Nothing wrong with that, but it helps to try for some semblance of order. Just the simple technique of planting at least three of one kind of plant and repeating the grouping more than once in a border or elsewhere will provide the appearance of a planned, organized design.

As your seeds sprout and later in the year as gardens are growing gloriously, look around your neighborhood and town. Note what's growing well.

Visit local nurseries, libraries, bookstores, and garden websites to learn the requirements of the plants you like. No matter what garden design and plants you select, your garden should reflect your personal preferences. Then, you can pick the seeds of plants you want to add to your garden in years ahead. Here are elements of some traditional types of gardens.

The **country garden or English Cottage garden** says old-fashioned with its plants and layout. For this style, select plants with an eye to their foliage texture, shape, and growth habit as much as to the colors of the blooms. Consider growing these plants for a cottage garden: bee balm, columbine, coneflower, daisy, delphinium, dianthus, English daisy, foxglove, hardy geranium, hollyhock, iris, lamb's ears, larkspur, lavender, phlox, peony, Russian sage, clematis, climbing rose, morning glory, and trumpet vine.

The old-fashioned **kitchen garden** was traditionally a garden by the back door that was handy for everyday use. A classic kitchen garden contains vegetables, herbs, and flowers for cutting. In colonial times, it would have held medicinal as well as culinary herbs, fruit trees, and berry shrubs. Plants for a kitchen garden include annual and perennial herbs such as basil, cilantro, oregano, parsley, rosemary, and thyme plus root, leafy, and vining vegetables. Include flowers for cutting such as bachelor's buttons, marigolds, snapdragons, and zinnias plus tasty flowers for eating such as calendulas, dianthus, pansies, marigolds, nasturtiums, and violas. For today's kitchen garden, you can start seeds to grow a rainbow of unusual colored and ornamental vegetables for eye appeal and your dinner table.

Natural gardens are another distinctive look. Think of a tall-grass prairie or a field of flowers and grasses swaying in the breeze. Today's field may be a sunny side yard, an area in the backyard surrounded with a split rail fence, a double border on either side of the front walk, or the entire front yard. To start a natural garden, remove sod and weeds to give native plants and seeds an opportunity to grow without competition from plant intruders. Plants for a natural garden include perennial and annual wildflowers indigenous to your area and ornamental grasses.

Rock gardens are another distinctive landscape idea. A rock garden usually is on a hillside or at least an incline, but you can create one on a level surface by mounding soil slightly and pressing rocks into the soil to make them look as if they forced their way above ground or have been worn down by wind and water. Plants for a rock garden include armeria, baby blue-eyes, candytuft, evening primrose, lupine, maiden pinks, phlox, rockcress, sanvitalia, snow-in-summer, sweet alyssum, sweet William, creeping thyme, viola, pansy, Iceland poppy, zinnia, and succulents such as sedums and sempervivum. You'll find fun ideas at the North American Rock Garden Society website: www.nargs.org.

Oriental gardens have sprouted as we all learn more about gardening around the world. Asian gardener friends explain that a sense of peace pervades an oriental-style garden, where careful placement of rocks and paths takes equal importance with plants. Function and ornamentation combine in stone benches, wooden bridges, and fences. Interest comes more from foliage texture and plant shapes than from colorful flower displays. Water plays a major role as a small pond, waterfall, or a trickle from a fountain made with bamboo. The primary color in an oriental garden is green, so plants for an oriental garden include agastache, asparagus densiflorus, fall-flowering chrysanthemum, flowering cabbage or kale, nicotiana, and decorative herbs such as basil, chives, dill, and thyme. Also consider using moss, ferns, and bamboo.

ENJOY INTERNATIONAL FLAVORS

American dining tastes are changing, and so are gardening tastes to provide the tempting foods from around the world to make more flavorful meals. Fortunately, seed companies combed their international sources to find suitable vegetables that would grow well in America and provide the foods for gardeners to grow and use. For example, seeds of many oriental vegetables are available from mail order firms. Nichols Seeds is a leader in providing many favorite international veggie varieties.

In fact, the National Garden Bureau celebrated a Year of Asian Vegetables that featured five popular Asian vegetables. Brief details follow, and then a much longer list of famed international veggies that give you new growing opportunities as you perfect your seed starting abilities.

Two vegetables for oriental meals are Asian eggplant and asparagus bean, also called the "yardlong" bean, and both are warm-weather crops. Daikon, pak choi or bok choi, and snowpeas are transitional crops grown best under spring or fall conditions. All are especially flavorful and fun to use in the kitchen, and they are easily grown from seeds.

Also worth starting from seed is edamame, or soybeans. For health-conscious folks, edamame is a nutritional powerhouse. Fresh soybeans are high in phytoestrogens, a natural plant estrogen. They are also rich in calcium and phosphorus and a good source of vitamin A.

As America's taste buds become more internationally sophisticated, millions of families are enjoying the delicious flavors that can be experienced from favorite foods grown around the world.

Finding the right vegetables and herbs for flavorful international cooking has been frustrating. Now, you have great growing opportunities to enjoy the freshest, finest, tastiest international flavors possible. Check out your favorite seed catalogs and write for others you'll find out about in chapter 18. Here are some examples of available favorite international vegetable varieties you can grow from seed, by starting some indoors and direct seeding others outdoors in your garden. Seed firms have been most helpful by providing detailed cultural directions, in their catalogs and of course with the seed packages they send. Try some new taste treats from the ground up in your garden and kitchen this year.

Chinese and Japanese

Sugar Snap Snowpeas

Chopsuey Greens, Shungiku

Mei Qing Choy

Flowering Pak Choi

Mizuna

Red Giant Mustard

Celtuce Malabar

Mei Qing Choy

Radish, Sakurajim Mammoth

Shogoin Turnip

Kikuza Squash

Yamato Extra Long Cucumber

Wong Bok

Purple Choy Sum

Pak Choi or Bok Choy

Joi Choi

Green-in-Snow Mustard

Minata Santo

Chinese Kale

Climbing Spinach

Chinese Winter Melon, Takiogtawa Long

Tokyo Market Turnip

Presto Turnip
Purple Eggplant
Celery, Chinese cabbage
Chinese Bitter Melon

French and Dutch
Shallots
Carrot Touchon
French Endive
Prelane Eggplant
Green Mignonette Lettuce
Charantais Melon
Sweet Pepper Ariane
Flageolet Beans
Celery Dinant
Cornichon vert du Massy Cucumber
Swiss Chard
White Bush Zucchini
Dutch Yellow Shallots

Italian
Green Sprouting Calabrese
Romano Pole Bean
Broccoli Raab, Rapini Promasa
Sicilian Purple Cauliflower
Asparagus Chicory
Blood Red Bottle Onion
Giant Italian Parsley
Lagenaria Longissimi Squash
Broccoli Romanesco
Aquadulce Fava Bean
Savoy Cabbage
Grumolo Chicory
Giulio Radicchio, Red Chicory
Wonder of Pompeii Onion
Pepperoncini Pepper
Viva Italia Paste Tomato

Mexican and Tex-Mex
Santa Maria Pinquito Beans
Montezuma Red Beans
Indian Flint Corn
Ground Cherry-Husk
Tomatillo, Salsa base
Tam Jalapeño
Serrano Hot Pepper
Hot Pickling Pepper
Long Black Spanish Radish
Heatwave Tomato
Sweet Spanish Onion
Black Aztec Corn
Mango Melon
Tomato Jicama
Tomatillo Purple
Habañero Pepper
Chili Jalapeño
Chili Ancho Pepper
Long Red Cayenne

Middle East and Russian
Egyptian or Walking Onions
Yardlong Armenian Cucumber
Russian Broadleaf Comfrey
Russian Beet Fakel
Amira Cucumber
Melon Gallicum
Red Russian Kale
Moscow Tomato

There are many, many more varieties becoming available every year! Grow international and feast on the world's favorite foods! Now, take a pledge to order some new catalogs, read them with your family, and begin expanding your growing horizons with treats from all around the world.

15

CONTAINER GARDENING

There's a colorful, tasty new trend growing up on porches, patios, balconies, and even rooftops all across America these days. It's container gardening. According to one recent survey, container gardening surpassed 26 million participating households. According to the National Gardening Association, container gardening is on a roll. Flower filled containers are perfect for the time- and space-strapped gardener. They add color to patios, and decks for those who don't have backyards or time to grow bigger gardens in beds and borders. Garden writing research I've done overseas during the past few years reveals that container gardening in America is approaching the extent of that popular practice in Europe.

Fact is, no matter where you live, in apartment or city condo, you can grow both delicious food and beautiful flowers and enjoy appealing colorful, tasteful container gardening. One secret to success is new hybrid seeds. Plant breeders have created wonderful new varieties that bear beautiful giant and profuse blooms on convenient, compact plants. You also can enjoy tasty harvests of full-size vegetables from plants and vines that grow well productively in containers. Another plus, new columnar fruit trees bear delicious fruits in tubs, buckets, or barrels. Strawberry barrels are useful too.

Garden authorities nationwide see the trend continuing to grow and thrive. Mississippi horticulturist Jim Perry noted there is a definite increase in container gardening in tubs, boxes, and on windowsills, especially for people in apartment complexes. Don Lacey of New Jersey reported wide use of conventional redwood tubs, ceramic pots, and barrels. Dr. Edwin Carpenter in Connecticut said he expects container gardening will become a major interest area for urban homes where space is at a premium. As we toured Europe, we learned that there are approximately 25,000 miles of windowbox gardens, based on horticulturist estimates.

In response to many people's desire to garden in cities, supply firms have come up with all you need, from attractive containers to soilless soil and liquid fertilizers. You'll learn the basics in this chapter and can grow from there to make container gardening a blooming asset where you live.

PICK THE BEST CONTAINERS

Experts say, somewhat jokingly, if it will hold soil, it is a container. Your choice of containers is attractively wide: wooden barrels, decorative ceramic tubs, glazed pots and planters, hanging fiberglass and plastic baskets, and buckets. Good old-fashioned windowboxes are back in style too. Our surveys revealed that people in apartment complexes are busily gardening with vegetables and flowers in many types of container plantings. Your choice is limited only by your imagination. Truly, anything that holds soil mix and provides proper water drainage will work. Look around. Garden centers and chain stores offer a wide range of shapes, sizes, and colors from purely functional to highly decorative. Shop flea markets and yard sales for old baskets, barrels, kettles, and buckets.

When you shop for containers, keep these points in mind. Container plants need more water than those in backyard gardens because of their restricted growing habitat, which means their roots cannot roam in search of moisture. They also are bombarded by sun and heat radiated from building walls. That doesn't mean just add more water. Proper drainage is especially important because

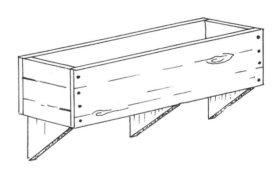

Pick up items at flea markets for flower displays.

Windowboxes are making a comeback, and you can easily make some yourself.

plants hate wet roots. Therefore, be sure your containers provide adequate drainage and escape of excess water. Soggy soil limits a plant's uptake of vital oxygen. Placing several inches of coarse gravel in the bottom before adding soil mixture is a basic move. This said, container plants still need close attention to their water needs, sometimes daily in dry periods.

Containers also are exposed to drying air on all sides. Check container soil daily by poking your finger deeply into the soil. If it remains dry, water well and deeply, because that encourages deeper rooting for sturdier plants. Light sprinkling only promotes shallow surface rooting. Water in mornings so plant have sufficient moisture during the hot, sunny time of day.

Avoid pouring water too rapidly that can disturb tender roots. Instead, use a watering can or fine-mist hose nozzle and soak soil thoroughly. Wick watering is useful too. You can insert one end of a fiberglass or felt wick into a container of water and the other end deeply into the soil of your container. Water will travel through the wick to keep soil supplied with moisture. Be sure to keep the reservoir filled or water can siphon back out of the soil. Try bottom wick watering too. Insert nylon or cord wicks from a water tray up into the draining holes of containers. Better yet, obtain containers with built-in watering systems. Best rule is to test soil of containers daily. If soil feels dry, water thoroughly.

Double potting is a useful idea. Plant in a large clay pot and put that into a larger decorative container. Put gravel on the bottom and fill the space between pots with sphagnum moss. That way you water the clay pot with plants, excess water drains away, and you have a good-looking container on the outside for eye appeal to complement your flowering plants.

Double potting—a clay pot containing a plant is placed inside a larger decorative pot—lets you fill the space between with sphagnum moss to give plant moisture while avoiding soggy roots.

As you shop, select pots with holes in the bottom or sides so excess water escapes. Raise containers without saucers off the surface of a deck or patio by placing them on decorative feet of wood or a moveable dolly. That lets you move containers around for parties and back to their best growing area. Larger containers reduce the need for watering but are heavy, even with soilless soil, so use dollies for convenience in moving large containers.

Before buying containers, envision your container garden area. For interest and to create depth, plan groupings of three to five different sized containers, such as one or two large pots with plants 2–3 feet tall, another with 18-inch plants, and some with smaller plants. That gives a three-dimensional look to your mini-garden. Veteran gardeners note that wood, plastic, or composition containers are better than terra cotta, common clay pots whose porous sides let water evaporate too fast.

FILLING CONTAINERS

One key to container growing success is "soilless" soil. Actually, this isn't a new development. Professional growers have used it with exceptional results for years and call it the ideal plant growing

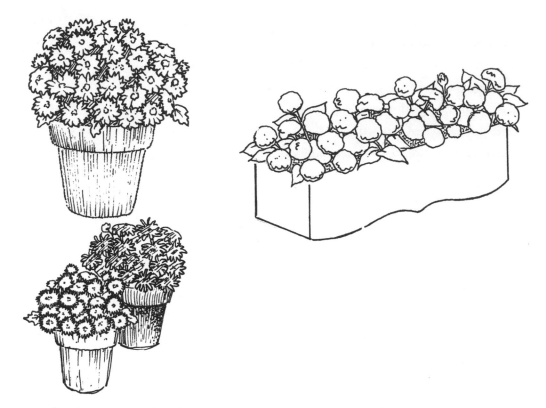

Consider both small and large pots and rectangular planters for container growing.

medium. Today you can easily obtain potting or growing soil mixes at local stores. They all have important advantages over typical backyard earth, which has soil bacteria, fungi, and insects in it and which can be too sandy or overly wet. The new container soil mixtures are scientifically prepared to give plants their optimum growing conditions. Many already have fertilizer elements included. If not, no problem. You can easily mix time-released fertilizer into the soil mix to help feed plants as they grow. Then, you can add granular or liquid feeding during the season as your plants need it.

Next step is planting. You can sow seed directly by following directions on the seed packets. Thin seedlings as specified. You also can use a starter kit and transplant seedlings to containers when ready. Or simply buy bedding plants locally to get a faster start on blooming time and vegetable or herb harvest.

With mini-gardens in containers, it pays to give more attention to color, texture, and flower form, the basic elements in designing your container garden. With color, just about anything goes. Select what appeals to you and your interior decor and grow with it. Texture is often best brought out by including foliage plants that have various shapes and forms. Flower forms range from tall ones like salvia spendens or snapdragons to mass forms of daisies, petunias, or marigolds with many small to larger flowers. Other dramatic forms include African marigolds and coneflowers and others with large, distinctive blooms. Another approach is to use masses of one flower and color in one pot contrasted with other colors and forms in another pot.

Expert container gardeners say that you should carefully choose your plant varieties. Some varieties have genetic capabilities to grow especially well in containers. Best bets for container flowers are ageratum, alyssum, bachelor's buttons, China asters, fibrous-rooted begonias, calendualas, candytuft, fragrant celosia, columbine, geraniums, lobelia, lupines, nasturtiums, pansies, dwarf phlox, various sizes of marigolds, stocks, sweet peas, and zinnias. Naturally, you can select other plants as you wish. Just pay attention to their needs. One common mistake is choosing the wrong combination of plants. Don't mix shade-loving plants with sun-loving plants in the same container.

How many plants should you use per container? If you provide enough soil and water, you can space plants closer together than usual recommendations for backyard gardens. In a larger pot, you could plant 9–12 transplants of flowers, depending on how spreading they are. Be careful not to overplant, or when the plants mature, they will overpower and overshadow one another and look too crowded. However, new varieties of cascading petunias will grow gloriously and spill over the sides of hanging baskets or windowboxes in colorful profusion.

TRY VEGGIES AND HERBS TOO

You can create entire gardens in containers using wooden half-barrels or large, 24-inch pots. Better yet, you can grow the ingredients for your favorite sauces and favorite vegetable dishes. Tomatoes are America's favorite vegetable, and many varieties will thrive and yield tasty tomatoes all season in containers. Smaller cherry types do especially well, but even larger varieties bear growing. Cucumbers are always appealing for salads, and new compact vine varieties are excellent for container growing. So are compact melon plants that yield full-size fruits. Don't overlook salad patches that keep on producing greens every time you cut some for meals. Harvest ripe fruits promptly so plants continue to produce new growth.

Here are some other ideas to whet your appetite. Consult garden catalogs to look up varieties that are recommended for container cultivation.

Try a **salsa garden** with bush-type tomato, jalapeño or hotter peppers, and cilantro. Sow the cilantro seeds around the edge of the container. If you want onions in your salsa, plant them in a separate, deep planter. Consider a **pesto pot** of basil, garlic, and parsley. For a colorful veggie treat, try a **rainbow array** of red, patio-type tomatoes, a purple or white eggplant, a couple of decorative yellow, orange, or purple sweet peppers, and green- and purple-leafed basils around the edge.

Don't overlook herbs. Combine **fines herbs** such as tarragon, chives, parsley, and chervil. Set the first two perennials toward the rear of the container, so you won't disturb their roots at the end of the season when you pull up the other herbs. If you enjoy oriental meals, grow a **stir-fry mix** of Chinese narrow eggplant, any hot pepper you like, snowpeas, and bok choy. Sow snowpeas and bok choy in early spring and again in midsummer for a fall harvest.

Of course, salads are popular all the time. For a **container salad bowl**, plant a patio tomato and sweet pepper in the center, and one or two cucumber plants near the edge so they can spill over. Add a few radishes and red- and green-leaf lettuce in the middle spaces. Another salad garden might include spring leaf lettuce, followed by summer beans on a teepee, succeeded by fall peas. Set up a teepee when you plant the lettuce seedlings. Sow beans and the bean plants will provide lettuce with a bit of shade from the summer sun. Sow peas in late summer where the lettuce was and while beans continue to produce.

Try a **soup mix** of lemongrass, thyme, parsley, chives, chervil, and scallions. For **pizza sauce**, grow bush tomatoes, sweet green peppers, onions or scallions, and oregano.

To **encourage children**, let them have their own container garden. Here's one approach with radishes, tomatoes, bush beans, basil, and carrots. Set a tomato plant in the center and alternate clumps of basil and bean seeds in a circle around the tomato. Mix seeds of radishes and carrots together and sow around the outer edge. Pick the radishes before the carrots need more space to grow. Better yet, ask children what they would prefer to grow. Radishes or carrots may not be their choice. Melons may be a better idea. Some kids may surprise you and want a flower garden instead. Grow it.

TIPS FOR CONTAINER CARE

Once you have selected the flowers, veggies, and herbs for your containers, note these cultivation and care tips. Container plants need more water than backyard plants because of their restricted growing habitat. Check your containers daily, especially smaller ones that can dry out faster. Poke a finger into the soil. If it feels dry, water well. Container gardens need deep watering to ensure that moisture gets to all parts of the soil mix, which encourages deeper rooting for sturdier plants. Wick and trickle watering systems are available to provide moisture on a regular basis, even when you are away. Some modern containers come equipped with their own bottom or wick watering systems.

Mulch will provide a decorative, finished appearance to any planting. More important, it helps the soil conserve moisture and prevents rain or hose water from splashing soil up onto plants' leaves. Choose any mulch that is readily available or that looks particularly attractive with your container, such as shredded bark.

Container plants need a balanced diet because their roots can't roam in garden ground in search of food. Fortunately, many balanced fertilizer mix-

tures are available for container plants. You have a choice of liquid fertilizer, granules, or slow-release pellets that feed plants over a longer period. Fertilize every 2–3 weeks unless you added a time-released plant food to the soil. Food is especially important when plants such as tomatoes and peppers begin to flower. It also boosts size and profusion of flowers. Always follow the directions for the type you use. Too much fertilizer can be as harmful as too little, especially in containers.

Near the end of the season, protect your container crops from sudden frosty nights by covering them with burlap or light blankets. If you tend only a few pots, bring them indoors when low night temperatures are forecast. Most vegetables slow their growth and fruit production as the heat and duration of sunlight subside going into fall. However, we harvested tomatoes well into winter, then next spring rolled the container tomato plants back on the deck, where they continued to bloom and bear. It's worth a try to have vine-ripe tomatoes year round. Keep the tomato plants in a sunny window but avoid an area that gets overly hot. Many herbs also will grow well all year and continue to form new leaves on a very sunny windowsill indoors.

One of America's most respected gardening groups, the National Gardening Association, based in Vermont, has focused on container gardening and extolled that trend. According to Charlie Nardozzi, senior horticulturist at NGA, "There are myriad possible plant combinations that home gardeners can use to create exciting container displays." For more container gardening information, go to NGA's website: www.garden.org. Or visit their National Garden Month website: www.nationalgardenmonth.org. This year, dig into the rewarding world of container gardening, wherever you live. You'll be abundantly pleased with what you can grow and enjoy.

GROW UP WHERE YOU LIVE

Back in the 1970s, the average backyard vegetable garden was about 1,000 square feet. Now it is typically 200 square feet. New houses tend toward

Sometimes it pays to grow *up* on fences or poles, even using cornstalks to support beans.

smaller yards, and people today, perhaps yourself, don't have the time for larger gardens. There are other ways and places to garden if you don't have much backyard room or landscape space. Raised beds and vertical gardening methods offer you opportunities to exercise your green thumb in productive ways and places. Here are ideas collected from around our country that you may transplant to your own home grounds.

Contemporary vegetable gardening borrows the best design ideas from the past, while incorporating new technology and materials to make smaller vegetable gardens easier to manage, and more productive. Two ways to coax more production from limited space are raised beds and vertical growing. Shifting a garden layout from rows to raised beds almost doubles the available growing areas, because most of the ground formerly devoted to paths is dedicated to production. Growing food vertically uses the airspace above the garden for your growing room, not along the ground. These systems also make it easier to use soaker hoses and trickle watering devices. You also can better use woven fabric mulches and other space-age materials to dramatically reduce the amount of work involved in growing crops.

TRY RAISED BEDS

Raised beds are basically permanent, rectangular plots containing soil that remains looser and better for plant roots because it is not compacted by foot traffic. From paths you leave between the beds, you can easily tend crops from all sides without much bending. It does take work initially to prepare a raised bed, making the box and adding soil mix, but the advantages are worth it, according to many who favor this growing system.

Instead of working to improve garden ground, you actually can purchase well-prepared, enriched

Some fruit lovers buy special barrels to grow strawberry gardens.

soil to fill the raised beds. Once set up, raised beds offer years of virtually instant bed preparation and easy planting each spring. Try one bed at first. Dig or till the ground in the fall when weather is cool. If you like the system, add more beds over time. Veterans say that you also can do more intensive planting in raised beds, so you don't need as much area for gardening.

To begin, lay out your bed's dimensions with stakes and string. A width of 3 or 4 feet is a comfortable reach from either side. Lengths of 8–12 feet seem good for the typical backyard. Then, begin digging and cultivating soil to a depth of at least 1 foot. Renting a rototiller is handy for this stage. Cut and remove turf. Then, after tilling the soil, work backward and dig shovels full of soil. Mound them in a loose pile within the measured dimensions of the bed. At this point, plan to incorporate organic material such as compost, peat moss, or chopped leaves into the soil. You may incorporate these by tilling under with a light tiller like a Mantis to blend soil and organic matter well.

Plan your path to be at least 3 feet around the bed, and remove the valuable top few inches of topsoil from the paths. Mound that soil on the newly dug bed to increase its height. You can use wood chips, old planks, or better yet, gravel in the path area to avoid muddy pathways. Next, rake and level the surface of the mounded soil in the bed. Now, if you wish, add purchased good, enriched topsoil and you are ready for planting come spring. To create a higher raised bed, add a support board system around the bed and bring in more topsoil.

Once you have your bed in place, add a layer of mulch or straw, chopped leaves, compost, or peat moss to protect the soil over the winter and discourage erosion of the mounded soil into the paths. A note about appearance. Boxing each bed with wooden planks prevents erosion, especially in heavy rains, makes beds easier to manage, and looks more attractive. Most experts recommend boxing raised beds. That also provides a way to attach watering systems, poles, fences, and other devices. Even with our low raised beds, we boxed them in with 2 x 10 boards.

Veteran gardeners affirm that raised beds provide a way to save space, maintain soil texture better, and avoid annual digging because the soil is in looser condition. You also gain easier cultivation with less bending, and you can even devise plastic or glass frame covers to extend your growing season.

GROW VERTICAL TOO

You also can save space by growing vertically. Vertical gardening offers several advantages: better air circulation, access to sunlight, fewer problems with moisture causing diseases, and easier harvest. By combining this idea with raised beds, you dramatically increase production. You can grow plants vertically more closely together and produce more

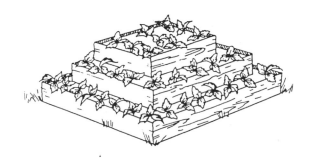

You can make pyramids for more growing space and fill with soil mixture.

in the rich, friable soil of a properly managed raised bed. Grown vertically, some crops take up only a few inches of surface soil, so you have lots of bed left to be intensively planted with low-growing vegetables. A key point is orienting beds on a north–south axis to ensure that plant-laden trellises do not block the sun from lower-growing plants as it moves from east to west during the day.

You can put a variety of vertical gardening devices to work. **Hoops of wire and wooden trellises** are available in garden centers. More advanced systems are featured in mail order garden catalogs. Free-standing devices provide flexibility in placement, but unless strong they can give way from the weight of maturing crops. Best bet is to attach supports to the planks that enclose a raised bed. You can probably devise your own trellis system, using cedar, redwood, or cypress, which resist rot. You also can erect tepees for beans, cukes, and flowering vines as decorative accents in your garden.

You have other options too. One useful method is to fasten 12-inch lengths of **PVC pipe**, 1.5–2 inches in diameter at 4-foot intervals along the insides of the long sides of the bed. Dig the PVC pipe into the soil so the opening is flush with the top of the board. Sturdy vertical poles, wooden or PVC, 6–8 feet long, fit easily and quickly into the PVC pipe fixtures and hold securely. Next step is to

Another version of a growing pyramid garden.

cut 4-foot lengths of furring strips, or better yet, 1 x 1 inch slats of redwood or cedar for crosspieces as panels for your trellis. Design it as you wish, with green plastic coated fence wire, heavy duty cord, or commercial netting. Give yourself room to reach in to pick the bigger veggies that grow inside your trellis or support system. By making frames and attaching wire or mesh to them, you can simply remove the frames and store them in a garage at the end of the garden season for reuse next year.

Tepees also are a simple vertical growing devise. Fasten three sturdy poles, even saplings, together at the top and set them into the ground, spacing out the legs for a 3-foot diameter. Plant seeds around each of the legs and let the plants grow up the poles naturally. Some gardeners prefer to weave stout cord between the poles or even use woven webs so plants grow up more easily.

Still another way to grow up is making **A-shaped frames** and covering them with coated wire fencing or cord webbing. Just plant on each side and let plants grow over the frames.

A number of vegetables and fruits perform well growing up. Try which you like and enjoy this new growing system. Consider pole snap beans and pole limas, cucumbers, melons, peas, various squash, and all types of tomatoes. Cherry, pear, and plum tomatoes do very well, but so do larger types. You also can grow these veggies in wire hoops or special vertical gardening frames now becoming more available in garden centers. It also is easy to make your own hoops from heavy-duty farm fencing. Just cut sections long enough to give you hoops with 18-inch diameters. Cut ends to stick into the ground, and attach fencing into hoops with their own wire strands.

In addition to getting more productivity out of a smaller space, growing plants vertically takes your vegetable garden out of the ordinary with interest-

You can find tubs and buckets for containers, but you may need wheeled dollies to move heavy pots full of soil.

Poles as a tepee, a wire fence, and wire hoops all let you save space growing *up*.

ing designs and makes your work easier with less bending. Fact is, trellises have been around for years as one of the favored ways to grow climbing roses and similar popular plants. Today, we're expanding their uses and coming up with more modern devises too.

As you grow up, also consider combining vining plants, such as beans and cucumbers or peas and gourds on the same support, whether a fence, A-frame trellis, or wire hoop to get multiple crops in the same space. In fact, use every bit of space to maximize results. Pole beans and peas will climb up just about anything, including other plants like corn. Think about the old time, "three sisters" method employed by Native Americans. They planted beans with corn and pumpkins. The corn stalks provide support for the beans to climb, while the pumpkins or other squash sprawl on the ground beneath as a living mulch to control weeds and help retain soil moisture.

Don't overlook hanging baskets.

Pole beans produce over a longer period than bush beans and continue to grow, flower, and fruit as long as you keep picking the pods. So do cucumbers, and many varieties climb well. Check catalogs for details about variety growth habits.

Peas are popular, and fresh peas beat store bought by miles for flavor. Most shelling or English peas produce short vines that need no support, but many of the edible-podded peas produce longer vines that readily climb string or netted trellises with their tendrils, so add them to your vertical garden plans. Peas grow best in cool weather, so combine them with later-maturing vegetables such as beans or cucumbers, or with a flowering vine to take their place during the hot, midsummer months. In late summer, sow peas again for a fall harvest.

Once you have your vining plants in mind, focus on melons or squash or even decorative tiny pumpkins that can cover the ground as a living mulch to thwart weeds. In fact, gourds grow up well, so use some to have fall decorations. Gourd tendrils carry the vines up while the fruits hang down, displaying their interesting shapes.

Space-saving cucumbers, in containers or in the ground, produce straighter, cleaner fruit when you grow them vertically. Sow seeds along a cage, netted A-frame, or flat trellis and guide the young plants up onto the netting. Once plant tendrils form, they naturally curl around on their own to climb your supports, but at first they need a bit of training help.

Melons are one of the favorite crops among gardeners, but often not grown because earlier varieties tended to need space for vines to crawl around the ground. Today, plant breeders have provided new varieties that love to climb. Check them out. Melons climb by means of tendrils, but their heavy fruit requires some extra support when you grow the plants vertically, to prevent their weight from pulling the vines down. You can make

For this system, simply sow pole bean seeds around bamboo or sapling tepees, along a netted trellis, or on an arbor. Or sow a few beans around corn planted in a hill system to support the beans. Be innovative. Try scarlet runner bean, with its appealing red flowers, on a fence or arbor. For very small gardens, try spacing individual poles in a row at the rear of the garden or bordering a back walk.

cloth slings and attach them to poles or a trellis to support melons and squash fruits too.

Tomatoes are America's favorite crop by far. A bit more focus for vertical gardening may help you grow more different varieties deliciously. Few gardeners let tomatoes wander in the garden. Most prefer training them up with wire hoops, commercial supports, or simple stakes. You'll need to encourage tomato plants to grow vertically, so tie them at intervals to a support with twist ties or garden cord. Staked tomatoes grow as well in a large container as they do in the ground, so try some of the taste-tempting different varieties, from heirloom favorites to newest hybrids. You'll be amazed at the difference in flavor that different varieties have.

Some final points to guide your vertical gardening success. As you plan for vegetables on trellises and other supports, grow them on the north side of your plot and toward the back of a row or bed so they don't block sun from low-growing plants. Also, think about the garden space you'll need overall. Wire hoops take about 3 feet of horizontal space. Most A-frame trellises are about 5 feet in length and 3 feet wide. Tepees require 3–5 feet of space. Single stakes and cages need 2–3 feet.

Don't overlook flowers to complement veggies in containers, raised beds, or vertical garden plots. Vines are good choices. Consider balloon vine (*Cardiospermum halicacabum*), black-eyed Susan vine (*Thunbergia alata*), cup-and-saucer vine (*Cobaea scandens*), moonflower (*Ipomoea alba*), morning glory (*Ipomoea tricolor*), nasturtium (*Tropaeolum*), and passion flower (*Passiflora caerulea*).

16

PROBLEM-SOLVING GUIDE

Gardening can be challenging and present problems. You won't find all the answers in this book, but this chapter is designed to cover some of the major problem areas and help you find answers. You'll also find answers to other common questions at the various clubs, organizations, and websites covered in chapter 18.

One worthwhile way to solve problems is to keep records, make notes, and track down answers for situations that develop. Thomas Jefferson, one of America's greatest early gardeners, was an avid record keeper. You too can have a garden book that will be helpful over the years to come.

One of the most heard comments among gardeners might be "I wish I could remember the name of that tomato I planted two years ago that was so good. I tossed the seed pack and cannot find my order form." Does that sound familiar? Keep records. Enter the name of each variety, the seed source, the lot number if available, the date planted, and the date harvested.

As you pick veggies and especially newer varieties as well as flowers, write down your evaluation. Record chemicals used, fertilizer analysis and use on various plants, and anything else of interest. Keep garden catalogs to compare your

results with pictures. Also save pictures to guide you in trying new varieties that will grace your land or provide tasty food for your table. All your notes will help plan next year's garden more efficiently. Here's a guide for what to record in a notebook:

Adaptability to area: How did the plant grow? Some varieties do well in parts of a given state or throughout it. The microclimate—the climate of the plant's immediate vicinity—may also affect the success of a particular variety.

Earliness: Did the plant grow as the seed packet said? The number of days from planting to maturity can vary considerably from one variety to another. In the future, consider successive plantings of the same variety, or of several varieties of different maturity dates planted at one time to extend your harvest season.

Maturity: Did it mature when expected? Note dates of first picking and quality through the season. Some varieties are determinate, which means they set one crop that ripens all at once. Other varieties are indeterminate, which means they continue producing over a period of time, provided plants are properly tended and the fruit is harvested as it matures. In short seasons, you want to get full crops before fall frost.

Productivity: Did you get the amount you expected? With the same care, some varieties yield considerably more than others. Usually hybrids outyield nonhybrids. Do some variety comparisons for yield to fill your table tastefully over many weeks.

Quality: How tasty or attractive was it really? Some varieties differ greatly in flavor, texture, keeping ability, and adaptability for canning and freezing. Read catalogs and compare newer varieties to find the best ones coming along.

Disease resistance: Did the variety grow well without problems? Plant breeders are working hard to build disease resistance into new varieties while retaining good flavors. Resistance to leaf and soil-borne diseases as well as nematodes is available in some varieties. In addition to vegetables, varieties of berries and tree fruits are available that resist common disease problems. They are all worth trying so you can save time, costs, and need for pesticide applications.

Add other points to your notebook and carry it with you as you garden. Highly successful veteran gardeners say they improved their skills over the years just from reviewing notes they made during periodic observations.

EVERYTHING OLD IS NEW AGAIN

It may seem curious that at the same time modern hybrid plants are getting attention, heirlooms are attracting much more interest among home gardeners. Often called rare or antique and even grandma's varieties, heirlooms are cultivated plant varieties that have been grown for at least 50 years, are time tested, and are open pollinated. Heirloom seeds have been passed down from one generation to the next. Through the centuries, people selected out and conserved seeds of plants with enhanced characteristics such as flavor, vigor, scent, and local hardiness.

Heirloom seeds were often among the treasured belongings immigrants brought to America. Many heirlooms are still being kept in families, and some are now available to gardeners everywhere. You may already be growing heirlooms and not realize it. As gardeners look globally for new growing adventures, they also seek reliable, proven favorites that have few problems. Fact is, more than 40 of the All America Selection (AAS) varieties can be considered heirlooms because after more than 50 years they are still available. Among the initial AAS introductions from the early 1930s was the Gleam Series of nasturtiums (*Tropaeolum majus*). Golden Gleam, with its brilliant gold flowers and spicy flavor, made its debut in 1933, followed by the handsome deep-red Scarlet Gleam and the Gleam Mix, both in 1935. Hollyhock Indian Spring (*Alcea rosea*), a 1939 AAS winner, bears single and semi-double blossoms in shades of pink, rose, and white on impressive 7-foot stems. A favorite pink cleome, Pink Queen (*Cleome Hasslerana*), came on the scene in 1942. In 1947, the ever-popular French marigold Naughty Marietta (*Tagetes patula*), with its bright yellow petals marked with maroon at their centers, made its debut.

The Persian Carpet zinnia (*Zinnia haageana*), also called Mexican zinnia, was an AAS selection for 1952, bearing variegated fully to semi-double flowers in shades of red, gold, and white; it is popular for attracting butterflies. Two favorite morning glories (*Ipomoea purpurea*), iridescent Pearly Gates and Scarlett O'Hara, date back to 1942 and 1939, respectively.

The AAS heirlooms include several classic vegetables: Straight 8 cucumber (*Cucumis sativus*) from

1935, Salad Bowl lettuce (*Lactuca sativa*) from 1952, Clemson spineless okra (*Abelmoschus esculentus*) from 1939, and Cherry Belle radish (*Raphanus sativus*) from 1949.

It may be a shock to realize seeds that were introduced during your childhood are designated as heirlooms. These open-pollinated varieties have withstood the test of time as AAS winners and heirlooms. Our thanks to Cathy Wilkinson Barash for providing these historic insights and to the Rotary Gardens, an AAS Flower Display Garden in Janesville, Wisconsin, for their extensive research on AAS flower winners still available commercially.

KNOW THE GOOD BUGS

Bad bugs give all gardeners trouble periodically. Yet many gardeners prefer to avoid undue use of chemical pesticides. You may not be an organic gardener but still want ways to fight insect pests without resorting to chemicals. Here are useful tips about good bugs that eat bad bugs. They are nature's way to balance the environment, naturally. Scientists call this natural balance of good insects against bad insects "biological control." Good insects help us by eating the insect pests that devour or damage our flowers, vegetables, trees, and shrubs. If one bad bug species increases, the insects that feed on that species will increase their own populations accordingly, because there is much more food available. Happily, the beneficial insects devour the pests. You can take advantage of this natural phenomena to put environmentally friendly allies to work for you, controlling the nasties in your gardens and home landscapes. These beneficial insects are available by mail from leading mail order garden firms.

The **praying mantis** gets its name from the form of its front legs, which are designed for seizing and holding prey. After mating in the fall, females deposit their eggs in a frothy secretion that hardens and protects eggs from predators and severe winter climates. These egg cases are attached to vegetation and may contain hundreds of eggs. You can buy these egg cases and set them out in your garden. Run a needle and thread through the outer surface of the case and tie the thread to a branch. For fun and a project with kids, you can hatch them

Insect pests can bug your plants and you. Don't forget to consult with the Cooperative Extension office in your county for the safest and most effective ways to control insect enemies.

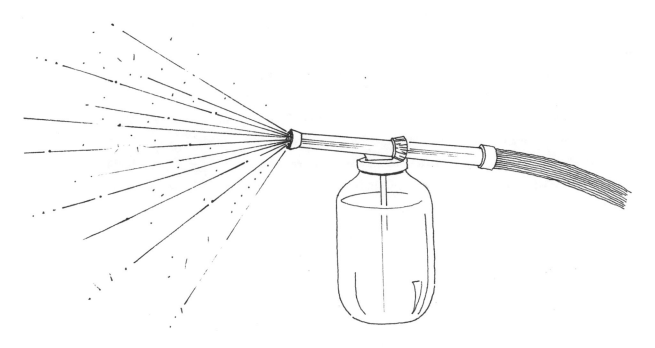

Plants need nutrients to grow well, and you can feed plants with water-soluble fertilizers in many different formulations.

indoors in a large glass jar with a screen top, but you must watch carefully for their hatching. As soon as they begin to hatch, scoop up the young and distribute them around your garden so they can begin their useful insect-eating work.

Ladybugs feed on tiny, soft-bodied insects as well as the eggs and small larvae of many other harmful insects. Their favorite food is aphids, those juice-sucking pests that can cripple young plants. They also consume scale insects, thrips, mealybugs, leafhoppers, leafworms, earworms, corn borers, and bean beetles. Good for them and you.

Ladybugs begin feeding on aphids and other tiny insects in spring. One larva will eat about 400 aphids during its larval period. In 3–4 weeks, larvae attach themselves to a leaf or twig and enter the pupal state, and in another week a hungry young ladybug emerges to begin feeding on harmful insects immediately. As an adult, one ladybug may eat 5,000 aphids. Then they lay eggs to produce more helpful ladybugs. Several generations may be pro-

Praying mantis, one of the beneficial insects for gardens.

duced in years with warm, favorable conditions. Ladybugs are available from biological insect control firms and mail order seed companies and usually are shipped as mature bugs that should be released immediately on arrival. Sprinkle the release area with water to give them a drink when you turn them loose. If releasing large quantities, gently scatter them so each bug can find food immediately.

The **green lacewing** is a beautiful, fragile, light-green insect with lustrous, golden eyes. Adults, which range from one-quarter to three-quarters of an inch long, place their eggs on foliage at the ends of short filaments as a means of protection. Lacewing larvae, also called aphid lions, emerge and begin eating a wide variety of aphids, mealybugs, cottony cushion scales, red spider mites, thrips, and eggs of many harmful worms. Green lacewings also are available from biological control firms and mail order seed companies that provide eggs. The tiny larvae that hatch look like minute alligators and should be released in your garden as soon as they arrive by mail. Hungry larvae will search almost 100 feet for their meals and can provide an effective, natural biological control in gardens. Put Mother Nature to work this year. These good bugs really are a natural boon to all home gardeners.

PLANTS FOR DIFFICULT AREAS

All of us have problem areas, which might include dry sandy spots, soggy and wet ground, shady areas where we want more color, and sun-baked places that challenge our gardening skills. It helps to know which plants are best suited for these difficult or problem areas. That's why the following lists are included, harvested from a range of top horticulturists and experts around our country. Each provides ideas for plants that are very tolerant of special conditions.

A common problem is what to plant in those shady areas of the garden. Two key plants come to mind: coleus and hosta. Coleus offer colorful leaves in variegated patterns that brighten our gardens where we can't get many flowers to bloom. Look through catalogs and you'll find an appealing variety of coleus as decorative accents for your grounds.

Hosta also offer an endless variety of foliage color and texture and are dependable perennials needing little care. Hosta grow best in rich, well-drained soil with uniform moisture and light shade. Some species may tolerate full sun as long as there is ample moisture available. Yellow-leaved and variegated forms need protection from direct sun, while bluish forms require partial shade. Hosta range in height from 10–36 inches and flower mid to late summer. Keep them moist because letting hosta to dry out is the quickest way to ruin a planting.

After those two basic plants, here are others you can select as you try to brighten shady areas or at least have some decorative plants to grace that part of your grounds.

Perennials for Shady Sites
Bugleweed (*Ajuga reptans*)
Snowdrop Anemone (*Anemone sylvestris*)
Columbine (*Aquilegia* x *hybrida*)
Jack-in-the-Pulpit (*Arisaema* spp.)
Wild Ginger (*Asarum canadense*)
European Wild Ginger (*Asarum europaeum*)
Astilbe, False Spirea (*Astilbe* spp.)
Heartleaf Bergenia (*Bergenia cordifolia*)
Siberian Bugloss (*Brunnera macrophylla*)
Lily of the Valley (*Convallaria majalis*)
Yellow Corydalis (*Corydalis lutea*)
Bleeding Heart (*Dicentra* spp.)
Foxglove (*Digitalis purpurea*)

Ferns (various species)

Sweet Woodruff (*Galium odoratum*)

Cranesbill (*Geranium* spp.)

Lenten Rose (*Helleborus orientalis*)

Coral Bells (*Heuchera sanguinea*)

Plantain Lily (*Hosta* spp.)

Lilyturf (*Liriope spicata*)

Cardinal Flower (*Lobelia cardinalis*)

Virginia Bluebells (*Mertensia virginica*)

Japanese Spurge (*Pachysandra terminalis*)

Lungwort (*Pulmonaria saccharata*)

Meadow Rue (*Thalictrum* spp.)

Foam Flower (*Tiarella cordifolia*)

Globeflower (*Trollius europaeus*)

You may also have problems with hot, dry areas around your home grounds. Here is a list of suggested plants to try. Check them out in mail order catalogs for pictures to see how they will look.

Perennials for Hot and Dry Sites

Yarrow (*Achillea* spp.)

Wall Cress (*Arabis caucasica*)

Sea Thrift (*Armeria maritima*)

Silver Mound Artemisia (*Artemisia schmidtiana* "Silver Mound")

Silver King Artemisia (*Artemisia ludoviciana* "Silver King")

Butterfly Weed (*Asclepias tuberosa*)

False Indigo (*Baptisia australis*)

Coreopsis (*Coreopsis* spp.)

Globe Thistle (*Echinops ritro*)

Coneflower (*Echinacea purpurea*)

Sea Holly (*Eryngium amethystinum*)

Blanketflower (*Gaillardia* x *grandiflora*)

Daylily (*Hemerocallis* spp.)

Candytuft (*Iberis sempervirens*)

Red Hot Poker (*Kniphofia* hybrids)

Blazing Star (*Liatris* spp.)

Maltese Cross (*Lychnis chalcedonica*)

Primrose (*Oenothera* spp.)

Russian Sage (*Perovskia atriplicifolia*)

Orange Coneflower (*Rudbeckia fulgida* var. *sullivantii*)

Rock Soapwort (*Saponaria ocymoides*)

Sedum, Stonecrop (*Sedum* spp.)

Veronica (*Veronica* spp.)

Plants for Moist or Damp Soils

Goatsbeard (*Aruncus dioicus*)

Astilbe, False Spirea (*Astilbe* spp.)

Clustered Bellflower (*Campanula glomerata*)

Pink Turtlehead (*Chelone lyonii*)

Delphinium (*Delphinium elatum*)

Hibiscus (*Hibiscus moscheutos*)

Hosta (*Hosta* spp.)

Siberian Iris (*Iris sibirica*)

Japanese Iris (*Iris ensata*)

Ligularia (*Ligularia* spp.)

Cardinal Flower (*Lobelia cardinalis*)

Gooseneck Loosestrife (*Lysimachia clethroides*)

Virginia Bluebells (*Mertensia virginica*)

Bee Balm (*Monarda didyma*)

Obedient Plant (*Physostegia virginiana*)

Rock Soapwort (*Saponaria ocymoides*)

Spiderwort (*Tradescantia* x *andersoniana*)

Globeflower (*Trollius europaeus*)

Great Blue Lobelia (*Lobelia siphilitica*)

Marsh Marigold (*Caltha palustris*)

Queen of the Prairie (*Filipendula rubra*)

Perennials for Poor, Sandy Soil

Yarrow (*Achillea* spp.)

Golden Marguerite (*Anthemis tinctoria*)

Butterfly Weed (*Asclepias tuberosa*)

Wild Indigo (*Baptisia* spp.)

Blackberry Lily (*Belamcanda chinensis*)

Daylily (*Hemerocallis* spp.)

False Red Yucca (*Hesperaloe parviflora*)

Lantana (*Lantana* spp.)

Texas Sage (*Salvia greggii*)

Yucca (*Yucca* spp.)

GOOD GROUND COVERS

Many times we have areas that really need a ground cover to give the area the proper look, such as on slopes, beneath some types of trees and shrubs, and in other applications. Here are some plants to solve those problem areas.

Goutweed (*Aegopodium podograria*)

Bugleweed (*Ajuga reptans*)

Wall Cress (*Arabis caucasica*)

Sea Thrift (*Armeria maritima*)

Beach Wormwood (*Artemisia stelleriana*)

Ginger (*Asarum* spp.)

Wild Ginger (*Asarum canadense*)

False Rockcress (*Aubrieta deltoidea*)

Snow in Summer (*Cerastium tomentosum*)

Leadwort (*Ceratostigma plumbaginoides*)

Lily of the Valley (*Convallaria majalis*)

Yellow Corydalis (*Corydalis lutea*)

Red Barrenwort (*Epimedium* x *rubrum*)

Sweet Woodruff (*Galium odoratum*)

Hosta (*Hosta* spp.)

FIND NEW, USEFUL PRODUCTS

As you review your home landscaping goals and search for ways to solve problem areas, you may find other exciting growing ideas. Here's one way to watch for news of award-winning plants and garden products that may fit right in with your growing plans. The Mailorder Gardening Association (MGA) Green Thumb awards highlight exciting product developments. These awards are presented annually. Check the MGA website at www .mailordergardening.com each year and you'll discover many good ideas.

MGA Green Thumb award winners are chosen by an independent panel of garden writers and editors and are picked based on their uniqueness, technological innovation, ability to solve a gardening problem or provide a gardening opportunity, and potential appeal to gardeners. The awards recognize outstanding new garden products available by mail or online.

Some of the recent winners in the Plants, Bulbs, and Seeds division were Prime Jan and Prime Jim, primocane-fruiting blackberries from Stark Bro's Nurseries; Ava's Hummingbird Mint (*Agastache* x "Ava") from High Country Gardens; Rumbo Hybrid Winter Squash from J. W. Jung Seeds; August Afternoons Perennial Garden from High Country Gardens; and Petunia Flambé from Park Seeds.

Honored in the Tools, Supplies, and Accessories division were the Seed Stick Planter from Johnny's Selected Seeds; the Watering Weed Mat from Gardener's Supply; Gardens Alive! Organic Garden Kit from Gardens Alive!; T8 Light Technology from Gardener's Supply; and the Complete Organic Potato Patch Kit from Wood Prairie Farm.

Prime Jan and Prime Jim blackberries produce berries on first-year canes as well as canes from the previous year. Ava's Hummingbird Mint, a hybrid of two native southwestern U.S. species, is rabbit resistant, deer resistant, and cold hardy. The Rumbo hybrid looks like a Cinderella pumpkin but tastes like a superior squash. The August Afternoons Perennial Garden includes ornamental grasses and three plant varieties for blue, pink, and ivory blooms that attract hummingbirds and butterflies. Petunia Flambé has large ruffled flowers with rose, lemon, and cream tones over white.

Johnny's Seed Stick Planter enables a gardener to plant seeds in the ground while standing up. The device moves one seed at a time from a hopper to the desired planting depth. The Watering Weed Mat controls weeds while it waters; it has a soaker hose woven into it and planting slots for rows of vegetables or other plants. The Gardens Alive! Organic Garden Kit contains four raised-bed corner joints, a weed barrier mat, two 16-quart bags of compost, a tomato support, plant growth enhancer, and a 2-pound bag of organic fertilizer. You add 2 by 6 boards and your own topsoil. The energy-efficient fluorescent T8 indoor lighting system offers optimum light for indoor plants and seed starting. The Complete Organic Potato Patch Kit has four different varieties of seed potatoes.

For other companies and organizations that can help you gather problem-solving ideas and products, see chapter 18.

PESTICIDE POINTERS

Another problem area for gardening is the proper use of pesticides. There are so many different brands and combinations of insecticides for different groups of insects that it isn't possible to provide the necessary details about them in this book. Also, many states have specific recommendations and rules governing use of pesticides by farmers and home gardeners too.

Therefore, it is best to ask your county agricultural agent or Cooperative Extension office for advice about proper and safe pest control in your area. Your local garden center owners also probably have the latest details about new pesticides they have available. Whenever you are concerned about pesticide use, be sure to ask questions and obtain full and adequate answers for your safety. If you are worried about handling chemicals, you may want to use pest control professionals in your area, or rely on the help of a trusted veteran gardener who knows how to use the best pesticides properly. And when you do use pesticides, always read, heed, and follow the directions exactly. These are chemicals designed to kill insects and plant diseases. Treat them with respect and care.

17

SHARE IDEAS, FOOD, AND FUN

Gardeners are sharing people by nature. Many began gardening when they were young and know the joys they experienced as they and their gardens grew. They know that sharing with their children can be particularly rewarding. Even the youngest toddlers can help plant their own little patch, tend it carefully, and marvel as life unfolds around them. Here are some useful tips for making gardening fun and safe for kids, your own or your grandkids.

GROW TOGETHER WITH KIDS

Before they plant, kids need some garden tools. High-quality, small-scale kid gardening tools such as a trowel, rake, and hoe are available to get them started right. Collect some of your favorite, colorful garden catalogs so you can capture their attention and build enthusiasm by thumbing through pages together. That way they get early input on what they like and want to plant.

Walk around your garden area with kids. Select a special area where a child can do as he or she pleases rather than part of your garden. Let them have "ownership" of their very own garden spot. This also avoids damaging prized plants in your garden. Key kids point: let children decide what they want to grow. They may choose plants they recognize, such as pumpkins and sunflowers. Larger seeds are easier for small hands to sow. Suggest growing foods they like, maybe a pizza garden containing tomatoes and peppers plus herbs such as basil and oregano.

Don't overlook growing projects that offer extra fun. How about setting up tall poles in a tripod for a tepee garden of beans or tomatoes or climbing flowers? Think about designing a red, white, and blue patriotic bunting garden using cascading blooms like petunias. How about a sniff and taste garden of culinary herbs. Kids love mint gum, so consider mint, sage, chives, and basil. Tomatoes come in dozens of shapes and sizes, so experiment with different ones from clusters of tiny toms to the biggest beefsteaks, plus plum shaped and yellow colored.

Make gardening fun, not work. Crawl around with kids so you see the growing ground and plants from their viewpoint, down near the good earth. Offer encouragement and how-to know-how. When kids see you tending the garden, they'll most likely want to imitate what you do. Setting an example is the best way to teach, as in show before tell.

Volunteer at schools and in your neighborhood, or lend a hand and your experience to help build gardening projects in your community. Gardening is growing in schools nationwide, thanks to the leadership of some national gardening groups and clubs. Sprouting beans and growing sunflowers are almost a rite of passage for kindergartners and first-graders. In the late 1990s, the California commissioner of education, Delaine Eastin, set the goal of creating a garden in every school. Happily, that concept has inspired teachers, administrators, and school board members across the country. In the process, the National Gardening Association launched their GrowLab Science Program to help children learn through gardening. That award-winning program has proved the power of plants to teach. Children learn fundamental science concepts better through the cultivation, care, and nurturing of plants than through just getting disconnected facts in the classroom.

The NGA program teaches children that an understanding of the natural world is required so future generations will be able to feed themselves and the rest of the world, and that an understanding of how to care for the environment begins with the care of one plant. And in today's electronic world of television, video games, and Internet surfing, hands-on real-life gardening teaches the interconnectedness of the earth, plants, and people.

The National Gardening Association has developed a School Garden Registry to document and highlight notable school garden projects and enable schools to contact one another about their gardens. To learn more, contact the NGA at 1100 Dorset St., South Burlington, VT 05403, or call them toll-free at 888-538-7476.

Here are other useful hints to introduce kids to gardening. Give them fun projects. We learned early that picking is one thing kids like to do, so we showed them how to pick raspberries and blackberries and then sell the surplus at the roadside. Nice thing about raspberries, only the ripe ones come off easily. They got to keep the profits, the extra money after paying for the plants and fertilizer. Our boys quickly realized that weeds competed for fertilizer, so they weeded and mulched and had bigger crops to pick and sell. They also learned a bit of mathematics, adding up costs of plants and growing them. That proved good things in life aren't free.

Pest control is vital in gardens. Learning about nasty bugs that eat vegetable and flower plants is one thing. Squashing those nasties was another project kids love. They learn to identify harmful insects, protect their gardens, and appreciate bug-free veggies and more attractive flowers without damaged leaves and petals. "Squash 'em" can be a catchphrase with kids. Other lessons can include use of beneficial bugs like the praying mantis, lady bugs, and parasitic wasps to control harmful insects. Kids would really focus on a poised mantis as it caught and ate its prey as they learned about natural balance in the garden.

Fetching is another teaching tool. When gardening, there is always something else you see that needs doing, so kids can fetch things. When we harvest a row, it's time to plant the next crop so that land has something else growing, so the kids fetch seeds to be planted or started seedlings to interplant. Each project offers opportunities to show and tell and teach more growing lessons as we share time in the garden.

Gardening also teaches basic lessons of life. City kids often have no idea where food comes from, except the supermarket. As you and your children grow together, they'll see tiny plants sprout, grow, and mature, and they'll get to enjoy eating them too. Try melons. Start some indoors in pots well before you can begin outdoor gardening. It's a treat to watch the enthusiasm as seeds sprout, plants grow, and kids are eager for their own garden spot outdoors. One way to boost enthusiasm is to enjoy a store-bought melon while seedlings are growing. Then guess how many melons the kids can grow on their vines. Plus, they get to try different types of melons. There are lessons melons offer. Watermelons and cantaloupes trace their roots to the Holy Land. Both were foods in ancient Egypt. Then you can add exotic Asian melons. In the process the children get to learn about other cultures and foods that come from all around the world. You'll find more details about growing wonderful international flavors of the some of the world's favorite veggies elsewhere in this book.

Do you recall that catchy cliché, "You are what you eat"? Kids can relate to that with your guidance. When children grow foods, they tend to eat them. As they do, they often want to try other foods. Good for them and you. They no longer look at food with no idea where it came from, who harvested it, or what was used to grow it. From that discovery, children can expand their growing world to a local produce stand or a farmers' market. Knowing what you eat is about planting and nurturing and harvesting food for yourself. It was well said by my friend, the late Robert Rodale, years ago: "When people begin to take the responsibility for their food literally into their own hands and when as a society we no longer rely on distant farms, wholesalers, or government inspectors to ensure that our food is safe to eat, we create a food system that is not only safe for our bodies but nourishing for our souls as well." A worthwhile thought.

INTERGENERATIONAL GARDENING PROJECTS

Here are some examples of intergenerational gardening experiences. What used to be a parking lot in a tough neighborhood in San Antonio is now the Avenida Guadalupe Garden, where fourth- and fifth-graders grow and harvest vegetables. With the help of local Master Gardeners the young people grow broccoli, beans, greens, lettuce, onions, peppers, squash, and tomatoes.

In another neighborhood, Master Gardeners helped juvenile offenders age 15–18 to create a vegetable garden and to mentor children younger than themselves in a program in which at-risk youths could learn about gardening, nutrition, and the environment.

Elsewhere, groups of Master Gardeners teach children about gardening techniques, pests, and plant problems, and they provide them with plants and seeds. Gardening is integrated into school curriculums through journal writing, charting growth, making drawings, cooking, and going on related field trips. When the Bexar County Master Gardeners joined with the Texas Agricultural Extension Service to involve urban children in gardening, the results included better school attendance, improvement in science and environmental studies, and parents who became more involved in school activities. If you would like more information about these Texas projects, write to Youth Gardening, Texas Agricultural Extension Service, 1143 Coliseum Rd., San Antonio, TX 78219. Or visit the National Gardening Association website at www.garden.org for articles about these and other projects nationwide.

David Els of National Gardening Bureau points out that gardening expands children's horizons globally. For the past five years, the statement on the front of the National Gardening Association's brochure has said, "Gardening is more than just a hobby." The NGB intends to prove their claim "by creating and supporting programs that demonstrate how gardening is so fundamental to life itself that it becomes a rejuvenating and sustaining experience. If gardening nurtures the environment, ourselves and each other, then it certainly qualifies as an important contribution to the new millennium."

For many, gardening is an activity that puts fresh vegetables on the dinner table, provides escape from our daily stresses, and helps us get in better touch with our earth. For millions of people around the globe, the family garden plot is much more than a hobby. It represents and sustains life itself. The NGB plans to expand their reach from North America to parts of the world where gardens are essential for survival. They aim to share their vision with the 25,000 teachers and 500,000 students who use the GrowLab program in about 10,000 schools nationwide to create a worldwide network of gardeners who better understand global interconnectedness.

Every home gardener can become involved in great new growing projects wherever they live. Thanks to the National Gardening Bureau, here is a brief checklist of how to start school gardens in your community. There, students can learn to work with teachers, parents, and neighborhood resident volunteers while growing plants and learning the relationship between people, plants, and wildlife. Talk with gardening friends and get involved. It's a winning scene for all.

Step 1: Form a Garden Committee to coordinate a program, be responsible for garden work, find support funds, schedule educational activities, recruit and train volunteers, and disseminate information. Look for volunteers among the school staff, parents, and local residents.

Step 2: Set up clear objectives. Every school garden must fulfill some need. All teachers will use the garden as a learning aid. For some it may reinforce natural science classroom studies while for others it may reinforce social studies.

Step 3: Lay out student garden activities. You will need to determine which groups of students will be doing what and when, and how garden space will be allocated. Experiences and input from your Garden Committee will be helpful to schedule specific activities or assign tasks to volunteers.

Step 4: Define a year-round plan. Decide: Who is going to keep the garden maintained until school starts? How do you want the garden to look on the first day of school? A year-round garden plan must take into account school breaks.

Step 5: Pick a permanent site and design the garden. The garden should be in an area that has adequate sunlight, good drainage, and a handy supply of water. It should be accessible to students, volunteers, and teachers with enough room for garden activities, tool storage, and students. Large gardens take too much effort. Be wise: at first, try a relatively small area.

Step 6: Build your gardens to a plan. The project matures when teachers, volunteers, students, and their parents pool their resources and build this permanent addition to the school.

As expected, other groups have been focusing on youth gardening. It is indeed a growing field, no pun intended. For more information, you may want to contact one of these other national organizations that targets programs to school gardens:

American Society for Horticultural Science
7931 East Boulevard Drive
Alexandria, VA 22308-1300

National Youth Gardening Symposium
International Reading Association, Special Interest
    Group
Gardeners and Readers Develop Naturally
Rt. 1, Box 1038
Ellensburg, WA 98926

National Gardening Association
1100 Dorset Street
So. Burlington, VT 05403

Many who grow up in rural areas are aware of the value of **4-H Clubs**. The 4-H association teaches children across the United States about agriculture, including home gardening. In 4-H, children learn not only about raising animals and plants, but also about responsibility and teamwork. You can contact 4-H Club offices in every county in America through your county Cooperative Extension office. Look them up in your phone book. I set my roots in 4-H when ten years old and can attest it continues to offer a solid foundation for gardening.

Many times people in cities don't have any backyard growing space. **Community gardens** are one answer. In these, gardening space is made available for those who need a plot of growing ground. As much of America's population moves to the suburbs, many inner city residential areas have suffered from neglect and misuse. Residents are often faced living amid high rates of crime, violence, and destruction of property. To fight this deterioration, many neighborhood residents have formed coalitions to improve their neighborhoods. Community gardens provide a way. Many neigh-

borhood groups are using vacant lots, areas near businesses, or even rooftops. These are a great way to get kids and adults involved in beautifying their shared neighborhood.

Actually, community gardens have existed for more than a century. In 1894, in response to an economic depression, Detroit's mayor created the first urban plots. The city gave 455 acres of land to 945 families who grew thousands of bushels of vegetables to feed their families. Other major cities began similar relief programs. When times improved, the gardens were neglected. Then, two world wars brought back community gardens because of the necessity to grow more food. Nearly 42 percent of the nation's vegetable production in 1944 was grown in Victory Gardens, which included community gardens, backyards, city parks, and town commons.

Community gardens got a major boost in 1972 when Lyman Wood created Gardens for All, precursor of the National Gardening Association. It began as an information resource about community gardening around the United States. Today the American Community Gardening Association carries on.

COMMUNITY GARDENING ASSETS

The American Community Gardening Association (ACGA) offers help to all as a national organization that oversees many of the community gardens in the nation. They have ideas and advice for starting and maintaining community gardens. Visit the ACGA website at www.communitygardens.com. Or contact them care of the Council of the Environment of New York, 51 Chambers St., Suite 228, New York, NY 10007, telephone: 212-275-2242.

The Neighborhood Gardens Association is another information source. Their goal is the long-term preservation of community gardens. Most community gardeners do not own the land they garden and are always at risk of being asked to leave. For some useful information, contact them at Philadelphia Land Trust, 100 N. 20th St., Suite 309, Philadelphia, PA 19103, telephone: 215-988-8797. Or visit their website at www.rigalandtrust .com.

Seeds of Hope is an operation of the Ohio State University and has marvelous, detailed community gardening details. Contact them at Ohio State University, 2490 Lee Blvd., Suite 108, Cleveland Heights, OH, telephone: 216-397-6000. The website is brightdsl.net/~coyahoga.

For other useful gardening activity sources, let your fingers do the walking on today's fast-action Internet. The American Horticultural Society is at www.ahs.org and has information on educational programs, including their annual Youth Gardening Symposium. To excite kids, you can try the Butterfly Garden Webster at www.mgfx.com/ butterfly/ for discussions and how-to projects. You'll find Discovery Gardens at www.mind-spring.com, with a wealth of information on de-signing and maintaining indoor and schoolyard gardens plus landscapes for kids. Gardening Education for Youth at www.pierce.wsu.edu/tex/ proggwp.html has information on early elementary studies, growing with plants, and garden and nutri-tion details. Let's Get Growing at www.letsgetgrow-ing.com is another net source for gardening education products and ideas.

Of course, the basic and major resource is the NGA with their Kids Gardening material. NGA has long been recognized as a national leader in gar-den-based education. Their Youth Garden Grants program, begun in 1982, has helped more than 1.2 million youngsters reap the rewards and lessons that green oases provide. With support from industry sponsors, they offer grants and awards that recog-nize exemplary school and community garden proj-ects and leaders and that help launch new programs. Their award-winning GrowLab Science Program has been implemented in 25,000 class-rooms. Telephone: 802-863-5251; FAX: 802-864-6889. Their websites are www.garden.org and http://kidsgardening.com.

COMMUNITY GARDENING KNOW-HOW

Community gardens are one of the best ways to en-able people without room to enjoy the benefits of gardening. Here's an overview from the successful ACGA and useful tips you can put to work. The ACGA is a national nonprofit organization of pro-fessionals, volunteers, and supporters of commu-nity greening in urban and rural communities. They recognize that community gardening im-proves the quality of life for people through com-munity development, social interaction, personal development, reducing family food budgets, and creating opportunities for recreation, exercise, therapy, and education.

Community "greeners" include gardeners, tree planters, and open space advocates. They know from their own experience that plants are good for people and for their communities. Research con-firms that people, even in this technological age, need plants for more than just food and need green space for more than just pleasure. "Nature is not just 'nice,'" University of Michigan psychologist Stephen Kaplan explains. "It is a vital ingredient in healthy human functioning." Much of the benefit comes from "people—plant interactions." Other research reveals that gardening can help you sleep better, and that street plantings reduce graffiti on nearby walls. One community gardener in

Dorchester, Massachusetts, described his green plot as "a little island in the madness."

Starting a community garden requires thoughtful planning. Some of the initial steps include answering key questions. Is there really a need and desire for a garden? What kind of garden should it be: vegetable, flower, trees, a combination? Who will the garden serve? Is space available and can sponsors be lined up? Site sponsorship is a major asset. Contributions of land, tools, seeds, fencing, soil improvements, or money are all vital to a successful community garden. Some community gardens charge fees, but for many a sponsor is essential. Churches, schools, citizens groups, private businesses, local parks, and recreation departments are all potential sponsors. Nearby companies may also offer financial help and encourage employees to garden too.

Finding an adequate site is basic. A site must have at least 6 hours of sun daily, pass soil tests to show adequate fertility levels, and be free of contamination or pollution. Be cautious near old landfills and shopping mall developments. A key consideration is whether the area can be leased or rented for 3–5 years so gardens can begin to take root. A membership organization is important to check all details, plan the design, assemble resources, work with sponsors, and otherwise get the gardens organized and operating. A communication system also is vital so members keep in touch and share duties. Poorly tended gardens can't be tolerated, since diseases and bugs can spread to others. Also, size considerations are needed and arrangements to allot garden plots. There's more work than you may realize, so check into this idea carefully. Simple things like who qualifies for plots and how to get rid of "bad apples" is another sticky point. Is insurance needed? What about theft and vandalism? Will children's plots be permitted?

Does the organization have by-laws, and can everyone live within them?

Don't become alarmed. Tens of thousands of community gardens operate successfully and happily all across America. Many are organized informally and well. Natural leaders often sprout to propose ideas and carry out tasks. Better yet, people make new friends among their fellow gardeners. It seems the most successful have an organizational structure, a system so that each person can participate fully and the group can perform effectively. Leadership must be responsive to the members. Basically, a community garden project should be kept as simple as possible, whether large or small, and should focus on the enjoyment of gardening.

There isn't space to cover all the points you need to know to organize or participate in community gardens. To get fullest details and questions answered, you can easily ask the leader of a local community garden. Or check out the ACGA website at www.communitygarden.org.

One interesting fact is that children included in community gardens often become champions of the cause rather than vandals. In fact, including children's gardens can help sell your idea to local scout troops, day care centers, foster grandparent programs, church groups, and other potential sponsors. For more details you should check with the Cooperative Extension Service in your county, local garden clubs, and state horticultural societies. There are an estimated 10,000 community gardens throughout the world. Checking around, we learned that experiences have varied widely, but thousands of highly successful community gardens have been in operation for a number of years. One of the factors that seems to be most important is a clearly thought out plan. And lots of volunteers! Check ACGA for many helpful hints.

THERAPY GARDENING TIPS

America is growing older, gracefully we hope. But for some seniors who have loved gardening, what once were simple tasks have become obstacles to gardening. These problems include arthritis, back injuries, accident disabilities, and other health problems that make gardening difficult if not impossible. Yet people with health problems are the ones who could benefit most from working in a garden. Gardening has proved therapeutic to many who take it up as a way to regain their health.

Therapeutic benefits of gardening have been well documented. Formal programs called horticultural therapy use the physical, mental, and spiritual benefits of gardening to help patients. Think how you feel after a hard day. Doesn't it feel good just to hang out in the garden, putter with a few plants, pick a few veggies, and smell a few flowers? Fortunately for many disabled people, gardening is an activity that can be adapted for various special needs. These include raised beds for people in wheelchairs or using walkers, and gardens for the blind that appeal to their other senses.

Here are some tips for "Enabled Gardens." Keep the garden in scale with the disabled gardener's preferences, motivation, and skill level. Start small so it won't be overwhelming. For people in wheelchairs or with walkers, provide smooth, wide pathways and beds built high enough for them to reach into easily. Beds should be designed so the center can be reached comfortably without stretching. Planting boxes and barrels are useful. About 12 inches is a good depth. Shallower boxes are satisfactory for many plants such as annual flowers and herbs.

Provide a place for tool storage nearby, either a small shed or perhaps a large mailbox mounted on a fence post. Rig tool pouches that can be hung from wheelchairs, walkers, and the edges of raised beds.

New garden hand tools have been introduced that are ergonomically correct for aching hands. Review garden catalogs for specially adapted hand tools.

Use drip irrigation or soaker hoses and mulches around plants to cut down on watering and weeding. Timers for automatic watering systems are useful too. Fertilizing can be done with water-soluble nutrients or by sprinkling granules around the plants. Provide a resting area out of the sun where gardeners can simply enjoy being in the garden, to sit and smell the roses, or whatever flower they prefer to grow.

One final point that can please disabled gardeners. Think fragrance. In other chapters, you'll find lists of fragrant roses, perennial shrubs, and flowers. Add them to plans for Enabled Gardens. A few whiffs of herbs also can bring back fond memories of youth as much as fragrant flowers. Inhale and plant sweet aromas to enjoy.

With thanks to the Washington State University Master Gardeners, here are some tips that apply to senior gardeners but are useful for all of us.

- Tie a cord around the handles of small tools to make retrieval easier if dropped.
- Use gloves to protect hands and help maintain your grip on tools.
- Carry a large magnifying glass to help you see small plants and seeds.
- Wear an apron or smock with large front pockets to carry seeds, tools.
- Use a piece of lightweight plastic pipe to help sow seeds without bending.
- Carry a whistle. A short blast can alert others if you need help.
- Rig hanging planters with a pulley to lower them for watering.
- Grow vining varieties of peas and beans on a trellis to make harvesting easier.

- Use containers or raised beds for planting to limit bending or stooping.
- Water with soaker hoses or drip irrigation in garden plots.

GARDEN HORTICULTURAL THERAPY

For more than 20 years, the Chicago Botanic Garden has been at the forefront of the horticultural therapy field. Their Horticultural Therapy Services is a major provider of training in this specialized profession and serves as an example throughout the world.

Visit their Buehler Enabling Garden online at www.chicagobotanic.org. This beautiful display garden demonstrates ways to make a garden fully accessible to people with disabilities and is a wonderful place to see the concept of barrier-free gardening put into practice. The 11,000-square-foot garden has many state-of-the-art elements such as raised beds, vertical gardens, hanging baskets, plants with sensory attributes, and a collection of enabling garden tools. Baskets in the garden can be lowered to a gardener's working height, then raised for display. Shallow beds built above the ground allow legroom for gardeners who sit while tending plants. For sensory enjoyment, the garden also has several fountains and uniquely designed water walls.

Since 1977, the Chicago Botanic Garden has assisted over 100 human service facilities to establish gardening programs for people of all ages. These facilities include rehabilitation hospitals, residences for older adults, special education schools, schools for people with visual disabilities, psychiatric hospitals, and correctional facilities. For further information, call 847-835-8250, or e-mail horttherapy@chicagobotanic.org.

PLANT A ROW FOR THE HUNGRY

Being a member of the professional Garden Writers Association (GWA) has enabled me to keep in touch with some of America's brightest and best horticulturists, plant breeders, and other talented garden writers. One of the most worthwhile programs of GWA has been their innovative Plant a Row for the Hungry (PAR), which encourages America's gardeners to plant millions more pounds of vegetables and foods for the hungry in our country. With thanks and a Big Salute to GWA and those who spearheaded this marvelous program, I am proud to include full details here. Perhaps you too will dig in and share your garden talents, ground, and produce with the hungry this year and in the future.

According to the U.S. Department of Agriculture, one in ten households in the United States experiences hunger or the risk of hunger. Many frequently skip meals or eat too little, sometimes going without food for an entire day. Approximately 25 million people, including 9.9 million children, have substandard diets or must resort to seeking emergency food because they cannot always afford the food they need. Research shows that hundreds of hungry children and adults are turned away from food banks each year because of lack of resources.

The purpose of PAR is to create and sustain a grassroots program whereby garden writers use their media position with local newspapers, magazines, and radio and TV programs to encourage their readers and listeners to donate their surplus garden produce to local food banks, soup kitchens, and service organizations to help feed America's hungry.

PAR's success hinges on its people-helping-people approach. The concept is simple. There are over 70 million gardeners in the United States alone, many of whom harvest more than they can consume. If every gardener plants one extra row of vegetables and donates the surplus to local food banks and soup kitchens, a significant impact can be made on reducing hunger. Food agencies will have access to fresh produce, funds earmarked for produce can be redirected to other needed items, and the hungry of America will have more and better food than is presently available.

PAR's role is to provide focus, direction, and support to volunteer committees who execute the programs at the local level. The local groups help gather the human resources necessary to form a nucleus for a local committee. Then GWA provides training and direction to enable the committee to reach out into the community. Finally, GWA assists in coordinating the local food collection systems and monitors the volume of donations being conveyed to the soup kitchens and food banks. PAR is proving that every individual can make a difference in his or her community.

A historic anecdote. PAR began in Anchorage, Alaska, in the garden column of Jeff Lowenfels, a former GWA president, when he asked gardeners to plant a row of vegetables for Bean's Cafe, an Anchorage soup kitchen. Since then, PAR has grown exponentially through continued media support, individual and company sponsorship, and volunteerism.

A group can hand out starter kits, organize community planting and harvest events, plant a community garden, and put together a glean team to harvest produce donated by local farms. Other projects include challenging other organizations to beat your goal, adopting a farm stand and organizing a team to collect the leftover produce and deliver it to a donation site. Businesses can organize a company-wide PAR campaign and also contribute "in-kind" or financial donations.

A large planting or bumper crop will mean a great deal to your local soup kitchen, shelter, or food pantry. Even one additional row of vegetables can make a difference in your community. A typical packet of snap bean seeds produces about 20 pounds of fresh, tasty produce. A packet of carrot seeds produces about 100 pounds. The average large tomato weighs about a pound. Flowers help brighten food shelter meals. Herbs add both flavor and nutrients to food. If you have no garden space or green thumb, help is also needed weighing and delivering produce, picking commercial farmers' surplus, and providing storage space for vegetables.

GWA established a supporting 501(c)(3) charity called the Garden Writers Association Foundation to administer and expand the PAR program. Their address is Garden Writers Association Foundation, Plant a Row for the Hungry, 10210 Leatherleaf Court, Manassas, VA 20111. You can also e-mail the group at par@gardenwriters.org. Or visit the GWA website: www.gardenwriters.org.

This year, expand your growing horizons in as many different directions as you wish. The ideas here can guide you to advice, opportunities, and new friendships that also will grow over the years.

18

SOURCES, CATALOGS, WEBSITES

Over the years, I've tapped the talents of marvelous people to give my readers the best growing knowledge available. Now it is time to share my great gardening sources in this handy book. Here's where you can find some of the best horticulturists, plant breeders, landscapers, and other plant experts who are glad to share their knowledge with you. Park your garden tractor and tiller. Let your fingers do the walking on your computer and your mouse do the pointing so you too can become an expert gardener. You can tap top talents and harvest bouquets of great growing information. Some sources have toll free numbers so you can get expert answers to your garden questions. Others offer answers by e-mail from experts at many seed, plant, and garden product firms. There's a wealth of information in cyberspace to be harvested. Pick what you wish.

Another major gardening source has been invaluable to me over the years: mail order garden catalogs. They have provided a wealth of growing ideas and advice, plus news of super new varieties worth trying. Each year I receive about 50 different garden catalogs. They range from the commonly known such as Burpee, Park Seed, and Johnny's to others that have heirloom plants and rare varieties.

In this chapter, you'll find out where to get free, illustrated garden catalogs from my favorite mail order firms. Many feature unique, hard-to-find varieties and special types of plants. Catalogs let you take a peek at beautiful flowers that you may wish to grow, learn about their habits, and find the best tips for growing each. Besides, colorful catalogs are inspirational reading when winter chills the garden and your bones. They give you new goals and boost your garden determination.

Check out the Mailorder Gardening Association (MGA), the world's largest group of companies that specialize in providing garden products via mail order and online. At MGA's periodically revised website, www.mailordergardening.com, you'll discover a bounty of helpful sources. They have more than 130 members who offer colorful, illustrated catalogs packed with tips and ideas. What you'll like especially about this site is the impressive list of member companies that are categorized by the types of products they provide, such as annuals, perennials, fruit trees, garden supplies, and fertilizer. More than 25 companies are listed under "bulbs" alone!

All you need to do is click on a company name and up pops a short description of the company's offerings, phone number, and address. Click on the hotlinks and you will be connected to the company's home page. From there you can shop around for whatever you wish to see and learn. This website is a super place to start when you want to find seed, plant, product, and accessory firms online. Even better, you can find toll free numbers of companies that offer answers to your personal gardening questions.

Another valuable place to shop for gardening information is the National Gardening Association (NGA) website: www.garden.org. NGA is the publisher of *National Gardening* magazine. You can read online articles from the magazine, find out about the NGA's Youth Garden Grants program, search their extensive library for gardening topics. There's even a seed swap section. If you want to ask some basic questions, go ahead. There are more than 16,000 questions already answered, so probably you'll find what you want to know there. Even better for those who like to swap information, you can sign up to become a Gardening Neighbor and share your know-how and exchange ideas with fellow gardeners with similar interests.

If you're looking for the right tool or piece of equipment and can't find it locally, check the Gardener's Supply Company, www.gardeners.com. This organization is devoted mostly to quality merchandise offered through their printed catalog, but the website often includes bargains not in the catalog. In addition you'll find an extensive Q&A library full of good growing tips. If you don't see an answer to your question, simply ask it and you should receive an answer by e-mail within 48 hours.

Would you like to learn about biblical plants of the Holy Land? It's easy to do. Online you can wander the biblical plant world and a 625-acre Biblical Garden Preserve in the Holy Land at www.neot-kedumim.org.il. Neot Kedumim is a labor of love, re-creating an extensive preserve with the flowers, herbs, vegetables, fruits, trees, and also some of the fauna mentioned in scriptures. For more about biblical gardens, see chapter 12. You can also find resources at local libraries. They may include my books on the topic: *Plants of the Bible and How to Grow Them*, *Flowers of the Bible and How to Grow Them*, and the newest, *Herbs of the Bible and How to Grow Them*.

For organic gardening enthusiasts, who are growing in number nationwide, look up *Organic Gardening* at www.organicgarden.com. They're America's experts and advice is plentiful. Happily, active gardeners have discovered the value of the Internet. There's a wealth of growing knowledge sprouting there every week. One way to find more information is to visit the Google website: www.google.com. Simply input the garden topic you want information about, and that search site will deliver dozens of sources, plus lead you to specialty clubs and organizations where you'll find myriad like-minded garden enthusiasts.

If you love houseplants, then check out www.incan-garden.com, which leads you to an index of houseplant-related articles written by dozens of houseplant experts. For herb enthusiasts, check www.wholeherb.com. For fruitful gardens, try www.starkbros.com. Stark Bro's has been selling fruit trees and berry plants for 180 years. Their site is a tasteful source for information about fruit trees, nut trees, and berry bushes. Miller Nurseries also has a handy website, www.millernurseries.com, with information about planting, pruning, harvesting fruit, and pest control.

Horticulture magazine's site is one of the better garden websites with a treasure chest of info. You can read stories from the magazine, track down online articles, find your horticultural zone, and plan your new gardens too. The Bulb Lady, Debbie Van Bourgondien, has a colorful spot, www.dutchbulbs.com, where you'll find timely articles about virtually every kind of bulb. She also will reply if you don't find answers to your questions on her site. Plus, you can order one of the best bulb catalogs from her.

If you love old gardens, there are Old World places to visit and historic sites too. Thomas Jefferson wrote that "the greatest service which can be rendered any community is to add a useful plant to its culture." By that standard, the Thomas Jefferson Center for Historic Plants is a natural treasure. At their website, www.monticello.org, you can browse a library of articles about Jefferson-related plants or look through an online catalog for eighteenth-century suggestions for your garden. Look up heirloom plants and landscape trees and other topics as you surf the Net and you'll discover many garden paths worth exploring.

TIPS TO FIND GARDEN WEBSITES

The high-tech world of computers provides abundant help to home gardeners. If you aren't familiar with the World Wide Web, perhaps some tips would help. Basically, the Web provides a contact or link to sites or places that provide a wide range of information. It is done over telephone or cable lines or wireless service. Once you are linked to the Internet through a computer, you can type in an address—such as www.gardens.org—and you'll be connected to that website.

You can also use a search engine to find information. Two popular search engines are Yahoo! at www.yahoo.com and WebCrawler at www.webcrawler.com. I prefer www.google.com. Once you pick one, type in a word such as rose, or garden, or even a company name, and you'll be taken to dozens of places filled with information. By using the Web addresses of firms and organiza-

tions, you'll be connected to their sites, packed full of great knowledge. It's a great growing world out there when you tap the Internet.

As you surf the Web, you'll find hundreds of articles, info pages, and other material you may wish to save. Most sites allow you to download and print out these pages of helpful ideas and advice that are of interest to you. Be aware that site and especially e-mail addresses change, as do contacts at these companies and gardening organizations. Fortunately, new gardening companies are sprouting, especially those with specialty plants and products. A time-honored biblical saying guides us to new growing ground: "Seek and ye shall find."

ALL AMERICA SELECTIONS

Avid gardeners are always looking for new and better varieties. Seed firms promote their newest varieties, but gardeners need to know which really are the best performers among the varieties being introduced. Fortunately, the All America Selections (AAS) provides a nationwide, reliable proving ground. That organization represents all major seed firms, who have put together an unbiased national network of trial grounds throughout North American climates where flower and vegetable varieties are grown and assessed by skilled, impartial judges. The seed trials accept only new, previously unsold varieties.

AAS trials have been conducted every year since 1932. New varieties are tested in trial grounds nationwide under various conditions of climate, soil, and growing environments. Their awards recognize a flower or vegetable for significant achievements, proven to be superior to all others on the market. In these comparison tests, vegetables are evaluated for flavor, quality, yield, earliness to harvest, appearance, ease of harvest, plant habit, texture, disease and pest resistance, production and space efficiency, nutrition, novelty value, and edible qualities. Flowers are judged for color, novel flower form, disease and pest tolerance or resistance, insect and weather stress, length of flowering season, uniformity, uniqueness, fragrance, and overall ornamental qualities. Bedding plant flower entries are judged for earliness, uniformity of flowering, flower quality, and size. There also are cool-season trails that evaluate frost-tolerant annuals from seed. Evaluations take place over the fall, winter, and spring.

Each trial ground has at least one official AAS judge, usually a horticultural professional, and the site is part of a seed company trial grounds, university, or horticultural institution. It is worth visiting these trial gardens to see for yourself what new varieties are coming along, how they compare with old-time favorites, and if they may fit into your gardening plans.

There are three types of AAS display gardens: for flowers and vegetables, for flowers only, and for vegetables only. You can find those sites by visiting the AAS website: www.all-americaselections.org. Seeing is believing, and a trip to these test and display gardens gives you a look at which varieties do best where you live.

ALLAN SWENSON'S FAVORITE GARDEN WEBSITES

Over the years as a garden writer, I have interviewed hundreds of leading horticulturists, botanists, and top gardeners nationwide. Today, many have established useful websites. So have America's prime garden mail order firms and manufacturers. I've found great growing tips and ideas on many sites and gladly share my favorites with you. Dig in and harvest more garden knowledge yourself.

All America Roses: www.roses.org

All America Selections: www.all-americaselections.org

Antique Flowers: www.selectseeds.com

Bartlett Tree Company: www.bartlett.com

Bluestone Perennials: www.bluestoneperennials.com

Burpee: www.burpee.com

Carnivorous Plants: www.peterpauls.com

Charley's Greenhouse Supply: www.charleysgreenhouse.com

Clyde Robin Wildflower Seeds: www.clyderobin.com

Cook's Garden: www.cooksgarden.com

Drip Rite Irrigation: www.dripirr.com

Dutch Gardens: www.dutchgardens.com

Garden to the Kitchen: www.gardentokitchen.com

Gardener's Supply Company: www.gardeners.com

Gardens Alive: www.GardensAlive.com

Gardenscape Tools: www.gardencapetools.com

Harris Seeds: www.harrisseeds.com

High Country Gardens: www.highcountrygardens.com

Johnny's Selected Seeds: www.johnnyseeds.com

Lilypons Water Gardens: www.lilypons.com

Mailorder Gardening Assn: www.mailordergardening.com

Mantis Tools: www.mantisgardentools.com

Miller Nurseries: www.millernurseries.com

Monticello: www.monticello.org

National Garden Bureau: www.ngb.org

National Gardening Association: www.garden.org

National Wildlife Federation: www.nwf.org

Neot Kedumim Biblical Gardens: www.neot-kedumim.org.il

Netherlands Bulb Assn.: www.bulb.com

Nichols Garden Nursery: www.pacificharbor.com/nichols

Old House Gardens: www.oldhousegardens.com

Organic Gardening: www.organicgardening.com

Park Seeds: www.parkseed.com

Raintree Nursery: www.raintreenursery.com

Seeds of Distinction: www.seedsofdistinction.com

Stark Bro's Nurseries: www.starkbros.com

Stokes Tropicals: www.stokestropicals.com

Territorial Seed Co: www.territorial-seed.com

Thompson & Morgan: www.thompson-morgan
.com

Van Bourgondien Bulbs: www.dutchbulbs.com

Vessey's Seed Co.: www.veseys.com

Water Gardens: www.watergarden.com

Wayside Gardens: www.waysidegardens.com

White Flower Farm: www.whiteflowerfarm.com

Wildseed Farms, Ltd.: www.wildseedfarms.com

ALLAN SWENSON'S FAVORITE GARDEN CATALOGS

Garden catalogs arrive about the time green thumbs begin to itch every winter. That's great timing to let all gardeners rejoice for the coming spring planting time. Over the years, I've found catalogs wonderfully uplifting and filled with new varieties worth trying. Here's my list of favorite, free garden catalogs.

Appalachian Gardens, PO Box 82, Waynesboro, PA 17268 (Rare trees/shrubs)

Bluestone Perennials, 7211 Middle Ridge Rd., Madison, OH 44057 (Nice variety)

Burpee, 300 Park Ave., Warminster, PA 18974 (Seeds, bulbs, plants)

Burgess Seed/Plant Co., 904 Four Seasons Rd., Bloomington, IL 61701 (Bulbs, seeds)

Clyde Robin Seed Co., PO Box 2366, Castro Valley, CA 9454 (Wildflowers)

Crystal Palace Perennials, PO Box 154, St. John, IN 46373 (Water garden plants)

Drip Rite Irrigation, 4235 Pacific St., Ste. H, Rocklin, CA 95747 (Irrigation supplies)

Dutch Gardens, PO Box 200, Adelphia, NJ 07710 (Dutch bulbs)

Flowery Branch Seeds, Box 1330, Flowery Branch, GA 30542 (Rare, heirloom, medicinal)

Forest Farm Nursery, 990 Tetherow Rd., Williams, OR 97544 (Good source)

Gardener's Supply Co., 128 Intervale Rd., Burlington, VT 05401 (Many gardening supplies)

Gardens Alive, 5100 Schenley Pl., Lawrenceburg, IN 47025 (Organic gardening source)

Harris Seeds, 60 Saginaw Dr., Rochester, NY 14692 (Old-line seed firm)

J. L. Hudson, Star Rt. 2, Box 337, La Honda, CA 94020 (Biblical plants)

Johnny's Selected Seeds, RR 1, Box 2580, Albion, ME 04910 (Seeds, wide variety)

Klehm's Song Sparrow Perennial Farm, 13101 East Rye Rd., Avalon, WI 53505 (Specialities)

Lilypons Water Gardens, PO Box 10, Buckeystown, MD 21717 (Great water garden source)

Ed Hume Seeds, Inc., PO Box 1450, Kent, WA 98035 (Short season varieties)

Mantis, 1028 Street Rd., Southampton, PA 18966 (Tillers and tools)

Mellinger's, 2310 W. South Range Rd., North Lima, OH 44452 (Variety)

Miller Nurseries, 5060 West Lake Rd., Canandaigua, NY 14224 (Great berry/fruit tree source)

Nichols Garden Nursery, 1190 N. Pacific Hwy. NE, Albany, OR 97321 (Asian, international)

Northwoods Nursery, 27635 S. Oglesby Rd., Canby, OR 97013 (Rare fruits, nuts, others)

One Green World, 28696 S. Cramer Rd., Modalla, OR 97038 (Rare international plants)

Park Seed, 1 Parkton Ave., Greenwood, SC 29647 (Major seed and plant firm)

Quality Dutch Bulbs, 13 McFadden Rd., Easton, PA 18045 (Many bulb flowers)

Roris Gardens, 8195 Bradshaw Rd., Sacramento, CA 95829 (Iris specialists)

Royal River Roses, PO Box 370, Yarmouth, ME 04096 (Rare, hardy, old-time roses)

Seeds of Perfection, PO Box 86, Station A, Toronto, Canada M9C 4V2 (Unique)

Select Seeds Antique Flowers, 180 Stickney Rd., Union, CT 06076 (Heirloom seeds, plants)

Stokes Seeds, Box 548, Buffalo, NY 15240 (Many varieties)

Stokes Tropicals, PO Box 9868, New Iberia, LA 70562 (Exotic tropical plants)

The Cook's Garden, PO Box 535, Londonderry, VT 05148 (Special salad/vegetable varieties)

Van Bourgondien, PO Box 1000, Babylon, NY 11702 (Major Dutch bulb specialist)

Vessey's Seeds Ltd., PO Box 9000, Calais, ME 04619 (U.S. and Canadian varieties)

Wayside Gardens, Hodges, SC 29695 (Major plant source)

White Flower Farm, PO Box 50, Litchfield, CT 06759 (Specialists in rare bulb flowers)

Wildseed Farms, 525 Wildflower Hills, Fredericksburg, TX 78624 (Wildflower specialists)

MAIL ORDER SHOPPING TIPS

While on the topic of mail order gardening, the Mailorder Gardening Association (MGA) provides some useful tips for shopping by mail and also for handling your plants when they arrive. With thanks to them, that helpful information follows.

Buy selections appropriate for your climate and garden setting. Most catalogs will provide zone ranges for each plant. Some will provide a map showing the zones so that you can determine which zone your home is in. If not, check with the company or your local Cooperative Extension Service to determine your zone.

Be ready when your order arrives. This means having the bed or ground tilled and ready for planting. The quicker you can get live plants into the ground, the better. Plants need immediate attention on arrival. Most mail order firms ship plants and bulbs to arrive at the appropriate planting time for your region. You should plant seeds when appropriate for your area. If you need help or have questions, call and ask. Most garden product mail order companies have customer service people available to answer questions. They can be very helpful and, as good gardeners, are happy to serve you.

Naturally, lots of good gardening information already is on websites. You'll often find "most frequently asked questions and answers" already posted to help gardeners solve basic problems. You can also contact many companies by telephone and e-mail.

Always order early by mail to avoid sold-out notices. Because seeds and planting stock are produced at least a season in advance, quantities often are limited. It pays to order early when a sale catalog arrives. Remember, it is a common practice for many mail order firms to substitute a similar item for one that is sold out. Usually there is a place on the order form to check if you prefer no substitutions. Specify clearly on the order form that you do not want substitutions made, unless you are more flexible to accept them.

Keep a record of your purchases: the product names, item numbers, prices, and dates to facilitate communications between you and the company if necessary. These firms receive thousands of orders every week, so they need your help to track your order with specific details if a problem occurs.

HANDY MAIL ORDER RECORD FORM

Here's a sample to copy and use for your mail ordering, again courtesy of MGA.

Company Name _____

Date of Order _____

Catalog/Brochure # _____

Ordering Phone # _____

Customer Account # _____

Customer Service Phone # _____

Items Ordered:

Item # _____ Name _____

Quantity _____ Price _____

Item # _____ Name _____

Quantity _____ Price _____

Item # _____ Name _____

Quantity _____ Price _____

Item # _____ Name _____

Quantity _____ Price _____

Shipping and Handling Charge $ _____

   Total $ _____

Discounts/coupons applied _____

Check # _____ Card used _____

Date Order Rec'd. _____

Invoice # _____

Condition of plants and notes _____

_____

Read and understand the company's guarantee policy. Most firms offer outstanding guarantees, but understandably there is a cut-off date by which a company must be notified of problems or plant failures. The date is generally set late enough to allow you ample time to plant your order and observe plant growth. Be sure to inform the company of plant failures or problems before the cut-off date.

Often plants can benefit from special fertilizers when planting or soon thereafter. It pays to order appropriate fertilizers and supplies with your plants. That way you'll have them when planting. Using the right starter fertilizer and soil amendments from the beginning ensures that plants have the best chance of prospering.

Finally, as you review the appealing mail order catalogs, look for tips and ideas to help you make the best choices. More gardening catalogs also offer useful tips for growing plants, especially to guide you to success with the more difficult ones. Take advantage of the catalogs' expertise to create a healthy, beautiful, and bountiful garden.

WHAT TO DO WHEN YOUR ORDER ARRIVES

Gardeners think they know this. But too often it is one area many people overlook in their busy lives. If they do, plants suffer. Here's a checklist, again thanks to MGA, that should prove helpful. Keep it handy with your order records. It can assure you better gardening results.

- Open the package and make sure your order is complete and correct. Check your order form to make sure all of the seed varieties, plants, supplies and other items have arrived. There may be a note stating that other packages will arrive later.
- Open any plants wrapped in plastic to allow air circulation. Don't be alarmed if you see dried foliage on dormant plants. Because they are dormant, dried foliage from the prior year is natural and will soon be replaced by new growth.
- Look for instructions for temporary handling. These are usually included as part of the planting

instructions. Handling varies from plant to plant, but you'll find general rules for different types of planting stock here.

· Plant as soon as possible. Until you do, give the planting stock proper care to maintain its viability. Follow the instructions provided with your shipment. Store seeds in a cool, dry place until it is time to plant outdoors, or start them indoors in pots and trays if you wish.

For bulbs, corms, rhizomes, and tubers follow these tips. Keep bulbs such as tulips and daffodils in a cool, dry spot with good air circulation until they can be planted. Remove them from the packaging and spread them in a single layer. Keep them dry and avoid temperature extremes. The ideal time to plant such bulbs is in the fall, after temperatures have permanently cooled and before the onset of winter freezes that harden the ground. You don't want to plant them too early, nor wait until the ground is unworkable. Remember, always plant bulbs pointy end up.

Lilies and other bulbs that are not winter hardy should be stored in the dark in a closed box and lightly sprayed with water occasionally to keep them moist until planted. Rhizomes, such as iris, can be kept in their packaging material as long as the shipping carton is open. Store them where they receive some light but are not exposed to direct sun or wind.

Bare-root stock is standard for mail order shipping. Many perennials, shrubs, and trees are shipped barefoot, without soil, in a dormant state. Until planting, keep the roots in their protective wrapping of plastic, newspaper, burlap, or wood shavings in which they were shipped. Moisten them frequently and keep them from exposure to direct sun. The greatest danger is excessive drying.

Before planting roses, shrubs, and trees, soak their roots in water for a few hours. Carry them to the garden in their water bucket and plant them directly from the water to avoid any drying prior to planting. If you are unable to plant for a longer period, a week or more, it is advisable to "heel in" bareroot plants.

Heeling-in is a form of temporary planting. Dig a V-shaped trench deep enough to hold the roots. Place the plants in the trench so they are sitting at about a 45-degree angle, and cover the roots with an equal mix of builder's sand and peat moss. If soil is workable, you can use it instead. Keep plants well watered, especially if temperatures are warm, until you are able to uncover and plant them where they will grow in your garden or landscape area.

Green plants need special attention. Green plants in nursery pots are in their growth cycle and require the most careful handling. Remove them from their packaging, water them, and place them where they receive the proper amount of light according to specific instructions, and the proper range of temperatures, especially if they are tender plants. Stock in small pots can dry out quickly, so keep close watch on them and plant as soon as possible. For container stock planted at midsummer, cut back tops by one-third to prevent die-back.

You can apply these tips to bulbs, roots, and plants you buy locally, of course, if you are faced with a tight work schedule and can't get them into the garden ground immediately. Too often many gardeners have a variety of ongoing projects that require attention. These tips will help you have more success with them as part of your good growing horizons.

SUPER GARDEN SOURCES

This chapter wouldn't be complete without a deserved salute to the NGA, undoubtedly one of the best sources for gardening information. Founded in 1972 as Gardens for All, the organization has become one of America's treasured garden websites. As they explain, NGA's mission is to renew the fundamental links between people, plants, and the earth. Through exemplary programs in schools and communities nationwide, they promote environmental stewardship and science literacy, and they create partnerships that restore and enhance communities. An original purpose was to spearhead the community garden movement. Today's NGA is best known for its educational programs, grant programs, websites, and research on gardening trends.

A key point is that gardening promotes responsible earth stewardship. In the words of the NGA, "Watching a seedling unfurl, discovering what makes plants thrive, observing how living things interact . . . these intimate experiences set the stage for caring about the Earth. As human activity affects ecosystems at an unprecedented rate, gardeners develop the understanding of natural systems, skills, and dispositions to be responsible environmental stewards and decision makers." They also emphasize that gardening promotes physical and emotional health, enhances local and global communities, and infuses beauty into our lives.

And a final key point is that gardens are learning environments. According to the NGA, "Gardeners are naturally inquisitive. The act of gardening entails observing cause-and-effect relationships, trying different problem-solving strategies, and absorbing the lessons the natural world offers. As gardeners learn from their own efforts, interactions with others, and via resources, they improve their practice and gain insight into the function of living systems. In schoolyard gardens and habitats, students discover important concepts as they think and act like scientists. Learning goals in history, economics, language arts, and a host of other subjects come to life. Perhaps more important are the vital life lessons—about cooperation, patience, persistence, and responsibility—that future decision makers absorb in the garden."

Their website, www.nga.org, offers a treasure of gardening insights, know-how, and growing enthusiasm. According to the Garden Writers Association Foundation, however, only about 20 percent of gardeners surveyed used the Internet as a frequent source of information. Many more used magazines and garden centers. One wag suggested gardeners prefer to get their hands into the dirt, not play with computers. Nevertheless, veteran gardeners do praise the wealth of useful knowledge now being made available on websites.

All Land Grant State Universities conduct Cooperative Extension programs. Many sites are brimming with information, free for the asking and downloading. Here are some of the best sites around the country.

- Colorado State University: www.ext.colostate.edu. Focuses on plants for Rocky Mountain gardens.
- Cornell University's Home Gardening: www.hort.cornell.edu/gardening. Provides searchable flower and veggie databases for selecting perfect plants for gardens, plus flower and vegetable fact sheets.
- North Carolina State University: www.ces.ncsu.edu/depts/hort/consumer. A marvelous site conveniently divided into plant groups, garden topics, plus hardiness zones, fertilizer, flowers, etc.
- Ohio State University: www.webgarden.osu.edu. Has 200 short gardening how-to videos and plant facts database, plus 600 frequently asked questions and answers.

- University of Illinois: www.etension.uiuc.edu. Has an Ask an Expert option.
- University of Wisconsin: www.uwex.edu/ces. Another fine gardening info site.

Don't overlook the federal government sources. Try www.plants.usda.gov, which is a national plant database. Also check the U.S. Department of Agriculture for a plethora of useful garden information and free literature.

There are many wonderful opportunities to learn more about gardening as a member of gardening clubs that relate to your special interest. You might begin by reviewing the clubs available. The National Garden Clubs (NGC) is a nonprofit educational organization headquartered in St. Louis, Missouri. It is composed of 50 State Garden Clubs, which include 7,183 member garden clubs and 221,943 members. The NGC encourages establishment and maintenance of botanical gardens, arboreta, and horticultural centers for the advancement of science, enjoyment, and education of the public, and the advancement of the study of gardening, landscape design, environmental issues, floral design, and horticulture, plus assisting deserving students through college scholarships in these fields of endeavor.

The Garden Club of America has a mission to stimulate the knowledge and love of gardening, to share the advantages of association by means of educational meetings and publications, and to protect the environment through educational programs and action in the fields of conservation and civic improvement. They are located at 14 East 60th St., 3rd Floor, New York, NY 10022, telephone: 212-753-8287.

There are Men's and Women's Garden Clubs linked around each state and nationally. You may find some in your area that have public meetings and welcome new members. In addition, check some of the specialty garden clubs. A few examples follow. Use Google or another search engine to find more. Enter the name of your favorite plant plus the word "club" and see what you can find. Gardeners are everywhere and most love to talk gardening with like-minded folks.

Garden Clubs and Organizations

American Daffodil Society: www.daffodilusa.org

American Orchid Society: www.orchidweb.org

American Rose Society: www.ars.org

Arnold Arboretum at Harvard: www.arboretum .harvard.edu

Atlanta Botanical Garden: www.atlantabotanical garden.org

Botanical Society of America: www.botany.org

Cornell Department of Horticulture: www.cals .cornell.edu/dept/flori

Massachusetts Horticultural Society: www.masshort .org

Missouri Botanic Garden: www.mobot.org

Morris Arboretum: www.upenn.edu/arboretum

National Council of State Garden Clubs: www .gardenclub.org

Ohio State University Department of Horticulture: www.hcs.ohio-state.edu

Scenic America: www.scenic.org

GREAT SOURCES FOR KIDS

Finally, dig in with kids and grandkids to some super sites. The award-winning National Gardening Association's www.kidsgardening.org offers treasures of gardening ideas and how-to fun projects. California has information about Life Lab school garden programs at www

.lifelab.org. The Great Plant Escape on Just for Kids is fun at www.urbanext.uiuc.edu. And you'll find herb and veggie ideas, tips, and recipes at www.vivagarden.com. For other resources and links, try www.thegardenhelper.com and www.gardenweb.com.

Keep looking and you'll keep learning to grow better with your gardens.

GLOSSARY

Every hobby has its own language of special terms. It helps to understand what these terms mean as you expand your own garden horizon. Garden catalogs are easy to read, but there are a few terms you frequently see that it helps to know. Here is a glossary of gardening words and phrases.

Acid: Soil with a pH less than 7 on the pH scale of 1 (acid) to 14 (alkaline).

Alkaline: Soil with pH greater than 7.0 on the scale.

Annuals: Vegetables or flowers that grow for only one season and need to be replanted from seed or plants each spring.

Award winners: This usually refers to honors awarded to superior new plant varieties. The All America Selection (AAS) awards for new flowers and vegetables and the All America Rose Selection (AARS) awards for new rose varieties are two major awards referred to in catalogs. Numerous other awards are given by plant societies. Gardeners can count on winners of such awards to be new varieties of special merit.

Bare-root plants: Planting stock shipped dormant without any soil around the roots. Roses, shrubs, berry plants, trees, and many perennials are often shipped in this form.

Biennial: Plants that require two growing seasons to complete their life cycle. The first year the plants mature and the second year flower and set seeds or fruit.

Bolting: A problem that may occur when greens, onions, and some other crops produce a flower stalk which is undesirable and usually linked with hot weather. Look for greens that resist bolting for a longer harvest.

Climate zones (hardiness zones): The U.S. Department of Agriculture has divided the country into "climate" or "hardiness" zones numbered 1 through 10, which are determined by average minimum temperatures. Catalog plant descriptions usually give a plant's zone range, so it is important to be sure your home zone is within the plant's range.

Common names: The popular, nonbotanical names used for a plant. For example, baby's breath is the common name for *Gypsophila*, its scientific name. Because common names may differ in different parts of our country, it is best to check the scientific name of the plants you want.

Compost: The end product of decomposition of organic matter into humus.

Corm: A modified underground stem that stores energy, such as a crocus corm.

Cultivar: This term is synonymous with variety, but it refers only to cultivated plants.

Days to maturity: This phrase in seed catalogs tells you about how long it takes a variety to produce fruits or vegetables. The day number is only approximate because local conditions vary. The number is most useful to determine which varieties require a longer or shorter season to reach maturity. In northern areas you should look for short-season maturity varieties.

Determinate or indeterminate: These terms refer to the growth habit of plants such as tomatoes and squashes. Determinate vines grow to a certain length and stop. Indeterminate vines continue to grow through the season, so they require more space.

Disease resistant or disease tolerant: Catalogs often indicate a variety's ability to tolerate or resist common diseases. Resistant means stronger than just tolerant, but neither indicates a plant will be totally immune.

Exclusives: Plant varieties offered in catalogs as "exclusives" means that they are offered only by that particular company. This usually applies to new introductions and patented plants developed by a company.

Field grown: This means rootstocks that are more mature because they have been grown in the ground for a full season or more. Conversely, rooted cuttings usually have been grown in pots.

Foliar fertilizer: A modern system of mixing fertilizer with water and applying directly to foliage to be absorbed by leaves to feed the plant. It also can be used on the ground and soaks in to nourish plants.

Grafted plants: Plants where the variety has been grafted onto a different rootstock, mainly used in reference to roses and trees. The upper portion of a grafted plant is the desired variety, while the rooted stock is another variety that imparts a desired characteristic such as dwarf growth habit, hardiness, or long life.

Genus: Closely related plants are grouped together under a single botanical name, known as their genus. Species are plants within a genus that can be identified by recognizable individual characteristics. In plant classification, the combination of genus and species names are the plant's official botanical name.

Germination: The growth of a plant embryo or sprouting of a seed.

Green plants: In contrast to bare-root stock, green plants are grown in a nursery and delivered actively growing in pots or other containers, rather than dormant. May simply be called potted plants.

Habitat: The region in which a plant is typically found growing wild.

Hardiness: This refers to a variety's ability to withstand winter temperatures. For northern area gardeners, the hardier the variety, the colder the temperatures it will tolerate. This relates to horticultural or climate zones given in most mail order catalogs for their plants.

Hybrid: A plant that is the offspring of two plants with different characteristics. Hybrids are often more vigorous than either parent and usually contain a combination of desirable characteristics, such as early fruit set and disease resistance.

Humus: The basic organic constituent of soil that persists after the decomposition of organic matter naturally or in the composting process.

Insecticide: A substance that kills insects by poisoning, suffocating, or paralyzing them. Pesticide is a synonym but also includes herbicides that kill weeds and fungicides that help control plant diseases.

Legume: A plant such as alfalfa, clover, pea, or bean that has nitrogen-fixing bacteria which can take nitrogen from the air and attach it with nodules on plant roots. These are especially valuable as cover crops to be tilled under to improve garden soil.

Mesclun: A mix of salad lettuces and greens that are grown as a cut-and-grow-again crop. Mesclun mixes usually contain several red and green lettuce varieties, mustard greens, arugula, curly cress, broccoli raab, baby bok choy, and other plants.

Naturalizing: Using plants or bulbs that are left to grow naturally. The plants are especially self-reliant and will come back year after year in increased numbers. Most daffodil varieties, species of wild tulips, and crocus are used for naturalizing to create a wildflower appearance rather than a cultivated garden look.

Open pollinated (OP): Refers to seeds that come from plants that have been naturally pollinated in the field. Unlike hybrid varieties, these plants will produce seeds that grow true to variety and will be the same as that of the parent.

Organic matter: Plant materials that were once living, which you can use in making compost to improve garden soil.

Pelleted: Seed so tiny it is coated to make it larger and easier to handle and plant.

Perennials: Plants that grow year after year from original bulbs or roots or from self-seeding. Typically, perennials are sufficiently hardy to be left in the ground over winter to grow again in the spring.

Pistil: The female reproductive structure of a plant that is found in the flower.

pH: This represents the hydrogen ion concentration by which plant scientists measure soil acidity. The pH chart ranges from I which is acid to 14 which is alkaline. The midpoint, 7, means neutral soil, neither acidic or alkaline. An important factor in gardening, because all plants have their own specific pH needs and tolerance.

Phosphorus: An essential nutrient for plant growth. It promotes root formation in plants.

Plant patent numbers: New plants can be patented, which protects the creator's ownership. The plant variety may be an exclusive and not available from other sources.

Potassium: Also called potash; a nutrient for plants that is vital for plant maturity, flower development, and hardiness.

Resistance: The plant's ability to withstand all or certain diseases for a length of time without suffering serious damage.

Rhizome: An underground horizontal stem that gives rise to roots and shoots or stems; similar to bulbs and corms.

Root divisions: Dormant harvested root clumps that are divided into viable portions for starting new plants.

Rooted cuttings: Plants propagated by making cuttings from other plants that then are rooted and grown in individual pots for replanting.

Species: TA group of individual plants that form a subdivision of a genus with similar characteristics but not differing from the genus enough to form a new genus.

Stamen: The reproductive organ of the male, pollen-bearing flower. The anther is the top part of the stamen.

Stigma: The terminal part of the reproductive organ of the female flowering plant that re-

ceives pollen, usually brought by bees and butterflies from the male portion of plants.

Terminal bud: The bud borne at the tip of a stem.
Side buds are at the sides. It helps to know these
terms when pruning plants.

Treated seeds: Seeds treated in some manner or
with a chemical for disease control. Handle
carefully.

Tuber: An underground modified stem that stores
large quantities of food for some plants, as do
corms and bulbs.

Variety name: The name of a particular plant
within a species; usually printed in roman type
within single quotation marks after the itali-
cized botanical name, as in *Helianthus annuus*
"Teddy Bear."

INDEX

ABOUT THE AUTHOR

Allan A. Swenson is the author of over 50 books on gardening as well as the nationally syndicated Gardener's Notebook newspaper column. He lives in Kennebunk, Maine.